A Calendar of American Poetry

A Calendar of

AMERICAN POETRY

*in the Colonial Newspapers
and Magazines and in the
Major English Magazines
Through 1765*

BY

J. A. LEO LEMAY

American Antiquarian Society

WORCESTER · 1972

Copyright © 1970 by American Antiquarian Society
Library of Congress Catalog Card Number 70-26435
Standard Book Number 0-912296-01-1
Designed by Klaus Gemming, New Haven, Connecticut
Manufactured in the United States of America
by the Davis Press, Inc., Worcester, Massachusetts

CONTENTS

INTRODUCTION

No ACCOUNT of American poetry of the colonial eighteenth century exists that is not shot through with the most glaring omissions and errors. Part of the reason for our ignorance of eighteenth-century American poetry is that most of it was published in newspapers and magazines—and since there has been no guide to this poetry, it has been effectually buried and lost in the mass of periodicals. The following calendar attempts to provide some control over the American poetry published in the colonial newspapers and magazines and in the major English magazines through 1765. For each poem, the following information is given: first, the date and place of publication (including volume and page references for magazines, and page and column references for the larger newspapers); second, the first line of the poem; third, the title (where the title is lacking I have usually supplied one within brackets); fourth, the number of lines; fifth, the author or pseudonym; and sixth, a note on the poem, which includes reprintings, accounts of the author, or any other information that I thought might be of wide interest to the user.

ACKNOWLEDGEMENTS

MUCH OF THE RESEARCH for the calendar was done during the summer of 1965 with the assistance of Grant No. 3970 from the Penrose Fund of the American Philosophical Society. I have extensively used the newspapers of the Harvard and Yale libraries; the Boston Public Library and the New York Public Library; the Massachusetts Historical Society, the New York Historical Society, and the Pennsylvania Historical Society; the Library Company of Philadelphia; the Maryland State Library; the Research Department of Colonial Williamsburg, Inc.; the Henry E. Huntington Library; and the Library of Congress. The libraries at UCLA have been long-suffering in borrowing and buying microfilms and Microprint of newspapers for me. Mr. Edward M. Riley of Colonial Williamsburg, Inc., and Mr. William M. E. Rachel of the Virginia Historical Society have kindly answered my questions and kept my interests in mind. My friends Whitfield J. Bell of the American Philosophical Society, Richard Beale Davis of the University of Tennessee, and Roger E. Stoddard of the Houghton Library have taken an interest in the calendar and have been unfailingly helpful. I am indebted to Mr. James E. Mooney, Editor of the American Antiquarian Society, and to Mr. Klaus Gemming, the Society's designer, for providing what I think to be an excellent solution to a difficult format. Finally, I am especially pleased that the American Antiquarian Society is publishing the calendar; for more reading has been done in its great collections of colonial newspapers than in any other library; and, without the massive bibliography of its former Librarian, Clarence S. Brigham, the undertaking would have been nearly impossible.

I · NOTES ON METHODOLOGY

1. *Criteria for Inclusion*

a. English Magazines

In scanning the English magazines looking for American poetry, it was necessary to have strict criteria for inclusion in the calendar. If any one of the following four conditions existed, the poem is listed: 1, if it contains American subject matter (e.g., poems about British generals currently serving in America, or, like Generals Braddock and Wolfe, killed in America, or about American Indians, etc.); 2, if it is dated from America (including the West Indies and Canada); 3, if the pseudonym suggests American authorship; and 4, if I knew or suspected that it was by an American. Nevertheless, a number of poems by Americans that were published in the English magazines must be omitted from the list, for Americans not infrequently wrote on such subjects as riddles, love, weather, or English politics. I have not, of course, been able to identify such poems as American—unless, as in the cases of Benjamin Waller and Robert Bolling (both of Virginia), holograph copies existed of the author's poems.

b. American Periodicals

Over half of the poetry published in the colonial periodicals was reprinted—usually without acknowledgment—from English periodicals. Since my concern was with American poetry only (partially because including English poetry would more than double the size of the bibliography), I had to try to distinguish between the American and English poetry in the American newspapers and magazines. The tests were not so rigorous as for the English magazines. Poetry with an English dateline or reprinted from English periodicals was excluded—unless it met the criteria sketched above for determining an 'American' poem. Familiar poems by English poets (Pope,

Addison, Swift, Young, Milton, Shakespeare, etc.) were also excluded. I omitted too some poems that seemed to me to be simply filler and were uninteresting in any way that I could imagine and that I suspected (but did not positively know) were borrowed from some English publication. (The place in the newspaper where a poem is printed often indicates whether it is American: e.g., if it is published among the English news items, one may usually assume that it is from an English newspaper.) Despite my attempt to exclude English verse, probably twenty percent of the poetry is English.

On the other hand, a few English poems published in American periodicals that had no American references and did not meet any of the above-mentioned criteria, but which seemed of special interest to the student of American literature and culture, were deliberately included. Thus I have listed a couple of poems by the early eighteenth-century thresher poet, Stephen Duck, and by Isaac Watts. A number of poems reprinted without acknowledgment from English sources have been included, simply to identify such poetry as English. Poems written by people who later emigrated to America, as well as poems that served as models for American poetry, are also included.

2. Omissions

American poetry, reprinted from English newspapers and magazines, that appeared in the colonial newspapers and magazines was probably frequently omitted; for poems reprinted from English periodicals are omitted, unless they are obviously American, even though poetry by Americans in the English magazines would have a better chance of being reprinted in American newspapers than the normal English poem. Snippets of poetry of less than five lines were omitted, unless such lines (e.g., no. 1151) seemed of special interest. Poems in foreign languages are also frequently excluded: I began the calendar purely for my own purposes, omitting foreign language poetry unless it was of particular interest or unless it was part of a literary exchange. German-language newspapers are not calendared. Surprisingly, more work has been done on the German-language newspapers than on those in English. The lack of a complete guide to Latin poetry will be more than compensated for by Leo Kaiser's forthcoming edition of the Latin poetry of colonial America. Finally, it is quite possible that, in scanning nearly all the extant newspapers of colonial America, I may have missed a few poems.

3. *Authorship*

a. Anonymous and Pseudonymous Verse

With some exceptions, eighteenth-century periodical poetry is anonymous or pseudonymous. It is almost always difficult and frequently impossible to identify the author. The use of initials, symbols, and pseudonyms was standard practice in Western literature from the Renaissance until well into the nineteenth century. Voltaire used at least 137 pseudonyms. Eighteenth-century writers assumed that their literary contemporaries would recognize their writings, and they generally believed that people who did not recognize their authorship did not deserve to know such information. Franklin used allonyms in several of his finest hoaxes and he expected his contemporaries to perceive his own pen behind the mock use of another's pseudonym. Moreover, such pseudonyms as 'Ruris Amator,' 'Philo-musae,' 'Martinus Scriblerus,' etc., frequently have a valuable literary function, indicating the author's attitude and *persona* in the poem. Sometimes the pseudonym will also indicate the genre of the work or will provide a reference to a source. Also, the use of a pseudonym could save an author from the charge of egotism in publishing his writings and might save him from criticism if the writing is judged faulty. Robert Bolling's comment on a poetical opponent (in a manuscript volume containing a copy of no. 1873A) reflects several of these reasons for anonymity: 'John Clarke was very indiscrete both in publishing a very incorrect copy of Verses and also in blazoning his name and abod to he knew not whom.'

b. Methods of Attribution

In some rare cases, the author's name is signed. More often—including poems by Mather Byles, Rev. John Adams, Samuel Davies, Nathanial Evans, Francis Hopkinson, Thomas Godfrey, Benjamin Young Prime, and Provost William Smith —I have been able to identify the author from later printings of the poems in books. A few authors, including Byles, Davies, and Joseph Green, have been identified from attributions in contemporary manuscript commonplace books. For some authors, including James Sterling, Joseph Shippen, and Byles, the identifications are the result of contemporary manuscript annotations on the periodicals. More frequently, the attribution is revealed by the hints of contemporary literary opponents; and often, the attribution is based on the dateline and the pseudonym itself. Thus a poem dated from Kent County, Maryland is almost positively by James Sterling; and one in a Maryland or Pennsylvania newspaper signed 'Philo-Musaeus' is very probably by Dr. Adam Thomson. Frequently the attributions made by previous scholars have provided the key to the identity of an author: Rufus Wilmot Griswold, Evert A. Duyckinck, Moses Coit Tyler, Lawrence C. Wroth, George Hastings, Lyon N. Richardson, and Richard Beale Davis are among the men who have done excellent work on some of the authors represented in the calendar.

c. Necessity for Attribution

Since the canon of practically no eighteenth-century American poet has been established with painstaking care, I have hazarded a number of tentative attributions. In such cases the author's name (followed by a question mark) is given within brackets, and the reasons for the tentative attribution are presented in the note. It is important to try to construct the canon of the American poets, and I know that future scholars with special knowledge will be able to add to (and I hope, in some cases, to confirm) my suggestions. Because I have recently completed a detailed study of the colonial Maryland writers, I have been more successful in identifying Maryland poets than those of other colonies.

d. Facts Concerning the Author

For well-known authors who are found in the *DAB* (e.g., Benjamin Franklin), I have not given any biographical data. If an author is not in the *DAB* or if he is comparatively obscure, the most recent account of value is cited in the first entry mentioning him; later entries do not repeat this information. If there is no published account of the poet, his birth and death dates (if ascertainable) are given, and reference is made to some work mentioning him. If I know nothing of an author, I say so.

4. Reprintings

The Note includes any later reprintings of the poem in the newspapers or magazines, as well as reprintings in modern anthologies and scholarly books and articles. Frequently, a topical poem (for example, an elegy on the death of General James Wolfe) was reprinted several times. The first entry for a poem lists all the contemporary reprintings, calling attention to such differences in the reprinting as a fuller title or a different pseudonym, or a revision of the poem. A reprinted poem also has an entry in the proper chronological order, but only the date and place of publication, the first line of the poem, and the information that this is a reprint of an earlier item is noted—unless the reprint differs in some important way; if so, this information is also given.

II · SOME SELECTIVE FINDINGS

1. New Attributions for Known Poets

All the major American poets of the mid-eighteenth century turn up in the calendar. The Rev. Mather Byles, for example, is represented by nineteen poems. Six are new attributions: of these, three are tentative (nos. 48, 92, and 296); one is based on Mather Byles' own manuscript notation in his file of the newspaper (no. 445); one is based on the near-contemporary attribution of Jeremy Belknap in a commonplace book (no. 160); and another is based on internal references (no. 156). Of the thirteen poems known to be by Byles from the fact that they are printed in his volume *Poems on Several Occasions*, (Boston, 1744), several were not located by C. Lennart Carlson when he edited a facsimile of Byles's *Poems* in 1940, and so the appearance of these items (although not new attributions) adds to our knowledge of his poetry.

The case of Byles's public nemesis, Joseph Green, is more interesting. Of the thirteen poems attributed to Green, nine are new additions to his canon. Three of these (nos. 969, 1187, 1255) are signed with the initials 'V.D.' (a pseudonym of Green). One of the other new poems (no. 976) is part of a controversy that 'V.D.' had with other Boston writers, and is signed 'J.G---ne.' (A contemporary has filled in the blanks with '*ree*,' thus spelling out '*Greene*.') Two early poems tentatively attributed to Green are satiric attacks on Mather Byles (nos. 144 and 298) and a later poem may be a reply to a poem by Byles (no. 1777). Two others, a satire on masonry (no. 990) and a satire on paper money (no. 1921), if not by Green, are imitations of his well known and popular poetic satires on these subjects. Finally, the free verse travesty of James Otis' speech in 1763 (no. 1922) is an early Loyalist literary expression of the Revolutionary Period; it is probably by Samuel Waterhouse or Joseph Green; and if it was not by Green, it at least expressed his late attitudes and political beliefs and imitated his early poetic burlesques of the speeches of Governor Jonathan Belcher. Another Boston poet—one whom Franklin praises in his *Autobiography*, Matthew Adams—has hitherto been known only as the author of a poem in James Franklin's *New England Courant* (no. 17). But, with the assistance of a key published in the last number of the 'Proteus Echo' essay-series, three more poems have been attributed to Adams (nos. 66, 83, and 87). There is also a suggested ascription (no. 933) to the Rev. Samuel Niles.

For John Maylem, there is, in addition to his one known newspaper poem (no. 1827A), a new poem which complements the information supplied in Lawrence C. Wroth's excellent article (see no. 1764), and a possible attribution (no. 1669A). The first publication of four anonymous poems that turn up in Benjamin Young Prime's *Patriot Muse* (London, 1764) is recorded (nos. 1274, 1529, 1807, and 1865A); and four new attributions to Prime are suggested (nos. 1283, 1859A, 1865B, 1866A). A series of poems by a Princeton alumnus (nos. 1548, 1575, 1596, 1597, and 1627) may also be by Prime.

A recent book claims that if Benjamin Franklin had died before 1750, he would be unknown in America today. But Franklin turns up more frequently in the calendar than any other person, and most entries are prior to 1750. Franklin's satire on the New England funeral elegy influenced critical American writing for the next several years. His coinage describing this 'new' and 'amazing' kind of poetry was used by at least six poets in the next two years—Franklin labeled it 'Kitelic' poetry, honoring, he said, the dead. References in other contemporary poems to the author of the elegy on Mrs. Mehitable Kitel make it possible to identify the author, whom Franklin referred to only as 'Dr. H-----k.' Although the editors of the *Papers* of Benjamin Franklin, following George Horner, suggest that it was Dr. Edward Holyoke, the author was actually Dr. John Herrick of Salem and Beverly (see Nos. 25 and 47).

Franklin's later 'Busy-Body' essay series was satirized by three poems (nos. 105, 109, 111).

Eight poems are ascribed to Franklin, six of which are new attributions. Of these, one (no. 1959) glosses a passage in the *Autobiography* that has been frequently misunderstood; another (no. 390) contains a savage satire similar to one of his news-note hoaxes; three (nos. 25, 161, and 865) reinforce his prose writings and help to clinch a point made in his accompanying essays; and one (no. 195) is prefaced by an editorial disclaimer by Franklin—a trick that he employed to dissociate himself from his own irreligious or coarse writings. For one of the two poems known to be Franklin's (no. 610), his source in an English poem of several years earlier (see no. 349) is located, and attention is called to an imitation of his poem, published several years later (no. 850). For his other known poem (no. 839), an additional contemporary reprinting is noted. Also, the reprinting of a number of poems from Franklin's *Poor Richard* is recorded.

In the middle colonies, Joseph Breintnall is well known as a poet because of Franklin's praise for him in the *Autobiography* —but his poetry is difficult to locate, not turning up in Evans, Sabin, Wegelin, or any other standard bibliography. But three poems positively by Breintnall (nos. 111, 386, and 544) and three others very possibly by him (nos. 509, 528 and 529) are listed. Provost William Smith is listed as the author of fourteen, including eleven new attributions. Two poems (nos. 1069, 1091) are ascribed to him because of internal references, three (nos. 1068, 1076, 1129) are attributed to him because they are called 'American Fables,' and he is elsewhere identified as the 'Author of the American Fables.' Three others (nos. 1062, 1063, and 1064) are ascribed to him because they were submitted by 'T.P.,' who, at the same time, was sending other poems by Smith to the same newspaper; and four (nos. 1190, 1222, 1223, and 1682) are tentative attributions, suggested because Smith, as Provost of the Philadelphia Academy, was the most logical author. The authorship of the two other poems (nos. 1347 and 1349) is revealed in the English reprintings. Although no new works by Nathaniel Evans have turned up, early printings are located of eight poems included in the volume published in 1772 by Provost William Smith. The first publication of five poems included in Thomas Godfrey's *Juvenile Poems* is recorded (nos. 1408, 1474, 1483, 1508 and 1894), and a new attribution of an interesting poem (no. 1667) is advanced. Joseph Shippen, another Pennsylvania poet, is represented in Griswold, Duyckinck, and Tyler as the author of two poems (nos. 1414 and 1740), but there are five other poems by him in the calendar (nos. 1416, 1417, 1418, 1419, and 1425) and reference is made to two more poems printed in the nineteenth century (see no. 1414).

In Maryland and Virginia, there are new poems by the Rev. Thomas Cradock, Rev. William Dawson, Rev. Samuel Davies, Charles Hansford, Richard Lewis, John Markland, and the Rev. James Sterling. In the Deep South, several poems are attributed to Charleston's Dr. Thomas Dale, including America's first extant prologue. I have also hazarded a guess concerning Dr. James Kirkpatrick's authorship. Like Dale, Kirkpatrick has been better known as a physician than as a poet. And seven poems published in England by Rowland Rugeley, who later emigrated to Charleston and published a volume of poetry in America, are located.

2. New Poets

Are there any new and important poets? Technically the answer is no, but pragmatically the answer is yes. I have already published an article on Richard Lewis that draws attention to his importance and significance in the history of American poetry (see no. 122). Lewis has certainly been known as an American poet—but he has been unappreciated, partially because his canon was unknown and his poetry unread. I have also published a pamphlet on John Markland of Virginia, pointing out that this poet first defended Addison from Pope's 'Atticus' lines—and thus deserves a minor place in English literary history (see no. 266). An elusive Virginia poet, Benjamin Waller, whose few extant manuscripts testify to his extensive literary interests and poetic ability, turns up in the *Gentleman's Magazine*. A Virginia lawyer and planter, John Mercer (see no. 1381) is identified by the pseudonym 'The Author of the Little Book,' which was the politic circumlocution for the 'Dinwiddiana,' a manuscript volume of savage poetic satire on Governor Robert Dinwiddie and his adherents. The 'mysterious Mr. Gardner,' who dominated the prose of the *New England Courant* and who, in my opinion, was the chief influence upon the prose (both for content and style) of Benjamin Franklin, contributed one poem (no. 20), and his identity is resolved. The author of the 'Virginia Centinel' essay series is another minor poet (see nos. 1324 and 1367) whose prose is of considerable importance, but who hitherto has not been identified. Evidence gathered from various reprintings of the essay series in other newspapers (only one number of the 'Virginia Centinel' is extant in the *Virginia Gazette*), suggests that the author (but there may have been two authors) was the Rev. James Maury, of Albemarle County, Virginia.

Two Americans for whom a considerable body of poetry exists are, in effect, new poets. Dr. Adam Thomson, who lived in Maryland, Virginia, Pennsylvania and New York, is not mentioned by Griswold, Duyckinck, Tyler, or any other literary historian of America or in any account of early American poetry—even though in the late nineteenth century George Seilhamer in his *History of the American Theater Before the Revolution* (Philadelphia, 1888) credited him with the authorship of a prologue, and though the *Papers of Benjamin Franklin*, VIII, 340, have recently noted that he wrote an essay which provoked one of Franklin's brilliant defenses of America. Fifteen poems by Thomson have turned up, thus making him one of the more prolific American poets of the mid-eighteenth-century. As a youth in Scotland, he wrote a play which was performed in Edinburgh; and in America too he was associated with the theater, writing the most popular prologue and epilogue of the day. Dr. Thomson's old Edinburgh school-fellow, Dr. Alexander Hamilton, in his critical essay on the literature of the *Maryland Gazette*, identified several of Thomson's poems, and others have been identified by the attacks of contemporary critics, by internal evidence, by references in Thomson's essays, and by the use of his usual pseudonym 'Philo-Musaeus.'

More prolific was Colonel Robert Bolling (1738–1775), a Virginia lawyer and planter. Although the *Virginia Gazette* is not extant for much of Bolling's productive literary life, yet he still is the most productive poet of mid-eighteenth-century America. Thirty-seven poems by him before the year 1766 are listed, and thirty-five of these are from English magazines (nos. 2031 and 2049 are the exceptions). Bolling dominated the poetry columns of the *Imperial Magazine* in 1762 and 1763, and he published frequently in the *London Magazine* and the *Universal Magazine*. Moreover, nearly all the attributions to Bolling are certain, for his own annotated file of the *Imperial Magazine* and four volumes of poetry in his holograph are extant. If a complete file of the *Virginia Gazette* existed, we would have many more of his poems. He is America's foremost satirical and occasional poet of the 1760's, replacing Joseph Green as America's primary practitioner of these dominant eighteenth-century genres. In any future evaluation of eighteenth-century American poetry, the works of Richard Lewis, Col. Robert Bolling and Dr. Adam Thomson will have major consideration.

3. Genres

a. Prologues and Epilogues

The prologues and epilogues of colonial America are an especially interesting group of poems and contain references both to the opposition to the theater in early America and to the *translatio studii* (i.e., the future glory of America) theme. Fourteen prologues and nine epilogues are included. Of these twenty-three poems, the authors of sixteen are identified. Dr. Thomas Dale wrote four, Rev. James Sterling wrote three, Provost William Smith wrote five, Dr. Adam Thomson wrote three, and John Singleton wrote one. Smith's are the least interesting of the group—but they were among the most frequently reprinted. One pair of his prologues and epilogues was reprinted four times. Dr. Thomson's excellent prologue, beginning 'To this New World, from fam'd Brittania's Shore' was the most frequently recited colonial prologue. Hallam first used it at the opening of the Philadelphia theater in the spring of 1754, when it was printed (no. 1184) in the *Pennsylvania Gazette* and reprinted in the *Gentleman's Magazine* (no. 1199). Five years later, Hallam declaimed a slightly revised version at the opening of the theater on Cruger's Wharf in New York at the end of 1758 (no. 1542). And Thomson revised it once again for Hallam three years later, and it was subsequently printed in the *New York Mercury* for January 11, 1762 (no. 1847). The epilogue that Thomson wrote for the opening of the theater in Philadelphia in 1754 went through an even more drastic process of revision. After it was printed in the *Pennsylvania Gazette* of April 25, 1754 (no. 1185) and reprinted in the *Gentleman's Magazine* (no. 1200), it grew from 27 to 55 lines for its delivery in New York in 1758 (no. 1543), and finally in 1762, it was once again revised and enlarged, now becoming a 68-line poem (no. 1848).

b. Travesties of Speeches

Perhaps the most interesting poetic genre in colonial America is the travesty of public speeches. Some of these were written in free verse and the genre may even be an American creation, for I have not been able to locate any English examples of the free verse parody. Parodies of speeches, like [Joseph Mitchell], *The Totness Address* (Dublin, 1727) were published in England, but the colonial American political scene afforded many opportunities for satirical paraphrases of speeches. So far as I know, these American poems are the earliest examples of satiric free verse in English poetry. The travesties of public speeches became common during the Revolutionary Period. I doubt that Walt Whitman's creation of free verse as a medium for elevated poetry owed anything to the free verse travesties of colonial and Revolutionary America—but it should be recognized that free verse existed in America over a century before Whitman wrote. Evidently Joseph Green created this genre with a series of burlesques of the speeches of Governor Jonathan Belcher in the early 1730s. None of these were published at the time, but manuscript copies of several of Green's free verse parodies (which seem to have circulated widely) survive. The earliest printed travesty of a speech is Benjamin Franklin's spoof of Sir William Gooch's speech (no. 839): Gooch's confused harangue seemed to blame the 'New-Light' revivalists for a fire that consumed the Virginia capitol building. Franklin's travesty immediately inspired a New York imitation (nos. 843 and 844), which uses the anapestic meter of Jonathan Swift (as in 'Mrs. Harris's Petition') rather than the free verse of Green and Franklin. Back in Virginia, an Anglican opponent (perhaps the Rev. John Robertson) of the Rev. Samuel Davies portrayed a speech by Davies (no. 1072A) before the General Court of Virginia, complaining of the repressive practices of the Established Church. In New York there appeared a hudibrastic satire of a speech asking for funds to prosecute the French and Indian War (no. 1572). Another

New York parody, this time on a speech of Massachusetts' Governor Francis Bernard, satirized the egotistic claims of Boston and Massachusetts (no. 1808) in protecting all the colonies from destruction. I have already mentioned the 1763 travesty (no. 1922) of James Otis's speech, which is probably by Joseph Green or Samuel Waterhouse. And three travesties (nos. 2035, 2060, and 2078), which anticipate the themes of the American Revolution, appeared in 1765, including Waterhouse's satire on 'Jemmy' Otis, 'Jemmibullero.'

c. Ut Pictura Poesis

The earliest American example of the *ut pictura poesis* genre is Mather Byles's poem praising Nathaniel Smibert, the artist who came to America with Bishop Berkeley. In 1753, a 'Dr. T.T.' wrote a poem 'On Seeing Mr. Wollaston's Pictures, at Annapolis' (no. 1125). John Wollaston, an itinerant British portrait painter, spent nearly a decade in America and had a major influence upon the development of eighteenth-century American art. Wollaston was probably the subject of a poem dated 'Philadelphia August 1753' (no. 1146), entitled 'To the Painter, on seeing the Picture of a Lady, which he lately drew.' Two years later, Francis Hopkinson praised Wollaston—and mentioned the young American artist Benjamin West—in his 'Verses inscribed to Mr. Wollaston' (no. 1486). A poem on Benjamin West himself is 'Upon seeing the Portrait of Miss **———**' [Anne Hollingsworth Wharton]. Although usually attributed to Joseph Shippen, the authorship is disputed, and the poem has also been ascribed to Francis Hopkinson and to William Hicks. The last poem specifically dealing with an American artist was, like the first, published in Boston, where Joseph Badger's painting of William Scott was mentioned in a minor literary war (no. 1956). In addition to the six poems that deal with specific American artists, there are seven more concerning art, three of which are in the 'Advice to a Painter' genre. One newspaper poem was illustrated: Joseph Green's

(?) satire on masonry (no. 990) was printed under a scurrilous cartoon.

I will not catalogue any further the genres and subjects of poetry, but if one wants to find poems on music, or elegies on the death of General Braddock, or poems on the French and Indian War, or poems on the Great Awakening, or on the Stamp Act or literary criticism or literary quarrels or satire— the subject and genre index furnishes a guide to such subjects.

NEWSPAPERS AND MAGAZINES
EXAMINED: ABBREVIATIONS

All of the magazines and most of the newspapers are available on microfilm. The greatest newspaper depositories are the American Antiquarian Society, the Massachusetts Historical Society, and the Library of Congress. All extant newspapers from colonial New York are available in photostatic copies at the New York Historical Society; and all extant newspapers from colonial Virginia are available in photostatic copies at the Research Department of Colonial Williamsburg, Inc. For full accounts of the publishing history of the various newspapers and for locations of individual copies, see the great bibliography by Clarence S. Brigham, *History and Bibliography of American Newspapers, 1690–1820,* 2 vols., Worcester, Mass., 1947 (abbreviated below as B). For the fullest discussion of the various early American magazines, see Lyon N. Richardson, *A History of Early American Magazines, 1741–1789,* New York, 1931 (abbreviated below as R).

ABBREVIATION	FULL NAME AND DATES	REFERENCE
Am Chron	*American Chronicle* (New York), 1762.	B, I, 607–608.
Am Mag	*American Magazine or a Monthly View* (Philadelphia) 1741.	R, pp. 363–4.
Am Mag	*American Magazine and Historical Chronicle* (Boston) 1743–46.	R, p. 364.
Am Mag	*American Magazine or Monthly Chronicle* (Phila.) 1757–58.	R, p. 365.
AWM	*American Weekly Mercury* (Phila.) 1719–49	B, II, 890–891.
	Annual Register (London) 1758–65.	
BEP	*Boston Evening Post* 1735–65.	B, I, 290–293.
BG	*Boston Gazette* 1719–65.	B, I, 297–303.
BNL	*Boston News Letter* 1704–65.	B, I, 327–331.
BPB	*Boston Post Boy* (*Boston Weekly Advertiser* in 1757–58) 1734–65	B, I, 335–339.

ABBREVIATION	FULL NAME AND DATES	REFERENCE
BWA	*Boston Weekly Advertiser*, 1757–58 (see *BPB*).	
	Boston Weekly Magazine 1743.	R, p. 364.
CC	*Connecticut Courant* (Hartford) 1764–65.	B, I, 22–27.
CG	*Connecticut Gazette* (New Haven) 1755–65.	B, I, 39–41.
	General Magazine (Phila.) 1741.	R, p. 364.
Gent Mag	*Gentleman's Magazine* (London), 1731–65.	
GG	*Georgia Gazette* (Savannah) 1763–65.	B, I, 125.
HG	*Halifax Gazette* (Nova Scotia: Mass. Hist. Soc. file)	
	Imperial Magazine (London) 1761–63.	
IA	*Independent Advertiser* (Boston) 1748–49.	B, I, 307.
	Instructor (New York) 1755.	B, I, 654.
Lon Mag	*London Magazine* 1732–65.	
MG	*Maryland Gazette* (Annapolis) 1727–34.	B, I, 218–219.
MG	*Maryland Gazette* (Annapolis) 1745–65.	B, I, 219–222.
NCG	*North Carolina Gazette* (New Bern), 1751–53.	B, II, 770.
NCG	*North Carolina Gazette* (Wilmington) 1764–65.	B, II, 782.
New Am Mag	*New American Magazine* (Woodbridge, N.J.) 1758–60	R, pp. 365–366.
NEC	*New England Courant* (Boston) 1721–27.	B, I, 322–323.
NE Mag	*New England Magazine* (Boston) 1758.	R, p. 366.
NEWJ	*New England Weekly Journal* (Boston) 1727–41.	B, I, 325–327.
NHG	*New Hampshire Gazette* (Portsmouth) 1756–64.	B, I, 471–477.
NLG	*New London Gazette* 1763–65.	B, I, 53–58.

ABBREVIATION	FULL NAME AND DATES	REFERENCE
NLS	*New London Summary* 1758–63.	B, I, 59–60.
NM	*Newport Mercury* 1758–65.	B, I, 997.
No Car Mag	*North Carolina Magazine* (New Bern) 1764–65.	R, p. 366.
NYEP	*New York Evening Post* 1744–51.	B, I, 629–630.
NYG	*New York Gazette* 1725–44.	B, I, 633.
NYG	*New York Gazette or Weekly Post Boy* 1747–65.	B, I, 635–638.
NYM	*New York Mercury* 1725–65.	B, I, 662–664.
NYWJ	*New York Weekly Journal* 1733–51.	B, I, 699–701.
NYWPB	*New York Weekly Post Boy* 1743–47 (for continuation, see *NYG* 1747–65)	B, I, 704.
PG	*Pennsylvania Gazette* 1728–65.	B, II, 933–937.
PJ	*Pennsylvania Journal* 1742–65.	B, II, 937–940.
ProvG	*Providence Gazette* 1762–65.	B, II, 1007–1111.
PM	*Portsmouth Mercury* 1765	B, I, 470–471.
RIG	*Rhode Island Gazette* 1732–33.	B, II, 1003.
SCG	*South Carolina Gazette* 1732–65 (all variations of this title published in the Charleston Lib. Soc. microfilm).	B, II, 1036–38, 1041–1042.
Scot Mag	*Scots Magazine* (Edinburgh) 1739–65.	
Universal Mag	*Universal Magazine* (London) 1747–65.	
VG	*Virginia Gazette* 1736–65.	B, II, 1158–61.
WNYG	*Weyman's New York Gazette* 1759–65.	B, I, 638–639.
WR	*Weekly Rehearsal* (Boston) 1731–35.	B, I, 349.

In addition to the above, several periodicals were examined that contained no poetry: the *Independent Reflector* (New York) 1752–53, B, I, 653; *John Englishman* (New York) 1755, B, I, 654; and *Occasional Reverberator* (New York) 1753, B, I, 674.

REFERENCE BOOKS AND ANTHOLOGIES
MENTIONED IN THE CALENDAR

CBEL—*The Cambridge Bibliography of English Literature*, ed. F. W. Bateson. 4 vols. Cambridge, England, 1941.

Crum—Margaret Crum, *The First-Line Index of English Poetry, 1500–1800, in Manuscripts of the Bodleian Library*. 2 vols. Oxford, 1969.

DAB—*Dictionary of American Biography*, ed. Allen Johnson and Dumas Malone. 20 vols. New York, 1928–37.

DNB—*Dictionary of National Biography*, ed. Leslie Stephen and Sidney Lee. 21 vols. London, 1885–1900.

Dodsley—Robert Dodsley, ed., *A Collection of Poems by Several Hands*. 6 vols. London, 1758.

Duyckinck—Evert A. Duyckinck and George L. Duyckinck, *The Cyclopaedia of American Literature*, ed. M. Laird Simons. 2 vols. Philadelphia, 1875.

Evans—Charles Evans *et al.*, *American Bibliography: A Chronological Dictionary*. 14 vols. Chicago, 1903–59.

Ford—Worthington Chauncey Ford, *Broadsides, Ballads, &c. Printed in Massachusetts 1639–1800*. Boston, 1922.

Franklin Papers—*The Papers of Benjamin Franklin*, ed. Leonard W. Labaree *et al.* 12 vols. (to 1969). New Haven, 1959–69.

Griswold—Rufus W. Griswold, *The Poets and Poetry of America*. New York, 1872.

Jantz—Harold S. Jantz, *The First Century of New England Verse*. New York, 1962.

Kettell—Samuel Kettell, ed., *Specimens of American Poetry*. 3 vols. Boston, 1829.

McCarty—William McCarty, ed., *Songs, Odes, and other Poems, on National Subjects*. 3 vols. Philadelphia, 1842.

Richardson—Lyon N. Richardson, *A History of Early American Magazines, 1741–1789*. New York, 1931.

Sabin—Joseph Sabin, *et al.*, eds., *A Dictionary of Books Relating to America*. 29 vols. New York, 1868–1936.

Shipton—Clifford K. Shipton, *Sibley's Harvard Graduates: Biographical Sketches of Those Who Attended Harvard*. 14 vols. (to 1969). Boston, 1873–1969. First three vols. by John Langdon Sibley.

Silverman—Kenneth Silverman, ed., *Colonial American Poetry*. New York, 1968.

Smyth—Albert H. Smyth, *The Philadelphia Magazines and Their Contributors 1741–1850*. Philadelphia, 1892.

Stedman & Hutchinson—Edmund C. Stedman and Ellen M. Hutchinson, eds., *Library of American Literature*. 11 vols. New York, 1888–90.

Stevenson—Burton Egbert Stevenson, ed., *Poems of American History*. Cambridge, Mass., 1922.

Tyler—Moses Coit Tyler, *A History of American Literature, 1607–1765*. Ithaca, 1949 (originally published, 1878).

Wegelin—Oscar Wegelin, *Early American Poetry* . . . *1650–1820*. Gloucester, Mass., 1965.

Weis, *Md.*—Frederick Lewis Weis, *The Colonial Clergy of Maryland, Delaware, and Georgia*. Lancaster, 1950.

Weis, *Middle Colonies*—Frederick Lewis Weis, *The Colonial Clergy of the Middle Colonies: New York, New Jersey, and Pennsylvania*. Worcester, Mass., 1957.

Weis, *New England*—Frederick Lewis Weis, *The Colonial Clergy and Colonial Churches of New England*. Lancaster, Mass., 1936.

Weis, *Virginia*—Frederick Lewis Weis, *The Colonial Clergy of Virginia, North Carolina, and South Carolina*. Boston, 1955.

A Calendar of American Poetry

1. Dec. 24, 1705 *BNL*.
'Gallica crux aequam flammam sentive coacta est.'
T: 'Boston; The Seminary at Quebeck, said to be burnt No. 84 [*BNL*, Nov. 26, 1705] was a large, fair, and costly Building. The flaming shingles of it flew to a distant Chappel, and set that on fire; By the near Neighbourhood of this little Chappel, a high Cross charged with a Crucifix, was surpris'd: Upon the Burning and Fall whereof, take this short Elegy; In Obitum Crucis.' ¶ No: 4 lines (Latin). ¶ A: [Samuel Sewall].
Note: First poem in any American newspaper. For Sewall's authorship, see Jantz, p. 254, no. 20. The poem is reprinted in Lyman Horace Weeks and Edward M. Bacon, *An Historical Digest of the Provincial Press* (Boston, 1911), pp. 278–279.

1721

2. Feb. 6, 1720/1 *BNL*.
'Tho Rome blaspheme the Marriage Bed.'
T: ['A Specimen of New-England Celibacy.'] ¶ No: 6 lines. ¶ A: 'S.S.' [Samuel Sewall].
Note: Dated 'Salem, Dec. 13, 1717.' The title is taken from no. 3. For authorship, see Jantz, p. 256, no. 40. On the death of Rev. Nicholas Noyes: cf. no. 3. Reprinted, see no. 4.

3. Feb. 13, 1720/1 *BNL*.
'Let Romes Anathemas be Dead.'
T: 'Boston, Our last gave you a Specimen of New-England Celibacy from Salem, December 13th, 1717 (When the Reverend Mr. Nicolas Noyes expired) and having since accidentally met with a like Number of Lines to the same purport, we thought it would not be ungrateful to subjoin them here to the former.' ¶ No: 6 lines. ¶ A: 'J.W.' [John Winthrop IV].
Note: For authorship, see Jantz, p. 256, no. 40.

4. Feb. 13, 1720/1 *BNL*.
'Tho *Rome* blaspheme the Marriage-Bed.'
Note: A reprint of no. 2.

5. Aug. 21, 1721 *NEC* ⚹3.
'Forgive the Scribler when he writes in Rhime.'
T: '*Jack Dulman* [i.e. James Franklin] to *John Campbell* (on his Satyrical Advertisement in his *Boston News-Letter* sendeth Greeting).' ¶ No: 27 lines. ¶ A: 'Jack Dulman' [James Franklin ?].

1

Note: Benjamin Franklin's attribution has been scratched out, but it looks like James Franklin. For an account of Benjamin Franklin's personal file of the *NEC*, in which manuscript attributions identify the authors, see Worthington C. Ford, 'Franklin's *New England Courant*,' Mass. Hist. Soc., *Proc.*, LVII (1923–24), 336–353.

6. Aug. 21, 1721 *NEC* #3.
   'No Wonder Tom thou wert so wroth.'
   T: [Reply to Rev. Thomas Walter.] ¶ No: 4 lines. ¶ A: ['John Checkley.']
   Note: Concluding part of Checkley's letter, in reply to Rev. Thomas Walter. Franklin's ms. attribution (see no. 5).

7. Aug. 28, 1721 *NEC*, 2/2.
   'Long had the Rulers prudent Care.'
   T: 'To the Author of the *NEC*. On the Distress of the Town of Boston, occasioned by the Small Pox.' ¶ No: 28 lines. ¶ A: ['James Franklin.']
   Note: Franklin's ms. attribution (see no. 5).

8. Sept. 4, 1721 *NEC* #5, 1/2.
   'We dare not own your Piece for Publick Use.'
   T: 'To Mr. C—l's Well-wishers, on their Malicious Letter inserted in his last.' ¶ No: 18 lines. ¶ A: 'Peter Columbus' ['James Franklin?']
   Note: Franklin's ms. attribution (see no. 5) has been crossed out.

9. Sept. 25, 1721 *NEC* #8, 1/2.
   'Beware, fond Youths, of Nymphs deceitful Charms.'
   T: 'A Caution to Batchellors.' ¶ No: 23 lines. ¶ A: 'Lucilius' ['James Franklin'].
   Note: Franklin's ms. attribution (see no. 5). Cf. nos. 10, 11, 13, and 14.

10. Oct. 2, 1721 *NEC* #9, 1/1.
    'Poor Swain! the Doubled say of Thee.'
    T: 'A Reply, in Doggrel Rhime, to his Caution to Batchellors.' ¶ No: 23 lines. ¶ A: 'Amelia.'
    Note: Franklin has crossed out the poem in his copy (see no. 5), perhaps because it was not local. Cf. no. 9.

11. Oct. 9, 1721 *NEC* #10, 1/2.
    'Dear Nymph, the Single say of thee.'
    T: 'Lucilius to Amelia.' ¶ No: 28 lines. ¶ A: 'Lucilius' [James Franklin?].
    Note: Franklin (see no. 5) has crossed out the attribution. Cf. no. 9.

12. Oct. 9, 1721 *BG* #98.
    'Fair P—r, sure 'twas wisely, bravely done.'

T: '—The following Lines were writ in Praise of the **Notable** Heroine, who spied him [a bear] first and attended him to his Execution.' ¶ No: 9 lines.

Note: Under date 'Phila., Sept. 28.'

13. Oct. 9, 1721 *NEC* ⚹10, 1/2.

'The Fool by his Wit.'

T: Reply 'to Lucilius, for his Caution to Batchellors.' ¶ No: 12 lines. ¶ A: 'Renuncles' ['*Madam* Staples'].

Note: This is a reply to 11, above. Cf. no. 9. B. Franklin's ms. attribution (see no. 5). I have not been able to identify Madam Staples.

14. Oct. 16, 1721 *NEC* ⚹11, 1/2.

'The round-headed Tribe.'

T: 'Lucilius to Renuncles.' ¶ No: 12 lines. ¶ A: 'Lucilius.'

Note: See no. 9. B. Franklin has crossed out his attribution (see no. 5).

15. Oct. 16, 1721 *NEC* ⚹11, 1/2.

'While in JEHOVAH's courts I trembling stand.'

T: [On behaviour in church.] ¶ No: 6 lines. ¶ A: 'AN DU. Spinst.'

Note: Dated 'Rhode-Island, Sept. 28, 1721.' With prefatory letter.

16. Nov. 13, 1721 *NEC* ⚹15, 1/1–2.

'Nature, 'tis true, has grac'd our Sex with Charms.'

T: 'In Praise of Matrimony.' ¶ No: 24 lines. ¶ A: 'Fidelia.'

Note: Not local; Franklin labels it 'Stolen' (see no. 5).

17. Nov. 27, 1721 *NEC* ⚹17.

'Now on the Town an Angel flaming stands.'

T: ['Lines, ... occasioned by the melancholy Prospect ... some Time since of the present doleful circumstances of the Place.'] ¶ No: 19 lines. ¶ A: ['Mr. Matthew Adams.']

Note: Dated 'An Evening Retirement, May 12, 1721,' with a prefatory letter, dated 'Boston, Nov. 4, 1721.' B. Franklin's ms. attribution (see no. 5). Matthew Adams (d. 1753), merchant, was once a partner with Nathaniel Gardner (1694–1770) in a tanyard, contributed with Mather Byles and the Rev. John Adams to the 'Proteus Echo' essay-series in the *NEWJ*, and is best remembered for lending books to the young Franklin.

18. Dec. 18, 1721 *NEC* ⚹20, 2/1–2.

'Once more, good Sir, indulge your Negligence.'

T: 'The Premium.' ¶ No: 13 lines. ¶ A: 'Timothy Turnstone' ['James Franklin'].

Note: '*Timothy Turnstone* of *Boston*, To *Nicholas Clodpate* Esq; of the Province of *New Hampshire* (on his Satyrical Advertisement

in the last Weeks *Gazette*) sendeth Greeting'—prefatory letter.
Cf. no. 42. B. Franklin's ms. attribution (see no. 5). The *BG* of
Dec. 11, 1721, #107, which contained the advertisement, is not
extant.

1722

19. Jan. 8, 1721/2 *NEC* #23, 1/1–2.
    'A famous Title now you boast on.'
    T: [Attack on N P[hilip] M[usgrav]e, Post-Master of Boston]. ¶
    No: 12 lines. ¶ A: 'Lucilius' ['James Franklin'].
    Note: Franklin's ms. attribution (see no. 5). cf. no. 21.

20. Jan. 29, 1721/2 *NEC* #26, 1/2.
    'Of Beauty's sacred, conquering Powers I sing.'
    T: 'If you see Cause to print the following Lines in *Emphatick
    Italick*, you will highly gratify the Fancy of you Friend and Con-
    stant Reader.' ¶ No: 22 lines. ¶ A: 'Corydon' ['Mr. Gardner'].
    Note: Praise for 'fair Eliza'—ugh. Franklin's ms. attribution (see
    no. 5). Nathaniel Gardner (1694–1770)—a brother-in-law of the
    poet Joseph Green, a skinner, one-time partner of Matthew
    Adams, and minor Boston official from 1715 to 1765—was the
    New England Courant's most prolific prose writer. Capt. Christo-
    pher Taylor supplied the key to Gardner's identity in the *BNL*,
    Feb. 4, 1722/3. He has usually been called 'the mysterious Mr.
    Gardner.'

21. Feb. 12, 1721/2 *NEC* #28, 1/2.
    '*Muzzey* may now *Courante's* Art defy.'
    T: 'To Jack Register Esq; on his Letter in The Last Week's Ga-
    zette.' ¶ No: 23 lines. ¶ A: 'Timothy Turnstone' ['James Frank-
    lin'].
    Note: *BG* Feb. 5, 1721/2, contains 'Jack Register's' letter. Frank-
    lin's ms. attribution (see no. 5). 'Muzzey' was probably Philip
    Musgrave; see no. 19.

22. Mar. 26, 1722 *NEC* #34, 2/1.
    'Bullies, like Dunghill Cocks, will strut and Crow.'
    T: [Attack on writer in *Boston Gazette*]. ¶ No: 9 lines. ¶ A: [Wil-
    liam Douglass?].
    Note: Part of his letter dated 'Hall's Coffee-House, March 19.'

23. April 16, 1722 *NEC* #37, 2/1.
    'If great Mens Frowns divert your Enterprize.'
    T: [Satire on a lawyer.] ¶ No: 14 lines.
    Note: Part of Captain Christopher Taylor's letter attacking a Boston

lawyer; 4 first lines are quoted, and the whole poem may be borrowed. On Taylor, see his obituary notice in the *WR* April 16, 1733, 1/2; and the information in Ford (see no. 5).

24. June 4, 1722 *NEC* #33, 1/2.
    'Long have the weaker Sons of Harvard Strove.'
    T: 'To Mrs. Silence Dogood, on her Letter in the Courant of the 14th Instant.' ¶ No: 17 lines. ¶ A: 'Crowdero.'
    Note: In support of Silence Dogood (Benjamin Franklin), dated 'Plymouth, May 22.'

25. June 25, 1722 *NEC* #47, 2/1–2.
    'Thou hast, great Bard, in thy Mysterious Ode.'
    T: 'To the Sage and Immortal Doctor H—k, on his Incomparable *ELEGY*, upon the Death of Mrs. Mehitabell Kitel, &c. A Panegyrick.' ¶ No: 32 lines. ¶ A: 'Philomusus' [Benjamin Franklin?].
    Note: Not bad poetry. Benjamin Franklin's satire on Kitelic poetry, 'Silence Dogood No. VII,' is in this issue of the *NEC*. Francis C. Davy, 'Benjamin Franklin, Satirist,' Ph.D. Thesis, Columbia, 1958, p. 21n, has suggested that this poem reinforces the 'Silence Dogood' essay and was written by Franklin. For further references to 'Kitelic' poetry, see nos. 26, 38, 39, and 51. 'Dr. H—k,' author of the elegy on Mrs. Mehitabell Kitel, is identified in no. 47 as Dr. 'Herwick.' In view of this information, Dr. H—k can not be Edward Holyoke (see the *Franklin Papers*, I, 26n). Rather Dr. H—k is almost certainly Dr. John Herrick (fl. 1697–1722) of Beverley (near Salem), Mass. Beverley is the town where Mrs. Kitel died.

26. July 9, 1722 *NEC* #49, 2/1.
    'In days of old, when Shepherdess and Swain.'
    T: 'The following Lines which are The Production of a Rhodian Muse, I desire you to insert in your next Courant; but not with a Design that they should be thought to run Parallel with the lofty *Kitelic* Strains which flow from those celebrated Bards, that have had the advantage of breathing a more Sublime Air than we, who are confined within these narrow Limits.' ¶ No: 20 lines. ¶ A: 'a Rhodian Muse.'
    Note: Dated 'Rhode-Island, June 25.' Cf. no. 28.

27. July 16, 1722 *NEC* #50, 1/1.
    'We justly Triumph in your righteous Fate.'
    T: 'O Rare Couranto!' ¶ No: 35 lines. ¶ A: [James Franklin?].
    Note: 'A Letter to Couranto, from some of his most eminent Friends, in the joyful News of his Imprisonment.' This letter and poem are included in James Franklin's defense of himself.

28. Aug. 6, 1722 *NEC* #53, 1/1.
    'Could I but emulate thy glorious Strain.'
    T: 'Having lately perused the Productions of your *Rhodean* Muse.' ¶
    No: 19 lines. ¶ A: 'Insulanus.'
    Note: Dated 'Newport on Rhode Island, July 13.' Good accompany-
    ing essay supporting Benjamin Franklin and attacking 'Harvard-
    ine Skill.' Cf. no. 26.

29. Sept. 17, 1722 *NEC* #59.
    'A Tract of Land of vast Extent.'
    T: [Poem attacking legislature for sentencing James Franklin.] ¶
    No: 106 lines. ¶ A: 'Dic. Burlesque.'

30. Oct. 29, 1722 *NEC* #65, 1/1.
    'Strange Aspects in New Haven late were seen.'
    T: [Preface to letter attacking the New Haven ministers.] ¶ No: 4
    lines. ¶ A: 'Nausawlander.'
    Note: On the Revs. Samuel Johnson, Timothy Cutter, and the other
    Congregational ministers who had caused an uproar by becoming
    Anglican ministers. Cf. no. 38.

31. Dec. 3, 1722 *NEC* #70, 2/2.
    'How now! proud *Queen*, what dost thou strutting here.'
    T: [On the eclipse.] ¶ No: 30 lines.

32. Dec. 3, 1722 *NEC* #70, 1/1.
    'Strephon, a Youth extremely modest.'
    T: ['Lines for the entertainment of our *Town Gallants*, who play *Bo-
    peep* at their Mistresses Doors.'] ¶ No: 106 lines. ¶ A: 'Amoroso.'
    Note: A versified version of James Franklin's essay signed 'Belinda,'
    NEC Mar. 19, 1721/2.

33. Dec. 24, 1722 *NEC* #73, 1/2–2/1.
    'Behold the Sons of *Antichristian* Saul.'
    T: 'A Testimony for the True Birth Day of Christ, and against the
    Popish Christmas.' ¶ No: 53 lines. ¶ A: 'Phinehas Micajah.'
    Note: Supposedly by a minister who lives 70 miles from Boston;
    with a reply by the editor.

34. Dec. 24, 1722 *NEC* #73, 1/1–2.
    'Long Time, alas! by our great Grandsire's Fall.'
    T: 'On Christmas Day.' ¶ No: 66 lines.

1723

35. Feb. 12, 1722/3 *AWM* #165.
    'The Great Jehovah from Above.'
    T: [On a charity school for negroes.] ¶ No: 8 lines. ¶ A: [Samuel
    Keimer.]

Note: First native verse in *AWM*. In this advertisement, Keimer offered to teach negroes to read 'without any Manner of Expence to their respective Masters or Mistresses.' He also advertised that he would confer with any religious people who were 'Truly concern'd for their Salvation.'

36. Feb. 21, 1722/3 *BNL*.
'Interdum Euphrates tribuit terrore dolores.'
T: 'Upon the River *Merrimak*, which at the Entrance, and upwards is the Boundary between the Towns of *Newbury & Salisbury*.' ¶ No: 2 lines (Latin). ¶ A: 'S.S.' [Samuel Sewall].
Note: For attribution, see Jantz, p. 257, no. 44. This is printed with 2 other brief Latin poems by Sewall, listed by Jantz as nos. 45 and 46.

37. Feb. 28, 1722/3 *BNL*.
'Libertas nomen; bonitas conjuncta colori.'
T: 'Upon the Reverend Mr. *Francis Goodhue*, who in his Journey from Jamaica on *Long-Island*, to Ipswich, was surprised with a Fever at Rehoboth, and there died Sept. 15, 1707.' ¶ No: 8 lines (Latin). ¶ A: 'S.S.' [Samuel Sewall].
Note: 'Aetatis 29.' See Jantz (no. 1), p. 255, no. 25.

38. Mar. 11, 1722/3 *NEC* ♯84.
'Oh! now alas, alas, what's come to pass.'
T: 'Poem ...occasioned by the late Revolution at Connecticut.' ¶ No: 148 lines. ¶ A: 'Hon. Major *James Fitch*, Esq; of Canterbury,' Ct.
Note: This poem is accompanied by an excellent essay, quoting Dryden and Norris on Pindaric poetry, burlesquing 'Dr. H—k' again for his invention of Kitelick poetry. The essayist claims that James Fitch has 'brought Kitelick Poetry to perfection. ... It has been communicated to me, with a Desire to have it made Publick, and I shall present it to my Readers as a perfect Pattern for all Kitelick Poets.' For Kitelic poetry, see no. 25. On the 'Revolution at Connecticut,' see no. 30. In a letter published in the *BNL* June 20, 1723, Ebenezer Fitch (1683–1724) of Windsor, Ct., protested against this satire of the poetry of James Fitch (b. 1649), son of the Rev. James Fitch of Saybrook, Ct. Cf. no. 41.

38a. Mar. 28, 1723 *BNL*, 2/1.
'*The Humble Springs of stately* Plimouth Beach.'
T: 'Upon the Springs issuing out from the foot of Plimouth Beach, and running into the Ocean.' ¶ No: 6 lines. ¶ A: 'S.S.' [Samuel Sewall].
Note: For attribution, see Jantz, p. 252, no. 1.

39. Apr. 1, 1723 *NEC* ♯87.
'Your's I received, but the Date.'

T: 'To the charming Phillis.' ¶ No: 36 lines. ¶ A: 'Amynter.'

Note: Conventional war of sexes poetry; refers to '*Lyrick* or *Kitelick* Verse ?'

39a. Apr. 11, 1723 *BNL*.

'Turbida nox Tenebras duplices dedit una Nov-Anglis.'

T: 'Upon the Reverend Mr. Samuel Pierpont and Mr. Benjamin Gibson ... their dying in one and the same night.' ¶ No: 8 lines (Latin). ¶ A: 'S.S.' [Samuel Sewall].

Note: See Jantz, p. 257, no. 47. The poem is reprinted in the *NEC* June 10, 1723, 1/1, with criticisms and emendations.

40. May 30, 1723 *BNL*, 1/1.

'The Prelates and their Impositions.'

T: [Elegy on Rev. John Wilson.] ¶ No: 4 lines. ¶ A: [Jonathan Mitchell.]

Note: Quoted from an elegy on Rev. John Wilson, in an article by 'Miso-Schismaticus.' The poem was printed in Nathaniel Morton's *New England's Memoriall* (Cambridge, Mass., 1669), pp. 185–188. Signed only 'J.M.,' the poem has been attributed to Mitchell by Jantz.

41. July 1, 1723 *NEC* #100.

'Hail wondrous Wit! Immortal Nezer!'

T: 'To Ebenezer Fitch of Windsor.' ¶ No: 20 lines. ¶ A: 'Janus' [James Franklin ?]

Note: With a long satirical prose paragraph replying to Fitch's letter in the *BNL* of June 27, 1723. Cf. *BNL* June 20, 1723, and no. 38.

42. July 22, 1723 *NEC* #103, 1/1–2.

'Rais'd on a Throne of Block-work see him sit.'

T: 'Justise Clodpate Characteris'd.' ¶ No: 79 lines. ¶ A: 'Mr. Steers' [Richard Steere ?]

Note: Copied, pp. 27–31, in Jeremy Belknap's 'A Collection of Poetry,' Belknap Papers 1720–1919, Massachusetts Historical Society. Richard Steere had died in 1721, but the prefatory note suggests that this poem had been in existence for some time: 'I have lately been favor'd with a manuscript, wrote by Mr. *Steers,* which is rarely to be found but in the closets of the Curious.' Reprinted, see nos. 874, 877. For Richard Steere (1643–1721), see Jantz, p. 261.

43. July 29, 1723 *NEC* #104.

'Aspiring men (swell'd with Ambition) rose.'

T: 'On the Rev. Mr. John Wise's Book, Entituled, The Churches Quarrel espous'd: Or a Reply in Satyr, to certain Proposals made, in answer to that Question, What further steps are to be taken,

that the Councils may have due Constitution and Efficacy in sup-
porting, preserving, and well ordering the Interest of the Churches
in the Country ?' ¶ No: 33 lines.

Note: No wise scholar seems previously to have noted this eulogy of
The Churches Quarrel espous'd. See George Allan Cook, *John Wise,
Early American Democrat* (New York, 1952), pp. 125–127.

44. Aug. 5, 1723 *NEC* №105, 1/2–2/1.
   'Great Bard, with bright Poetic Notions Fir'd.'
   T: 'To the very ingenious Mr. J[ohn] C[alef] of Newbury, on his
   three incomparable Elegies, occasion'd by the much lamented
   Death of Mr. Daniel Holbrook; By the Great Mortality in the
   Family of Mr. Henry Clark; And by the Death of Mr. Edmund
   Titcomb, all of Newbury.' ¶ No: 33 lines. ¶ A: 'Dic. Rymer.'
   Note: Joshua Coffin, *A Sketch of the History of Newbury, Newburyport
   and West Newbury, from 1635 to 1845* (Boston, 1845), p. 193, says
   that Calef (son of John Calef of Newbury) wrote these poems at
   age 19. An essay in the same issue of the *NEC* by 'Tibullus'
   quotes from and satirizes Calef's elegies.

45. Aug. 22, 1723 *BNL.*
   'To fix the Laws, and Limits of these Colonies.'
   T: 'Ad Regem.' ¶ No: 7 lines. ¶ A: 'John Winthrop' IV.
   Note: 'At Boston in America, the First of August: Spoken Extem-
   pore by John Winthrop Esq; before his Honour the Lt. Gov., and
   in the presence of divers Gentlemen and Ladies, and several of the
   Clergy: Being the Happy Accession of His Sacred Royal Majesty
   King GEORGE to the Imperial Throne of Great Britain.' Re-
   printed, no. 45a. Cf. nos. 46, 47, and 48.

45a. Aug. 26, 1723 *NEC* №108, 1/1–2.
   'To fix the Laws, and Limits of these Colonies.'
   Note: A reprint of no. 45, in a satirical essay on the poem.

46. Aug. 26, 1723 *NEC* №108.
   'Hail Bard Seraphick! Tell what Generous Fire.'
   T: 'To the Worshipful John Winthrop Esq; on his inimitable Genius
   to *Extempore Poetry*.' ¶ No: 19 lines. ¶ A: 'Philo Poesis-Extem-
   porarii.'
   Note: A satire on no. 45. Cf. no. 47 and the reply, no. 48.

47. Aug. 26, 1723 *NEC* №108.
   'What if your Muse to Royal *George* does fly.'
   T: 'To John Winthrop Esq; on his Poetical Address to King George
   spoken Extempore Aug. 1, 1723.' ¶ No: 16 lines. ¶ A: 'Spoken
   Extempore by DINGO.'
   Note: 'And if you mean to drive the Rhyming Trade, / Call in *Law,*

Fitch, and *Herwick* to your Aid;' (ll. 13–14); i.e., Tom Law, James Fitch, and Dr. John Herrick. Cf. no. 45, and the reply, no. 48.

48. Sept. 2, 1723 *NEC* ⚹ 109, 1/2.
   'Tell me, poor peevish Bard! What Muse in spight.'
   T: 'Cum Natura negat, facit indignatio Versus.' ¶ No: 35 lines. ¶ A: 'Philo-Satyricus' [Mather Byles?].
   Note: An excellent attack on Janus; defends John Winthrop IV with an essay on the nature of satire; good scurrilous 18th century poetry. A reply to nos. 46 and 47.

49. Oct. 24, 1723 *BNL*.
   Londini domus est in Nigris Fratribus, Hunsdon.'
   T: 'Upon the downfall of the Papists at *Black Friers, London*, October the Twenty sixth 1623. being the Lords Day, and the Fifth of November, New Style; Mr. *Drury* the Preacher not having finished his Sermon.' ¶ No: 14 lines. ¶ A: 'S.S.' [Samuel Sewall].
   Note: For attribution, see Jantz, p. 257, no. 43.

1724

50. April 6, 1724 *NEC* ⚹140.
   'Alas, poor Soul! Those youthful Days are fled.'
   T: [On the poet's melancholy.] ¶ No: 18 lines. ¶ A: 'Philanthropos.'
   Note: With a prose paragraph.

51. April 6, 1724 *NEC* ⚹140.
   'Have you e'er seen the raging stormy Main.'
   T: 'To all curious CRITICKS, and Admirers of Verse and Prose.' ¶ No: 17 lines. ¶ A: 'Janus' [James Franklin?].
   Note: With a long accompanying attack on critics and reference to *Kitelick* Numbers.

52. June 22, 1724 *NEC* ⚹151.
   'There was an old Dame aged Ninety and Eight.'
   T: 'A Parable of the Old Woman and Friar, occasion'd by a Pulpit Harangue at the Funeral of a Lawyer.'
   Note: An attack on Roman Catholicism, perhaps not local.

53. July 2, 1724 *AWM* ⚹237.
   'Marino! – – – welcome from the Western Shore.'
   T: 'A Poem to the Memory of Aquila Rose.' ¶ No: 89 lines. ¶ A: Elias Bockett of London.
   Note: A pastoral elegy in dialogue. For a bibliography and a brief account of Elias Bockett (1695–1735), see Joseph Smith, *A Descriptive Catalogue of Friends' Books*, I (London, 1867), 289–293. Cf. no. 57. Reprinted (with expanded title), no. 396.

54. Aug. 10, 1724 *NEC* ⋕158.
'Here lies old Cole; but how or why.'
T: 'The Epitaph.' ¶ No: 10 lines.
Note: On Mr. Israel Cole of Eastham: it satirizes his sons' treatment of their father; with a news notice of Cole's death.

55. Sept. 1, 1724 *NEC* ⋕164.
'Think what you list, yet he that trains.'
T: [On military preparation.] ¶ No: 10 lines. ¶ A: 'Scanderbeg.'
Note: The poem prefaces an article which is continued from the *NEC* of Sept. 14.

56. Dec. 7, 1724 *NEC* ⋕175.
'Rachel appears with bleating Flocks afar.'
T: [On the marriage of Rachel and Jacob.] ¶ No: 9 lines.
Note: Dated 'Newport, R.I. Dec. 3. 7 a Clock, PM.' Allegorical.

1725

57. Mar. 4, 1725 *AWM*.
'Stream on my Eyes, with generous Grief o'erflow.'
T: 'On sight of *MYRIS* Tomb; an ELEGY.' ¶ No: 87 lines. ¶ A: [Elias Bockett ?].
Note: 'The following Verses were lately left with the Printer, by an intimate Friend of A[quila] R[ose], deceased, who touching at Philadelphia, on his Way to *Great Britain*, had but Time to hear a relation of his Friends Death, view the place of his Interment, and write these line, without revising 'em, which he entituled ...' The concluding lines tell that Rose left 2 children; cf. no. 53.

58. May 27, 1725 *AWM*.
'In Vain is all you speak, and all you Write.'
T: 'A Dream, Written by the Widow R—lt.' ¶ No: 10 lines.
T: [With] 'The Answer, By a Lady.' ¶ No: 12 lines.
Note: These two poems form a unit.

1726

59. Jan. 25, 1725/26 *AWM*.
'Vainest of Mortals crub [curb] thy mad Career.'
T: 'To S.[amuel] K.[eimer]. ¶ No: 88 lines. ¶ A: J.[acob] T.[aylor].
Note: Accompanies Taylor's attack on Keimer; Keimer had published a *Compleat Ephemeries* for 1726 under Taylor's name. Taylor (d. 1746), a friend of George Webb, Joseph Breintnall, and Franklin, was an almanac-writer, printer, poet, teacher, and sometime Surveyor-General of Pa. See his obituary in the *PG*, March 11, 1745/6, and the *Franklin Papers*, III, 101n.

60. Feb. 12, 1725/6 *NEC.*
    'To You, *dear Sir*, whom all the Muses own.'
    T: 'To my Friend, occasioned by his Poem on Eternity, dedicated to
    me.' ¶ No: 107 lines. ¶ A: 'By a Harvard Muse' [Mather Byles].
    Note: Prefatory letter by 'Philomusus' [Matthew Adams or Byles
    himself?] calls the poem on 'early Production of a Harvard Muse.'
    A revised and expanded version of this complimentary poem ap-
    peared in the *NEWJ* (no. 65) and was reprinted in Mather Byles,
    Poems on several Occasions (Boston, 1744), pp. 49–57. The poem
    [by Byles!] on eternity is no. 64.

61. April 30, 1726 *NEC.*
    'Thro' all Mankind impatient Ardours reign.'
    T: 'Horace, Ode the XVI. Lib II, to Grasphus.' ¶ No: 63 lines. ¶ A:
    [Rev. John Adams.]
    Note: Dated 'Cambridge, April 25, 1726.' Reprinted in Adams,
    Poems (Boston, 1745), pp. 67–69; Evans 5527. Adams (1705–
    1740), nephew of Matthew Adams and a contributor to the 'Pro-
    teus Echo' essay series in the *NEWJ*, graduated from Harvard in
    1721. See Shipton, VI, 424–427.

62. July 28, 1726 *AWM.*
    'Would you attempt to lash a guilty Age.'
    T: 'To the most Ingenious Pamphleteer, author of the He-Monster.'
    ¶ No: 51 lines. ¶ A: 'a Gentleman, dwelling at a considerable
    Distance from this Place.'
    Note: The pamphlet is Evans 2757. The poem refers to Andrew
    Bradford and Samuel Keimer.

1727

63. Mar. 9, 1726/7 *BNL.*
    'Parthanissa's Beauty blooming.'
    T: 'On the Celestial Parthanissa.' ¶ No: 24 lines.
    Note: Reprinted in *A Collection of Poems* (Boston, 1744), pp. 37–38,
    with the title 'Parthanissa. Dedicated to the admirers of the
    Italian Opera.'

64. May 15, 1727 *NEWJ.*
    ''No more of murm'ring Streams, or shady Groves.'
    T: 'Eternity, A Poem. Dedicated to the Instructor of my Muse.' ¶
    No: 125 lines. ¶ A: 'R.S.' [Mather Byles].
    Note: Reprinted in Mather Byles (see no. 60), pp. 106–111. C.
    Lennart Carlson's facsimile edition of *Poems on Several Occasions*
    discusses these poems (nos. 64 and 65) on pp. xiii–xiv.

65. June 5, 1727 *NEWJ.*

'To You, Dear Youth, whom all the Muses own.'

T: 'To my Friend: Occasioned by his Poem on Eternity, dedicated to the Author.' ¶ No: 150 lines. ¶ A: 'Z' [Mather Byles].

Note: Very good—with two prefatory letters: 'An imperfect Publication of them [these verses] has been already made [in the *NEC*, see above, no. 60] when they stole into the World without the consent of the Author; who imagines, that if the Lines are still bad, yet at least in that incorrect Dress, they were worse.' Reprinted in Byles (see no. 60), pp. 49–57. 'Not I, but mighty POPE inspir'd thy muse': Praises Pope at length.

66. July 3, 1727 *NEWJ.*

'Now his last level Rays the Sun hath cast.'

T: 'The Sequel of Commencement.' ¶ No: 155 lines. ¶ A: 'AE:' [Matthew Adams].

Note: Number XIII of 'Proteus Echo' series. 'You may please to remember, that the Poem on Commencement that was published the last Year, concluded at the Colledge with a Complement to the Members of that learned Society. I have presumed to march off the prodigious Swarms that were then left at Cambridge, and conduct them thro' their various Pastimes & Divertisements, down to their several Districts and Habitations: promising myself your Protection, and candid Examination of the Performance.' The authorship is determined by a key provided in 'Proteus Echo' no. 52, 1 Ap 1728, *NEWJ.*

67. Aug. 14, 1727 *NEWJ.*

'Oh! the sad Day, when the exhausted Store.'

T: 'Lines ... composed ... by a Gentleman in his last Hours, and under the dismal Prospects of that Catastrophe which is the great Subject of his poetical Meditation.' ¶ No: 54 lines.

Note: On Judgement Day.

68. Aug. 21, 1727 *NEWJ.*

'Had I, O had I all the tuneful Arts.'

T: 'Verses Written in Milton's Paradise Lost.' ¶ No: 186 lines. ¶ A: 'L' [Mather Byles].

Note: The American Antiquarian Society's copy of this newspaper has Byles' ms. corrections. The poem was reprinted in Byles (see no. 60), pp. 25–34.

69. Sept. 4, 1727 *NEWJ.*

'Say, mournful Muse, declare thy rising Woe.'

T: 'A Poem on the Death of King George I, And Accession of King George II.' ¶ No: 126 lines. ¶ A: [Mather] 'Byles.'

Note: 'Proteus Echo' essay series no. 22; see below, no. 83, for Matthew Adams' superior poem on the same subject. Reprinted in Byles (see no. 60), pp. 61–68. This poem was also printed separately, probably in 1727: see Evans 2846 and Wegelin 40.

70. Oct. 9, 1727 *NEWJ.*
 'Hail! charming Poet whose distinguish'd lays.'
 T: 'To a Gentleman on the sight of some of his POEMS.' ¶ No: 141 lines. ¶ A: 'T.' [Rev. John Adams].
 Note: Reprinted in *A Collection of Poems by Several Hands* (Boston, 1744), pp. 3–8. For authorship, see C. Lennart Carlson, ed., Mather Byles *Poems on Several Occasions*, p. xxviii; the key in 'Proteus Echo' no. 52, Ap. 1, 1728, *NEWJ*; and the manuscript attributions (evidently by Mather Byles) in the copies of *A Collection of Poems by Several Hands* at the Mass. Hist. Soc. and at the Lib. Co. of Phila.

71. Oct. 30, 1727 *NEWJ.*
 'Great Pontiff, James the Chevalier.'
 T: 'A Dialog between the Pope and Cardinal Ottoboni.' ¶ No: 48 lines.
 Note: This is probably not local, but it's copied in Jeremy Belknap's 'A Collection of Poetry,' Belknap Papers, 1720–1919 (013.9[b]), at Massachusetts Historical Society, pp. 9–11.

72. Nov. 6, 1727 *NYG.*
 'Most Gracious Sovereign Lord, May't please.'
 T: 'The Oxford Man of Wars Address to the KING's Most Excellent Majesty.' ¶ A: [Rev. John Rhudde?]
 Note: Not local, but first poetry in *NYG*. For Rhudde, see nos. 1145 and 1221.

73. Nov. 6, 1727 *NEWJ.*
 'Thy dreadful Pow'r, Almighty God.'
 T: 'The God of Tempest.' ¶ No: 56 lines. ¶ A: 'Z' [Mather Byles].
 Note: Part of Proteus Echo, no. 31; reprinted in Byles (see no. 60), pp. 4–8; and in Kettell, I, 129–131.

74. Nov. 20, 1727 *NEWJ.*
 'O Bless the Lord, *my Soul*, with Rapture sing.'
 T: 'The Hundred and Fourth Psalm, Paraphrased.' ¶ No: 132 lines. ¶ A: 'R' [Rev. John Adams].
 Note: Number 33 'Proteus Echo,' prefatory paragraph: '... I need not observe to the Gentlemen who are acquainted with Sir Richard Blackmore's noble Poem on the *Creation*, that the following Translation is written for Style, Diction, and Sentiment, in imitation of that admiral [!] Piece; of which they will perceive it bears a very

nice Similitude and Resemblance.' Signed 'O'. The authorship is determined by the key in 'Proteus Echo' no. 52, Ap. 1, 1728, *NEWJ.*

75. Dec. 18, 1727 *NYG.*
'Rise Heavenly Muse, but rise with *heavy* Wings.'
T: 'An Elegy upon Mrs. Burnett.' ¶ No: 56 lines.
Note: Competent, first local poem in *NYG.* Reprinted, see nos. 77, 78, and 80. She was the wife of *Gov.* William Burnet.

1728

76. Jan. 1, 1727/8 *BG.*
'Oh, say what it is that Thing calld Light.'
T: 'The following Lines having been made by a poor Blind Boy upon himself, I therefore desire you'll give 'em a Place in yr Paper.' 'T.B.' ¶ No: 20 lines. ¶ A: 'T.B.' [Colley Cibber].
Note: Copied in J. Belknap's (see no. 71) 'A Collection of Poetry,' p. 16. For Cibber (1671-1757), see *CBEL*, II, 430. The earliest printing that R. S. Crane knew was 1734; see Crane's *Collection of English Poems*, 1660-1800 (New York, 1932), p. 293.

77. Jan. 2, 1727/8 *AWM.*
'Rise Heavenly Muse, but rise with heavy Wings.'
Note: A reprint of no. 75.

78. Jan. 8, 1727/8 *NEWJ.*
'Rise Heav'nly Muse, but rise with heavy Wings.'
Note: 'The following Lines being publish'd in the New York Gazette, on the Death of the Virtuous Consort of His Excellency Governour Burnett, we take leave to insert them here.' A reprint of no. 75.

79. Jan. 11, 1727/8 *BNL.*
'Aequore germanos glacies infida relinquens.'
T: [On the drowning of George and Nathan Howell.] ¶ No: 4 lines.

80. Jan. 15, 1727/8 *BG.*
'Rise Heavenly Muse, but rise with heavy Wings.'
Note: A reprint of no. 75.

81. Jan. 15, 1727/8 *NEWJ.*
'Rouze up my Soul, awake thy active Pow'rs.'
T: 'Lines ... written upon the Death of a fine Gentlewoman, who was well known in the Town, and by their Soft and Passionate Strain, confess their Author to be but too nearly and tenderly concerned in the loss.' ['On the Death of Mrs. Mascarene']. ¶ No: 34 lines.

Note: Contained in 'Proteus Echo' number 41. Entitled 'On the Death of Mrs. Mascarene' in J. Belknap's 'A Collection of Poetry' (see no. 71), pp. 21–22. In Jan. 22, 1727/8 *NEWJ* 'Proteus Echo' notes, 'I have received the Letter No. 2. with the inclosed, which I presume is from the unknown Author of the Copy of Verses inserted in our last Paper.' Mrs. Mascarene, the wife of Paul Mascarene, died on January 2; her obituary appeared in *BG*, Jan. 8, 1727/8. Reprinted, see no. 82. For Paul Mascarene's thanks, see no. 85.

82. Jan. 22, 1727/8 *BG*.
'Rouze up my Soul, awake thy active Pow'rs.'
Note: A reprint of no. 81.

83. Feb. 12, 1727/8 *NEWJ*.
'Now, O ye Nine ! if all your Pow'rs can paint.'
T: 'A Poetical Lamentation, occasioned by the Death of His Late Majesty King George the First.' ¶ No: 143 lines. ¶ A: 'M' [Matthew Adams].
Note: Proteus Echo ⌗ 45; excellent local poetry; the 'M' identifies Matthew Adams as the author. See no. 69 for Mather Byles' poem on the same subject. C. Lennart Carlson, in his edition of Byles' *Poems on Several Occasions*, p. ix, said that this poem (no. 83) was never published. In the poem, Adams compliments Byles. It is reprinted in *A Collection of Poems* (Boston, 1744), pp. 19–24; Mather Byles identifies the author with ms. attributions in the copies at the Mass. Hist. Soc. and the Hist. Soc. of Penna.

84. Feb. 13, 1728 *AWM*.
'Oh Say what is that thing call'd Light.'
Note: A reprint of no. 76.

85. Feb. 26, 1727/8 *BG*.
'What strange Conceits attend on real Grief.'
T: [Mascarene thanks the elegist who wrote on his wife.] ¶ No: 12 lines. ¶ A: 'P.M.' [Paul Mascarene].
Note: See no. 81. For Major-General Paul Mascarene (1684–1760), Governor of Annapolis Royal, Nova Scotia, whose son John graduated from Harvard in 1741, see the *DNB*.

86. Mar. 4, 1727/8 *NEWJ*.
'O'er that sad sacred Tomb where B—t lies.'
T: 'On B—t's Elegy by J.H.' ¶ No: 20 lines. ¶ A: 'J.H.' (or is J.H. the author of an elegy on B—t that this poem is satirizing ?).
Note: Part of Proteus Echo number 48; '... The following very beautiful Lines, written by a Young Gentleman too accomplished to lye hid in the Obscurity, which his Modesty at this Time de-

sires. There seems to be in it, a fine Vein of genteel Satyr, a variety of Poetical Thoughts, a Purity and Richness of Language, wrought into very numerous & flowing verse.'

87. Mar. 18, 1727/8 *NEWJ.*
'As once the Shame of *Gath* with impious Boast.'
T: 'A Letter: The following Epistle, was sent some years since, to an ingenious Gentleman, upon his being challeng'd to a Dispute with a person of such Principles, as are subversive of that Liberty we have now mentioned, as well as the noble Designs of Civil and Ecclesiastical Government.' ¶ No: 59 lines. ¶ A: 'S' [Matthew Adams].
Note: Part of 'Proteus Echo' number 50; contains references to Charles Lesley and to Robert Dodsley's *Epistle*. The key in 'Proteus Echo' no. 52, Ap. 1, 1728, *NEWJ*, identifies Adams as the author.

88. Apr. 1, 1728 *NEWJ.*
'Let grov'ling rhymers court an awkward Muse.'
T: 'To a Young Lady. Written with a Pen presented by Her to the Author.' ¶ No: 26 lines. ¶ A: 'Z' [Mather Byles].
Note: Reprinted in Byles (see no. 60), pp. 96–97.

89. Apr. 15, 1728 *BG* #438.
'Again fair Nymph, you charm our wond'ring eyes.'
T: 'To Florinda.' ¶ No: 24 lines. ¶ A: 'Tim. Vainlove.'
Note: With accompanying letter; good *carpe diem* poem.

90. July 8, 1728 *NEWJ.*
'When the proud Philistines for war declar'd.'
T: 'Goliah's Defeat.' ¶ No: 89 lines. ¶ A: 'Your hearty Friend' [Mather Byles].
Note: Pref. letter: '... the Lines are written in imitation of Statius; and therefore if there appear any Metaphors in it, too bold and forced; or if the Lines run in any places, more rough and grating than ordinary, it must be imputed, not to the Author, but to the Poet he intends to imitate. Those strokes which would otherwise have been unpardonable considered in this Light, will be allowed Beauties: and I persuade myself, all who are acquainted with Statius' Sentiment and Manner, will here see some Resemblance of him.' The poem is also found in pp. 12–15 in Belknap (see no. 71), where it is attributed to 'M.B.,' which stands for Mather Byles in this commonplace book. Reprinted in Byles (see no. 60), pp. 18–23.

91. July 25, 1728 *BNL* #82, 1/2–2/1.
'Immortal William sav'd the British Isle.'

T: 'A Gratulatory Poem received from a Friend the Day after the Arrival of His Excellency Governour Burnet.' ¶ No: 47 lines.

Note: William Burnet, formerly Governor of New York and New Jersey, had just been appointed Governor of Massachusetts.

92. July 29, 1728 *NEWJ* #71.

'Burnet, To Thee the darling Muse would sing.'

T: 'A Congratulatory Poem, etc.' ¶ No: 88 lines. ¶ A: [Mather Byles?].

Note: Welcoming William Burnet as Gov. of Mass. Mather Byles wrote 'A poem presented to His Excellency William Burnet ...' [Boston, 1728], Evans 3004, which is not the same as the present poem. Although I am not positive that the present poem is by Byles, the Library of Congress card for Evans 3004 notes 'Not the same as the poem by Mr. Byles published in the *NEWJ* July 29, 1728.'

93. Aug. 5, 1728 *NEWJ* #72.

'Long has *New England* groan'd beneath the Load.'

T: 'On reading the POEM to His Excellency, by Mr. *Byles.*' ¶ No: 24 lines. ¶ A: [Dr. John Perkins.]

Note: Fulsomely complimentary poem. This poem may refer either to no. 92 or to Evans 3004. Reprinted in *A Collection of Poems* (Boston, 1744), pp. 13–14; Mather Byles' ms. notes in the copies at the Massachusetts Hist. Soc. and the Hist. Soc. of Penna. identify the author.

94. Aug. 26, 1728 *BG* #457.

'What heat of Learning kindled your desire?'

T: '... Lines occasioned by the Burning of a Grammar-School ...' ¶ No: 28 lines. ¶ A: 'T.W.'

Note: Copied in Belknap (see no. 71), pp. 17–18. Crum W487 notes that it was printed in *Wit and Drollery* (London, 1661), p. 104, where it is attributed to 'T. R.'

95. Nov. 25, 1728 *NEWJ* #88.

'Hail sacred Art! Thou Gift of Heaven, design'd.'

T: 'A Poem on the Art of Printing, which was wrought at the Printing Press carry'd before the Corporation of Stationers in their Cavalcade with the other Companies of Dublin.' ¶ No: 26 lines. ¶ A: [Constantia Grierson.]

Note: This was printed with no. 96, which is by James Sterling, a poet who later emigrated to America. It is dated Dublin, Aug. 10. Reprinted, nos. 97, 1118, 1122, 1128. The Dublin broadside containing these two poems was reprinted several times. There is a facsimile in E. R. M'Clintock Dix, 'An Early Eighteenth-Century

Broadside on Printing.' *Royal Irish Academy Proceedings*, XXVII
(1908–9), 401–403. Crum H97.

96. Nov. 25, 1728 *NEWJ* #88.
'Say, Cadmus, by what Ray divine inspir'd.'
T: 'Second Poem' [On the Art of Printing]. ¶ No: 54 lines. ¶ A:
[James Sterling.]
Note: Like no. 95, this is reprinted from a Dublin broadside. Sterling
later emigrated to America. The poem, slightly revised, is in *The
Poetical Works of the Rev. James Sterling* (Dublin, 1734), pp. 118–
121. Reprinted, no. 98. In America, Sterling revised and enlarged
the poem, and dedicated it to Samuel Richardson, see no. 1426.
On Sterling, see Lawrence C. Wroth, *James Sterling: Poet, Priest
and Prophet of Empire* (Worcester, 1931) an offprint from the *Pro-
ceedings* of the Am. Antiquarian Soc. XLI (1931), 25–76.

97. Dec. 24, 1728 *AWM* #468.
'Hail sacred art! Thou Gift of Heaven design'd.'
Note: Reprint of no. 95.

98. Dec. 24, 1728 *AWM* #67.
'Say, Cadmus, by what Ray divine inspir'd.'
Note: Reprint of no. 96.

99. Dec. 24, 1728 *MG* #67.
'What means this Mourning, Ladies, has Death led.'
T: 'An Elegy [on] the Death of the Honourable Nicholas Lowe,
Esq.' ¶ No: 40 lines, with a 9-line epitaph. ¶ A: 'E. Cooke,
Laureat.'
Note: Reprinted in Bernard C. Steiner, ed., *Early Maryland Poetry*
(Baltimore, 1900), pp. 53–54. 'Laureat' refers to Ebenezer
Cook(e)'s title, Poet Laureate of Maryland.

100. Dec. 30, 1728 *NEWJ* #94 [93 really!], pp. 1–2.
'At Ten this Morn, Dear Friend, Your most.'
T: 'A Letter to a Gentleman, in Answer to a Latin Epistle, written
in a very obscure Hand.' ¶ No: 129 lines.
Note: A satirical rejoiner (in the form of a vision-essay) to this
poem is in *NEWJ* #95, Jan. 13, 1728/9, 1–2.

1729

101. Jan. 7, 1728/9 *PG* #3.
'All which, by full Experience plain doth show.'
T: [Against drinking rum.] ¶ No: 4 lines. ¶ A: [S. Keimer?].

102. Jan. 13, 1728/9 *BG* #477.
'While fair Belinda's various Strains conspire.'

T: 'Lines occasioned by having heard a Young Lady play on the *Spinet.*' ¶ No: 14 lines. ¶ A: 'Tim Constard.'

Note: Dated 'Boston, Jan. 9.'

103. Jan. 21, 1728/9 *PG* #5.

'Too long have Party-Broils usurpt the Song.'

T: [On Pennsylvania.] ¶ No: 45 lines. ¶ A: 'Jack Careless.'

Note: Poem in praise of Penna, concluding with adulation of Addison. Prefatory note says: 'Mr. Keimer, Upon reading an advertisement in your *Gazette*, No. 4 [where Keimer asks for contributions], I send you the following epitome of something far more universal 1 had form'd of the Kind, which (if this meets with a generous Reception) may in Time see the Light. By inserting it, you may hear further from Jack Careless.'

105. March 13, 1728/9 *PG* #12.

'Since you've provok'd my humble Rage.'

T: 'An Answer to the Busy-Body.' ¶ No: 33 lines. ¶ A: 'Morisini' [Samuel Keimer].

Note: Couplets: 'You hinted at me in your Paper,/Which now has made me draw my Rapier.' This seems to be Keimer's reply to Franklin.

106. Mar. 17, 1728/9 *NEWJ* #104.

'Tho' Angels could infuse their holy Fire.'

T: 'A Paraphrase—XIII. Chap. of the I. Corinthians.' ¶ No: 56 lines. ¶ A: [Rev. John Adams.]

Note: Reprinted in Adams, *Poems* (Boston, 1745), pp. 57–59; Evans 5527.

107. Mar. 30, 1729 *NEWJ* #106.

'Dreams, on whose fleeting shades our fancy's rove.'

T: '... Translations from Petronius.'

Note: No. IX of an essay series. For another poem by the same author, see no. 110.

108. Apr. 3, 1729 *AWM* #482.

'Once *Cupid* on Summer's Day.'

T: 'Cupid Wounded, The Hint Taken from Theocrotus' [sic]. ¶ No: 50 lines. ¶ A: 'Damon.'

Note: There is 'A Comment on ['Cypid Wounded'] the verses in Bradford's Mercury) #482' in *PG*, Apr. 10, 1729, #16. Accompanying the poem, there is the following note: 'N.B. The Author of this piece desires to inform the Gentlemen of Taste, that according as they shall think proper to receive this Trifle, they shall meet with some little diverting Papers of this kind, that may be of a little amusement to 'em, in their leisure Hours.' Reprinted, see no. 113. In the *AWM*, June 19, 'Damon' writes in, saying he has heard of the criticism of his poetry.

109. Apr. 10, 1729 *PG* ⚹16.
'We mourn your Fate, unhappily severe.'
T: 'Epitaph for Busy-Body.' ¶ No: 7 lines. ¶ A: [S. Keimer].
Note: Keimer wrote a news notice about the cessation of the 'Busy-Body' essay series and this epitaph.

110. Apr. 21, 1729 *NEWJ* ⚹109.
'Oft has my anxious mind been rack'd to know.'
T: 'The Publick having paid so great and just applause to the Translation from *Petronius* [see no. 107,] which I lately gave them; ... a Version of a very beautiful passage in the second Book of *Claudian's Rufinus* ...' ¶ No: 31 lines.
Note See no. 107.

111. May 15, 1729 *AWM* ⚹488.
'Five Times Ten Miles from Town, a clyme there lies.'
T: '... [lines] written by way of grateful Return for some kind and hospitable Entertainment receiv'd at his Friend's Habitation ...' ¶ No: 22 lines. ¶ A: 'Philomusus' [Joseph Breintnall].
Note: Part of 'Busy-Body ⚹13'. Breintnall wrote the 'Busy Body' essay series (excepting Benjamin Franklin's contributions), and he was a poet. On Breintnall (d. 1746), see the *Franklin Papers*, I, 114n.

112. May 19, 1729 *NEWJ* ⚹113, p. 1.
'In some calm midnight, when no whisp'ring breeze.'
T: 'The Conflagration, A Poem.' ¶ No: 123 lines. ¶ A: [Mather Byles].
Note: This was included in Byles (see no. 60), pp. 100–106. A prefatory note says that the author wrote it when he was 15. Reprinted in Kettell, I, 126–129.

113. May 27, 1729 *MG* ⚹89.
'Once Cupid on a Summer's Day.'
Note: Reprint of no. 108.

113a. May 27, 1729 *MG*.
'Go forth my Muse, and be not thou dismay'd.'
T: [On Determining Longitude.] ¶ No: 10 lines. ¶ A: John Smith.
Note: Dated 'Cecil County [Maryland], May 22, 1729.'

114. June 12, 1729 *AWM* ⚹492.
'What brought me here, —Custom and Fancy flee.'
T: 'Serious Reflections at Church, on Sunday, the 9th of June, in the Morning.' ¶ No: 16 lines. ¶ A: 'Damon.'
Note: First of three poems by 'Damon' in this issue (see nos. 115 and 116).

115. June 12, 1729 *AWM* #492.
    'Now will I Guard against my Morning Fall.'
    T: 'In the Afternoon at the P[resbyteria]n Meeting.' ¶ No: 6 lines.
        ¶ A: 'Damon.'
    Note: Cf. nos. 114 and 116.

116. June 12, 1729 *AWM* #492.
    'Passing those Fields where Negroe slaves are found.'
    T: 'In the Evening's Walk.' ¶ No: 43 lines. ¶ A: 'Damon.'
    Note: See nos. 114 and 115.

117. June 19, 1729 *AWM* #493.
    'At Delaware's broad Stream, the View begin.'
    T: ['a plain Description of one single Street (Market Street) in this
        City.'] ¶ No: 59 lines. ¶ A: [Joseph Breintnall.]
    Note: The poem describes the courthouse, Friends' meeting house,
        and prison in Market Street; part of Busy-Body #18. See no. 111
        for attribution. Reprinted in Silverman, pp. 374–375.

118. June 19, 1729 *AWM* #493.
    'Make 'way for Hymen with his Lights.'
    T: 'On seeing a Wedding at the Rev'd Mr. Cum[ming]s on Monday
        last, when the good Woman's Apron gave large Testimonies that
        Connubial liberties had been taken, and the Ill natur'd Crowd
        laugh'd the poor Fellow out of Countenance.' ¶ No: 30 lines. ¶
        A: 'Damon.'

119. June 24, 1729 *MG* #93.
    'Let other Pens th' ungrateful News declare.'
    T: 'Mr. Blackamore's *Expeditio Ultramontana*, render'd into Eng-
        lish Verse. Inscrib'd to the Honourable the Governour [Alex-
        ander Spotswood].' ¶ No: 197 lines. ¶ A: Rev. George Seagood's
        English translation of Rev. Arthur Blackamore's poem.
    Note: Reprinted by Lyon G. Tyler, ed., *William and Mary Quarter-
        ly*, 1st ser., VII, 30–37; and by Earl G. Swem, ed. *Mr. Blacka-
        more's Expeditio Ultramontana* (Richmond, Va., 1960). A few
        lines of the original Latin (which has since disappeared) were
        translated by Godfrey Pole in *Southern Literary Messenger*, II
        (March, 1836), 258. Reprinted in Silverman, pp. 317–322. On
        Blackamore, see R.B. Davis, 'Arthur Blackamore: The Virginia
        Colony and the Early English Novel,' *Va. Mag. of Hist. and
        Biog.*, LXXV (1967), 22–34.

120 June 26, 1729 *AWM* #494.
    'You who in London youthful Passions fir'd.'
    T: 'To Madam —.' ¶ No: 63 lines. ¶ A: 'Damon.'

121. July 3, 1729 *PG* #28.
'How is my honest Soul oppress'd!'
T: [Poem written in Prison.] ¶ No: 52 lines. ¶ A: 'S. Keimer.'
Note: Keimer was in prison for debt; cf. no. 124.

122. July 3, 1729 *AWM* #495, 3/1–2.
'Let Philadelphia's generous Sons excuse.'
T: 'We have received the following Lines out of the Country from an unknown Hand, Occasioned by some of our fomer [i.e., former] Publications.' ¶ No: 44 lines. ¶ A: 'T.Z.' [Richard Lewis or George Webb?].
Note: This contains the first statement of the important *translatio studii* theme (i.e., future glory of America) in American newspaper verse. Cf. no. 182 for another poem signed 'T.Z.' For an account of Richard Lewis, see J. A. Leo Lemay, 'Richard Lewis and Augustan American Poetry,' *PMLA*, LXXXIII (1968), 80–101. George Webb (c. 1706–1732?), whom Franklin characterizes in the *Autobiography*, was a poet and printer. He drops out of sight after his *Batchelors-Hall; a Poem* (Philadelphia, 1731; Evans 3485) appeared; and he probably is the printer who died in S.C. early in 1732.

123. July 3, 1729 *AWM* #495.
'Reynard for Cunning is Renown'd.'
T: 'On Seeing a Fox get Drunk with Punch, on Board the Olive-Branch, at Capt. Birch's Departure.' ¶ No: 10 lines. ¶ A: 'Damon.'

124. Sept. 4, 1729 *PG* #36.
'Alas poor Shad.'
T: [To Tom Shad, a Philadelphia Creditor.] ¶ No: 6 lines. ¶ A: S. Keimer.
Note: Part of Keimer's diatribe against creditors. cf. no. 121.

125. Oct. 6, 1729 *NEWJ* #133, p. 1.
'Of all the Draughts of heavenly Art.'
T: 'The Gospel.' ¶ No: 28 lines.
Note: This is 'a Specimen of a Collection of Miscellany Poems.' Cf. no. 126.

126. Oct. 6, 1729 *NEWJ* #133, p. 1.
'With Majesty and Glory clad.'
T: 'A paraphrase on the former Part of the Ninety-Seventh Psalm.' ¶ No: 37 lines.
Note: Second example of 'A Specimen of a Collection of Miscellany Poems'; see no. 125.

127. Oct. 13, 1729 *NYG* #206.
'In Mournful Lays let Melpomene sing.'

T: 'An ELEGY upon his Excellency William Burnet, Esq., who departed this Life September 7th, 1729 AETat. 42.' ¶ No: 66 lines with 10 line epitaph.

1730

128. Jan. 6, 1729/30 *NYG* ⚡218.
'Let this give Notice to my Friends.'
T: 'Daniel Dood of Newark in New Jersey, Surveyor, designs to remove to another place and therefore gives publick Notice in his own State of Poetry, viz:' ¶ No: 24 lines. ¶ A: 'Daniel Dood.'

129. Jan. 13, 1729/30 *PG* ⚡61, pp. 1–2.
'Long since I bad the pleasing Muse adieu.'
T: '*To Mr.* Samuel Hastings, (ship-wright of Philadelphia) *on his launching* the Maryland Merchant, *a large ship built by him at* Annapolis.' ¶ No: 219 lines. ¶ A: [Richard Lewis].
Note: 'From the *Maryland Gazette*, December 30' (which is not extant). See no. 130.

130. Jan. 14, 1729/30 *AWM* ⚡523, pp. 3–4.
'Long since I bade the pleasant Muse adieu.'
Note: Although the *AWM* printing does not acknowledge it, the poem is evidently reprinted (like no. 129), from a non-extant copy of the *MG.*

131. *circa* Jan. 1729/30 *BG.*
"Ages our Land a barb'rous Desert stood.'
T: 'To Mr. Smibert on the sight of his Pictures.' ¶ No: 80 lines. ¶ A: [Mather Byles].
Note: Reprinted in *AWM*, Feb. 19, 1729/30 (see no. 133), so a Boston printing in January may be presumed. The *BG* for the first part of 1730 is not extant, and the reply to it (see no. 144) is in the *BG* for Apr. 13, 1730, suggesting that Byles' poem had appeared in that paper. Reprinted in the London *Daily Courant* for Apr. 14, 1730; in part in George Vertue, *Note Books*, III (Walpole Society, Vol. XXII, 1934), 42; reprinted from London *Daily Courant* in Henry Wilder Foote, *John Smibert, Painter* (Cambridge, 1950), pp. 54–55; and reprinted by Byles (see no. 60), pp. 89–93 and misdated by C. Lennart Carlson in his facsimile edition as 1735, pp. xii–xiii. Reprinted in Silverman, pp. 235–237.

133. Feb. 19, 1729/30 *AWM* ⚡528.
'Ages our Land a barb'rous Desert stood.'
Note: Reprint of no. 131.

134. Feb. 24, 1729/30 *PG* #67.
'Masters should have sound Wit, and Documents that's plain.'
T: [To the muse who fosters knowledge.] ¶ No: 19 lines. ¶ A: 'John Lloyd.'
Note: 4 lines, then 3 of Latin, then 12 more lines. Lloyd was a schoolmaster (in Arch Street, Phila.) and this is part of his advertisement.

135. Mar. 9, 1729/30 *NEWJ* #155.
'Say muse, what Numbers shall relate.'
T: ['Nanny' refuses Benjamin for love of Sampson.] ¶ No: 32 lines. ¶ A: 'J.W.' [John Winthrop IV ?].
Note: A prefatory note is dated 'Boston, March 7, 1729/30.' 4 stanzas of 8 lines each. Reprinted, see no. 142.

136. Mar. 16, 1729/30 *BG* #536.
'Others their Beauty heighten and improve.'
T: 'To Miss S— W—.' ¶ No: 9 lines.
Note: Perhaps not local. Copied in Belknap (see no. 71), pp. 18–19.

137. Mar. 17, 1729/30 *MG* #131.
'When God was pleas'd with Truth divinely bright.'
T: 'Verses on St. Patrick's Day: Sacred to Mirth and Good-Nature.' ¶ No: 97 lines. ¶ A: 'Somerset English.'
Note: Dated 'March 16, 1729/30.' Reprinted, no. 181.

138. Mar. 30, 1730 *BG* #538.
'Clos'd are those Eyes, that beam'd Seraphic Fire!'
T: 'Epitaph on a Young Lady lately Dead.' ¶ No: 16 lines. ¶ A: 'R.S.' [Richard Savage].
Note: Reprinted, see no. 150. Reprinted in *Polyanthes*, I (Jan 1806), 133–134; and in Clarence Tracy, *The Poetical Works of Richard Savage* (Cambridge, Eng., 1962), pp. 159–160.

139. Mar. 30, 1730 *NEWJ* #158.
'In a thick Shade, the Owl, the Bat.'
T: 'The Night-Birds and the Sun, A Fable.' ¶ No: 17 lines with a 2 line application.
Note: Reprinted, see nos. 151, 223, and 906.

140. Mar. 31, 1730 *MG* #133.
'Tell me, Old Man, with stooping Head.'
T: 'The Aged Creole: Or, The Way to Long Life in Jamaica. A copy of Verses, Occasioned by a Conversation with an Ancient Person of that Island.' ¶ No: 88 lines.

141. Apr. 6, 1730 *NEWJ*.
'Oh lead me where my Darling lies.'

T: 'Written on the Death of an only Daughter.' ¶ No: 16 lines.
Note: Copied on pp. 22–23 in Belknap (see no. 71).

142. Apr. 9, 1730 *AWM* ⸭536.
'Say muse, what Numbers shall relate.'
Note: A reprint of no. 135.

143. Apr. 9, 1730 *PG* ⸭73.
'Let gloomy Groves, let awful Rocks and Hills.'
T: 'On the Death of Mr. Austin Paris.' ¶ No: 20 lines.
Note: 5 stanzas, couplets, terminal refrain. 'Last night [25 Mar]
died suddenly, Mr. Austin Paris of this City, Founder'—*PG* ⸭71,
Mar. 26, 1730.

144. Apr. 13, 1730 *BG*.
'Unhappy Bard ! Spring in such Gothic Times.'
T: 'To Mr. B[yles], occasioned by his verses to Mr. Smibert on
seeing his Pictures.' ¶ No: 12 lines. ¶ A: [Joseph Green?].
Note: Reply to no. 131. This issue of the *BG* is missing, but the poem
was copied by Jeremy Belknap (see no. 71), p. 18. Reprinted
Mass. Hist. Soc. *Proc.*, LIII (Dec, 1919), 59, and in Henry Wilder
Foote, *John Smibert, Painter* (Cambridge, 1950), p. 56.

145. Apr. 20, 1730 *NEWJ* ⸭161.
'To yonder Hills of sacred Bliss.'
T: 'A Paraphrase on Psalm CXXI.' ¶ No: 16 lines.

146. Apr. 27, 1730 *NEWJ* ⸭162.
'To Spheres above, and distant Hills.'
T: 'A Paraphrase on the CXXI Psalm.' ¶ No: 28 lines.
Note: Reprinted, see no. 154.

148. June 18, 1730 *AWM* ⸭546.
'In various Shapes have I been shewn.'
T: 'Cupid, On Seeing himself painted by a young Lady.' ¶ No: 52
lines.
Note: 'From the Boston Gazette.' This issue of the *BG* is not extant.

150. June 25, 1730 *AWM*.
'Clos'd are those Eyes, that beam'd Seraphic Fire!'
Note: A reprint of no. 138.

151. June 25, 1730 *AWM*.
'In a Thick Shade, the Owl, the Bat.'
Note: A reprint of no. 139.

152. June 29, 1730 *NEWJ*.
'How vain is Man! how fickle his estate!'
T: 'An Elegy On a Report of the *Pretender's* Death.' ¶ No: 32 lines
plus 8 line epitaph.

153. June 29, 1730 *NEWJ*, 1/1.
  'Lucida, qui novit numeris constringere justis.'
  T: [Elegy.] ¶ No: 9 lines (Latin).
  Note: Accompanied by an essay on poetry, which praises the poem,
    the subject and the author.

154. July 2, 1730 *AWM*.
  'To Spheres above, and distant Hills.'
  Note: A reprint of no. 146.

155. July 13, 1730 *NYG*.
  'The Dean would visit Market-Hill.'
  T: 'The Lady weary of Dean Sw—ft.'

156. Aug. 11, 1730 *NEWJ*.
  'You ask, Dear Friend, that I ressume the Lyre.'
  T: 'A Letter to Mr. —.' ¶ No: 32 lines. ¶ A: [Mather Byles].
  Note: The poem refers to the author's poems on Gov. William
    Burnet, and on the coming of Gov. Jonathan Belcher.

157. Aug. 13, 1730 *PG*.
  'Go, favourite Man, spread to the Wind thy Sails.'
  T: 'To his Excellency Jonathan Belcher, Esq, in London, appointed
    by his Majesty King George II, to the Government of New Eng-
    land, and now returning Home.' ¶ A: 'I[saac] Watts.'
  Note: Dateline: 'Boston, July, 27. We have had published here the
    following congratulatory Poem, lately communicated from *Lon-
    don.*' The poem is dated 'March 31, 1730.' Evidently the Boston
    newspaper of July 27 is no longer extant. Cf. no. 159. The poem
    was reprinted in Watts, *Horae Lyricae* (New York, 1750), pp.
    224–226.

158. Aug. 17, 1730 *NEWJ*.
  'My Muse uncall'd, starts forth; not vainly fir'd.'
  T: 'A Congratulatory Poem to his Excellency Governour Belcher,
    at his Arrival.' ¶ No: 78 lines. ¶ A: 'J.P.' [Dr. John Perkins?].
  Note: A note on Perkins (1698–1783?) as a poet may be found in
    Alonzo Lewis, *The History of Lynn* (Boston, 1829), p. 183.

159. Sept. 7, 1730 *NEWJ*.
  'He comes! great Watts, he comes! (thy Vows prevail).'
  T: 'To Dr. Watts, Upon the Arrival of His Excellency Jonathan
    Belcher, Esq; to his Government of New England.' ¶ No: 38
    lines.
  Note: Cf. no. 157.

160. Sept. 21, 1730 *NEWJ*.
  'Ye tuneful Nine, who all my Soul inspire.'
  T: 'Belinda. A Pastoral.' ¶ No: 78 lines. ¶ A: [Mather Byles.]

Note: Copied in Jeremy Belknap's 'A Collection of Poems' (see no.
71), pp. 56–57, where the poem is entitled: 'Belinda, a Pastoral,
written by Rev. Mr. Byles, Sent to Miss Rogers of Portsmouth
afterwards the amiable wife of Rev. Mr. John Taylor of Milton.'
Reprinted in the *Boston Mag*, I (Mar. 1784), 197–198.

161. Sept. 24, 1730 *PG*.
'If Bees a Government maintain.'
T: 'The Rats and the Cheese, a Fable.' ¶ No: 42 lines. ¶ A: [B.
Franklin?].
Note: Franklin's prefatory letter: 'In our last we gave our Readers
the most material Paragraphs of Governor *Belcher*'s Speech to the
Assembly of his other Government of *New-Hampshire*; and in our
next shall insert his Speech at large to the Assembly of *Massachu-
setts*, which we have by this Post, It may suffice at present to ob-
serve it, that he has brought with him those very instructions that
occasion'd the Difference between Governor *Burnet* and that
People, which were what he went home commission'd as Agent
for the Country, to get withdrawn, as an intolerable Grievance.
But by being at Court, it seems, he has had the *advantage* of seeing
Things in another Light, and those Instructions do now appear to
him highly consistent with the Privileges and Interest of the
People, which before, as a Patriot, he had very different Notions
of.' As Francis X. Davy (see no. 25), p. 49, has noted, this poem
is inspired by Bernard Mandeville's 'The Grumbling Hive.'

162. Sept. 24, 1730, *PG*.
'Myrtle unsheath'd his shining *Blade*.'
T: 'The Fright.'
¶ No: 12 lines.

163. Oct. 20, 1730 *MG*.
'Melpomene, assist my mournful Theme.'
T: 'An Elegy, On the Death of Miss Elizabeth Young, late of Cal-
vert County. Gentlewoman.' ¶ No: 48 lines. ¶ A: 'By a Wel-
wisher, to the Memory of the Deceas'd.'
Note: Sent in by 'incogniti.' Poor verse.

164. Nov. 2, 1730 *NYG*.
'Our Fathers crost the wide Atlantick Sea.'
T: 'The following Lines were put over the Door of the General
Court, viz.' ¶ No: 8 lines.
Note: Reprinted in *New Jersey Archives*, XI, 225, and in Kenneth
Scott, ' "Rattling" Verses on Royal Prerogative,' *N.Y. Folklore
Quart.*, XIII (1957), 195–203. Occasioned by Jonathan Belcher's
demand for a fixed salary as Governor of Massachusetts. For con-

temporary reprints and replies, see nos. 165, 166, 167, 168, 170, 172, 176, 177, 178A. Cf. no. 769B. Crum O1262.

165. Nov. 2, 1730 *NTG.*
'Their Fathers crost the wide Atlantick Sea.'
T: 'A Stranger passing by, and seeing several Persons reading the above lines, caused him to stop, and having perused the same, he took a piece of Calk [sic], and writ under-neath the Lines following, viz.' ¶ No: 8 lines.
Note: A satirical reply to no. 164; reprinted in *New Jersey Archives,* XI, 225, and K. Scott (see no. 164). For replies, see nos. 167 and 168. Crum T1642.

166. Nov. 5, 1730 *PG.*
'Our Fathers pass'd the wide Atlantick Sea.'
T: 'Something since the following Lines were found stuck on the outside of the Door of the Council Chamber.'
Note: A reprint of no. 164.

167. Nov. 5, 1730 *PG.*
'Their Fathers crost the wide Atlantick Sea.'
T: 'To which a Gentleman in New York has wrote the following Answer.'
Note: A reprint of no. 165. B. Franklin added this note in the *PG* on the religious reasons for emigrating to New England: 'Whatever Wit there may be in this Answer, it contains one Reflection not altogether just: Since 'tis certain, that the greatest Part of the Settlers of New-England removed thither on no other Account than for the sake of enjoying their Liberty, especially their religious Liberties, in greater Security: Being persecuted at home, as *Puritans* in the Reign of *James I,* and among all other Dissenters in the Reign of Charles II.'

168. Dec. 7, 1730 *NTG.*
'Presumptuous Traytor, we can make't appear.'
T: 'I am a Boston Man by Birth, and meeting with your last Weeks Gazette, I there found a Satyr on the New-England Verses, wrote by a Gentleman passing thro 'Perth-Amboy, I reading them, called for Pen, Ink and Paper, and wrote the following answer to it, and seeing it is Poetry, I wrote this in his own Stile, viz.' ¶ No: 24 lines.
Note: Dated 'Connecticut, Dec. 3.' Reply to no. 165; reprinted in *New Jersey Archives,* XI, 230–231 and in K. Scott (see no. 164). 'Now should a salary be fix'd out-right/On him that's appointed to guide us Right,/Then all our Dear-bought Freedom takes its Flight' (11. 16–18).

169. Dec. 22, 1730 *PG.*
'Phoebus, Wit-inspiring Lord!'
T: 'An Invitation to the Hall.' ¶ No: 8 lines.
Note: 'To the Publisher of the Gazette. A gentleman the other night
gave these Lines to my Hand: They carry an Air of good Reading,
easy Versification, and the sprightly Turn of Epigram. 'Tis a well
turn'd Compliment to *Batchelors Hall,* and I think will make a
handsome Appearance in your Paper.' This compliments George
Webb's *Batchelors-Hall* (Philadelphia, 1731). Reprinted, see no.
175.

170. Dec. 22, 1730 *NYG.*
'Hail happy Man! *New -England's* genuine Son.'
T: 'One who has a just Value for the Connecticut Poetry in your
Gazette, Number 267. Takes Leave to congratulate the Poet on
extraordinary Performance.' ¶ No: 10 lines.
Note: Dated 'Richmond, Dec. 8, 1730.' A reply to no. 168. Re-
printed in *New Jersey Archives,* XI, 232, and in K. Scott (see no.
164), p. 199.

1731

171. Jan. 4, 1730/1 *NYG.*
'In Scenes confus'd the busy Year we've past.'
T: [New Year's verses—title cut off]. ¶ No: 30 lines.
Note: A portion quoted in K. Scott (see no. 164), p. 200.

172. Jan. 18, 1730/1 *BG.*
'Our Fathers pass'd the great Atlantic Sea.'
T: 'A Letter from one in the County to his Friend in Town.' ¶ No: 9
lines. ¶ A: 'T.S.'
Note: See no. 164. This is contained in an essay urging, in effect, the
Massachusetts legislature to fix the Governor's salary. Reprinted
in K. Scott (see no. 164), p. 200.

173. Jan. 26, 1730/1 *AWM.*
'E'er the full Vigour of the rip'ning Year.'
T: 'To Caelia.' ¶ No: 24 lines. ¶ A: 'Ignavus.'
Note: Typical war of sexes poetry. Reprinted, no. 180.

174. Jan. 26, 1730/1 *PG.*
'The grateful Tribute of these rural Lays.'
T: 'The Thresher's Labour.' ¶ No: 283 lines. ¶ A: Stephen Duck.
Note: Benjamin Franklin also printed Duck's poem on Poverty in
#116, Feb. 2, 1730/1 (see no. 190), and 'The Shulamite' in #122,
Mar. 18, 1730/1.

175. Feb. 1, 1730/1 *BG*.

'Phoebus, Wit-inspiring Lord!'

Note: A reprint of no. 169.

176. Feb. 2, 1730/1 *NYG*.

'All Hail, My Sons, who can so justly Trace.'

T: 'Lu[cife]r to the People of B[osto]n.' ¶ No: 12 lines.

Note: Dated 'Hellgate, Jan. 24, 1730'; on Massachusetts politics, with letter; reprinted in K. Scott (see no. 164), p. 201. Cf. no. 164.

177. Feb. 9, 1730/1 *NYG*.

'Mine, and the F[ur]ies Sons, why are your Lyres.'

T: 'Pluto from H[ell] gate to his expected Gusts from B[osto]n.' ¶ No: 15 lines.

Note: Dated Feb. 4, 1730/1; reply to preceding; reprinted in K. Scott (see no. 164). Cf. no. 164.

178. Feb. 9, 1730/1 *PG*.

'Say, mighty Love, and teach my Song.'

T: 'Few Happy Matches.' ¶ No: 54 lines. ¶ A: [Isaac Watts.]

Note: Reprinted, nos. 186, where 'J. W—l' is given as the author, and 224. Printed in *Horae Lyricae*. Crum S96.

178a. Feb. 16, 1730/1. *NYG* ⚹277.

'Take Courage, Friends, for in This G[loom]y shade.'

T: [Satirical Reply To Proprietary Party Poetry.] ¶ No: 18 lines.

Note: Prefatory letter: 'P[roserpi]na D[aught]er to Ju[pite]r and C[er]es, as also W[i]fe to Pl[u]to and Q[uee]n of H[e]ll, desires the following may be Recommended to B[osto]n in her behalf, without any alteration, but just as they were given into the hands of A P[oor?] L[ittle?] D[evil?] at H[ell] G[a]te, February 12, 1730/1.' This is the last poem in the series occasioned by Belcher's request for a fixed salary. Reprinted in Scot (see no. 164), p. 202.

179. Mar. 1, 1730/1 *NYG*.

'One Thing I of Paturia must confess.'

T: —. ¶ No.: 14 lines. ¶ A: 'Robt. Cowsturd.'

Note: With a long accompanying letter.

180. Mar. 8, 1730/1 *BG*.

'E're the full Vigour of the rip'ning Year.'

Note: A reprint of no. 173.

181. Mar. 25, 1731 *PG*.

'When *God* was pleas'd, with Truth divinely bright.'

¶ A: 'Philanthropos.'

Note: Despite the signature 'Philanthropos,' this is a reprint of no. 137 (which is signed 'Somerset English').

182. April 8, 1731 *PG* ✻*125*, 3/2–4/1.
     'No more a willing Muse her Aid bestows.'
     T: [Poem in praise of Penna.] ¶ No: 121 lines. ¶ A: 'T.Z.'
     Note: Prefatory note: 'By inserting the following Lines in your
          Paper, when you have Room, you will oblige ... M.M.' The poem
          uses the *translatio imperii* theme, especially lines 50 onward;
          praises Governor Patrick Gordon and William Allen; and refers
          to Waller's 'Bermudas': 'Bright as *Bermudas* seems in Waller's
          Lines.' 'T.Z.' was also the author of no. 122.

183. May 6, 1731 *AWM.*
     "'Twas when a gloom my pensive Soul o're spread.'
     T: 'The *Wits* and *Poets* of Pennsylvania, A Poem, Part I.' ¶ No: 74
     lines. ¶ A: 'E.M.' [E. Magawley?].
     Note: This issue of the *AWM* is incorrectly numbered 594; it is ac-
          tually 592. Very good poetry; prefaced by 2 lines from Horace.
          The author is probably the 'E. Magawley' (a woman) who corre-
          sponded with Joseph Norris in June, 1730 (J. Norris Commonplace
          Book, The Huntington Library). The poem critically evaluates
          Samuel Keimer, Jacob Taylor, Joseph Breintnall, George Webb,
          and Henry Brooke. See 'Wits of Pennsylvania,' *Am. Notes &
          Queries*, IV (1965–66), 9, 41, 72–73. Reprinted in Silverman, pp.
          378–380.

184. May 20, 1731 *PG*, pp. 1–3.
     'At length the wintry horrors disappear.'
     T: 'A Journey from Patapsco to Annapolis.' ¶ No: 387 lines. ¶ A:
     [Richard Lewis].
     Note: For contemporary reprintings, see nos. 187, 198 (revised and
          slightly enlarged), 215, 252a, 253a, and 258. This first extant
          version may well be a reprinting from a now lost issue of the
          Maryland Gazette. Cf. nos. 557, 564.

185. May 20, 1731 *AWM.*
     'I know you Lawyers can, with Ease.'
     T: 'Fable. The Dog and the Fox. To a Lawyer.' ¶ No: 112 lines. ¶
     A: [John Gay].
     Note: This is Gay's Fable I of the Second Series. See *The Poetical
          Works of John Gay*, ed. G.C. Faber (London, 1926), pp. 277–278.
          The first 20 lines were reprinted in Franklin's *POOR RICH-
          ARD*, 1740; see *The Franklin Papers*, II, 254; in *Bickerstaff's
          Boston Almanac*, 1778 (Danvers, Massachusetts, 1777?); and in
          Samuel Bullard, *An Almanack for the Year—1793* (Boston, 1792?)
          Burton J. Konkle, *The Life of Andrew Hamilton* (Philadelphia,
          1941), p. 137, thought the poem pointed at Hamilton. Reprinted,
          no. 303.

186. June 7, 1731 *BG*.
  'Say, mighty Love, and teach my Song.'
  ¶ A: 'J. W—l.'
  Note: A reprint of no. 178.

187. June 21, 1731 *NYG*, pp. 1–2; cont., June 28, pp. 1–2.
  'At length the Wintry Horrors disappear.'
  T: 'The Spring and Summer' [i.e., 'A Journey from Patapsco to Annapolis']. ¶ A: 'P.L.' [Richard Lewis].
  Note: With prefatory letter. An abridged reprint of no. 184.

188. June 28, 1731 *NEWJ*, p. 1.
  'Of ancient Streams presume no more to tell.'
  T: ['Food for Criticks.'] ¶ No: 147 lines. ¶ A: [Richard Lewis?].
  Note: A different version of this poem is listed below, see no. 232. I have suggested that this version, no. 188, and the later one, no. 232, may be revisions of an earlier poem by Richard Lewis that appeared in an issue of the *Md. Gaz.* (which is not extant), sometime before May, 1731. See 'Richard Lewis and Augustan American Poetry,' *PMLA*, LXXXIII (1968), 89–90. Excerpts from the poem are quoted in Duyckinck, I, 77–78. The title is taken from no. 232. Freneau's 'Indian Burial Ground' may imitate this poem.

189. June, 1731 *Gent Mag* I, 261–262.
  'A common Theme a flatt'ring Muse may fire.'
  T: 'An Elegiac Poem by Mr. H. On his only daughter, who dy'd aged 11.' ¶ No: 172 lines. ¶ A: 'Mr. H.'
  Note: For an American reprinting, see no. 216.

190. July 19, 1731 *BG*.
  'There is no Ill on Earth which Mortals Fly.'
  T: 'On Poverty.' ¶ No: 75 lines. ¶ A: 'C.W.' [Stephen Duck].
  Note: This is either an early version or a reworking of Stephen Duck's 'On Poverty,' which in Duck's *Poems on Several Occasions* (London, 1738), pp. 4–7, begins 'No Ill on Earth we Tim'rous Mortals fly.' Cf. no. 174. 'On Poverty' is reprinted in Titan Leeds, *The American Almanac for … 1732* (Phila., 1731).

191. July 26, 1731 *NYG*.
  'This day young Mars in wedlock Bands was ty'd.'
  T: ['Epithalamion.'] ¶ No: 38 lines.
  Note: Dated 'NY, July 20, 1731,' with accompanying note. See no. 192.

192. Aug. 9, 1731 *NYG*.
  'Hail Critick! from whose furious scorching Tongue.'

T: 'To the Author of the Criticism upon the Epithalamion in the last Gazette.' ¶ No: 32 lines. ¶ A: (By the author of no. 191).
Note: Very good. See no. 191. Evidently the criticism was not published.

193. Aug. 23, 1731 *NEWJ*.
'How gaily is at first begun.'
T: 'The Progress of Life.' ¶ No: 45 lines. ¶ A: 'Written by a Female Hand.'

194. Sept. 2, 1731 *PG*.
'Long had mankind with darkness been oppress'd.'
T: 'Verses on the Art of Printing.' ¶ No: 75 lines. ¶ A: [Rev. Thomas Birch.]
Note: Especially praises the printing of Oldus. The poem appeared in James Ralph, *Miscellaneous Poems* (London, 1729), pp. 36–39 (Case 354), in the London *Weekly Register*, Sept. 9, 1732, and in the *Lon Mag* for Sept. 1732 (I, 309). For American reprintings, see nos. 237, 241, and 246.

195. Nov. 4, 1731 *PG*.
'My dearest Daphne, charming Maid.'
T: 'Apollo and Daphne, A Dialogue.' ¶ No: 8 lines. ¶ A: [Benjamin Franklin?].
Note: 'To oblige Subscribers we are sometimes under a kind of Necessity to insert some Things, which to serious People may not seem altogether proper.' Franklin typically used such editorial disclaimers when he printed his own irreligious or salacious writings. See *The Franklin Papers*, I, 122 and 195; II, 28, for other editorial disclaimers.

196. Nov. 4, 1731 *PG*.
'Why how now, old Grandsir, what is it you mean.'
T: 'Good Advice to an old Miser.' ¶ No: 43 lines. ¶ A: 'Musophilarguros.'
Note: 'By inserting the following Lines in your next, you will much oblige one of your constant Readers. It is long since they were design'd by a better Pen, for the Use of certain *European* Idolaters.'

197. Nov. 29, 1731 *BG*.
'Ye Ladies who to Boston-Town are come.'
T: 'To the Ladies at Boston, in New England.' ¶ No: 113 lines.
Note: Contains a number of local allusions.

197a. Dec. 13, 1731 *WR*, 4/1.
'Whilst Celia sings, let no intruding breath.'

T: 'On a Lady, Singing.' ¶ No: 48 lines. ¶ A: 'a young Gentleman in the Country.'

Note: Prefatory note: 'The following Lines are inserted at the Request of a Friend, who says they are the Production of a young Gentleman in the Country.' Reprinted in *Stedman and Hutchinson*, II, *334–35*.

1732

198. Jan. 1, 1731/2 (London) *Weekly Register*.
  'At length the *wintry* Horrors disappear.'
  T: '*A Journey from* Patapsco to Annapolis, April 4, 1730.' ¶ No: 390 lines. ¶ A: (Richard Lewis.)
  Note: This is a slightly revised version of no. 184.

199. Jan. 3, 1731/2 *WR*.
  'To my dear Wife.'
  T: 'Some time since died here Mr. Matth. A—y, in a very advanc'd Age, he had for a great Number of Years served the College here, in quality of Bed maker and Sweeper. Having left no child, his Wife inherits his whole Estate which he bequeathed to her by his last Will and Testament as follows.' ['Father Abbey's Will']. ¶ No: 84 lines. ¶ A: [John Seccomb.]
  Note: Dated 'Cambridge, Decemb. 1731.' See George T. Goodspeed, 'Father Abbey's Will,' *Proc.* of the Mass. Hist. Soc., LXXIII (1963), 18–37. Reprinted in Duyckinck, I, 137, and in Stedman and Hutchinson, II, 352–54. 'Father Abbey's Will' was a popular poem and Goodspeed gives the best account of the broadside editions. Goodspeed also reprints the poem, pp. 19–22. Goodspeed did not note the contemporary newspaper reprintings, see nos. 203, 204, 219, 225 and 226. The poem remained popular throughout the century. When the widow finally died in 1762, the *BEP* of Dec. 13, 1762 printed this obituary: 'Cambridge, Dec. 10. Yesterday died here in a very advanced age, Mrs. Abdy ... She was the Relict of the late Matthew Abdy, Sweeper, well known to the learned world by his last Will and Testament. [Father Ab–y's Will may be had of the Printer hereof.]' For a reply, see no. 202. Imitated by no. 345.

200. Jan. 8, 1731/2 *SCG*.
  'I'm not High-Church, nor Low Church, nor Tory, nor Whig.'
  T: 'To all, whom it may concern to know me.' ¶ No: 30 lines. ¶ A: [Henry Baker.]
  Note: This poem is from Henry Baker's *Universal Spectator*, No. 1, Oct. 1728. Franklin reprinted the poem in an advertisement of his

Poor Richard, Nov. 16, 1733, *PG* (see no. 277), and thus it has been attributed to him. See *The Franklin Papers,* I, 347n. Reprinted, nos. 277, 520.

201. Jan. 22, 1731/2 *SCG.*
'Who dare affirm, my Pow'r is weak.'
T: 'A Riddle.' ¶ No: 30 lines. ¶ A: A 'Fair Correspondent.'
Note: See the reprint, no. 228, and replies, nos. 229 and 230.

202. Feb. 7, 1731/2 *WR.*
'Mistress A—y.'
T: 'To the Author of the Rehearsal' [Proposal to Mistress Abbey].
¶ No: 66 lines. ¶ A: [John Seccomb? or John Hubbard?].
Note: 'New Haven, January 24' 'Our Sweeper having lately buryed his Spouse, and accidentally hearing the Death and Will of his deceas'd *Cambridge Brother,* has conceiv'd a violent Passion for the Relict. As Love softens the Mind, and disposes to Poetry, he has eas'd himself in the following Strains, which he transmits to the charming Widow, as the first Essay of his courtship.' See Goodspeed's article (no. 199), pp. 22–23, for a reprinting and an account of the broadside editions. For contemporary reprintings, see nos. 212, 220, 231, and 235. For an imitation, see no. 981. Reprinted in Duyckinck, I, 137–138; and in Stedman and Hutchinson, II, 354–356.

203. Feb. 8, 1732 *AWM.*
'To my dear Wife.'
T: [Father Abbey's Will.]
Note: A reprint of no. 199.

204. Feb. 8, 1731–2 *PG.*
'To my dear Wife.'
T: [Father Abbey's Will.]
Note: A reprint of no. 199.

205. Feb. 12, 1731/2 *SCG.*
'My Son, th' Instruction that my Words impart.'
T: 'The Seventh Chapter of the Proverbs, in a poetical Dress, being the Description of a Harlot.' ¶ No: 62 lines. ¶ A: 'Lucretia.'
Note: Reprinted (revised), no. 1258. Crum M885.

206. Feb. 19, 1731/2 *SCG.*
'From Courts remote, and Europe's pompous Scenes.'
T: [On an American pastoral nymph.] ¶ No: 13 lines. ¶ A: 'Secretus.'
Note: See reply, no. 207.

207. Feb. 25, 1731/2 *SCG.*
'Since, th'am'rous Bard has thus essay'd.'

T: [To Secretus.] ¶ No: 28 lines. ¶ A: 'Belinda.'
Note: Answer to no. 206. Cf. no. 213.

208. Mar. 4, 1731/2 *SCG.*
'*Twenty-Third*, did I say! no—that will be *Sunday.*'
T: 'The Valient Company of Volunteers, who have engaged in a desperate Attempt upon Fort Jolly, on the 23ᵈ Day of April next, being St. George's Day, command the Printer to insert the following Lines, by way of Advertisement, to all concern'd in that honourable Engagement. They are penn'd by their Mightyness no less courageous than rhyming Laureat Doggeril.' ¶ No: 16 lines. ¶ A: 'Dismal Doggrel' [Thomas Dale?].
Note: For an account of the celebration of St. George's day, see *SCG*, Apr. 29; cf. no. 253. Dr. Thomas Dale (1700–1750) wrote light verse and was a member of the Charleston St. George's Society. See R. E. Seibels, 'Thomas Dale, M.D., of Charleston, S.C.' *Ann. Med. Hist.*, n.s. III (1931), 50–57.

209. Mar. 11, 1731/2 *SCG.*
'If what the curious have observ'd be True.'
T: 'The Cameleon Lover.' ¶ No: 8 lines.
Note: See the reply, no. 211. Reprinted in Silverman, p. 322.

210. Mar. 11, 1731/2 *SCG.*
'Tho' heav'nly Musick dwelt upon my Tongue.'
T: 'a Sort of poetical Version of Part of the 13th Chapter of St. Paul's 1st Epistle to the Corinthians.' ¶ No: 26 lines.

211. Mar. 18, 1731/2 *SCG.*
'All Men have Follies, which they blindly trace.'
T: 'The Camelion's Defence.' ¶ No: 14 lines. ¶ A: 'Sable.'
Note: A reply to no. 209. Reprinted in Silverman, p. 323.

212. Mar. 23, 1732 *PG.*
'Mistress A—y.'
Note: A reprint of no. 202.

213. Mar. 25, 1732 *SCG.*
'Cou'd I the grateful Tribute pay.'
T: [To Belinda.] ¶ No: 12 lines. ¶ A: 'Dorinda.'
Note: Dated 'Santec, Mar. 7, 1731.' Cf. no. 207.

214. Mar. 27, 1732 *BG.*
'Happy the Man! Thrice happy he!'
T: 'The Bean; an Ode.' ¶ No: 22 lines. ¶ A: 'Tim Timewell.'

215. Mar. 1732 *Gent Mag*, II, 669–671.
'At length the wintry Horrors disappear.'
Note: A reprint of no. 198.

216. April 3, 1732 *WR.*
    'A Common Theme a flatt'ring Muse may fire.'
    T: 'An Elegaic Poem by Mr. H. on his only Daughter, who dy'd
      aged 11.'
    Note: A reprint of no. 189.

217. Apr. 3, 1732 *NYG.*
    'Begin, just Satyr, lash those who pretend.'
    T: [Praise of satire.] ¶ No: 30 lines.

218. Apr. 22, 1732 *SCG.*
    'Learning, that Cobweb of the Brain.'
    T: [The Encumbrance of Learning.] ¶ No: 26 lines. ¶ A: 'Ralpho
      Cobble ... a good honest Makanike.'
    Note: With an accompanying burlesque, dialect letter.

219. May 6, 1732 *SCG.*
    'To my dear Wife.'
    Note: 'from the *PG*, dated Feb. 8, 1731/2' (no. 204). A reprint of
      no. 199.

220. May 20, 1732 *SCG.*
    'Mistress A—y.'
    Note: A reprint of no. 202.

221. May 20, 1732 *SCG.*
    'Since we see the long Surplice, and eke the short Cloak.'
    T: [On religious denominations.] ¶ No: 14 lines. ¶ A: '* * *'
    Note: Says high and low church are the same.

222. May 25, 1732 *PG.*
    'Distracted with Care.'
    T: '... I was about to send for *Dommet,* and put him upon making a
      new Ditty on this Affair; but a friend of mine has furnish'd me
      with an old one, which methinks suits the Occasion indifferent
      well ,...' ¶ No: 33 lines. ¶ A: [William Walsh.]
    Note: John Dommet (d. 1739) was a teacher and a hack poet of
      Philadelphia. See nos. 528, 529, 530. For Walsh (1663-1708),
      a friend of the young Alexander Pope, see CBEL, II, 287.

223. May 25, 1732 *AWM.*
    'In a Thick Shade, the Owl, the Bat.'
    Note: A reprint of no. 139.

224. May 27, 1732 *SCG.*
    'Say, mighty Love, and Teach my Song.'
    Note: A reprint of no. 178.

225. May 1732 *Gent Mag*, II, 770.
    'To my dear Wife.'
    Note: A reprint of no. 199.

226. May 1732 *Lon Mag*, I, 87–88.
     'To my dear Wife.'
     Note: A reprint of no. 199.

227. June 17, 1732 *SCG*.
     'Say, I conjure Thee, Damon, say.'
     T: 'Florella to Damon.' ¶ No: 24 lines. ¶ A: 'Florella.'

228. June 19, 1732 *PG*.
     'Who dare affirm my Pow'r is weak.'
     Note: A reprint of no. 201. For replies, see nos. 229 and 230.

229. June 26, 1732 *PG*.
     'Hail! great Instructor of Mankind.'
     T: [Answer to no. 228]. ¶ No. 38 lines. ¶ A: 'M.B.'
     Note: Not as good as 'The Pow'r of Letters...' (no. 230: Although
       it should happen that in the following Lines I have expounded the
       Riddle put forth in your last Paper, yet I shall not think my self
       entitled to the Reward; that being only due to the Person who
       explains you in good Verse, which I am sensible my Performance
       falls infinitely short of. Yours, &c. M.B. 'M.B.' was also the
       author of no. 355.)

230. June 26, 1732 *PG*.
     'The Pow'r of LETTERS can't be weak.'
     T: [Answer to no. 228]. ¶ No: 28 lines. ¶ A: [a 'Female Hand'].
     Note: Last 2 lines: 'Your Gazette thus this Verse secures,/For
       they're at least as good as yours.' Franklin's editorial note of
       July 3, 1732, says that the author was a woman.

231. June 1732 *Gent Mag*, II, 821.
     'Mistress A—y.'
     Note: A reprint of no. 202.

232. July 17, 1732 *PG*.
     'Of ancient streams presume no more to tell.'
     T: 'Food for Criticks.' ¶ No: 146 lines. ¶ A: [Richard Lewis?].
     Note: A re-worked version of no. 188.

233. Aug. 17, 1732 *AWM*.
     'Welcome to us, thou happy one of three.'
     T: 'On the arrival of the Honourable Thomas Penn, Esq; one of the
       Proprietors of the Province of Pennsylvania.' ¶ No: 43 lines. ¶
       A: 'T.M.' [Thomas Makin?].
     Note: For Thomas Makin (1665?–1733), see the brief sketch in *Pa.
       Mag. of Hist. and Biog.*, XXXVII (1913), 369–374. Cf. no. 234.

234. Aug. 21, 1732 *PG*.
     'I praise their Ardor, that with generous Pride.'

T: 'Congratulatory Verses, wrote at the Arrival of our Honourable PROPRIETARY.' ¶ No: 44 lines. ¶ A: [Richard Lewis?].

Note: Excellent occasional poem, with a catalogue of rivers. A news-story of Thomas Penn's arrival is in *PG*, Aug. 14, 1732, ※194. Prefatory note: 'The following congratulatory Verses, wrote at the arrival of our Honourable Prporietary, came to hand too late to be inserted in our last.' Cf. no. 233.

235. Aug. 1732 *Lon Mag*, I, 256.
'Mistress A—y.'
Note: A reprint of no. 202.

236. Sept. 14, 1732 *AWM*, pp. 1–2.
'To bring the various Doctrines of the Schools.'
T: 'A Poem, Sacret [sic] to the Memory of the Honourable ROBERT CARTER, Esq; late President of His Majestys Council, in the Colony of Virginia. Who departed this Life on Friday, the 4th of August, 1732, in the 69th year of his Age.' ¶ No: 148 lines. ¶ A: 'Lycidas Philensis' [William Dawson?].
Note: This very good elegy may have been reprinted from a now lost issue of the *Maryland Gazette*. It seems probable that Dawson would have written an elegy for Carter, who was perhaps the most outstanding Virginian of the day. For Dawson, see Harold L. Dean, 'An Identification of the "Gentleman of Virginia,"' *Papers of the Bibliographical Soc. of Am.*, XXXI (1937), 10–20. Cf. no. 454.

238. Oct. 26, 1732 *PG*.
'The bleak Norwest begins his dreaded Reign.'
T: 'The Rape of Fewel. A Cold-weather Poem.' ¶ No: 98 lines.

239. Oct. 30, 1732 *NEWJ*.
'Soar now, my Muse, exert thy utmost Lays.'
T: 'A Poem, Address'd to his Majesty on his Birth-Day.' ¶ No: 96 lines.

239a. Nov. 16, 1732 *RIG* ※8, 1/1–2.
'He that to *Wit* has no pretence.'
T: 'The Scatterwaters.' ¶ No: 46 lines. ¶ A: 'Will Rusty.'
Note: Dated 'New Haven, Oct. 31, 1732.'

240. Nov. 30, 1732 *AWM*.
'One Evening I courted my Muse.'
T: [On the muse.] ¶ No: 24 lines.

240a. Dec. 21, 1732 *RIG* ※13, 1/1–2.
'My anxious Hours roll heavily away.'
T: 'Lines to a beautiful Lady.' ¶ No: 51 lines. ¶ A: 'Young Gentleman.'
Note: Dated 'Newport, Decem. 21, 1732.'

241. Dec. 25, 1732 *NEWJ.*
'Long had mankind with darkness been oppress'd.'
Note: With a prefatory essay; a reprint of no. 194.

1733

1733
242. Jan. 25, 1732/3 *PG.*
'Agrippa next, a Bard unknown to Fame.'
T: 'I have sent you some Verses taken out of a Manuscript that I
have by me: Tho' the Author seems not to be of Copernicus'
opinion, yet perhaps there has not hitherto been made a more true
Discovery of the wonderful Force that those heavenly Bodies (the
Stars) have on this Earth, and its Inhabitants, than what is con-
tained in the following Lines, tho' meanly drest.' ¶ No: 16 lines.
¶ A: 'N.D.'

243. Feb. 6, 1732/3 *AWM.*
'Cold as the Arctick Pole in Winter Time.'
T: 'On the instant cold Weather.' ¶ No: 56 lines.
Note: Writer arouses sympathy for the poor. Local, sentimental
verse.

244. Feb. 9, 1732/3 *MG.*
'A Swain who musing on the various Cares.'
T: 'A Rhapsody.' ¶ No: 126 lines. ¶ A: [Richard Lewis].
Note: *A Rhapsody* was originally published on a folio sheet, printed
on both sides, on March 1, 1731/2 (Annapolis, William Parks,
1732). Reprinted, no. 321.

245. Feb. 10, 1732/3 *SCG.*
'While generous O—g—p's unwearied Pain.'
T: ['An Address to James Oglethorpe, Esq; on his settling the colo-
ny in Georgia.'] ¶ No: 100 lines.
Note: The *SCG* of Feb. 3, 1732/3, contained this notice: 'A Poem,
is received, on the settling of Georgia, and will be communicated
in our next.' Reprinted, see nos. 256 (from which the title is
taken), 261, and 300. See Richard C. Boys, 'General Oglethorp
and the Muses,' *Ga. Hist. Quart.*, XXXI (1947), 19–30. Re-
printed in Hennig Cohen, 'Two Colonial Poems on the Settling
of Georgia, *Ga. Hist. Quart.*, XXXVII (1953), 131–134.

246. Feb. 17, 1732/3 *SCG.*
'Long had Mankind with Darkness been oppress'd.'
A: 'By the Rev. Mr. Birch.'

Note: A reprint of no. 194, but this is the first printing that has supplied the author. Perhaps the information came from Dr. Thomas Dale, a friend and correspondent of the Rev. Thomas Birch.

247. Feb. 17, 1732/3 *SCG.*
'When Israel's Daughters mourn'd their past Offences.'
T: 'Epigram.' ¶ No.: 6 lines.

248. Feb. 24, 1732/3 *SCG.*
'In the sprightly Month of May.'
T: 'The Milk-Maid.' ¶ No: 82 lines.

249. Feb. 24, 1732/3 *SCG.*
'You know where you did despise.'
T: 'By Mr. A. Pope. On his being banter'd by a Lady, for his little Size.' ¶ No: 10 lines. ¶ A: 'A. Pope.'
Note: Crum Y284 supplies the title 'Lines in a letter to Henry Cromwell, June 24, 1710' and notes that it was printed in Edmund Curll's *Miscellanea*, I (London, 1727), 37.

250. Feb. 1733 *Gent Mag*, III, 92–93.
'Hail Raleigh! Venerable Shade.'
T: 'The Convert to Tobacco. A Tale.'
Note: 'From a MS.'

251. Feb. 1733, *Gent Mag*, III, 93.
'While, yet, Unripe, the glowing Purpose lay.'
T: 'Georgia and Carolina.' ¶ No: 20 lines.
Note: This also appeared in a shortened, altered version in the *Norfolk Poetical Miscellany* (London, 1744), I, 131, as 'On Giving the Name of Georgia to a Part of Carolina.' See Boys (no. 245).

252. Mar. 22, 1732/3 *PG.*
'Now blessed be this present Age.'
T: On the 'Queen's placing the Busto's of certain great Men deceas'd, in her Hermitage.' ¶ No: 18 lines. ¶ A: 'By a Lover of Reason and Virtue.'
Note: Dated 'Allenton, Feb. 19, 1732/3.' 'Meeting with what you published in your Paper [poem in *PG*, Mar. 15, #224] from the *London Journal*, concerning the Queen's placing the Busto's of certain great Men deceas'd, in her Hermitage, it not only pleas'd me exceedingly, but put me upon writing the following Lines, which crave a Place in your Paper.' Poor verse.

252a. Apr. 7, 1733 (London) *Weekly Register.*
'At length the wintry horrors disappear.'
Note: A reprint of no. 198, but with the author named: 'By Mr. R. Lewis.'

253. Apr. 14, 1733 *SCG*.
'The Twenty-third of April is ever the Day.'
T: [On St. George's Day]. ¶ No: 16 lines. ¶ A: [Thomas Dale ?].
Note: See no. 208, for an earlier poem celebrating St. George's Day.
The *SCG* for Apr. 28, 1733 contains an account of Charlestown's
St. George's Society.

254. Apr. 14, 1733 (London) Eustace Budgell's *Bee* (I, 393–404).
'At length the wintry horrors disappear.'
Note: A reprint of no. 198, but with the author named: 'By Mr.
Lewis.'

255. Apr. 23, 1733 *BG* ⚹694, 2/3–3/1.
'What did inspire the Fair to cross the Main.'
T: 'The following Lines (by an unknown Hand,) on the Lady *Balti-
more's* Voyage hither, being sent to the Press, we hope will be
agreeable to our READERS.' ¶ No: 20 lines.
Note: 'From the *Maryland Gazette*, of the 23ᵈ of *March last*' (not
extant). Mediocre verse.

256. Apr. 1733 *Gent Mag*, III, 209.
'While generous Oglethorpe's unwearied pain.'
T: 'An Address to James Oglethorpe, Esq; on his settling the Colo-
ny in Georgia.'
Note: A reprint of no. 245, though it is unlikely that no. 245 could
have been the source for this poem.

257. Apr. 1733 *Gent Mag*, III, 209–210.
'If in wish'd progress, thro' these wide domains.'
T: 'A Description of Maryland, extracted from a Poem, entitled,
Carmen Seculare, addressed to Ld Baltimore, Proprietor of that
Province, now there. By Mr. Lewis, Author of the beautiful Poem
inserted in our 4ᵗʰ Number entitled, a Journey from Patapsco to
Annapolis.' ¶ No: 11. 48–98 and 232–292 of the poem. ¶ A:
Richard Lewis.
Note: *Carmen Seculare* was published in Annapolis, 1732. Cf. no.
259.

258. Apr. 1733 *Lon Mag*, I, 204–207.
'At length the wintry horrors disappear.'
T: 'A Journey from Patapsko to Annapolis by Mr. R. Lewis, April
4, 1730.'
Note: 'Taken originally from the *Weekly Register*.' A reprint of no.
198.

259. May 1733 *Gent Mag*, III, 264.
'Such, gracious sir, your province now appears.'

T: 'Further Extract of the Poem addressed to Ld Baltimore.' ¶ No:
Ll. 99–194 of *Carmen Seculare*.
Note: Cf. no. 257.

260. July 12, 1733 *PG*.
'Gently stir and blow the fire.'
T: 'Gently touch the warbling Lyre; Burlesq'd by Sir W—Y—.' ¶
No: 18 lines. ¶ A: 'Sir W.Y.' [Sir William Young?].
Note: 'Attempted in Latin, Line motum perfla socum.' Not Ameri-
can.

261. July 16, 1733 *NEWJ* #330.
'While generous Oglethorpe's unwearied Pain.'
Note: A reprint of no. 245.

262. July 28, 1733 *SCG* #80.
'At Midnight when the Fever rag'd.'
T: 'By a Person recovered of a fit of SICKNESS.' ¶ No: 48 lines.
Note: Crum A1829 gives the title 'An Ode . . . Jan. 22, 1732'.

263. July 30, 1733 *NEWJ* #332.
'A Pritty Bird did lately please my sight.'
T: 'A Lamentation &c. On the Death of a Child.' ¶ A: 'a Tender
Mother.' ¶ No: 31 lines.
Note: 'The following Lines (compos'd by a Tender Mother, not far
from this Place,) on the Death of a most forward, amiable, and
hopeful child, was lately left with us for Publication, without her
Knowledge, and without the least Alteration.' An excellent poem,
suggesting the influence of Ann Bradstreet.

264. July 30, 1733 *BG* #708.
'Byfield beneath in peaceful slumber lies.'
T: 'Epitaph' [on Nathaniel Byfield]. ¶ No: 10 lines. ¶ A: [Mather
Byles.]
Note: 'An Epitaph taken off the tomb stone of the Hon. Col. [Na-
thaniel] Byfield lately deceas'd.' Reprinted, see no. 268. As Sam-
uel G. Drake, *The History and Antiquities of Boston* (Boston,
1856), p. 595n, points out, a revision of this epitaph is in Byles,
Poems on Several Occasions (Boston, 1744), pp. 95–96. For Judge
Nathaniel Byfield (1653–1733), see Drake, pp. 593–594.

265. July 1733 *Lon Mag*, I, 359.
'Not ev'ry Temper rural scenes delight.'
T: 'Warbletta: A Suburban Eclogue.' ¶ No: 110 lines.
Note: Reprinted, see no. 285.

266. Aug. 9, 1733 *AWM* #710.
'Amidst the vast Profusions of Delight.'
T: 'To the Right Honourable Charles, Lord Baron of Baltimore,

Absolute Lord and Proprietary of the Province of Maryland, and Avalon.' ¶ No: 84 lines. ¶ A: [John] Markland.

Note: Reprinted in J. A. Leo Lemay, *A Poem by John Markland of Virginia*, (Williamsburg, 1964).

267. Aug. 13, 1733 *NEWJ* #334.
'Tho' now we may with Transport gaze.'
T: 'To Olivia, on her Birth Day, Entring into her 21st Year of her Age.' ¶ No: 21 lines.
Note: Copied, pp. 23–24, in J. Belknap's 'A Collection of Poetry' (see no. 71).

268. Aug. 16, 1733 *PG* #246.
'Byfield beneath in perfect slumber lies.'
Note: A reprint of no. 264.

269. Aug. 20, 1733 *NYG* #408.
'For once let me ask you a Question, good Sir.'
T: [On the poor state of Trade]. ¶ No: 17 lines.

270. Sept. 7, 1733 *PG* #249.
'Once unconfined and light as Air.'
T: [Courtship verse.] ¶ No: 18 lines.
Note: Probably reprinted from a Boston newspaper of Aug. 13.

271. Sept. 17, 1733 *WR* #103.
'At Milton, near the Paper-Mill.'
T: [advertisement verse.] ¶ No: 20 lines.

272. Sept. 28, 1733 *PG* #252.
'Happy's the Man, who with first Thoughts, and clear.'
T: 'Against Party-Malice and Levity, usual at and near the Time of Electing Assembly-Men.' ¶ No: 208 lines. ¶ A: 'Pennsylvanus' [Benjamin Franklin?].
Note: 'N.B. The citations are from Pope's Essay on Criticism.' 'Pennsylvanus' is also the pseudonym of the writer in *PG* Dec. 20, 1733 of the essay (which has been authoritatively attributed to Franklin) on brave men who put out fires. This poem is pro-Hamilton. Although the pseudonym and views suggest Franklin's authorship, he was in Boston, Sept.–Oct., 1733.

273. Sept. & Oct. 1733 *Gent Mag*, III, 490–491 and 546.
'The nymphs of Plaistow fields begin my Song.'
T: 'Plaistow, A Poem.' ¶ No: 282 lines. ¶ A: 'J.D. Esq' [Jeremiah Dummer].
Note: Begins with a compliment to Pope, and refers to 'Windsor Forest.' A recent note on Dummer is Calhoun Winton, 'Jeremiah Dummer: The "First American"?' *Wm. & Mary Quart.*, XXVI (1969), 105–108.

274. Oct. 18, 1733 *AWM* ⚹720.
    '[I] Know thee Janus, both what thou art, and who.'
    T: 'Seasonable Advice to the Gazeteers late Correspondent.' ¶ No:
    30 lines. ¶ A: 'J.D.' [John Dommet].
    Note: 'Thy dull Attack on *Black Gowns* shows small skill' (line 7).
    For Benjamin Franklin's earlier slur on 'Black Gowns' (i.e.,
    ministers), see the *Franklin Papers*, I, 197.

275. Oct. 25, 1733 *PG* ⚹256.
    'Artist, that underneath my Table.'
    T: 'On a Spider and a Poet.' ¶ No: 28 lines. ¶ A: [Edward Littleton.]
    Note: Crum A1426 notes that the poem was printed in Anthony
    Hammond's *Miscellany* (London, 1720), p. 147. For Littleton
    (d. 1733), see the *DNB*, which notes that this was his best-known
    poem. It is in Dodsley, VI, 298.

276. Nov. 5, 1733 *NYWJ* [*Oct.* misprinted for *Nov.*].
    'Victorious Wisdom whose supreme Command.'
    T: 'On Wisdom.' ¶ No: 60 lines. ¶ A: 'Philo-sophia.'
    Note: Accompanies an Addisonian essay. Crum V35.

277. Nov. 16, 1733 *PG* ⚹259.
    'I'm not High-Church, nor Low-Church, nor Tory nor Whig.'
    Note: Reprinted in *PG* Nov. 29, ⚹261. The poem is found in Frank-
    lin's advertisement for *Poor Richard*. A reprint of no. 200.

278. Nov. 29, 1733 *PG* ⚹261.
    'Some purchase Land, some stately Buildings raise.'
    T: [Epitaph.] ¶ No: 8 lines. ¶ A: 'Thomas Meakins' [Makin].
    Note: 'Phila. Nov. 24. On Monday Evening Last, Mr. Thomas
    Meakins fell of[f] a Wharff into the Delaware, and before he
    could be taken out again, was drowned. He was an ancient Man,
    and formerly liv'd very well in this City, teaching a considerable
    School; but of late Years was reduc'd to extreme Poverty. The
    following Lines were made by himself some time since.' 4 heroic
    couplets, poor. Reprinted in James Mulhern, *A History of Second-
    ary Education in Pennsylvania* (Philadelphia, 1933), p. 41.

279. Nov. 1733 *Lon Mag*, I, 579.
    'In David's psalms, an oversight.'
    T: 'on Mr. B[yles]—'s singing an Hymn of his own composing at
    Sea, on a Voyage from *Boston* to an Interview with the *Indians* in
    New England.' ¶ No: 32 lines. ¶ A: [Joseph Green].
    Note: A prefatory poem to a burlesque of Mather Byles (see no. 281).
    Reprinted (with no. 251 and Byles' original hymn) in Kettell, I,
    135–136; Griswold, p. 28; Duyckinck, I, 131 (where Byles'
    scurrilous rejoinder may also be found); Stedman and Hutchinson,
    II, 433–34; and in numerous anthologies in this century.

280. Nov. 1733 *Lon Mag*, I, 579.
    'Oppress'd with grief, in heavy strains I mourn.'
    T: 'The Poet's Lamentation for the Loss of his Cat, which he used to
    call his Muse.' ¶ No: 44 lines. ¶ A: [Joseph Green].
    Note: Dated 'Boston in New England, Sep. 4, 1733.' Another of
    Green's satires on Byles. Reprinted, no. 1494. Reprinted in Duy-
    ckinck, I, 132–133; in Stedman and Hutchinson, II, 434–5.

281. Nov. 1733 *Lon Mag*, I, 579–80.
    'With vast amazement we survey.'
    T: 'The Hymn.' ¶ No: 24 lines. ¶ A: [Joseph Green].
    Note: The burlesque of the hymn by Byles. Byles' hymn was printed
    in his *Poems* (see no. 60), pp. 48–49. Byles' hymn and Green's
    burlesque are reprinted in all the sources cited in no. 279.

282. Dec. 14, 1733 *AWM* #728.
    'Now lay your Politics aside.'
    T: 'Since the Gazetteer has unkindly omitted this Postscript to the
    Conversation in his paper of the 16th of November, I desire you
    to publish it.' ¶ No: 8 lines + refrain 'Down, down ...'
    Note: This attack on Andrew Hamilton, leader of Pennsylvania's
    Popular party, replies to Franklin's 'Half-hour's Conversation
    with a Friend,' Nov. 16, 1733. See *The Franklin Papers*, I, 333,
    and Anna J. DeArmond, *Andrew Bradford* (Newark, Del., 1949),
    p. 90. See also no. 287.

283. Dec. 31, 1733 *NYG* #427, 2/2.
    'Music has Power to melt the Soul.'
    T: 'Written at a Concert of Music, where there was a great Number
    of Ladies.' ¶ No: 12 lines.

1734

284. Jan. 7, 1733/4 *NYG* #428, 1/2–2/1.
    'Cosby the Mild, the happy, good and great.'
    T: [Defense of Governor William Cosby]. ¶ No: 6 lines.
    Note: In reply to 'the last *Weekly Journal*.'

285. Jan. 1733/4 *AWM* #733.
    'Not ev'ry Temper rural scenes delight.'
    T: 'Warbletta: A Suburban Eclogue.'
    Note: Prefatory note: 'The following *Eclogue* was written by a
    gentleman of some reputation is Parnassus, Tho he is now de-
    scended into the suburbs ...' A reprint of no. 265.

286. Jan. 23, 1733/4 *PG* #268.
    'Virtue, thou ornament of human life.'
    T: 'In Praise of Virtue.' ¶ No: 12 lines.

287. Jan. 29, 1733/4 *AWM* #735.
    'Tho' unconfin'd Spinosa rov'd abroad.'
    T: 'To a certain Gentleman who is pleas'd, for what reason he best
       knows, to apply to himself the characters of Spinoso, Sejanus, and
       Protesilaus.' ¶ No: 30 lines.
    Note: Andrew Bradford, publisher, cuts off the poem arbitrarily at
       line 30. The Poem's title refers to a passage in a letter of Jan. 22
       in the *AWM*, which continues the attack on Hamilton. Cf. no.
       282.

288. Jan. 29, 1733/4 *AWM* #735.
    'What is the Thing our Nature doth require.'
    T: 'The Credit and Interest of America, Considered: Or, The Way
       to Live above Want, Wherein Temperance is Commended for her
       Decency, and being Provident.' ¶ No: 180 lines.
    Note: In the genre of Benjamin Franklin's *The Way to Wealth*.

289. Feb. 7, 1733/4 *PG* #270.
    'Your sage and moralist can show.'
    T: 'The Cobler, A Tale. For the Benefit of the Hisphy Cripshy.' ¶
       No: 285 lines. ¶ A: 'By the Revd Saml Wesly'—in MS.
    Note: Reprinted, nos. 368, 546. For Wesley, see the *DNB*. Re-
       printed also in the *Am Mag*, I (Nov. 1745), 501–504, and in the
       New Am Mag., II (Sept. 1759), 619–621.

290. Feb. 26, 1733/4 *AWM* #739.
    'While other Bards of Grecian Heroes Treat.'
    T: 'Upon Prince Madoc's Expedition to the Country now called
       America, in the 12th Century. Humbly inscrib'd to the worthy
       Society of Ancient Britons, meeting at Philadelphia, March the
       1st, 1733-4.' ¶ No: 125 lines. ¶ A: 'Philo Cambrensis' [Richard
       Lewis].
    Note: Dated 'Jun [Jan] 29, 1733–4.'

291. Mar. 2, 1733/4 *SCG*.
    'Against my Negro man nam'd Parris.'
    T: [Advertisement.] ¶ No: 10 lines. ¶ A: 'Fran. Le Brasseur.'

292. Mar. 2, 1733/4 *SCG*.
    'While conscious Aura curls the dimpled Tyde.'
    T: 'The Voyage. A descriptive Canto on the Union of the Rose and
       Orange. In the Spirit of Tasso.' ¶ No: 56 lines. ¶ A: 'N.R. of
       Trinity Col., Cambridge.'

293. Mar. 3, 1733/4 *NYG* #488, 1/1–2.
    ''Tis sometimes absent curst Mankind admires.'
    T: 'Discontent.' ¶ No: 28 lines.

294. Mar. 15, 1733/4 *MG* ✳60.
'Beneath the baleful Yews unfruitful Shade.'
T: 'An Elegy on ... Charles Calvert ... formerly Governor ... of Maryland.' ¶ No: 221 lines. ¶ A: [Richard Lewis].
Note: Cf. no. 701.

295. Mar. 21, 1733/4 *PG* ✳276.
'This Town would quickly be reclaim'd.'
T: [Poem against drinking]. ¶ No: 12 lines. ¶ A: 'R.W.'
Note: Poor verse. 'Mr. Franklin, If you insert these few following Lines in your Gazette, I do not doubt they will be very well accepted by some of your Readers.' See the reply, no. 297.

296. Mar. 25, 1734 *NEWJ* ✳365.
'To Thee, my Fair, I string the Lyre.'
T: [Poem to his wife]. ¶ No: 44 lines. ¶ A: [Mather Byles].
Note: With prefatory paragraph. Reprinted, nos. 304, 312. Cf. no. 298, which suggests Byles was the author. Byles married Anna Noyes Gale on Feb. 14, 1732/33.

297. Mar. 28, 1734 *PG* ✳277.
'This Town would quickly be reclaim'd.'
T: 'An Answer to R.W.' ¶ No: 12 lines. ¶ A: 'W.R.'
Note: Clever. A reply to no. 295.

298. Apr. 1, 1734 *BG* ✳743, 3/1.
'Illustrious Bard! (whoe'er thou art).'
T: 'To the Author of the Poetry in the last Weekly Journal.' ¶ No: 32 lines. ¶ A: [Joseph Green?].
Note: Ridicules no. 296. 'To the Publisher of the *BG*: Sir, when I wrote the following Lines; agreeable to a common Custom, I desired a Friend to bestow an Encomium on them; which he declined; telling me I might as well do it my self; and that not without a late Example. [Probably a reference to Byles.] This I took for a friendly Intimation that they did not deserve one. However, have ventured to send them to you; and if you'd allow them a place in your Paper, you'd oblige.' An excellent, humorous poem, satirizing no. 296. It seems likely that Joseph Green (who delighted in his role as Byles' poetic nemesis) was the author.

299. April 4, 1734 *AWM* ✳744.
'A, stands for Andrew, the Saint so renown'd.'
T: 'An Alphabetical Key, explaining all the dark Innuendo's, Hyeroglyphicks, Magic and Conjuration of that Caitiff, Mr. Bradford his late Papers.' ¶ No: 22 lines.
Note: Reprinted, no. 301.

300. Apr. 4, 1734 *PG* #278.
     'While the generous Oglethorp's unwearied Pain.'
     Note: A reprint of no. 245. With this prefatory note: 'We doubt not
       but the following Copy of Verses, published in The South-Caro-
       lina Gazette at Charlestown, will with pleasure to most of our
       Readers, supply the place of Foreign News.'

301. Apr. 15, 1734 *NYWJ* #24, 2/2–3/1.
     A, stands for A—w, the Saint so renown'd.'
     Note: A reprint of no. 299.

302. Apr. 15, 1734 *NYG* #442, 3/2–4/1.
     'Since Scandal and ill Nature take their Rounds.'
     T: [Defense of Governor William Cosby]. ¶ No: 49 lines.

303. Apr. 18, 1734 *AWM* #746.
     'I know you Lawyers can with Ease.'
     Note: 'Second ser. fable 1.' A reprint of no. 185.

304. Apr. 18, 1734 *PG* #280.
     'To Thee, my Fair, I string the Lyre.'
     Note: A reprint of no. 296.

305. Apr. 20, 1734 *SCG* #12.
     'Oh! how I tremble for thy Virgin Heart.'
     T: 'To a young Lady.' ¶ No: 57 lines.

306. Apr. 27, 1734 *SCG*.
     'Compassion proper to our Sex appears.'
     T: [Sensibility.] ¶ No: 14 lines. ¶ A: 'Atram.'
     Note: These lines accompany an essay.

307. May 18, 1734 *SCG*.
     'In this our Town I've heard some Youngsters say.'
     T: 'Verses, on an old Lover of a young Lady.' ¶ No: 22 lines.

308. June 3, 1734 *NYWJ* #31, 2/2.
     'At length we see the Day auspicious shine.'
     T: 'On the Marriage of the Prince of Orange and the Princess
       Royal.'
     Note: Cf. no. 313.

309. June 8, 1734 *SCG* #19.
     'Hail! pious, learn'd and eloquent Divine.'
     T: 'To the Reverend and Learned Doct Neal, on his excellent Ser-
       mon preached at Charlestown, on Sunday, the 26th of May, 1734.'
       ¶ No: 35 lines. ¶ A: 'Philanthropos' [James Kirkpatrick?].
     Note: See *SCG*, #68. Since the poem praises Pope and has a reli-
       gious bent, it is perhaps by Kirkpatrick. Dated 'June 1, 1734.'
       The subject is evidently the Rev. Lawrence O'Neill, who had just

emigrated to America. See Weis, *Virginia*, p. 86. For an account of Dr. James Kirkpatrick (c. 1690–1770), see Joseph I. Waring, 'James Killpatrick and Smallpox Inoculation in Charlestown,' *Ann. Med. Hist.*, n.s. (1938), 301–308.

310. June 10, 1734 *NEWJ* #374.
'Whilst an Industrious Company of Swains.'
T: 'A Paraphrase on seven Verses in the second Chapter of Luke, beginning at the eighth.' ¶ No: 34 lines. ¶ A: 'The following Lines were compos'd by a Young Gentleman in a neighbour Colony; and sent to an Acquaintance of his here; who desires a publication of them in this Paper.'

311. June 15, 1734 *SCG.*
'From fair Cypria's Fane I'm forced away.'
T: [To Flavia]. ¶ No: 29 lines. ¶ A: 'a young Person.'

312. June 22, 1734 *SCG.*
'To Thee, my Fair, I string the Lyre.'
Note: A reprint of no. 296.

313. June 24, 1734 *NYG* #452, 1/2–2/1.
'From distant Climes, and desart Woods, where no.'
T: 'Lines on the Prince of Orange's Marriage with the *Princess* Royall.' ¶ No: 55 lines. ¶ A: 'American Genius.'
Note: Excellent. Cf. no. 308.

314. June 29, 1734 *SCG.* #22.
'How gaily is at first begun.'
T: 'The Progress of Life.' ¶ No: 45 lines. ¶ A: A 'fair Correspondent.'
Note: Same author wrote no. 315.

315. June 29, 1734 *SCG.*
'Ye Virgin Pow'rs defend my Heart.'
T: 'The Virgin's Prayer.' ¶ No: 16 lines. ¶ A: Same author wrote no. 314.
Note: Crum Y151 lists the more interesting title 'A Song, by a Lady, mistrustful of her own strength.'

316. July 1, 1734 *BG* #756, 3/1.
'Now Nature with her various Verdure glows.'
T: 'A Poem to Amanda, on May.' ¶ No: 20 lines.
Note: Good.

317. July 1, 1734 *NYWJ* #35, 2/1–2.
'How pleasant is it, to behold on shore.'
T: 'A Receipt to be Happy.' ¶ No: 26 lines. ¶ A: [William Somervile.]
Note: Crum H1498. For Somervile (1675–1742), see *CBEL*, II, 328.

318. July 1, 1734 *WR* ✻144.
   'What a Pity it is that *some* modern Bravadoes.'
   T: 'The Sorrowful Lamentation of *Samuel Keimer*, Printer of the *Barbados Gazette*.' ¶ No: 34 lines. ¶ A: Samuel Keimer.
   Note: 'From the Barbados Gazette, May 4th.' For Keimer, see no. 35. The poem mentions the salaries of the printers of the various colonies. Printed in Duyckinck, I, 110. Reprinted, see no. 327.

319. July 15, 1734 *NEWJ* ✻379.
   'Hail! Sol supream the glory of the skies.'
   T: [On the sun and nature]. ¶ No: 29 lines.
   Note: With a prefatory paragraph.

320. July 27, 1734 *SCG* ✻26.
   'An Irish Mungrel, lately Run away.'
   T: 'A Hue and Cry, after an Irish Dear Joy.' ¶ No: 48 lines.

321. July 1734 *Gent Mag*, IV, 385.
   'A Swain who musing on the various cares.'
   Note: 'The following was sent us long since from Maryland and we hope the author will have timely notice of our proposed prize, to be a candidate.' A reprint of no. 244.

322. Aug. 12, 1734 *BG* ✻762, 3/2.
   'When on Thy ever blooming charms.'
   T: 'To Miss —.' ¶ No: 16 lines.

323. Aug. 19, 1734 *BG* ✻763, 3/1.
   'How sweetly opening with the blushing morn.'
   T: 'The Prospect.' ¶ No: 50 lines. ¶ A: 'Q.T.'
   Note: Excellent Thomsonian nature verse; perhaps not local.

324. Aug. 29, 1734 *PG* ✻299.
   'Attwood, while those, whose yearly Thousands bring.'
   T: 'The Pokeamouth [Puckermouth—corrected on manuscript] Apple. To Capt. Attwood.' ¶ No: 76 lines.
   Note: Pretty good, local; refers to Milton. 'The following copy of Verses, describing a very strange and valuable Apple, is published for an Information to the curious Persons who of late have been and are generously industrious in the Propagation of the best Fruits.' 'O, Attwood, haste, Is *Price* the Message told?/ Shall he, in Lewes, such a Treasure hold?'

325. Sept. 9, 1734 *WR* ✻154.
   'Here are such rare Conceits and Merriment.'
   T: [Puff for book]. ¶ No: 6 lines in advertisement. ¶ A: Edward Williams.
   Note: 'Just Published' 'In a few Days will be published, (and sold at the *Heart* and *Crown* in *Boston*) The *Five Strange Wonders of the*

World; Or, a new merry Book of *All Fives*. Which was written on purpose to make all the People of *New England* Merry, who have no Cause to be Sad. By *Edward Williams*, who was an *English* Slave in *Turkey* Eleven Years.' Evans 3858. The microcard published by the American Antiquarian Society notes for Evans 3858: 'Title taken by Haven from an adv. not now located. No other reference to this title known.' Sabin 104194 (citing Evans). If the book was published, it may have been an American edition of an English jest book, and it is doubtful that Edward Williams existed.

326. Sept. 25, 1734 *PG* ⚹303.
'Blest husbandman! whose horny hands have Till'd.'
T: 'The Old Man of Verona. Translated from Claudian.' ¶ No: 27 lines.
Note: Jeremy Belknap copied this poem in his 'Collection of Poetry' (see no. 71), pp. 25–26.

327. Sept. 25, 1734 *PG* ⚹303.
'What a Pity it is that some modern Bravadoes.'
Note: A reprint of no. 318.

328. Sept. 30, 1734 *NYWJ* ⚹48, 2/2–3/1.
'The Counsel of a Friend Belinda hear.'
T: 'Advice to a Lady.' ¶ No: 90 lines. ¶ A: 'A.B.' [George Lyttleton.]
Note: Crum T429. Printed in Dodsley, II, 41. For Lyttleton, 1st Baron of Frankley (1709-1773), see *CBEL*, II, 321.

329. Sept. 1734 *Gent Mag*, IV, 505.
'Fading are laurels won in martial fields.'
T: 'To the honourable James Oglethorpe, Esq, On his Return from Georgia.' ¶ No: 50 lines. ¶ A: [Moses Browne ?].
Note: Boys, p. 25 n16 (see no. 245), speculates that the author is Moses Browne. See also Georgia Historical Society *Collection*, v. 2 where this poem is printed, along with the one in *A New Voyage to Georgia* (London, 1735). The author is evidently the 'Benevolus' who wrote on Oglethorpe in the *Weekly Miscellany*, Aug. 31, 1734; the poem has been amended by the *Gent Mag* editors; it probably first appeared in the *Weekly Miscellany*.

330. Oct. 19, 1734 *SCG* ⚹38.
'Your Petitioners being reduc'd to a wretched Condition.'
T: 'The Petition of some of the inhabitants of the Province of G[eorgi]a, to the P[rovince] of S.C[arolina] SHEWETH, That ...' ¶ No: 33 lines. ¶ A: 'Incognito.'
Note: Reprinted, no. 365.

331. Oct. 21, 1734 *BG* ⚹772, 2/1.
     'While Sir in merry mood you choose.'
     T: 'To Mr. Tho. C— upon his late Poetic Essay on Buxdorf's
     Hebrew Grammar.' ¶ No: 42 lines. ¶ A: 'A—s.'
     Note: A 'T. Cox' was a Boston bookseller in 1733 and 1734: see
     Evans 3624, 3719, 3765. There is a reference to Miss W[alli?]s
     (rhymes with 'small is'). Hudibrastic satire.

332. Oct. 28, 1734 *WR* ⚹161.
     'A famous Prophet in this Year appears.'
     T: [Part of ad for James Franklin's *Poor Robin*]. ¶ No: 8 lines. ¶ A:
     [James Franklin?].

333. Nov. 18, 1734 *NEWJ* ⚹399, 1/1.
     'Conceal the flame, dear Charmer, from the Swain.'
     T: [Despairing lines on love.] ¶ No: 32 lines.

334. Dec. 5, 1734 *PG* ⚹ 313.
     'O Cruel Fate, could'st thou not miss!'
     T: 'An Epitaph' on Richard Lewis. ¶ No: 6 lines and 4 lines in
     Latin. ¶ A: 'W. Byfield.'
     Note: See no. 335.

335. Dec. 5, 1734 *PG* ⚹313.
     'This City's lost their Pedagogue of Arts.'
     T: 'An Elegy on the much to be lamented Death of Mr. RICHARD
     LEWIS, late Master of the Free-School of the City of ANNAP-
     OLIS.' ¶ No: 17 lines. ¶ A: 'W. Byfield, late of New-Castle upon
     Tine.'
     Note: This poem is ridiculed in an excellent accompanying essay
     which is probably by Joseph Breintnall. Cf. no. 334. The essayist
     praises Lewis and satirically mentions John Dommet and other
     poor poets of the day.

336. Dec. 9, 1734 *NEWJ.*
     'All Attendants, apart.'
     T: 'A Letter wrote by a young Lady to some others with whom she
     had agreed to take up a Protestant Nunnery, but some Time after
     altered her mind—(for the better).—' ¶ No: 24 lines. ¶ A: [Miss
     Soper.]
     Note: Printed in Dodsley, VI, 232, under the title 'Repentance.'
     Crum A904 gives the date July 11, 1730. Copied in Jeremy Bel-
     knap's 'A Collection of Poetry' (see no. 71), pp. 26–27.

337. Dec. 12, 1734 *PG* ⚹314.
     'A Table, Chairs, and pair of Bellows.'
     T: 'A List of Wants/From a Gentleman in the Fleet Prison to his
     Friend.' ¶ No: 30 lines.
     Note: Hudibrastic, evidently not local.

338. Dec. 19, 1734 *PG* #315.
   'The kingly ruler of the plain.'
   T: 'An Enquiry after True Pleasure. A Fable.' ¶ No: 172 lines. ¶ A:
   'By Mr. Dodsley.'
   Note: For Robert Dodsley, see the *DNB*.

339. Dec. 21, 1734 *SCG*.
   'The Zeal that in Thy Godlike Bosom glows.'
   T: 'To James Oglethorpe, Esq; on his late Arrival from Georgia.' ¶
   No: 52 lines.
   Note: Excellent verse; note line 3: 'Let Twickenham's Bard, in his
   immorral [sic] Lays.' The reprint, no. 362, has a dateline 'London,
   Oct. 5.'

340. Dec. 24, 1734 *AWM* #782.
   'In vain th'Indulgence of the warmer Sun.'
   T: 'Written Extempore, on Reading the News.' ¶ No: 21 lines.
   Note: Dated 'Singr[ ]nce Coffee-House.' 'From the NE Weekly
   Journal.'

341. Dec. 30, 1734 *NYWJ* #60, 4/2.
   'Neptune! be kind, and calm the raging Sea.'
   T: 'A Coppy of Verses upon Col. Morris's Voyage to England.' ¶
   No: 16 lines.
   Note: For Gov. Lewis Morris. Cf. nos. 344, 350. Reprinted in the
   New Jersey Archives, XI, 408–409. Reprinted, see no. 347.

342. Dec. 31, 1734 *AWM* #783.
   'Fear God, Honour the King.'
   T: 'A New Year—Gift.' ¶ No: 31 lines.

1735

343. [Jan. 1, 1734/5] *AWM*.
   'There's not an Ear that is not deaf.'
   T: [Carrier's Verse, 1734/5.] ¶ No: 40 lines.
   Note: This half sheet is included in the Historical Society of Penn-
   sylvania's microfilm of the *AWM*.

344. Jan. 6, 1734/5 *NYWJ* #61, 4/2.
   'Aid me Phoebus, aid me ye sacred nine.'
   T: 'On Coll. Morris' going for England.' ¶ No: 14 lines.
   Note: Cf. no. 341. Reprinted in *New Jersey Archives*, XI, 409. Re-
   printed, see no. 346.

345. Jan. 16, 1734/5 *PG* #319.
   'Since all men must.'

T: 'Ned Wealthy's last Will.' ¶ No: 90 lines.

Note: Reprinted from the *Lon. Mag.* of Aug. 1734; an imitation of no. 199.

346. Jan. 21, 1734/5 *AWM* ⚹786.
'Aid me Phoebus, aid me ye sacred Nine.'
Note: A reprint of no. 344.

347. Jan. 21, 1734/5 *AWM* ⚹786.
'Neptune be kind, and calm the raging Sea.'
Note: A reprint of no. 341.

348. Jan. 27, 1734/5 *WR* ⚹174.
'Unerring Nature learn to follow close.'
T: '... The inclosed Extract from a Pamphlet entituled *Health*, a Poem; which may be had at Mr. *Benjamin Eliot's* ...' ¶ No: 43 lines. ¶ A: [Darby Dawne?]
Note: Quotes Dr. Bayard's advice to his godson. The prefatory note refers to several contemporary poets: 'I confess that Poetry does not look over graceful in a *News-Paper*—Yet there is Reason to hope the following ingenious Performance may prove at least as useful and acceptable, as some Pieces which have lately been published in our most celebrated Papers, Tho' pompously introduced and recommended, whether *New-Haven* Nuptial Songs, *Biddiford* Presentments, or even the Lays of a Lady of superior Genius at *Portsmouth*.' The poem probably refers to another edition of Darby Dawne's *Health, A Poem*; see Evans 2521.

349. Jan. 1735 *Gent Mag*, V, 44.
'Arah, dear joy, suave all your faushes.'
T: 'Teague's Orashion.' ¶ No: 78 lines.
Note: Cf. Benjamin Franklin's poem, no. 610, which was evidently modeled upon this one.

350. Feb. 3, 1734/5 *NYWJ* ⚹65, 4/1.
'No more, great Jove, let angry Neptune reign.'
T: 'Upon Coll. Morris's Voyage to London.' ¶ No: 34 lines. ¶ A: 'The Performance of a rural Muse.'
Note: Written in 'Cape-May in New Jersey.' Sent in by 'I.S.' Cf. no. 341.

351. Feb. 4, 1734/5 *PG* ⚹322.
'Let groveling Misers count their sordid store.'
T: 'To Mr. Greenwood, Hollisian Professor of Mathematics and Astronomy at Cambridge, Occasioned by his late astronomical Lectures.' ¶ No: 64 lines.
Note: Prefaced by 6 lines from Horace; under the dateline 'Boston, Dec. 16.' On Isaac Greenwood, see Shipton, VI, 471–482. This

poem was probably reprinted from the *BG* of December 16, 1734, which is no longer extant.

352. Feb. 8, 1734/5 *SCG* #54.
    'Encourag'd by your Smiles again we dare.'
    T: 'Prologue to the Orphan, acted at Charlestown, Febr 7, 1734–5.'
    ¶ No: 48 lines. ¶ A: [Thomas Dale.]
    Note: Cf. nos. 354 and 356. Reprinted by Robert A. Law, *Nation* XCLIII (April 23, 1914), 464. Law speculates that Febr 7 was a misprint for Febr 4.

353. Feb. 8, 1734/5 *SCG* #54.
    'Thy heavenly Notes, like Angel's musick cheer.'
    T: 'To the Horn-Book.' ¶ No: 14 lines.
    Note: At conclusion of essay.

354. Feb. 8, 1734/5 *SCG* #54.
    'When first Columbus touch'd this distant Shore.'
    T: 'Prologue spoken to the Orphan, upon it's being play'd at Charlestown, on Tuesday the 24th of Jan. 1734/5.' ¶ No: 32 lines. ¶ A: [Thomas Dale.]
    Note: Cf. no. 352. Reprinted by Law (see no. 352), pp. 463–4 and by Silverman, pp. 323–324. Reprinted also by John H. Johnston, 'The Early American Prologue and Epilogue,' in *West Va. Univ. Philological Papers*, XVI (1967), 33.

355. Feb. 18, 1734/5 *PG* #324.
    'How mighty silly your Resolves.'
    T: 'Verses ... design'd as a Piece of Advice to a very good Friend of mine and one of yours.' ¶ No: 16 lines. ¶ A: 'M.B.'
    Note: See prose reply by 'AA' Mar. 4, 1734/5, *PG* #326; 'M.B.' also wrote no. 229.

356. Feb. 22, 1734/5 *SCG* #56.
    'By various Arts we thus attempt to please.'
    T: 'Epilogue to the Orphan, Spoken after the Entertainment at Charlestown.' ¶ No: 30 lines. ¶ A: [Thomas Dale?]
    Note: Reprinted by Law (see no. 352), p. 464; and by Johnston (see no. 354), pp. 34–35.

357. Feb. 25, 1734/5 *AWM* #791.
    'Were you, good Sir, a Friend of mine.'
    T: 'Mr. Bradford, Sir, The following Lines may serve as an answer to those in the last Weeks Gazette.' ¶ No: 20 lines.
    Note: Poem answers the letter by 'S.' on 'Matches made by Parents for their Children, without their Inclination' in *AWM* #789, February 11, 1734/5.

358. Feb. 25, 1734/5 *NYG* #487, 4/1.
'The Tuneful Muse in lofty strains.'
T: [Satire on Political Writers.] ¶ No: 45 lines. ¶ A: 'Z.D.'
Note: This hudibrastic satire concludes an essay which mentions the 'Morris-Dancers' and mocks the writers who have been praising Lewis Morris.

359. Feb. 1735 *Lon Mag*, III, 96.
'Painters shall use Their fading arts no more.'
T: 'To Septimia, on a Picture wrought by her in Silk.' ¶ No: 10 lines. ¶ A: [William Dawson.]
Note: Reprinted from Dawson's *Miscellaneous Poems on Several Occasions* (London, 1735 [1734]), p. 8.

360. Mar. 11, 1734/5 *AWM* #793.
'My charming Youth! why flies —'
T: 'On a Negro Girl making her Court to a fair Youth.' ¶ No: 12 lines.
Note: 'From the *BG*.' See the companion poem, no. 361.

361. Mar. 11, 1734/5 *AWM* #793.
'Negro, complain not, that I fly.'
T: 'The Youth's Answer.' ¶ No: 14 lines.
Note: 'From the *BG*.' See the companion poem, no. 360.

362. Mar. 20, 1735 *PG* #327.
'The Zeal that in Godlike Bosum glows.'
Note: A reprint of no. 339, but dated 'London, Oct. 5.'

363. Mar. 20, 1734–5 *AWM* #794.
'Would you be concern'd to know.'
T: 'From Chester County in the Province of Pennsylvania. To a Friend at Oxford.' ¶ No: 97 lines. ¶ A: 'Ruris Amator.'
Note: Good verse containing interesting references; the writer had been at Oxford. With a prefatory letter. Cf. nos. 369, 424, 427.

364. Mar. 1735 *Gent Mag*, V, 154.
''Tis what will in some hands work wonders.'
T: 'An Extempore Explication of the Riddle taken from the Gentleman's Magazine of June 1734, and inserted in the Barbadoes Gazette, Nov. 23.' ¶ No: 20 lines. ¶ A: 'Blan.'

365. Apr. 24, 1735 *PG* #333.
'Your Petitioners being reduc'd to a wretched Condition.'
Note: A reprint of no. 330.

366. May 12, 1735 *NEWJ* #423, 1/1–2.
'Let all the Works of Heaven's External KING.'

T: 'An Imitation of the 148th Psalm.' ¶ No: 84 lines. ¶ A: [Rev. John Adams.]

Note: Reprinted in Adams, *Poems* (Boston, 1745), pp. 3–6.

367. May 12, 1735 *NYWJ* #79, 2/3.
'Man was a happy Favourite above.'
T: [On Woman.] ¶ No: 46 lines.
Note: Included within an essay on women by 'Francis Ready.'

368. May 17, 1735 *SCG* #68.
'Your sage and moralist can show.'
Note: A reprint of no. 289.

369. June 5, 1735 *AWM*.
'From luxury and care, from dear quadril.'
T: *To the Fair* Camilla.' ¶ No: 26 lines.
Note: Chester County correspondent, cf. no. 363. 'I received the following Piece from a Correspondent in Chester County; about the beginning of April, but had the unhappiness for some time past to have it mislaid.' Refers to Thomson's *Spring*.

370. June 23, 1735 *BG* #807, 2/1–2.
'Almighty Monarch! How Thy glorious Name.'
T: 'Psalm VIII.' ¶ No: 36 lines.
Note: Dated 'Boston, May 30, 1735.'

371. June 23, 1735 *NEWJ* #429, 1/1–2.
'And is old Merrymak come to an End?'
T: 'Connecticutt's Flood, on Merrymak's Ebb.' ¶ No: 38 lines. ¶ A: 'J.W.' [John Winthrop, IV.]
Note: 'Extempore, March 10, 1720/21.' See no. 372.

372. June 23, 1735 *NEWJ* #429.
'Long did *Euphrates* make us glad.'
T: 'Upon the drying up of that Ancient River, the River Merrimak.' ¶ No: 36 lines. ¶ A: 'S.S.' [Samuel Sewall].
Note: Dated 'Jan 15, 1719,20.' See no. 371. Listed in Jantz, p. 257, no. 42.

373. July 12, 1735 *SCG* #76.
'Would you, as sure you would, with utmost care.'
T: 'The Advice.' ¶ No: 17 lines.

374. July 21, 1735 *BPB* #36.
'Poor Pompy's dead! and likewise skin'd,'
T: 'An Epigram made on a Ladys Lap-Dog called Pompey.' ¶ No: 14 lines.
Note: Reprinted, see no. 377.

375. Aug. 7, 1735 *PG* #348.
    'His Host (as Crouds are superstitious still).'
    T: 'On the Occasion of Cato's marching at the Head of an Army
       thro' the Desarts of *Africa* near the Temple of Jupiter Ammon.' ¶
       No: 114 lines.
    Note: A translation, with Lucian's original.

376. Aug. 7, 1735 *AWM*.
    'France, Spain, and Sardinia, together conspire.'
    T: 'The Tripple Alliance. An EPIGRAM.'

377. Aug. 7, 1735 *AWM* #814.
    'Poor Pompy's dead! and likewise skinn'd,'
    Note: A reprint of no. 374.

378. Aug. 30, 1735 *SCG* #83.
    'When on the Banks of Babel's rolling Flood.'
    T: 'The 6 first Verses of the 137th Psalm paraphrased.' ¶ No: 31
       lines.

379. Sept. 6, 1735 *SCG* #84.
    'Two Hotspurs unnoted for martial adventures.'
    T: [A Duel of Dunghill Soldiery.] ¶ No: 14 lines.

380. Sept. 13, 1735 *SCG* #85.
    'The Russ loves Brandy, Dutchman beer.'
    T: 'For the Honour of Old England.' ¶ No: 24 lines.

381. Sept. 18, 1735 *AWM* #830.
    'May none but fair and pleasant Gales.'
    T: [On John Penn's voyage.] ¶ No: 8 lines.
    Note: John Penn was sailing back to England. The poem is included
       in the news account.

382. Sept. 1735 *Gent Mag*, V, 549.
    'Pensive my Thoughts descend to shades below.'
    T: 'Verses from New England, by O.B.T. in his 14th Year.' ¶ No:
       14 lines. ¶ A: 'O.B.T.'
    Note: Ugh.

383. Oct. 1735 *Lon Mag*, IV, 565.
    'While, ripening slow, the future *purpose* lay.'
    T: 'On giving the Name of Georgia, to a Part of Carolina.' ¶ No: 10
       lines ¶ A: ['Ensebuis'?]
    Note: This poem evidently first appeared in *Howgrave's Stamford
       Mercury*, #37 (Feb. 22, 1733). See R.M. Wiles, *Freshest Advices*
       (Ohio State, 1965), p. 313.

384. Dec. 29, 1735 *NYWJ* #112, 4/2.
    'What Doubts if all sufficient Providence?'

T: 'An Endeavour for an Imitation by another Hand.' ¶ No: 25 lines.

Note: With Latin verse, and a 'Low-Dutch' poetic translation.

1736

385. Jan. 6, 1736 *PG* #370.
'What sounds harmonious strike the ears!'
T: 'Hymn, on the Nativity of Christ.' ¶ No: 31 lines.
Note: Reprinted, no. 1843.

386. Jan. 6, 1736 *PG* #370.
'Where Nature does her greatest Gifts bestow.'
T: 'An acquaintance of Jacob Taylor's perusing the Reading in Jacob's Almanack for the Year 1736, had the following thoughts.' ¶ No: 30 lines. ¶ A: [Joseph Breintnall].
Note: The poem, prefaced by two lines from Pope, praises Taylor. For the attribution, see J. Philip Goldberg, 'Joseph Breintnall and a Poem in Praise of Jacob Taylor,' *Pa. Mag. of Hist. and Biog.*, LXXXVI (1962), 207–209.

387. Jan. 6, 1735–6 *PG* #370.
'Stop Passenger, until my Life you read.'
T: 'An Epitaph on Margery Scott, who died at Dunkill in Scotland, February, 1728.'
Note: A riddle; evidently not American. Crum S1218.

388. Jan. 13, 1735/6 *NEWJ* #458.
'Now mantled with an hoary Garb, the Earth.'
T: 'On the Twelve Months of the Year.' ¶ No: 48 lines. ¶ A: 'Composed by a young Gentleman not far from Boston.'
Note: Four lines for each month.

389. Jan. 15, 1735/6 *PG* #371.
'For these nocturnal thieves, huntsman prepare.'
T: 'Fox-Hunting.' ¶ No: 142 lines.

390. Jan. 19, 1735/6 *BEP* #23, 2/2.
'Things that are bitter, bitterer than Gall.'
T: [Savage verse on women's tongues.] ¶ No: 8 lines. ¶ A: [Benjamin Franklin?]
Note: From *Poor Richard's Almanack* for 1736. Printed in *The Franklin Papers*, II, 139. This is similar to Franklin's news-note *jeu d'esprit* (not reprinted in the *Franklin Papers*) in the *PG* Feb. 15, 1731/2, on a husband who bit off part of his wife's tongue.

391. Jan. 20, 1736 *AWM* #838.
    'Behold how Papal Wright with Lordly Pride.'
    T: 'A copy of Verses sent from *London* to a Gentleman here.' ¶ No:
    32 lines. ¶ A: [---Baker.]
    Note: Crum B211 gives the title 'On the Presbyterian Clergy, 1736'
    and the attribution.

392. Jan. 20, 1736 *AWM* #838.
    'Immortal Bard! for whom each Muse has wove.'
    T: 'A Letter from Mr. Littleton to Mr. Pope.' ¶ A: [John Whaley.]
    Note: The poem, ostensibly by George, Lord Lyttleton, is in
    Whaley's *Poems* (London, 1732), p. 77. Crum I1183 gives the
    title 'An Epistle to Mr. Pope, from a Young Gentleman at Rome,
    May 7, 1730.' On Whaley (1710-1745), see *CBEL*, II, 332.

393. Jan. 1736 *Gent Mag*, VI, 52.
    'When Pharoh's sins provok'd th'Almighty's hand.'
    T: 'To Feria. Epigram I.' ¶ No: 8 lines. ¶ A: 'Americanus.'
    Note: Reprinted from *Barbados Gazette*, Oct. 1, with long prefatory
    letter addressed 'To Mr. T. F.' Cf. nos. 394, 395.

394. Jan. 1736, *Gent Mag*, VI, 52.
    'As Sir Toby reel'd home, with his skin full of wine.'
    T: 'Epigram II.' ¶ No: 12 lines. ¶ A: 'Americanus.'
    Note: Cf. no. 393.

395. Jan. 1736 *Gent Mag*, VI, 52.
    'Since, as the serious preach, and prudent say.'
    T: 'Epigram III.' ¶ No: 4 lines. ¶ A: 'Americanus.'
    Note: Cf. no. 393.

396. Jan. 1736 *Lon Mag*, V, 41–42.
    'Marino!—welcome from the western shore.'
    T: 'A Poem. To the Memory of Aquila Rose, who dy'd at Phila-
    delphia, in Pennsylvania, August the 22d, 1723. Aetat 28.'
    Note: A reprint of no. 53.

397. Feb. 2, 1735/6 *BPB* #64.
    'Blest martyr, for whose fate.'
    T: 'An Ode on the 30th of January.' ¶ No: 50 lines.
    Note: Reprinted, see no. 400.

398. Feb. 5, 1735/6 *PG* #374.
    'A Good repute, a virtuous name.'
    T: 'A Tale of the Travellers.' ¶ No: 72 lines.
    Note: On literature; mentions Nathaniel Lee, Sir Richard Black-
    more, Milton, Shakespeare, John Gay, Jonathan Swift.

399. Feb. 16, 1735/6 *NYWJ* #119, 3/1.
'Toby a Dog of Sport.'
T: 'Poor Toby's Fate, Or, a Farewell to Courtiers, To the Tune, of Daphne our dearest Bitch. O bone, o bone.' ¶ No: 45 lines + refrain. ¶ A: 'Tho. Right.'
Note: Reprinted, see no. 470.

400. Feb. 24, 1735/6 *NYG* #538, 1/1–2/1.
'Blest Martyr, for whose Fate,'
Note: A reprint of no. 397.

401. Mar. 16, 1736 *AWM.*
'Hail happy virgin of celestial race.'
T: 'On the noted & celebrated Quaker Mrs. Drummond.' ¶ A: 'By a young Lady.'
Note: May Drummond (d. 1772) was set at the peak of her fame in 1736. See Joseph Smith, *A Descriptive Catalogue of Friends' Books,* I (London, 1867), 543–545.

401a. Mar. 22, 1735/6 *BEP* #32, 2/2.
'Here lies our Captain and Major.'
T: [Epitaph on Humphry Atherton.] ¶ No: 12 lines.
Note: The verses were 'taken off a Grave Stone in the burying-ground at Dorchester.' See Jantz, p. 288, no. 14. In addition to the reprintings cited by Jantz, the poem is copied in a thick, light green clasp notebook in The Belknap Papers 1720–1919 at the Massachusetts Historical Soc. (call no. 013.9b); in John Farmer and Jacob Bailey Moore, *Collections, Historical and Miscellaneous* II (1823), 144; and below, no. 1816.

402. Mar. 23, 1735/6 *AWM* #847.
'Oh! thou eternal wisdom, who surveys.'
T: 'On God's omnipotency.' ¶ No: 22 lines.

403. April 5, 1736 *NYG* #544.
'Farewel you gilded Follies, pleasant Troubles.'
T: 'Sir Kenelm Digby's Farewell to the World.' ¶ No: 44 lines. ¶ A: [Sir Henry Wotton?]
Note: Allegorical? Crum F216 gives the title 'Valediction' and tentatively ascribes the poem to Wotton (1568-1639), for whom, see *CBEL,* I, 426.

404. April 15, 1736 *AWM* #850.
'Permit, lamented shade, an humble Muse.'
T: 'Verses, to the Memory of Henry Brooke, Esq; Who departed this Life on Friday, February 6th and was Buried in the Church at Philadelphia, on Saturday, February 7th, 1735, 6.' ¶ No: 50 lines.
Note: Not bad verse. Cf. note to no. 420. Reprinted (with fuller title), no. 612.

405. May 27, 1736 *AWM* ∦856.
    'Ton Pegase est un franc cheval.'
    T: Epigramme. A Monsieur [Webbe]. ¶ No: 6 lines. ¶ A: 'Dalmas,'
    [John Salomon?]
    Note: An attack on John Webb[e]. Salomon, a Philadelphia school
    teacher, wrote poems in French. See nos. 418 and 419.

406. May 29, 1736 *SCG* ∦122, 2/1.
    'How cruel Fortune, and how fickle too.'
    T: 'On the Sale of the Theatre.' ¶ No: 8 lines.

407. May 1736 *Lon Mag*, V, 269.
    'Let *Rome* no more her antient Triumphs boast.'
    T: 'A new Prologue (wrote by Mr. Sterling) to the Conscious
    Lovers, which was acted, in Goodman's Fields, in Honour of the
    Royal Wedding.' ¶ No: 30 lines. ¶ A: [James] Sterling.

408. May 1736 *Gent Mag*, VI, 288.
    'In Truth, dear ladies! 'Tis a curious matter.'
    T: 'Epilogue to the Recruiting Officer, written by Thomas Dale,
    M.D., and spoken by Silvia in Man's Cloaths, at the Opening of
    the New Theatre, in Charles-Town in South-Carolina.' ¶ No: 25
    lines. ¶ A: Dr. Thomas Dale.
    Note: Dale sent a letter containing this poem to his friend the Rev.
    Thomas Birch, dated February 29th 1735 [6], commenting: 'We
    are building here a fine Theater, which was opened this season,
    they opened with the Recruiting Officer and the Epilogue was
    made for Sylvia and spoke by her in man's cloathes. I send it you
    to divert you tho' I think it is my first attempt in Rhime in this
    Country and you know what slender acquaintance I have with the
    Muses ... If you and some of our old Friends should think the epi-
    logue worth printing, you may give a Copy to Charles Ackers for
    his magazine.'—British Museum MS. 4304. Robert A. Law re-
    printed selections from the poem in 'Thomas Dale, an Eighteenth
    Century Gentleman,' *The Nation*, C1 (Dec. 30, 1915), 773, and in
    A' Diversion for Colonial Gentlemen,' *Texas Review*, II (1916–
    17), 84.

409. June 8, 1736 *NEWJ* ∦479.
    'Indulgent Death, prepare thy gentle Dart.'
    T: 'Lines' on death. ¶ A: 'A Gentlewoman, yet living in the West of
    England.'

410. June 14, 1736 *NYG* ∦554, 2/1–3/2.
    'No questions mov'd about your claim.'
    T: 'Expostulation.' ¶ No: 76 lines.
    Note: An attack on Lewis Morris.

411. July 17, 1736 *SCG* #129, 3/1.
'It can't be Treason in our own Defence.'
T: [The Dictates of Common Sense and Law.] ¶ No: 14 lines.
Note: A political poem.

412. July 31, 1736 *SCG* #131, 2/2.
'From your own taste don't judge another's Gou'st.'
T: [The Variety of God's Creation.] ¶ No: 8 lines.

413. July 31, 1736 *SCG* #131, 2/1.
'Here, wife, let's see my slippers, cap and gown.'
T: 'A Dialogue between a proud, idle, foppish Husband, and a scold-
ing Wife.' ¶ No: 34 lines.

414. Aug. 7, 1736 *PG* #400.
'Blest Leaf, whose Aromatick Gales dispense.'
T: 'Tobacco, In Imitation of Mr. Pope.' ¶ No: 20 lines. ¶ A: [Isaac
Browne.]
Note: From *Lon Mag.*, Nov. and Dec., 1735. Printed in Dodsley, II,
284. Crum B446.

415. Aug. 7, 1736 *PG* #400.
'Criticks avaunt! Tobacco is my Theme.'
T: 'Tobacco, In Imitation of Dr. Young.' ¶ No: 22 lines. ¶ A:
[Isaac Browne.]
Note: From *Lon. Mag.*, Nov. and Dec., 1735. Edward Young, poet.
Printed in Dodsley, II, 283. Crum C776.

416. Aug. 7, 1736 *PG* #400.
'O Thou matur'd by glad hesperian Suns.'
T: 'Tobacco, In Imitation of Mr. Thompson.' ¶ No: 26 lines. ¶ A:
[Isaac Browne.]
Note: From *Lon. Mag.*, Nov. and Dec., 1735. James Thomson,
poet. Printed in Dodsley, II, 282. Crum O868.

417. Aug. 7, 1736 *PG* #400.
'Pretty Tube of mighty power.'
T: 'Tobacco, In Imitation of Mr. Phillips.' ¶ No: 18 lines. ¶ A:
[Isaac Browne.]
Note: From *Lon. Mag.*, Nov. and Dec., 1735. Ambrose Philips,
poet. Printed in Dodsley, II, 285. Crum P383.

418. Aug. 7, 1736 *PG* #400.
'Oui, je l'ai dit cent fois, ce n'est que fiction.'
T: 'Sonnet.' ¶ No: 14 lines. ¶ A: 'J.S.' [John Salomon.]
Note: With prefatory letter—also in French.

419. Aug. 19, 1736 *AWM* #868.
'Ciel, grand Gouverneur, ne vous avoct fuit naitre.'

T: 'Sonnet.' ¶ No: 14 lines. ¶ A: 'John Salomon.'
Note: On the death of Gov. Patrick Gordon.

420. Sept. 2, 1736 *AWM*.
'[P]lain, Gen'rous, Honest, Merciful, and Brave.'
T: 'Verses to the Memory of the Honorable Patrick Gordon, Esq;
the Lieutenant-Governor of Pennsylvania, and of the three Lower
Counties on Delaware.' ¶ No: 12 lines.
Note: Dated August 14th, 1736; Gordon's obituary is reprinted in
the *Franklin Papers*, II, 159. The poem is similar to 'Verses to the
Memory of Henry Brooke' (no. 404) and they both may be by the
same author. Another poem 'On the Death of Gov. P. Gordon
Aug. 5, 1736' is in Joseph Norris, Commonplace book, leaf 11
(1st line—'The last Inexorable Debt[']s discharg'd'), at the
Huntington Library.

421. Sept. 6, 1736 *NYWJ* #148, 1/1.
'Fate Shapes our Lives as it divides the Years.'
T: [On Behaviour in Good or Bad Fortune.] ¶ No: 14 lines.

422. Oct. 1, 1736 *VG* #9.
'Welcome, fair Princess, to the Shore.'
T: 'To Her Highness Princess Augusta, landing at Greenwich.' ¶
No: 12 lines.
Note: First poem in *VG*.

423. Oct. 1, 1736 *VG*.
'Ye Muses, Hail the Roial Dame.'
T: 'An Ode presented to their Roial Highnesses the Prince and
Princess of Wales, in Richmond-Gardens, May 6.' ¶ No: 24 lines.
¶ A: 'By Mr. Stephen Duck.'
Note: Crum Y94.

424. Oct. 14, 1736 *AWM* #876.
'Lonely Chloe, pretty creature.'
T: 'To my absent Chloe.' ¶ No: 12 lines. ¶ A: 'Ruris Amator.'
Note: Cf. no. 363.

425. Oct. 22, 1736 *VG*.
'Custom, alas! doth partial prove.'
T: 'The Lady's Complaint.' ¶ No: 16 lines. ¶ A: ['E.R.']
Note: 'Mr. Parks, The following Lines were some Years ago, pre-
sented to me by a Lady; and as I don't remember I ever saw them
in print, your inserting them in your Paper will, I dare say, oblige
many of your Readers, as well as your humble Servant.' Reprinted,
No. 690 (where the initials 'E.R.' are given).

426. Oct. 29, 1736 *VG*.

'Dame *Law*, to maintain a more flourishing State.'

T: 'The Call of the 14 new Serjeants, mentioned in our Gazette, No. 9 gave Birth to the following Lines.' ¶ No: 6 lines.

Note: Crum D11.

427. Nov. 4, 1736 *PG* #412.

'From Delawarian banks, the Muses seat.'

T: 'On Mrs. M—y D—bis; going from Philadelphia to B—l, by Water.' ¶ No: 42 lines. ¶ A: 'R.A.' [Ruris Amator?]

Note: Dated 'From the Country, Novem. 1, 1736. Mr. Franklin, as this is the first, so in all probability it may be the last trouble I shall give you: ... R.A.' Cf. no. 363.

428. Nov. 12, 1736 *VG*.

'All hail, ye Fields, where constant Peace attends.'

T: [Against Worldly Vanities.] ¶ No: 40 lines.

Note: These verses are from the 'Monitor' no. 13, an American essay series.

429. Nov. 15, 1736 *BG* #879, 3/1.

'In the immense Expance above.'

T: [Religious verse.] ¶ No: 16 lines.

Note: Dated 'Boston, Nov. 9, 1736.'

430. Nov. 18, 1736 *PG* #414.

'There are a number of us creep.'

T: 'Paraphrase' [from Horace, part of an essay 'The Waste of Life.'] ¶ No: 15 lines.

Note: Reprinted, no. 439.

431. Nov. 19, 1736 *VG*.

'Awful Hero, Cato, rise!'

T: 'Cato, and his Genius.' ¶ No: 16 lines.

Note: An American imitation of Addison's *Cato* and Leonard Welsted's poem 'The Genius' (in Dodsley, IV, 276).

432. Dec. 3, 1736 *VG*.

'When first I tun'd the Lyric Strings.'

T: 'This Imitation of the 15th Ode of the 4th Book of Horace, is humbly addressed to the Honourable William Gooch, Esq; Governor of this Colony.' ¶ No: 50 lines. ¶ A: 'David Mossom, Jun.' Probably the son of the Rev. David Mossom: see Lundie W. Barlow, 'The Rev. David Mossom of Mass. and Va.,' *Va. Genealogist*, V (1961), 170–171.

433. Dec. 10, 1736 *VG*.

'Scarse Egypt's Land more dire Disasters knew.'

T: 'A Rapsody, occasioned by a Review of the Common Misery of Human Kind, especially in that Part of the World called Great-Britain.' ¶ No: 62 lines.

434. Dec. 10, 1736 *VG.*
'A New Creation charms the ravish'd Sight.'
T: 'The following Lines were wrote by a Gentleman of Virginia.' 'To a Lady. On a Screen of Her Working.' ¶ No: 28 lines. ¶ A: 'By a Gentleman of Virginia' [William Dawson].
Note: See the more specific title in no. 436.

435. Dec. 28, 1736 *AWM* #887.
'Accomplish'd *Gurney* charms my ravish'd ear.'
T: 'Verses on several of the Quakers Teachers.'
Note: 'From the London Magazine for August.'

436. Dec. 1736 *Lon Mag,* V, 694.
'A New creation charms the ravisht sight!'
T: 'To Mrs. G—: On a Screen of her own working.' ¶ A: 'W—m D–ws–n' [Wm. Dawson].
Note: See no. 434. Reprinted in *Va. Hist. Register,* VI, 30–31.

1737

437. Jan. 4, 1736/7 *NYG* #582, 2/1–2.
'Tho' Rhyme serves the thoughts of great Poets to fetter.'
T: 'The Prodigy. A Letter to a Friend in the Country.' ¶ A: 'By Mrs. Barber.'
Note: Mrs. Mary Barber of Dublin.

438. Jan. 15, 1737 *SCG* #155, 2/1.
'Life's but a Feast; and when we die.'
T: [Paraphrase of Horace.] ¶ No: 8 lines.

439. Jan. 15, 1737 *SCG* #155, 2/1.
'There are a Number of us creep.'
Note: A reprint of no. 430.

440. Jan. 21, 1736/7 *VG* #25.
'I, Who long since did draw my Pen.'
T: 'The Monitor admonished: A new Song: To the Tune of, *To all ye Ladies now at Land.*' ¶ No: 30 lines. ¶ A: 'Zoilus.'
Note: Dated 'Jan. 12, 1736/7.' With a prefatory letter. See the reply, no. 442. Cf. nos. 447, 451.

441. Jan. 24, 1736/7 *NYWJ* #167, 2/1–2.
'As sounding Brass and Tinkling Cymbals ring.'
T: [Religion necessary in true love.] ¶ No: 27 lines.
Note: Sent in by 'Constanter.'

442. Jan. 28, 1736/7 *VG.*
'Since injur'd Wit is thus reliev'd.'
T: 'The Monitor to Zoilus: A New Song: To the Tune of, To all ye Ladies new at Land, &c.' ¶ No: 42 lines & chorus.
Note: 2 Parts of the Monitor #19. A reply to no. 440.

443. Jan. 31, 1737 *BG* #890.
'Dear *Collen* prevent my warm Flushes.'
T: 'The Request of an Old Maid by a Declaration of her Passion.' ¶ No: 16 lines. ¶ A: 'L.Z.'
Note: See accompanying poem, no. 444. Reprinted, see no. 452. The 'Old Maid' is supposedly Frances Seymour, Countess of Hertford. The poem was written on the occasion of Lord William Hamilton's marriage. Crum D73.

444. Jan. 31, 1737 *BG* #890.
'Good Madam, when Ladies are willing.'
T: 'The Answer.' ¶ No: 16 lines. ¶ A: 'L.Z.' [Lady Mary Wortley Montagu.]
Note: See no. 443. Reprinted, see no. 452. See Robert Halsband's edition of the *Complete Letters of Lady Mary Wortley Montagu*, III (Oxford, 1967), p.187 and n.4. In Dodsley, VI, 230-231, these two poems are misleadingly entitled 'Lady Mary W[ortley Montagu] to Sir W[illiam] Y[onge]' and 'Sir W[illiam] Y[onge]'s Answer.' The *DNB* article on Yonge (d. 1755) mistakenly attributes the latter poem to Yonge.

445. Feb. 1, 1736/7 *NEWJ* #513.
'That with all dazzling Splendor strike the Eye.'
T: ['Verses on Sleep.'] ¶ No: 51 lines, 6 by Milton. ¶ A: [Mather Byles?]
Note: Poem begins with a quotation of 6 lines from Milton, Book 4: 'O Thou! who, with surpassing crown'd,' Mather Byles' copy of this newspaper at the American Antiquarian Society has the MS. addition of the title, 'Verses on Sleep.'

446. Feb. 3, 1736/7 *NYG* #586 1/1-3/2 & cont. in Feb. 10, 1/1-4/2.
'What is this Life we strive with anxious care.'
T: 'A Poem on Life, Death, Judgment, Heaven and Hell.'

447. Feb. 4, 1736/7 *VG.*
'I knew that the Song, which I lately did send.'
T: [Zoilus to the Monitor.] ¶ No: 20 lines. ¶ A: 'Zoilus.'
Note: See no. 440.

448. Feb. 8, 1736/7 *NEWJ* #514.
'Oh! lapsed Nature's fixt, but righteous Laws.'

T: 'Lachrymae Patris. An Elegy on a Son suppos'd to be lost at Sea.' ¶ No: 106 lines. ¶ A: 'A.Z.'

449. Feb. 10, 1737 *PG* #426.
'When to cold Winter Fruitful Autumn yields.'
T: 'A Paraphrase on Cursus Glacialis.' ¶ No: 24 lines. ¶ A: 'I.P.'
Note: The Latin verses are also printed.

450. No verse.

451. Feb. 11, 1736/7 *VG*.
'How hard is my fate!—to be thus over match'd.'
T: 'The Monitor, to Zoilus.' ¶ No: 16 lines. ¶ A: 'The Monitor.'
Note: See no. 440.

452. Feb. 21, 1736/7 *NYWJ* #171, 1/1.
'Dear Collen prevent my warm Flushes.'
Note: Reprint of nos. 443 and 444.

453. March 1, 1736/7 *NEWJ* #517.
'Let loftier Bards the Hero's Acts relate.'
T: 'The Fate of the Mouse: A Tragic-comic Poem, occasioned by a mouse that was caught and killed by an Oyster.' ¶ No: 96 lines.
Note: An excellent poem.

454. April 8, 1737 *VG*.
'My Muse, Great Caesar, can't attend your Hearse.'
T: 'On the Death of the Hon. Sir John Randolph, Knt.' ¶ No: 62 lines. ¶ A: [William Dawson?]
Note: A trans. of no. 455. Cf. no. 236.

455. April 8, 1737 *VG* #36.
'Non ego jam planctu decorem tua funera sero.'
T: 'In Obitum, Hororandi Viri Johannes Randolphi, Equitis.' ¶ No: 46 lines, Latin. ¶ A: [William Dawson?]
Note: See no. 454. For Randolph's Latin epitaph, see no. 525. The Rev. James Blair, as minister of Bruton Parish Church (of which Randolph was a vestryman) would have been the logical person to write an elegy on Randolph, but Blair was in his 80's and held no high opinion of the deistic Randolph's religion. The natural person associated with William and Mary College (where Randolph was buried) to write the elegy and to assist Blair at the funeral would have been Blair's successor, both as President of the College of William and Mary, and as Commissary of the Virginia clergy, the Rev. William Dawson.

456. April 29, 1737 *VG*.
'How sweet a Face, what magic Charms.'
T: 'On modern Courtship.' ¶ No: 16 lines. ¶ A: 'Amintor.'

Note: 'Mr. Parks, I send you an Essay on the *modern Way of Wooing.*' Dated: April 28, 1737. Cf. no. 589.

457. April 1737 *Lon Mag*, VI, 210.
'Belcher, once more permit the muse you lov'd.'
T: 'To his Excellency Governor Belcher (of New England) on the Death of his Lady. (See p. 108) An Epistle. By the Rev. Mr. Byles, his Excellency's Nephew.' ¶ No: 56 lines. ¶ A: Mather Byles.
Note: Printed previously in *To His Excellency Governor Belcher* B(oston, 1736); Evans 3999. Reprinted in Byles, *Poems* (see no. 60), pp. 76–79; in Kettell, I, 131–32.

458. May 16, 1737 *NYWJ*, 1/1–2.
'To Thee my Spouse.'
T: 'Will of one — Solom' ¶ No: 84 lines.

459. May 30, 1737 *BG* ✳907.
'Virtue here lyes, a Pattern for any.'
T: 'Epitaph' [on] Mrs. Elizabeth Tothill. ¶ No: 4 lines. ¶ A: 'M.M.'
Note: Dated 'Narraganset, May 10, 1737.'

460. June 3, 1737 *VG* ✳44.
'Sweetness and Strength in Silvia's Voice unite.'
T: 'Verses occasioned by a young Lady's singing to the Spinnet.' ¶ No: 8 lines. ¶ A: 'By a young Gentleman in Virginia.'
Note: Reprinted, see no. 477.

461. June 10, 1737 *VG*.
'The coolest Time in a Summer's Day.'
T: [A riddle.] ¶ No: 4 lines.

462. June 11, 1737 *SCG* ✳176, 3/1.
'As blustering Winds disturb the calmest Sea.'
T: [On Tyrants and Rebellion.] ¶ No: 18 lines.
Note: Dated 'North Carolina, May 18, 1737.' Imitated by no. 471. Reprinted in Richard Beale Davis, 'Three Poems from Colonial North Carolina,' *No. Car. Hist. Rev.*, XLVI (1969), 34–35.

463. June 17, 1737 *VG* ✳46.
'When *Talbot* ravag'd all the Plains of France.'
T: 'A Tale: Extracted from Shakespear.' ¶ No: 40 lines. ¶ A: 'Musaephilus.'
Note: With a prefatory note. Cf no. 516.

464. July 1, 1737 *VG*.
'Would *Heaven* propitious with my Wish comply.'
T: 'The Wish.' ¶ No: 136 lines.
Note: With a prefatory letter.

465. July 7, 1737 *AWM* #914.
    '*Two Limbs of the Law* (so capricious is Fate!)
    T: 'An Epigram, Occasion'd by the News of the Transportation of
        Two Lawyers from England, the one for Stealing Books out of a
        publick Library in Oxford, the other for Robbing on the High-
        way.' ¶ No: 12 lines. ¶ A: 'By a Gentleman of St. *Christophers.*'
    Note: 'From the Barbados Gazette.'

466. July 8, 1737 *VG*.
    'Among some Roses, with dull sleep opprest.'
    T: 'Cupid and the Bee.' ¶ No: 12 lines.
    Note: A translation of *Anacreon.*

467. July 16, 1737 *SCG* #181, 2/2.
    'Good unexpected, Evil unforeseen.'
    T: [The Ebb and Flow of Fortune.] ¶ No: 12 lines.
    Note: Dated 'Charlestown.'

468. July 18, 1737 *NYG*, 2/1.
    'Would you lead a peaceable, undisturb'd life.'
    T: 'A Charm, to ward against that dangerous Creature, the TALE-
        BEARER.' ¶ No: 16 lines. ¶ A: 'Timothy Forecast.'

469. July 22, 1737 *VG*.
    'Whilst I lov'd thee, and thou wer't kind.'
    T: 'Hor. Ode IX. Carmin. 1. 3. Dial. Hor & Lydia.' ¶ No: 24 lines.
        ¶ A: 'Helena Littewit.'
    Note: Local verse with a prefatory letter.

470. July 25, 1737 *NYWJ* #194, 1/2–2/1.
    'Toby a Dog of Sport.'
    Note: This 'doleful dull Dity, tho' fashionable,' is included in an ex-
        cellent skit (which mentions Lewis Morris and Gov. William
        Cosby) on New York politics, which began in the *NYWJ*, July
        18, 1737, 1/1–2/2, and was continued in this issue, 1/1–2/2.

471. July 25, 1737 *NYWJ* # 194, 2/2.
    'As stormy Winds disturb the calmest Sea.'
    T: [On the reasons for rebellion.] ¶ No: 21 lines.
    Note: An adaptation of no. 462. This poem is contained in the same
        political essay as no. 470.

472. July 29, 1737 *VG*.
    'In the name of Good Liquor, Amen. I J—n C—s—y.'
    T: [Mock-will] ¶ No: 22 lines. ¶ A: J.C. J[oh]n C—s—y.
    Note: Dated 'Hanover, July 25, 1737.'

473. July 30, 1737 *SCG* #183, 3/1.
    'The solid Joys of human Kind.'
    T: 'On a Good Conscience.' ¶ No: 24 lines.

474. July, 1737 *Lon Mag*, VI, 394.
'When first the seals the good lord King resign'd.'
T: 'On the late News from England, of the Death of the Lord Chan-
cellor Talbot, and the Appointment of Lord Chief Justice Hard-
wicke in his Room.' ¶ No: 22 lines.
Note: Dated 'Barbadoes, April 23, 1737.' On Charles Talbot and
Philip Yorke, first Earl of Hardwicke.

475. Aug. 4, 1737 *AWM* ⍟918.
'What silly Wretch would prostitute his Name.'
T: 'Lines ... for the Benefit of my Friend W—b.' ¶ No: 8 lines. ¶ A:
'B.L.'
Note: 'B.L.' had written one of the articles on Andrew Hamilton.
See *AWM*, Dec. 29, 1733. On John Webb[e].

476. Aug. 19, 1737 *VG*.
'The Friend, who proves sincere and true.'
T: 'On Friendship: In Imitation of the 22d Ode, of the First Book ot
Horace.' ¶ No: 30 lines.

477. Aug. 26, 1737 *VG*.
'Sweetness and Strength in Silvia's Voice unite.'
Note: A reprint of no. 460.

478. Sept. 19, 1737 *BG* ⍟923, 1/2–2/3.
'And has Charissa her whole Heav'n of Charms.'
T: 'Epithalamium.' ¶ No: 94 lines.

479. Sept. 22, 1737 *PG* ⍟458.
'Unhappy Day! distressing Sight!'
T: 'David's Lamentation over Saul and Jonathan Sam. i. 19, &c.
Paraphrased.' ¶ No: 69 lines.
Note: 'I have seen it several times in an *English* Dress, but none of
them have given me any more Satisfaction, than perhaps I shall
give to those who read mine. 'Twas a mere admiration of this
Hebrew Song that set my imagination at work, in this attempt to
imitate.'—prefatory letter.

480. Oct. 20, 1737 *AWM*.
'With spotless Innocence, that chears the Mind.'
T: 'Verses, Occasioned by a Letter in the *PG* ⍟459' [Sept. 29, 1737;
the letter was written by a member of the Proprietary party.] ¶
No: 22 lines.
Note: Heroic couplets; pretty good. Contemporary ms. copy in
Joseph Norris (1698/9–1733), Commonplace Book, leaf 11 verso,
The Huntington Library.

481. Nov. 1737 *Gent Mag*, VII, 697.
'How great, how just Thy zeal, advent'rous youth!'

T: 'To the Rev. Mr. Whitfield, on his Design for Georgia.' ¶ No: 34 lines.

Note: Dated 'Gloucester, Nov. 1.'

482. Dec. 1, 1737 *SCG* #201, 1/2.

'Orpheus to seek his Wife decreed.'

T: 'An Explication of the Fable of Orpheus and Eurydice, by a Batchelor.' ¶ No: 16 lines.

Note: Cf. accompanying poem, no. 483.

483. Dec. 1, 1737 *SCG* #201, 1/2.

'Orpheus to seek his Wife 'tis said.'

T: 'Another Explanation by a Marry'd Man.' ¶ No: 16 lines.

Note: Cf. no. 482.

484. Dec. 9, 1737 *VG*.

'Ever constant to her Friend.'

T: 'An Acrostick upon Miss Evelyn Byrd, lately deceased.' ¶ No: 10 lines. ¶ A: [William Byrd of Westover?]

Note: 'On Tuesday [Nov 29] last, died Miss Evelyn Byrd, eldest Daughter of the Honour. William Byrd, Esq'—*VG*, Dec. 2, 1737. The acrostic has been reprinted several times, including Richmond C. Beatty, *William Byrd of Westover* (Boston, 1932), p. 119; and Maude H. Woodfin, ed., *Another Secret Diary of William Byrd ... 1739–1741* (Richmond, 1942), p. 382, where an attribution to Byrd is suggested.

485. Dec. 29, 1737 *PG* #472.

'Some Husbands on a Winter's Day.'

T: 'The Obedient Wives, A Tale.' ¶ No: 208 lines. ¶ A: [William Dawson?]

Note: Reprinted, nos. 487A, 1120, 1605 (with a different title). No. 929, by 'A Gentleman of Virginia' is called 'a Sequal to *The Pig*,' which is the later title of this poem.

486. Dec. 1737 *Gent Mag*, VII, 760.

'Low, in the gloomy vale of thought, confin'd.'

T: 'To the Right Hon. Lord Baltimore.' ¶ No: 32 lines. ¶ A: [Thomas Brerewood, Jr.?]

Note: For the attribution, see Mrs. Russell Hastings, in the *Md. Hist. Mag.*, XXII (1927), 342 n. Brerewood (1694?–1747) was in Maryland from 1734 to 1737. See *ibid.*, p. 343n. Reprinted, no. 493.

1738

487. Jan. 10, 1738 *AWM*.

'Do thou, O God, in Mercy help.'

T: [On distress.] ¶ No: 48 lines. ¶ A: 'Rebecca Richardson.'

Note: A Biblical paraphrase.

487a. Jan. 30, 1737/8 *BEP* ⁑129, p. 1.
    'Some Husbands on a Winter's Day.'
    Note: 'From a Paper published in a neighbouring Government.' A
       reprint of no. 485.

488. Feb. 6, 1737/8 *BG* ⁑943, 2/2.
    'Had I a field, it soon should be.'
    T: 'Hor. Ode XVIII.' ¶ No: 36 lines.

488a. Feb. 10, 1737/8 *VG.*
    'If the Angel you court.'
    T: [On a rejected proposal of marriage.] ¶ No: 12 lines. ¶ A: 'J.R.'

489. Feb. 17, 1737/8 *VG.*
    'When a Comet presumes.'
    T: 'On a Comet.' ¶ No: 12 lines.
    Note: 'The following Lines were written extempore by a Gentle-
       man, on a Comet, that lately appear'd in Pennsylvania.'

490. Feb. 20, 1738 *BG* ⁑945, pp. 1 and 2.
    'Oft, as my lonely Hours return.'
    T: [On the departure of a clergyman, who removed to a 'neighbor-
       ing Government.'] ¶ No: 133 lines.
    Note: Included in no. 6 of an essay series.

491. Feb. 21, 1737/8 *NYG*, 3/1.
    'Rejoyce not in Beauty, ye Masons, beware.'
    T: [Reply to a Free Mason] ¶ No: 8 lines.
    Note: Doggerel. Cf. nos. 500, 501.

492. Mar. and April 1738 *Gent Mag*, pp. 158, 213–214.
    'You ask me how this sultry clime.'
    T: 'The Pleasures of Jamaica. In an Epistle from a Gentleman to his
       Friend in London.' ¶ No: 147 lines.

493. Apr. 14, 1738 *VG.*
    'Low, in the gloomy vale of Thought, confin'd.'
    Note: A reprint of no. 486.

494. Apr. 14, 1738 *BNL* ⁑1777, 2/1.
    'Long us'd this World's vain Greatness to despise.'
    T: 'On the Death of the Queen.' ¶ No: 8 lines.
    Note: The wife of George II. Cf. nos. 495, 506.

495. Apr. 24, 1738 *BG* ⁑954.
    'No more, ye Fair, of withering Charms complain.'
    T: 'An attempt towards an Epitaph on her late most Excellent
       Majesty Queen Caroline.' ¶ No: 14 lines.
    Note: Cf. nos. 494, 506. Reprinted, see no. 497.

496. May 5, 1738 *VG.*
'Unus'd to Love's Imperial Chain.'
T: 'The Discovery.' ¶ No: 15 lines. ¶ A: 'By a Youth, of the Frontiers.'

497. June 1, 1738 *PG* #494.
'No more, ye Fair, of withering charms complain.'
Note: A reprint of no. 495.

498. June 8, 1738 *AWM.*
'If there are Muses they the Verse attend.'
T: 'Verses to the Memory of Joseph Growdon, Esq; Late *Attorney-General* of this Province.' ¶ No: 22 lines.
Note: Heroic couplets; not bad. Growdon's obituary is in *AWM,* #960, May 25, 1738. Reprinted, see no. 499. The poem was reprinted by Samuel Keimer and so appears in *Caribbiana* (London, 1741), II, 276.

499. June 19, 1738 *BG* #962, 2/2.
'If there are Muses they the Verse attend.'
Note: A reprint of no. 498.

500. June 26, 1738 *NYG*, 3/1.
'Rejoyce, O ye Masons,! and cast away Care.'
T: 'A Song for the Free-Masons.' ¶ No: 8 lines.
Note: Cf. nos. 491, 501.

501. June 26, 1738 *NYG*, 3/2.
'Rejoyce, O ye *Ladies*, and cast away Care.'
T: 'A Parody of the same Verses for the Ladies.' ¶ No: 8 lines.
Note: Cf. no. 500.

502. July 3, 1738 *NYWJ* #242, 1/1–2.
'Well may the Cypress now my Brows adorn.'
T: 'Lines ... on the Departure of a deserving Young Lady from this City.' ¶ No: 50 lines. ¶ A: 'By a young Gentleman' ['Ezekiah Salem'].
Note: Sent in by 'Rachel Salem.' Cf nos. 508, 513 (where this author is called 'Ezekiah Salem'), 518.

503. July 6, 1738 *SCG* #232, 3/2.
'While boundless ambition and turbulent care.'
T: 'A Song.' ¶ No: 20 lines. ¶ A: 'Philomusus.'

504. July 10, 1738 *NYWJ* #243, 2/2–3/1.
'To my Ditty good People give ear.'
T: 'The Masque of Life.' ¶ No: 64 lines. ¶ A: 'Non Ignotus.'

505. July 20, 1738 *AWM* #968.
'No more of Comick Sports, or Childish Toy's.'
T: 'A Poem on the Spanish Depredations.' ¶ No: 45 lines.

506. July 1738 *Lon Mag*, VII, 356–7.
  'While from each soul the sorrows copious flow.'
  T: 'On the Death of the Queen. To his Excellency Governor Belcher.
  By the Rev. Mr. Byles.' ¶ No: 82 lines. ¶ A: Mather Byles.
  Note: Cf. nos. 494, 495. Reprinted in Byles (see no. 60), pp. 81–86.

507. Aug. 10, 1738 *AWM* #971.
  'Hypocrisy, the Thriving'st calling.'
  T: 'Hypocrisy.' ¶ No: 21 lines. ¶ A: 'A.B.'

508. Aug. 14, 1738 *NYWJ* #248, 1/1–2.
  'Sweet Philomel renew thy sacred strains.'
  T: 'Verses, wrote by the same Hand as the former, upon the same
  Lady's Return.' ¶ No: 52 lines. ¶ A: ['Ezekiah Salem'].
  Note: Sent in by Rachael Salem. Cf. nos. 502, 513, 518.

509. Aug. 24, 1738 *PG* #506.
  'Hence ye Prophane, ye puny Slaves retire.'
  T: 'Madness. An Ode.' ¶ No: 133 lines. ¶ A: [Joseph Breintnall?]
  Note: The seventh verse paragraph (ll. 104–117) praises Coper-
  nicus; and the eighth (118–133) makes local American references.
  The style, subject matter, and place of publication suggest Breint-
  nall's authorship.

510. Sept. 4, 1738 *BG* #972, 3/2–4/1.
  'Father of all! in every Age.'
  T: 'The universal Prayer.' ¶ No: 52 lines. ¶ A: [Alexander Pope.]
  Note: Crum F235. Printed in Norman Ault and John Butt, *Minor
  Poems* (Oxford, 1954), p.145.

511. Sept. 11, 1738 *NYWJ* #261, 3/1–4/1.
  'Damon Thy look presages me no good.'
  T: 'A Pastoral Elegy, on the Death of a Virtuous young Lady.' ¶
  No: 86 lines. ¶ A: 'Philantus.'

512. Oct. 9, 1738 *NYWJ* #264, 4/1–2.
  'When Phebus had lain off his Golden Vest.'
  T: 'A Pastoral Elegy.' ¶ No: 59 lines.
  Note: The author says it is his first poem and asks to be spared
  criticism.

513. Oct. 15, 1738 *NYWJ* # 265, 3/2.
  'When I consider my Disgrace.'
  T: 'Salems Complaint. Hymn the XVIII.' ¶ No: 28 lines. ¶ A:
  'Nahab Din.'
  Note: 'As many of the performances of my well beloved Friend
  Ezekiah Salem have been Joyfully received ... I beg you would do
  his Memory the Honour to insert his XVIII Hymn ...' Cf. no. 502.

514. Oct. 19, 1738 *SCG* #297, 3/2.
     'Hail, Carolina, hail! Fill up the Bowl.'
     T: [Advertisement of goods.] ¶ No: 38 lines. ¶ A: 'James Reid.'
     Note: Not bad. Reprinted Nov. 2, where there is reply; repeated
     again Nov. 9, where the reply of Nov. 2 is also reprinted.

515. Nov. 2, 1738 *SCG* #248, 3/2.
     'I'm no Poet or Critick, yet this I can tell.'
     T: [Reply to James Reid]. ¶ No: 34 lines.
     Note: See 514. For another burlesque of Reid, see no. 1097.

516. Nov. 24, 1738 *VG*.
     '—Once, beneath a Myrtle Grove.'
     T: 'Fable. Bacchus and the Satyr.' ¶ No: 20 lines + 6 line moral. ¶
     A: 'Musiphilus.'
     Note: Dated, 'Nov. 1, 1738.' 'Sir, The Hint of the following *Fable*
     was taken from the Arch Bishop of Cambray,' The first word of
     the first line is missing in the only extant copy of this issue. Cf.
     no. 463.

1739

517. Jan. 8, 1738/9 *BEP* #178, 1/1.
     'Right Trusty and expert Commanders.'
     T: 'To the honoured Commanders of—' [on vanity]. ¶ No: 82 lines.
     Note: Ford no. 347, conjectures a broadside of 1714. 'F.T.' sent in
     the poem, saying that it was published 'here' in 1714.

518. Jan. 8, 1738/9 *NYWJ* #265, 4/1–2.
     'By what I know and ye perceive.'
     T: 'A Letter from Rebecca Salem in the County to her Husband in
     Town.' ¶ No: 52 lines. ¶ A: 'Rebecca Salem' [i.e., 'Nahab Din'].
     Note: This is really by 'Nahab Din' and part of a literary war. Cf.
     nos. 512, 508, 513.

519. Jan. 22, 1738/9 *NYG*.
     'The Mind oppress'd, with heavy cares of state.'
     T: 'When I first put Pen to Paper, I proposed to send you my
     Thoughts upon the Elaborate Performance which was handed
     about Town the other Day, Entitled (Witt's) alias (Lack Witts
     Journal)'. ¶ No: 14 lines. ¶ A: 'Z.'

520. Feb. 5, 1738/9 *BG* #994.
     'I'm not High Church nor Low Church, nor Tory nor Whig.'
     Note: A reprint of no. 200.

521. Feb. 5, 1738/9 *NYWJ* #269.
  'Oh cruel Death, why did you take from hence.'
  T: 'Upon the Death of Mrs. Margaret Smith, aged about 13 years,
  who Departed this Life the 19th of Jan. 1738/9.' ¶ No: 18 lines.

522. Feb. 13, 1738/9 *NEWJ* #617.
  'Hail! Joyful Bride, your Eyes are brought to see.'
  T: 'An address to a Lady on the Day of her Marriage, Jan. 11th,
  1738, 9.' ¶ No: 5 lines.

523. March 14, 1739 *AWM* 1738/9 #1002.
  'What Bard shall Fame to Rosalinda give.'
  T: 'On the Departure of a Lady to a Foreign Country.' ¶ No: 28
  lines. ¶ A: 'J.R.'

524. April 2, 1739 *BEP* #190, 2/1.
  'Ye Quacks be gone, with all your Ills.'
  T: [On Rum—'Sir Richard.'] ¶ No: 22 lines.

525. April 20, 1739 *VG*.
  'Hoc juxta Marmor S.E.'
  T: [Epitaph for John Randolph.] ¶ No: 6 lines. ¶ A: [William Daw-
  son?]
  Note: Cf. nos. 454 and 455.

526. May 1739 *Lon Mag*, VIII, 249.
  'What first demands our care, 'Tis hard to tell.'
  T: 'To Mrs. Belcher, on viewing her curious Shell-Work.' ¶ No: 56
  lines.
  Note: If the poem is on Mrs. Jonathan Belcher (d. 1736), Byles may
  well have written it.

527. July, 1739 *Gent Mag*, IX, 378.
  'When pale Disease th'affected blood assails.'
  T: 'A Copy of Verses presented to E. Waller, M.D. and Fellow of
  St. John's College, Cambridge, April 18, 1739.' ¶ No: 64 lines. ¶
  A: 'By a young Gentleman of the same College.'

528. Aug. 2, 1739 *AWM* #1022.
  'So Fam'd for Rhymes, for Mockery and Myrth.'
  T: 'An Elegy, on John Dommett, Who dy'd at *White-Marsh*, on the
  22d of *July*, 1739.' ¶ No: 19 lines + 4 line epitaph.
  Note: Dommett was a drunk who wrote doggerel for pay: 'That our
  good CHIEFS, no more perhaps may hear,/Publick Events, in
  Rhymes amuse the Ear;/His thirst of Liquor's quencht, he'll now
  no more/Caress them come, or dying them adore.' Breintnall
  elsewhere (see no. 335) satirizes Dommett. Cf. nos. 529, 530.

529. Aug. 2, 1739 *AWM*.
'Wealthy while Rum he had, was John, yet Poor.'
T: 'His Epitaph' [i.e., John Dommett's] ¶ No: 4 lines.
Note: The 'Epitaph' reveals that Dommett was born in England. Cf.
no. 528.

530. Aug. 9, 1739 *PG* #556.
'The Fate of Dommett is not singly hard.'
T: 'To the Memory of John Dommett, the unborn Poet, lately de-
ceased.' ¶ No: 37 lines.
Note: Good verse, containing oblique references to other local poets
and poems. An extract reprinted, no. 532.

531. Aug. 27, 1739 *NYWJ* #298, 1/1–2.
'Contented thus I lead a rural life.'
T: 'Thyrses and Menalcas, A Pastoral.' ¶ No: 70 lines.

532. Sept. 10, 1739 *NYG*.
'If to be ragged, poor and stock'd with Lice.'
T: 'On the Death of John Dommett.' ¶ No: 8 lines.
Note: 'From the *PG*': an extract from no. 530.

533. Sept. 14, 1739 *VG*.
'Who wou'd have thought that Bella's Frown.'
T: 'Occasionally written to a Friend.' ¶ No: 60 lines.
Note: Sent in by 'H.P.,' a friend of the poet.

534. Sept. 21, 1739 *VG*.
'Pensively pay the Tribute of a Tear.'
T: 'An Epitaph, on Miss M. Thacher, (Daughter of *Col.* Edwin
Thacher, of Middlesex) who Dy'd at Williamsburg, on Wednes-
day last.' ¶ No: 6 lines.
Note: Reprinted in Henry Howe, *'Historical Collections of Virginia*
(Charleston, S.C., 1845), p. 332. Cf. no. 535.

535. Sept. 28, 1739 *VG*.
'Shall virtuous Molly unlamented die.'
T: 'On the Death of Miss M. Thacher.' ¶ No: 82 lines.
Note: Cf. no. 534.

536. Nov. 19, 1739 *NYWJ* #310, 4/1–2.
'Begin the high celestial Strain.'
T: 'Part of the 148th Psalm Paraphras'd.' ¶ No: 32 lines. ¶ A: 'S.W.'
Note: Reprinted, no. 1842. Crum B173 gives the title 'Hymn 2
Collect. Poems.'

537. Nov. 20, 1739 *NEWJ* #657, 1/1.
'Beat on proud Billows! Boreas blow.'
T: [On being in jail.] ¶ No: 60 lines. ¶ A: Sir Hammond [i.e.,
Roger] L'Estrange.

Note: Sent in by 'J.N.' 'Wrote by Sir Hammond L'Estrange, while he was under Confinement for his unshaken Loyalty to K. Charles I in Cromwell's Time.' Crum B100. See *Notes and Queries*, March 26, 1904, p. 250.

538. Nov. 29, 1739 *PG* ⚹572.
'Whitefield! That great, that pleasing Name.'
T: 'Lines, on the Rev. Mr. Whitefield.' ¶ No: 28 lines. ¶ A: 'Juventus.'
Note: A reprint from the *NYWJ* of Nov. 26 (no longer extant). Reprinted, see nos. 539, 540, 541, 548.

539. Dec. 3, 1739 *NYG*, 3/1–2.
'Whitfield that great, that pleasing Name.'
Note: A reprint of no. 538.

540. Dec. 6, 1739 *AWM*.
'Whitefield! that great, that pleasing Name.'
Note: 'From the *NYWJ*.' A reprint of no. 538.

541. Dec. 11, 1739 *NEWJ* ⚹660.
'Whitefield! that great, that pleasing Name.'
Note: A reprint of no. 538.

542. Dec. 13, 1739 *AWM* ⚹1041.
'Sing the Hero in strains so sublime, O my Muse.'
T: 'The Modern Goliah: Or Hero of Heroes. A Panegyric, humbly address'd to the venerable and worthy set of Free-Thinkers.' ¶ No: 56 lines.
Note: An attack on the Philadelphia deists.

543. Dec. 28, 1739 *VG*.
'Great Jove, ambitious of immortal Name.'
T: 'The Temple of Virtue.' ¶ No: 264 lines.

1740

544. Jan. 3, 1740 *AWM*, ⚹ 1044.
'Salkeld, from silent Sitting, slow would rise.'
T: [Elegy accompanying obituary of John Salkeld, a Quaker.] ¶ No: 18 lines. ¶ A: [Joseph Breintnall.]
Note: For the attribution to Breintnall, see J. Comly, ed., *Friends Miscellany*, III, 69–70; and Joseph Smith, *A Descriptive Catalogue of Friends' Books*, I (London, 1867), 316. Reprinted, see no. 551.

545. Jan. 4, 1739/40 *VG*.
''If the good-natur'd, hospitable Man.'
T: 'To the King' [On Gov. William Gooch and Virginia]. ¶ No: 10 lines.

Note: 'Mr. Parks, The following Lines were written last Year by a Gentleman who was then in *England*. Please to insert them in your next Paper.' Reprinted, no. 597.

546. Jan. 7, 1739/40 *NYWJ* ※ 317, 1/1–3/2.
'Your sage and moralist can show.'
Note: A reprint of no. 289.

547. Jan. 15, 1739/40 *AWM* ※ 1046.
'Quoth modest S[mi]th in me combine.'
T: 'A late Conversation in NY abridg'd. The Lawyer, Orator, Divine.' ¶ No: 3 lines.
Note: This is probably reprinted from a New York paper and contains references to William Smith, Rev. George Whitefield, and Jonathan Arnold. Cf. nos. 550 and 554.

548. Jan. 18, 1739/40. *VG*
'Whitefield! That Great, that pleasing Name.'
Note: A reprint 'from the NYWJ' of no. 538.

549. Jan. 26, 1740 *NYWJ*, 4/1.
'Whilst thirst of fame and dreadful War's charms.'
T: 'Silvia to Philander.'

550. Jan. 28, 1739/40 *BPB* ※ 303, 2/1.
'The Lawyer, Orator, Divine.'
T: [On the New York Whitefield controversy.] ¶ No: 12 lines.
Note: Cf. no. 547.

551. Jan. 28, 1739/40 *BPB* ※ 303, 3/1.
'Salkeld, from silent Sitting, slow would rise.'
Note: A reprint of no. 544.

552. Jan. 28, 1739/40 *NYWJ* ※ 320, 4/1.
'Of Seven Parts they me compose.'
T: 'Riddle, for the Month of January.' ¶ No: 14 lines.
Note: See the reply, no. 555.

553. Feb. 1, 1739/40 *VG*.
'Thy Pow'r, O Lord, in the great Deep is shown.'
T: 'The following Lines, which were written at Sea, by the Rev. Mr. Hartswell, on a Voyage to Virginia, in the Year 1739, are Humbly Inscrib'd To *Sir* Yelverton Petton, Bart.' ¶ No: 14 lines. ¶ A: Rev. Richard Hartwell.
Note: For the Rev. Richard Hartwell, see Philip Slaughter, *A History of Bristol Parish, Va.* (Richmond, 1879), pp. 15–16, who cites Blair's letter, May 29, 1740. Hartwell was ordained by the Bishop of Rochester, Sept. 21, 1735. See also Churchill Gibson Chamberlayne, ed., *The Vestery Book and Register of Bristol Parish, Va., 1720–1789* (Richmond, 1898), p. 98: on May 26, 1740 'Mr.

Richard Heartswel be received Minister of this Parish.' On May 27, he declared himself unsatisfied with the salary and so was discharged. Weis, *Virginia*, p. 24.

554. Feb. 5, 1740 *AWM* ⚹ 1049, 1739/40.
'Awake O Arnold from Thy drousie Den.'
T: [Acrostic on [Jonathan] Arnold]. ¶ No: 6 line anagram +2 line tag. ¶ A: 'M. F.' [Magnus Falconar].
Note: In Falconar's ad of 'forty sheets from several Famous authors.' 'Beside ... there will be added the whole Letters, &c. that has been Printed between Mr. *Arnold* and Mr. *Smith*.' For William Smith's [N.Y. lawyer] letters, see *AWM*, Jan. 15, 1740; for Jonathan Arnold's, see *AWM*, Jan. 8, 1740; for Falconar's 'Animadversions' on them, see *AWM*, Jan. 15, 1740.
Falconar advertised teaching navigation and astronomy in *AWM*, Jan. 29, 1740. He is listed as 'of Botness, in Scotland,' in *AWM*, Jan. 28, 1739, ⚹ 1017. Cf. no. 547. The advertisement was reprinted in *AWM* Mar. 4, 1739/40.

555. Feb. 11, 1739/40 *NYWJ* ⚹ 322, 2/2–3/1.
'The January Riddle I swear by Jove.'
T: 'Solutions to the Riddle for the Month of January.' ¶ No: 14 lines.
Note: Contains 2 solutions. A reply to no. 552.

556. Feb. 12, 1739/40 *NEWJ* ⚹ 669.
'In heav'nly Choirs a Question rose.'
T: 'Heavenly-Strife: Or the only Contention of sacred Souls in the State of Glory. One of the Gospel Sonnets.' ¶ No: 96 lines. ¶ A: Rev. Ralph Erskine of Scotland.

557. Feb. 19 & 26, 1740 *AWM* ⚹ 1051 and 1052.
'O Heavenly Muse my darling Breast inspire.'
T: [An imitation of Richard Lewis' 'Journey from Patapsco to Annapolis.'] ¶ No: 241 lines. ¶ A: 'Enroblos.'
Note: Good topographical verse; an imitation of Richard Lewis, see no. 184 (as his prefatory note acknowledges); repeats Lewis' mocking-bird passage (in continuation of poem *AWM*, Feb. 26, 1740); echoes Addison's 'Ode'; ends with a tribute to William Allen. 'Mr. Bradford, Reading a few Years ago a Poem in one of the New's Papers, entitled, a walk from Annapolis to Potapsico: It furnish'd me with a Hint, whereupon I have digested the following, which however deficient to that Piece, may if you think proper, be inserted in your New's Papers, I am your constant Reader, Enroblos.' This Pennsylvania poet describes a watersnake, black-snake, garter snake & rattle snake; and includes local scenery.

558. March 3, 1739/40 *NYWJ* ✳ 325.
     'Within this tomb of water, not of stone.'
     T: [Elegy.] ¶ No: 20 lines.

559. March 10, 1739/40 *NYWJ* ✳ 326, 1/1–2.
     'Why should our Joys transform to Pain.'
     T: 'The Indian Philosopher.' ¶ No: 60 lines. ¶ A: Sent in by 'O.P.'
     Note: On Indians in India, not American Indians.

560. March 11, 1739/40 *NYG* ✳ 744, 3/2.
     'Now Mars with double Fury has arose.'
     T: [On English valor.]

561. March 23, 1740 *NYWJ* ✳ 381, 3/2–4/1.
     'Peggy, Pride of heav'nly Muses.'
     T: 'The New York Charmer.' ¶ No: 20 lines. ¶ A: 'Philanthus.'
     Note: With pref. note—an imitation of 'The London Charmer.' For
        a parody, see no. 562.

562. March 30, 1740 *NYWJ* ✳ 382, 3/1–2.
     'S[awne]y Pride of Grubstreet Muses.'
     T: 'Parodia.' ¶ No: 20 lines.
     Note: A parody of no. 561.

563. April 14, 1740 *NYWJ* ✳ 331, 3/1.
     'Fly hence ambition far from hence be gone.'
     T: 'Against Ambition.' ¶ No: 59 lines.
     Note: Sent in by 'X'.

564. May 12, 1740 *NYWJ* ✳ 336, 1/1–2.
     'Begin; ye Muses, that delight to rove.'
     T: 'Description of the Spring.' ¶ No: 52 lines. ¶ A: 'By S. W.'
     Note: A plagiarism of Richard Lewis' 'Journey' (no. 198).

565. May 24, 1740 *SCG* ✳ 326, 1/1–3.
     'But lest you think me deaf or rude.'
     T: '... part of a poetical Epistle from a Gentleman of this Town to a
        Friend, which may serve as an Epilogue to the late Polemical
        Writings on Religion ...' ¶ No: 122 lines. ¶ A: 'C---'
     Note: Pref. letter signed 'T---'; poem dated 'Charlestown, May 20,
        1740'; anti-Whitefield poem; very good. Cf. no. 567.

566. June 5, 1740 *AWM* ✳ 1066.
     'Plainman and Truman cease your hate.'
     T: 'To Mr. Obadiah Plainman and Mr. Thomas Truman.' ¶ No: 12
        lines.
     Note: 'Obadiah Plainsman' and 'Thomas Truman' are pseudonyms
        of writers in preceding *AWM* numbers.

567. June 7, 1740 *SCG* ✳ 328, 2/2–3/1.
     'Near Philip's Church without controul.'

T: [On Whitefield controversy.] ¶ No: 33 lines. ¶ A: 'Z**'
Note: Dated 'Charlestown, May 29, 1740.' An attack on no. 565.

568. June 26, 1740 *SCG* ✳ 330.
'Great miracle of modesty and sence.'
T: 'The Congratulation. Humbly address'd to the Rev. Mr. White-
field on his 68 Preachments in Forty Days, with the great and
visible Effect of Meat and Money that ensued therefrom, &c.' ¶
No: 16 lines. ¶ A: 'Misanaides.'
Note: An attack on Whitefield, Reprinted, see nos. 572, 573. See
the replies, nos. 574, 575.

569. June 30, 1740 *NYWJ* ✳ 343, 1/1–2.
'Dic mihi, musa, verum sacci qui gloria nostri.'
T: 'In Augustissemun Ludovicum Morris, Caesareae Novae Clype-
um, Encomium.' ¶ No: 41 lines.
Note: Dated 'Novi Brunsvici.' Reprinted in *New Jersey Archives*,
XII, 33–35.

570. July 18, 1740 *SCG* ✳ 334, 2/2–3/1.
'Serene as Light is *Whitefield's* soul.'
T: [Lines adapted from Watts, defending Whitefield.] ¶ No: 46
lines.

571. July 25, 1740 *SCG* ✳ 335.
'Whilst th'*Arian* Preacher *Christ* his God denies.'
T: [Attack on Rev. Alexander Garden and defense of Whitefield.] ¶
No: 35 lines. ¶ A: 'T. Z.'
Note: Reprinted, no. 598.

572. Aug. 4, 1740 *BPB* ✳ 329.
'Great Miracle of Modesty and Sense.'
Note: A reprint of no. 568.

573. Aug. 21, 1740 *AWM*.
'Great Miracle of Modesty and Sense.'
Note: A reprint of no. 568. Cf. no. 574.

574. Aug. 28, 1740 *AWM*.
'Pharaoh's proud Heart was not with Wonders mov'd.'
T: 'To the Meat and Money Gods of South Carolina, &c. An An-
swer to the Congratulatory.' ¶ No: 18 lines.
Note: A reply to no. 568.

575. Sept. 1, 1740 *BPB* ✳ 333.
'Whilst God inspir'd the pious fervent Youth.'
T: 'Eusebius to Misanaides on his Congratulation of Mr. White-
field.' ¶ No: 22 lines. ¶ A: 'Eusebius.'
Note: A reply to no. 568.

576. Sept. 22, 1740 *BPB* ✳ 336, 3/1.
     'If ever Dram to thee was dear.'
     T: 'Epitaph on Landlord [John] Doggett, Innholder at Attlebor-
     ough.' ¶ No: 8 lines.

577. Oct. 13, 1740 *BEP* ✳ 271, 1/1–2.
     'To Thee my Friend, tho' now perhaps disgrac'd.'
     T: 'A Letter from Don Blas de Lezo, the Spanish Admiral at Car-
     thagena, to Don Thomas Geraldino, late Agent for the King of
     Spain in London.' ¶ No: 120 lines. ¶ A: 'A Gentleman at
     Jamaica.'
     Note: Reprinted, nos. 578, 579, 594. For a mock reply, see no. 614.
     Propaganda in the War of Jenkins' Ear.

578. Oct. 30, 1740 *PG* ✳ 620.
     'To Thee my Friend, tho' now perhaps disgrac'd.'
     Note: 'From the Boston Evening Post.' A reprint of no. 577.

579. Oct. 30, 1740 *AWM* ✳ 1087.
     'To thee my Friend, Tho' now perhaps disgrac'd.'
     Note: A reprint of no. 577.

580. Nov. 20, 1740 *AWM.*
     'When foolish Calves in Forests walk astray.'
     T: [An attack on Jacob Taylor.] ¶ No: 10 lines. ¶ A: Jacob Taylor.
     Note: Ten lines are quoted from Taylor's almanac for 1741, in a
     satire on Taylor and his poetry.

581. Dec. 15, 1740 *NYWJ* ✳ 367, 3/2–4/1.
     'Stay gentle Nymph, nay, pray thee stay.'
     T: 'The Hearty Old Man.' ¶ No: 16 lines.

582. Dec. 18, 1740 *AWM* ✳ 1094.
     'Long have the learned Pastors of the age.'
     T: 'On George Whitefield's Preaching at the New Building.' ¶ No:
     48 lines.
     Note: Reprinted, nos. 584, 600, 605.

583. Dec. 18, 1740 *AWM* ✳ 1094.
     'Whitefield to what End do you preach.'
     T: 'To The Reverend Mr. Whitefield, on his Preaching Faith Alone.
     ¶ No: 6 lines. ¶ A: 'W. W.'
     Note: 'Mr. Bradford, As you have inserted several things in your
     Mercury in praise of the Rev. Mr. Whitefield, and nothing on the
     Contrary, makes it believed you are Partial, which is thought not
     according to the Custom of [the ?] Printer, Your inserting the fol-
     lowing EPIGRAM will highly oblige many of your Readers, and
     particularly, W. W.'

584. Dec. 18, 1740 *PG* ⌗ 627.
  'Long have the learned Pastors of the Age.'
  Note: A reprint of no. 582.

1741

586. Jan. 19, 1740/1 *BPB* ⌗ 354, 3/2.
  'Auspicious *Chiefs**, your great Designs pursue.'
  T: [On *Admiral* Edward Vernon & *Lord* Cathcart.] ¶ No: 14 lines.
  Note: Reprinted, no. 606.

587. Jan. 22, 1740/1 *PG* ⌗ 632.
  'Mayst Thou, Breat Man, withstand a misled throng.'
  T: 'On Mr. John Wesley's Sermon on Free Grace.' ¶ No: 18 lines.
  Note: Benjamin Franklin had just published Wesley's Sermon, so
    this poem is a puff. Reprinted, see no. 595.

588. Jan. 25, 1741/2 *NYWJ* ⌗ 426, 3/1.
  'My Neighbour Gravelook to preserve his Store.'
  T: —. ¶ No: 32 lines. ¶ A: 'T. P.'
  Note: There is a prose reply by 'E. B.' in *NYWJ* Feb. 1, p. 1. Re-
    printed, no. 652.

589. Jan. 1741 *General Mag* I, 57.
  'With close attack, I lately woo'd a Maid.'
  T: 'Ovid's Cure' (translation from *The Art of Love*) with Latin. ¶
    No: 14 lines. ¶ A: 'Amintor.'
  Note: From the *VG* Dec. 12, 1740. Cf. no. 456.

590. Jan. 1741 *General Mag* I, 62.
  'Anxious and trembling for the future Hour.'
  T: [Religious verse.] ¶ No: 25 lines.

591. Jan. 1741 *General Mag* I, 62–3.
  'Native of *Africa's* far coast.'
  T: 'A Riddle.' ¶ No: 34 lines. ¶ A: 'Sphinx.'
  Note: Cf. 'Answer,' no. 611.

592. Jan. 1741 *General Mag* I, 63.
  'Awake, Britannia's Guardian Pow'r.'
  T: 'On the War.' ¶ No: 16 lines.
  Note: 'Printed at New York.'

593. Jan. 1741 *General Mag* I, 63–4.
  'As, near *Porto Bello* lying.'
  T: 'Admiral Hosier's Ghost, To the Tune of Come listen to my
    Ditty.' ¶ No: 63 lines. ¶ A: [Richard Glover.]

Note: Cf. no. 613. Richardson, p. 34, gives the author. Crum A1609.
On Glover (1712–1785), see *CBEL*, II, 317.

594. Jan. 1741 *General Mag* I, 65–7.
'To thee, my Friend, tho' now perhaps disgrac'd.'
Note: A reprint of no. 577.

595. Jan. 1741 *General Mag* I, 67–8.
'Mayst Thou, Great Man, withstand a misled Throng.'
Note: 'From the *PG*.' A reprint of no. 587.

596. Jan. 1741 *General Mag* I, 68.
'Hail, happy Pair, for you these Vows ascend.'
T: 'To W. G. *jun.* Esq; and Mrs. E. B. on their Marriage.' ¶ No: 10
lines.
Note: On the marriage of William Gooch, jr. (d. 1744) and Eleanor
Bowles. Reprinted from the *VG*.

597. Jan. 1741 *General Mag* I, 68.
'If the good-natur'd, hospitable Man.'
Note: A reprint of no. 545.

598. Jan. 1741 *General Mag* I, 68.
'Whilst the *Arian* Preacher Christ his God denies.'
Note: 'From the *SCG*.' A reprint of no. 571.

599. Jan. 1741 *General Mag* I, 69.
'O Happy Virgin Land! still Self-producing.'
T: 'To the Author of the Poor Planter's Physician.' ¶ No: 29 lines.
¶ A: 'Philanthropos.'
Note: 'From the VG.' Compliments Dr. John Tennent.

600. Jan. 1741 *General Mag* I, 70.
'Long have the learned Pastors of the Age.'
Note: 'From the PG.' A reprint of no. 582.

601. Feb. 1, 1741 *NYWJ* ⚹ 427, 3/1.
'As soon as the bless'd Sabbeth dawns, and all.'
T: 'Epistle to Hezekiah Salem.' ¶ No: 31 lines. ¶ A: 'Philander.'
Note: Cf. no. 604.

602. Feb. 8, 1741 *NYWJ* ⚹ 428, 2/2.
'Last Wednesday Night L—'e you know.'
T: 'To Mr. L—le, on his good Wine.' ¶ No: 18 lines. ¶ A: 'Jean De
Malbranche, Procurateur de Poitore.'
Note: Written in a mock French accent. See reply, no. 603.

603. Feb. 15, 1741 *NYWJ* ⚹ 429, 3/1.
'Est il donc vrai Monsieur le Sot.'

T: 'A ce Cocquin de Melbranche le Procureur,' ¶ No: 12 lines. ¶ A: 'C—le L—le'
Note: A reply to no. 602.

604. Feb. 15, 1741 *NYWJ* ⚹ 429, 3/1.
'Your Riddle I, observed to be.'
T: 'To the Sixth Son of Salem.' ¶ No: 6 lines. ¶ A: 'Philander.'
Note: Cf. no. 601.

605. Feb. 17, 1740/1 *NEWJ* ⚹ 722.
'Long have the learned Pastors of the Age.'
Note: A reprint of no. 582.

606. Feb. 19, 1740/1 *PG* ⚹636.
'Auspicious *Chiefs*, your great Designs pursue.'
Note: A reprint of no. 586.

607. Feb. 19, 1740/1 *AWM* ⚹1103.
'From a small Acorn see the Oak arise.'
T: 'English Oak.' ¶ No: 8 lines.
Note: Crum F645 gives the title 'De minimus maxima,' and the attribution 'Latin verses by L. Duncombe of Merton College, translated by another hand.'

608. Feb. 19, 1741 *AWM* ⚹1103.
'Whilst Thirst of fame and dreadful War's alarms.'
T: 'Sylvia to Philander.' ¶ No: 45 lines.

609. Feb. 19, 1741 *BNL* ⚹1296, 2/1.
'Unwise and thoughtless! impotent and blind!'
T: 'An Epigram, intended to restrain the Folly of Man.' ¶ No: 10 lines.

610. Feb. 26, 1740/1 *PG* ⚹637.
'Arra Joy! My monthly Macasheen shall contain sheets four.'
T: 'Teague's Advertisement.' ¶ No: 21 lines. ¶ A: [Benjamin Franklin.]
Note: See A. Owen Aldridge, 'A Humorous Poem by Benjamin Franklin,' Am. Philosophical Soc., *Proc.*, XCVIII (1954), 397–399. Reprinted in *The Papers of Benjamin Franklin*, II, 305. Cf. no. 349 for Franklin's source; and see no. 850 for an imitation.

611. Feb. 1741 *General Mag* I, 136.
'This is to let you know, That I have seen.'
T: [Answer to 'A Riddle,' no. 591]. ¶ No: 10 lines. ¶ A: 'T. J.'

612. Feb. 1741 *General Mag* I, 136-7.
'Permit lamented Shade! an humble Muse.'

T: 'Verses to the Memory of Henry Brooke, Esq; who departed this Life, at Philadelphia, on Friday, Feb. 6, 1735, 6, in the 57th Year of his Age.'

Note: A reprint of no. 404.

613. Feb. 1741 *General Mag* I, 137–8.
'Hosier! with indignant Sorrow.'
T: 'Vernon's Answer to Hosier's Ghost.' ¶ No: 40 lines.
Note: Cf. no. 593.

614. Feb. 1741 *General Mag* I, 138–143.
'If yet confin'd within thy Walls, O Chief!'
T: 'A Letter from Don Thomas Geraldino, in Answer to Don Blas de Lezo's, at Carthagene. Faithfully translated by Britannicus. Printed at Jamaica, 1740.' ¶ No: 283 lines. ¶ A: 'Britannicus.'
Note: A mock reply to no. 577.

615. Mar. 3, 1740/1 *NEWJ* #724.
'O Blessed Man, great Tennent! what shall we.'
T: 'On the Departure of the Rev. Mr. Gilbert Tennent from Cambridge.' ¶ No: 132 lines.
Note: Cf. no. 616. Reprinted in *New Jersey Archives*, XII, 71–75.

616. Mar. 5, 1740/1 *BNL* #1928, 2/1.
'Adieu! Thou Saint of God, Adieu!'
T: 'Upon the Rev. Mr. Tennent's departure from Boston.' ¶ No: 30 lines. ¶ A: 'Farewell.'
Note: Cf. no. 615. Reprinted, no. 637.

617. Mar. 17, 1740/1 *NEWJ* #726.
'See Heaven born Tennent from Mount Sinai flies.'
T: 'The following Lines are humbly Dedicated to the Rev. Mr. Gilbert Tennent, by Mrs. S. M. upon hearing him display both the Terrors of the Law and blessed Invitations of the Gospel, to awaken Sinners, and comfort Saints.' ¶ No: 63 lines. ¶ A: 'Mrs. S. M.'
Note: Dated 'Boston Feb. 28th, 1740/1.' Reprinted, *New Jersey Archives*, XII, 76–78. Reprinted, no. 631.

618. Mar. 19, 1740/1 *AWM* #1101.
'Rowse Haddock, rowse thee from inglorious Sleep.'
T: 'To Admiral Haddock, on the Success of Admiral Vernon.' ¶ No: 48 lines.

619. Mar. 1741 *General Mag* I, 207.
'No longer Orphean Melody.'
T: 'On Divine Psalmody.' ¶ No: 12 lines. ¶ A: 'G. H.'

620. Mar. 1741 *General Mag* I, 208–9.
'While Britain's Lyon, couchant seem'd to lay.'
T: 'On the taking Porto-Bello by Admiral Vernon.' ¶ No: 69 lines.
Note: 'From the BPB' (not extant).

621. Mar. 1741 *General Mag* I, 209–10.
'Say, smiling Muse, what heav'nly strain.'
T: 'To the Rev. Dr. Watts, on his Divine Poems.' ¶ No: 48 lines. ¶
A: 'Mather Byles.'
Note: 'Verses prefix'd to the late Boston Edition of Dr. Watts'
Hymns.' Dated 'New England, Boston, March 15.' Reprinted in
Byles' *Poems* (see No. 60), pp. 86–89.

622. Mar. 1741 *General Mag* I, 210–1.
'The Raven *Phoebus'* fav'rite Bird was long.'
T: 'The Raven's Colour changed. Ovid. Met. Lib. 2.' ¶ No: 44 lines.

623. Mar. 1741 *General Mag* I, 211–12.
'From whence this Horror at the Thought of Death.'
T: 'On Death. An Irregular Ode.' ¶ No: 40 lines + 4 line refrain.

624. Mar. 1741 *General Mag* I, 112.
'Mauginio says, I am a Fool, and I.'
T: 'An Epigram.' ¶ No: 4 lines.

625. Mar. 1741 *General Mag* I, 213.
'Who on the Earth, or in the Skies.'
T: 'The Comparison, the choice, and the Enjoyment.' ¶ No: 40
lines. ¶ A: 'M. Byles.'
Note: 'Printed at Boston.' Religious verse. Reprinted in Byles,
Poems on Several Occasions (Boston, 1744), pp. 13–15.

626. April 9, 1741 *AWM* ⚹1110.
'Those who, quite careless, leave unshut my Gate.'
T: 'The Gardners Curse for such Visiters as leave his Gate open.' ¶
No: 26 lines.

627. April 1741 *Lon Mag* X, 201.
'In vain, *Almeria*, do you this way strive.'
T: 'To the antiquated Almeria, shewing her Picture that was drawn
when she was but sixteen.' ¶ No: 14 lines. ¶ A: [William Daw-
son.]
Note: Reprinted from William Dawson, *Miscellaneous Poems on
Several Occasions* (London, 1735), p. 14.

628. April 1741 *General Mag* I, 276–8.
'Thy Frowns, O Fortune, I contemn.'

T: '*Solomon's* Pursuit after *Content*.' ¶ No: 114 lines. ¶ A: 'Joseph
   Dumbleton.'
Note: 'From the *VG*.' With a prefatory note, quoted from the *VG*.
   All that is known of Joseph Dumbleton (the name may be a pseu-
   donym) is that he was a poet of ability who contributed to the
   VG and the *SCG* from 1740 to 1750. The information on his
   poems (see nos. 746, 927, 928, 955) is slightly more complete
   than Hennig Cohen, 'The Poems of Joseph Dumbleton, 1740–
   1750,' *Bull. of Bibliog.*, XX (1952), 220.

629. April 1741 *General Mag* I, 278–9.
   'Flavia complains of dull Restraint.'
   T: [War of sexes.] ¶ No: 32 lines. ¶ A: 'A. B.'
   Note: 'From the Virginia Gazette.'

630. April 1741 *General Mag* I, 279–80.
   'Muse, extend thy sable Wing.'
   T: 'On the Death of a young Lady.' ¶ No: 40 lines. ¶ A: 'Strephon.'
   Note: 'From the *BPB*, No. 352.'

631. April 1741 *General Mag* I, 281–2.
   'See Heaven-born Tennent from Mount *Sinai* flies.'
   Note: A reprint of no. 617.

632. April 1741 *General Mag* I, 282–3.
   'A Gentleman whilst walking in his Ground.'
   T: 'A Mathematical Question.' ¶ No: 23 lines.
   Note: A riddle.

633. April 1741 *General Mag* I, 283.
   'The great Jehova is my Friend.'
   T: 'A new Version of the 23rd Psalm.' ¶ No: 24 lines.

634. May 18, 1741 *NYWJ* #389, 1/2.
   'Poverty's bitter, but a wholesome Good.'
   T: 'Solution.' ¶ No: 16 lines.
   Note: 'From the *Barbados Gazette*.'

635. May 1741 *General Mag* I, 348–50.
   'The wond'rous Draught, the Pencil's daring Stroke.'
   T: 'A Translation of Mr. Addison's Latin Poem, on a Picture of the
      Resurrection, in Magdalen College Chappel at Oxford.' ¶ No:
      134 lines.
   Note: 'From the Virginia Gazette.'

636. May 1741 *General Mag* I, 350-1.
'Shall Blazing Stars drop from their Spheres.'
T: 'Verses to the Memory of Benjamin Needler, Esq.' ¶ No: 20 lines.
Note: 'From the Virginia Gazette.'

637. May 1741 *General Mag* I, 351.
'Adieu! Thou Saint of God, Adieu!'
Note: A reprint of no. 616.

638. June 1741 *General Mag* I, 417-9.
'Candide doctarum praeses, Cytharacde, sororum.'
T: 'Illustrissimo & Praestantissimo viro Georgio Thomae, Armigero Pensylvaniae Provinciae, & Agrorum Novicastelli, Cantii & Suffexiae Praefecto. Carmen Gratulatorium.' ¶ No: 147 lines. ¶ A: [William Loury.]
Note: Attribution is given by J. F. Fisher, 'Some Account of the Early Poets and Poetry of Pennsylvania,' *Memoirs* of the Hist. Soc. of Pa., II, pt. 2 (Phila.) 79–80. I know nothing of Loury.

639. June 1741 *General Mag* I, 420.
'Bold Heroes, who undaunted dare engage.'
T: 'To the Querists.' ¶ No: 47 lines.
Note: Attack on Whitefield.

640. June 1741 *General Mag* I, 421.
'A Man of Wisdom may disguise.'
T: 'A True Tale of a Country Squire.' ¶ No: 126 lines.
Note: Scatological poem. 'From the Virginia Gazette.' Reprinted, no. 801.

641. June 1741 *General Mag* I, 423.
'Rowe, like the Queen of Love, would studious save.'
T: 'On Mrs. Rowe's Friendship in Death, and Letters moral and entertaining.' ¶ No: 26 lines. ¶ A: [Benjamin Colman?]
Note: Dated 'America, May, 1741.' The Rev. Benjamin Colman, a friend and correspondent of Mrs. Rowe, wrote the long obituary on her in the *BNL* of April 27, 1737. As he frequently wrote occasional poetry, he may well have written this elegy. See Clayton H. Chapman, 'Benjamin Colman and Philomela,' *New Eng. Quart.*, XLII (1969), 214–231.

642. July 20, 1741 *BPB* #381.
'A Monkey, to reform the Times.'
T: 'A Fable. The Monkey who had seen the World.' ¶ No: 46 lines. ¶ A: [John Gay.]

Note: A shortened version of Gay's Fable 14, First Series. See *The Poetical Works of John Gay*, ed. G. C. Faber (London, 1926), pp. 246–247.

643. July 23, 1741 *AWM* #1125.
'Captain Whole-Bones is now come in.'
T: 'Some Remarks on the valient behaviour and noble conduct of Capt. F[rankland], or if you please a second Capt. Wholebones.' ¶ No: 24 lines. ¶ A: 'Written by a Lad in South Carolina.'
Note: Reprinted, no. 646. On Captain Thomas Frankland. Cf. the poems praising Frankland, nos. 663, 691, 767, and 770.

644. July 1741 *Lon Mag*, X, 354–7.
'Arise! my Muse, extend thy trembling wing.'
T: 'A Poem on the late Successes of Admiral Vernon in the West-Indies.' ¶ No: 351 lines. ¶ A: 'By a Lady residing at Jamaica.'
Note: Incomplete.

645. Aug. 3, 1741 *NYWJ* #400, 4/1–2; cont. Aug. 10, 4/2.
'Beauteous Venus Queen of Love.'
T: 'On the loss of Celia, to Venus.' ¶ No: 108 lines.
Note: Sent in by 'Delon.'

646. Aug. 17, 1741 *BEP* #315.
'Captain *Whole-Bones* is come in.'
Note: Accompanying news-note from Charleston: 'we have had one of our Men of War out and in for about this two Months past, but every Day he is seen off our Bar as if he thought the Privateers would come to him.' A reprint of no. 643.

647. Sept. 8, 1741 *NEWJ* # 976 [!]
'When the old World was sunk in Vice.'
T: 'Upon hearing the Rev. Mr. Whitefield Preach, and afterwards various Sentiments concerning him.' ¶ No: 48 lines.

648. Oct. 22, 1741 *BNL* #1961, 4/2.
'Peter his Lord and Master, did deny.'
T: 'The following Piece was lately found in the Room where the above Committee were transacting the Partners [in the Manufactory Scheme] affairs.' ¶ No: 19 lines.
Note: On the Land Bank currency scheme.

649. Nov. 23, 1741 *NYWJ* #417, 3/2–4/1.
'For heaps of Gold let plodding misers Toil.'
T: 'An Epistle from the Country.' ¶ No: 74 lines.
Note: Retirement theme urged in dialogue.

1742

650. Feb. 8, 1741/2 *NYWJ* #428, 3/1.
'As soon as to the Temple you retire.'
T: 'The second Son in the House of *Salem* to Philander.' ¶ No: 32 lines. ¶ A: 'Second Son of Salem.'
Note: Cf. nos. 601, 604, 651, 656.

651. Feb. 8, 1741/2 *NYWJ* #428, 3/1.
'I am a thing of ugly form.'
T: 'A Riddle for the Month of February. To L. M.' ¶ No: 10 lines. ¶ A: 'Sixth Son of Salem.'
Note: Cf. nos. 601, 604, 650.

652. Feb. 11, 1741/2 *AWM* #1154.
'My Neighbour Gravelook to preserve his Store.'
Note: A reprint of no. 588.

653. Feb. 17, 1741/2 *PG* #688.
'Unde nova haec rerum facies miserabiles? eheu!'
T: 'De Morte Luctuosa Celeberrimi Andreae Hamiltonis, Armig. Qui obüt IV. Augusti MDCCXLI Elegia Threnodia Prima.' ¶ No: 32 lines. ¶ A: [William Loury.]
Note: Sent in by 'R. C.'; reprinted with translation in B. A. Konkle, *The Life of Andrew Hamilton* (Phila., 1941), pp. 143–149. Fisher (See no. 638), p. 79, attributes the poems to Loury. B. A. Konkle, p. 143, mistakenly (I believe) attributes the poems to James Logan. 'A copy of the following Elegy happening lately into my Hands, I send it to you, with a Request that you would afford it a place in your Paper. The too great Modesty of the Author, is, I am told, the Reason it has lain so long unpublished.' 'R. C.' The first of three elegies on Andrew Hamilton. Cf. nos. 654, 655.

654. Feb. 17, 1741/2 *PG* #688.
'Nasonis fletus gemebundi, sive Tibulli.'
T: 'Threnodia Secunda.' ¶ No: 34 lines. ¶ A: [William Loury.]
Note: Cf. no. 653.

655. Feb. 17, 1741/2 *PG* #688.
'Candidus, ah! Sociis grato officiusus Amico.'
T: 'Threnodia Tertia.' ¶ No: 32 lines. ¶ A: [William Loury.]
Note: Cf. no. 653.

656. Feb. 22, 1741/2 *NYWJ* #430, 4/1.
'Hail! House of Salem, let it, pray, be shown.'
T: 'To the House of Salem.' ¶ No: 4 lines.
Note: Cf. 650.

657. Mar. 1, 1741/2 *NYWJ* #431, 1/1–2.
'Miss Bett,--pray, what think you'd the reason.'
T: 'An Apology for the Censorious in a familiar Epistle to a Female Friend.' ¶ No: 44 lines. ¶ A: 'R. D.'
Note: Cf. no. 982.

658. Apr. 5, 1742 *NYWJ* #436, 2/2–3/1.
'Come, let us join our God to bless.'
T: 'The Orphans Hymns.' ¶ No: 20 lines.
Note: 'From the American Historical Chronicle'; also 'Before going to Work' 20 lines; and 'For Their Benefactors' 16 lines: three brief hymns sung by the orphans at Whitefield's Georgia asylum.

659. Apr. 19, 1742 *NYWJ* #438, 3/2.
'Damon, no more implore the fair.'
T: 'Advice to Mr. —.' ¶ No: 16 lines. ¶ A: 'Eucerius.'

660. Apr. 26, 1742 *BEP* #351, 3/2.
'Among the Divines there has been much Debate.'
T: [Practical Verses on the Nature of the World.] ¶ No: 8 lines. ¶ A: [Benjamin Franklin?]
Note: From *Poor Richard's Almanack* for 1742. Reprinted, The *Franklin Papers*, II, 338.

661. July 19, 1742 *BPB* #396.
'Hail! D[aven]p[or]t of wondrous fame.'
T:[Attacks 'New Light' preachers.] ¶ No: 86 lines.
Note: Good satire on the *Rev.* James Davenport.

662. Aug. 5, 1742 *AWM* #1179.
'That you Salute me on one Cheek alone.'
T: [Part of a short essay against the custom of men kissing one another.] ¶ No: 4 lines.

663. Aug. 16, 1742 *SCG* #438, 2/1.
'To you, great Sir, who justly Merit praise.'
T: 'To Captain Thomas Frankland, Commander of His Majesty's Ship The Rose, lately arrived (from a Cruise) at Charles-Town, with another Spanish Privateer, &c.' ¶ No: 18 lines. ¶ A: 'Mechanism.'
Note: Cf. no. 643. Reprinted, no. 665.

664. Oct. 14, 1742 *AWM* #1189.
'O Mournful One of Nine, ne'er known to smile.'
T: 'On the Death of Mr. Robert Jordan, who departed this Life the 5th of this Instant October.' ¶ No: 22 lines.
Note: Cf. no. 686.

665. Nov. 15, 1742 *BEP* #380, 3/1–2.
  'To You, *great Sir*, who justly merit Praise.'
  Note: A reprint of no. 663.

666. Dec. 20, 1742 *NYWJ* #474.
  'Since no Adven'trous Muse her voice will raise.'
  T: 'To His Excellency, James Oglethorpe, Esq; ... On his Success in
    having defeated the *Spaniards* in their attack upon Georgia, whose
    naval Force consisted of 36 Sail of Vessels and 5000 Men with
    little more than so many Hundred disciplin'd Forces. Occasioned
    by a malicious Misrepresentation of that glorious Action.' ¶ No:
    94 lines. ¶ A: 'Philanthropos.'
  Note: An attack on South Carolinians; refers to Col. Alexander
    Vander Dussen's flight in the expedition against St. Augustine.

667. Dec. 27, 1742 *BEP* #386, 2/1.
  'Ah, modest M[oorhea]d, vain are all'
  T: 'On John M—d's stiling himself, The Rev'd John M—d' ¶ No: 8
    lines.
  Note: On John Moorhead.

1743

668. Jan. 4, 1742/3 *PJ* #5.
  'Hail the dear Angels of the Lord.'
  T: [On the birth of Christ.] ¶ No: 48 lines.

669. Jan. 10, 1743 *BEP* #388, 1/2–2/1.
  'Hibernian Jack, the saddest D–g.'
  T: 'Unlucky Jack. A Tale.' ¶ No: 64 lines.

670. Jan. 24, 1742/3 *NYWJ* #479, 2/2–3/1.
  'In what a maze of Errour do I stray.'
  T: [Religious verse.] ¶ No: 73 lines.
  Note: Sent in by 'Σ'. Reprinted, no. 675.

671. Jan. 31, 1743 *BEP* #391, 1/2.
  'A Year of Wonders now behold!'
  T: 'From Poor Richard's Almanack for the Year 1743.' ¶ No: 9
    lines. ¶ A: [Benjamin Franklin?]
  Note: Reprinted, the *Franklin Papers*, II, 372.

672. Jan. 31, 1743 *BEP* #391, 1/2.
  'A Muskito just starv'd, in a sorry Condition.'
  T: 'On Idleness, and Strolling.' ¶ No: 8 lines. ¶ A: [Benjamin
    Franklin?]

Note: 'From Poor Richard's Almanack for 1743.' Reprinted, *The Franklin Papers*, II, 372.

673. Jan. 31, 1743 *BEP* #391.
'A Town fear'd a Siege, and held Consultation.'
T: 'Every Man for himself.' ¶ No: 8 lines. ¶ A: [Benjamin Franklin?]
Note: 'From Poor Richard's Almanack for 1743.' Reprinted, *The Franklin Papers*, II, 369–370.

674. Jan. 31, 1743 *BEP* #391, 1/2.
'From *Georgia* t'*Augustine* the General goes.'
T: 'On the Florida War.' ¶ No: 6 lines. ¶ A: [Benjamin Franklin?]
Note: 'From Poor Richard's Almanack for 1743.' Reprinted *The Franklin Papers*, II, 367.

675. Feb. 1, 1742/3 *PJ* #9.
'In what a maze of Error do I stray.'
Note: A reprint of no. 670.

676. Feb. 2, 1742/3 *PG* #738.
'Tu commissa diu fuerat cui masculo Pubea.'
T: 'Alsoppus Nicholao suo, Scholae Westmonasteriensis Proto-Didascalo, S. Epithalamium.' ¶ No: 35 lines.

677. Mar. 2, 1743 *Boston W. Mag*, pp. 6–7.
'Dear Kitty! now my Counsel take.'
T: 'To a Poetical Lady.' ¶ No: 48 lines.

678. Mar. 9, 1743 *Boston W. Mag*, p. 12.
'No more, ye Muses, tell of Verdant Plains.'
T: 'Verses made at Sea.' ¶ No: 32 lines.

679. Mar. 9, 1743 *Boston W. Mag*, p. 12.
'To point out Faults, yet never to offend.'
T: 'The Man of Sense.' ¶ No: 10 lines.

680. Mar. 10, 1742/3 *BNL* #2032, 2/1.
'Heu! Generosus abest Faneuil. Et temperet ulluo.'
T: 'In Obitum, Virs valdè Generosi, Petri Faneiul, Armigeri, Hodierno Die in Tumulo, sepulturi.' ¶ No: 10 lines.
Note: 'Data Bostonȳ, Die Decimo; Martij, 1741, 3'; follows obituary of Peter Faneuil.

681. Mar. 16, 1743 *Boston W. Mag*, p. 22.
'Hail, glorious God! thou goodness' source.'
T: 'A Hymn to the Author of the Universe.' ¶ No: 24 lines.

682. Mar. 16, 1743 *Boston W. Mag*, pp. 22–3.
     'We tremble, when we hear the fame.'
     T: 'An Ode.' ¶ No: 28 lines.

683. Mar. 16, 1743 *Boston W. Mag*, p. 23.
     'Hail mighty Sires! whose bright Refulgence shines.'
     T: 'A Question on Wit, with the Answer.' ¶ No: 39 lines.

684. Apr. 18, 1743 *NYWJ* #491, 1/1–2.
     'I Lov'd no King in forty one.'
     T: 'The Religious Turncoat, or The T—g P—n.' ¶ No: 72 lines +
     4 line chorus.
     Note: Pref. quotation: 'Let the Gaul'd Herse wince; our Whithers
     are unwrung.—Androb.' From Gov. Robert Hunter's *Androboros*
     ([New York], 1714), pp. vi–vii. Chorus—'A turncoat is a cunning
     Man.'

685. May 26, 1743 *PG* #754.
     'Thy formost Sons of War.'
     T: 'David's Lamentation on the Death of Saul and Jonathan. 2 Sam.
     i. 17–27.' ¶ No: 144 lines.

686. June 2, 1743 *PG* #755.
     'From Hearts devout the Tear sincerely falls.'
     T: 'Sacred to the Memory of Mr. Robert Jordan, late of *Philadel-
     phia*, deceased, a Preacher among the People called *Quakers*.' ¶
     No: 56 lines.
     Note: Cf. no. 664.

687. June 30, 1743 *PJ* #31, 2/2.
     'Why should the Nations angry be?'
     T: [Religious verse.] ¶ No: 28 lines.

688. July 1743 *Gent Mag* XIII, 360.
     'A Slice of pudding, once, a man divine.'
     T: 'Found written in a Volume of Waller's Poems.' ¶ No: 12 lines.

689. July 1743 *Lon Mag* XII, 352.
     'From native *Britain's* verdant plains.'
     T: 'SONG, extempore, by a young Gentleman now in America, at
     his leaving New York, Dec. 11, 1742, in order to proceed to
     Maryland.' ¶ No: 42 lines. ¶ A: 'E. K.' [Edward Kimber].
     Note: Poem compliments 'Miss Kath. Laurence' of N.Y. 'Tune, In
     vain dear chloe, &c.' On Edward Kimber (d. 1769) who toured
     America 1742–1744, see Sidney A. Kimber, 'The Relation of a late
     expedition to St. Augustine, with biographical and bibliographi-
     cal notes on Isaac and Edward Kimber,' *Papers* of the *Bibliog.*

Soc. of Am., XXVIII (1934), 81–96; and Frank G. Black, 'Edward Kimber: Anonymous Novelist of the Mid-Eighteenth Century,' *Harvard Studies and Notes in Philology and Lit.*, XVII (1935), 27–42.

690. Aug. 15, 1743 *SCG* #490, 3/1.
  'Custom, alas! doth partial prove.'
  A: 'E. R.'
  Note: Reply, no. 692. A reprint of no. 425.

691. Aug. 22, 1743 *BEP* #420, 1/1.
  'From peaceful Solitude, and calm Retreat.'
  T: 'To Capt. Thomas Frankland, Commander of His Majesty's Ship Rose, Now in Boston.' ¶ No: 28 lines.
  Note: Cf. nos. 643, 663.

692. Aug. 22, 1743 *SCG* #491, 3/1.
  'Dear Miss, of Custom you complain.'
  T: 'Lines ... on reading *The Ladies Complaint.*' ¶ No: 16 lines.
  Note: A reply to no. 690.

693. Sept. 5, 1743 *SCG* #493, 2/2–3/1.
  'Well Sirs, what think ye now of Cato's Fate?'
  T: 'An Epilogue to the Tragedy of Cato.' ¶ No: 36 lines. ¶ A: 'S. C.' [wrote by a young Man, then about 17 years of Age, for his own Amusement'].

694. Sept. 8, 1743 *PG* #769.
  ''Tis strange how Things, that singly disagree.'
  T: 'A gentle Hint to a few *Gentlemen-Rakes*, occasionally written by a Sufferer, August 28th, 1743.' ¶ No: 19 lines.
  Note: Reprinted, no. 698.

695. Sept. 15, 1743 *AWM* #1236.
  'Unhappy Youth, that could not longer stay.'
  T: 'An Apology for the young Man in Goal, and in Shackles, for ravishing an old Woman of 85 at Whitemarsh, who had only one Eye, and that a red one.' ¶ No: 20 lines.
  Note: Excellent ribald poetry.

696. Sept. 29, 1743 *BNL* #2052, 2/1.
  'Descend my Muse to sing the noble Fray.'
  T: 'On the late Victory obtain'd by His Majesty over the French at Dettingen.' ¶ No: 40 lines.
  Note: Dated 'Boston, Sept. 27, 1743.' Reprinted, nos. 699, 700.

697. Sept. 1743 *Am Mag* I, 34.
   'To you fair maidens, I address.'
   T: 'A Riddle for the Ladies.' ¶ No: 36 lines.
   Note: See the reply, no. 705. A poem with the same first line, Crum
      T3225, is entitled 'A Riddle on a Needle given me by Miss Betty
      Bennet, Jan. 6, 1748/9.'

698. Sept. 1743 *Am Mag* I, 35.
   ''Tis strange how Things, that sinply disagree'
   Note: A reprint of no. 694.

699. Sept. 1743 *Am Mag* I, 36.
   'Descend my Muse to sing the noble Fray.'
   Note: A reprint of no. 696.

700. Oct. 13, 1743 *PJ* #46, 2/2.
   'Descend my Muse to sing the noble Fray.'
   Note: A reprint of no. 696.

701. Oct. 1743 *Am Mag* I, 74.
   'Essare, Sepulchrale Marmor.'
   T: 'Inscription on a Tomb Lately Erected at Annapolis in Maryland.
      ¶ No: 28 lines.
   Note: On Gov. Charles Calvert of Maryland, Cf. no. 294.

702. Oct. 1743 *Am Mag* I, 74–76.
   'The Man that Happiness enjoys, is he.'
   T: 'The Pleasures of a Country Life. A Translation from Hor. Ep.
      2d.' ¶ No: 66 lines.
   Note: By the author of 'The Razor'; see no. 708.

703. Oct. 1743 *Am Mag* I, 76.
   'With a White Stone, Macrinus, mark This Day.'
   T: 'The Second Satire of Persius.' ¶ No: 150 lines. ¶ A: Translated
      1737, 'By a young Student of Harvard-College.'
   Note: Crum W2536.

704. Oct. 1743 *Am Mag* I, 80.
   'Brethren, This comes to let you know.'
   T: 'A Charge to the Clergy. Occasioned by hearing a Sermon
      preach'd very hastily.' ¶ No: 64 lines.

705. Oct. 1743 *Am Mag* I, 80.
   'If she shall first be made a wife.'
   T: 'In Answer to the Riddle for the Ladies.' ¶ No: 20 lines.
   Note: Reply to no. 697.

706. Nov. 21, 1743 *SCG* #504, 2/2.
'How wretched is a Woman's Fate.'
T: 'Verses ... on Women born to be controul'd!' ¶ No: 24 lines. ¶
   A: 'Written by a young Lady.'
Note: Cf. no. 707.

707. Nov. 21, 1743 *SCG* #504, 3/1.
'How happy is a Woman's Fate.'
T: 'The Answer: By a Gentleman.' ¶ No: 28 lines.
Note: Cf. no. 706.

708. Nov. 1743 *Am Mag* I, 120–122.
'Of noisy rattling Drums and clattering Shields.'
T: 'The Razor, A Poem.' ¶ No: 104 lines. ¶ A: By the author of
   'The Pleasures of a Country Life,' no. 702; see ed. note, *Am Mag*,
   I, 88, where editor says that 'The Razor' by the author of 'The
   Pleasures' has been received.

709. Nov. 1743 *Am Mag* I, 122–3.
'Whilst with glad Voice united Nature sings.'
T: 'A Hymn On the late Anniversary Thanksgiving.' ¶ No: 49 lines.

710. Nov. 1743 *Am Mag* I, 123–4.
'Assist, my muse, while I with fear relate.'
T: 'The Plague.' ¶ No: 46 lines.

711. Nov. 1743 *Am Mag* I, 125–6.
'Grant me gods, a *little* seat.'
T: 'A Little Wish. In Imitation of the Great Mr. Philips.' ¶ No: 68
   lines. ¶ A: 'Ben. Drake.'
Note: Evidently an imitation of Ambrose Philips, who was known
   for his trochaics addressed to children, reprinted, no. 1856A. I
   cannot identify Ben Drake. Crum G439 gives the source 'from the
   Old Whig Jan. 15, 1735/6.' Printed in Dodsley, IV, 250.

712. Dec. 5, 1743 *SCG* #506, 2/2.
'In Virtue's Cause to draw a daring Pen.'
T: 'On Good and Ill-Nature.' ¶ No: 18 lines.

713. Dec. 1743 *Am Mag* I, 166–7.
'While weeping Friends around thy Funeral mourn.'
T: 'Attempted from the Latin of an American Indian, a Junior Soph-
   ister at Cambridge, Anno 1678. On the Death of the Rev. and
   Learned Mr. Thacher.' ¶ No: 50 lines. ¶ A: 'Philo Muses' [Dr.
   Adam Thomson?]

Note: Eleazar, an American Indian, wrote the Latin elegy on the Rev. Thomas Thacher. See Jantz, p. 207. Dr. Adam Thomson (1712?–1767), a physician, poet, playwright, and political author, emigrated from Scotland to America about 1741 and is remembered for his 'American method' of inoculation and for several literary quarrels. See Henry Lee Smith, 'Dr. Adam Thomson, the originator of the American method of inoculation for smallpox,' Johns Hopkins U. Hospital *Bull.*, XX (1909), 49–52; The *Franklin Papers*, IV, 80n, and VIII, 340n; and Francisco Guerra, *American Medical Bibliography* (New York, 1962). George O. Seilhamer, *History of the American Theatre Before the Revolution* (Philadelphia, 1888), p. 74, has previously called attention to Thomson as a poet. Since he used the pseudonym 'PhiloMusus' and sent at least one poem to the *Am Mag* (see no. 793), this poem may be by him. On the other hand, the subject and place of publication also suggest an attribution to the Boston 'Philo Musus' (see no. 806).

1744

714. Jan. 1, 1743/4 *PJ.*
   'Time's Measurer, The radiant Sun.'
   T: *The Verses of the Printer's Boy that carries about the Pennsylvania Journal, 1743–4.*
   Note: In Pa. Hist. Soc. microfilm of the *PJ.*

715. Jan. 2, 1744 *SCG* ₴510, 2/2.
   'Continual Wars I wage without Expence.'
   T: 'Aenigma.' ¶ No: 5 lines. ¶ A: 'A. Z.'

716. Jan. 1744 *Lon Mag* XIII, 43–4.
   'See dusky clouds, the welkin overspread.'
   T: 'On the Death of Mrs. Alice K[imbe]r, who dy'd in childbed, October 24, 1742.' ¶ A: 'By her Brother, in Foreign Parts' [E. Kimber].

717. Jan. 1744 *Am Mag* I, 212.
   'Ye Nymphs! That boast your Charms, see here.'
   T: 'On the Death of a Young Lady.' ¶ No: 42 lines.
   Note: Dated 'Dec. 13, 1743.' An abridgement reprinted, no. 1521.

718. Jan. 1744 *Am Mag* I, 213–4.
   'I stroll'd one day into a room.'
   T: 'A College Room.' ¶ No: 80 lines. ¶ A: 'L. M.'
   Note: 'A. L. M.'—with the *A* added in contemp ms.

719. Jan. 1744 *Am Mag* I, 214–215.
    'Surprizing Being! Which we Nature call.'
    T: 'Nature.' ¶ No: 38 lines.

719A. Feb. 6, 1743/4 *NYWPB* ⚹55, 1/1.
    'With youth and perfect Beauty blest.'
    T: 'A Riddle.' ¶ No: 32 lines.

719B. Feb. 13, 1743/4 *NYWPB* ⚹56, 1/1.
    'From fam'd *Barbados* on the western Main.'
    T: 'A Receipt for all young Ladies that are going to be married, to
    make a Sack Posset.' ¶ No: 18 lines.

720. Feb. 16, 1743/4 *PJ* ⚹64, 1/1–2.
    'It grieves me much to hear my Friend complain.'
    T: 'An Answer to a Letter from a Friend under Affliction.' ¶ No: 57
    lines.
    Note: 'Lately written ... by a Person of our own Province, who,
    though he has not had the advantage of a liberal Education; and
    his common Employment will not permit him to bestow much
    Time upon the Improvement of his Genius.'

721. Feb. 20, 1743/4 *BEP* ⚹446.
    'Descend, Urania, and inspire my verse.'
    T: 'The Comet: A Poem.' ¶ No: 64 lines. ¶ A: [Mather Byles].
    Note: 'A few Days ago the following Poem was published here,
    (with a curious Cut representing the *Comet*, the *Sun*, &c.) and is
    to be sold by B. Green and Company in *Newbury-street*, and D.
    Gookin, at the Corner of *Water-street*, Cornhill. (*Price Four
    Pence*.)' Reprinted, see nos. 725, 727A, 728. This broadside is not
    in Ford. Reprinted in *A Collection of Poems* (Boston, 1744), pp.
    14–17.

722. Feb. 22, 1743/4 *PG* ⚹793.
    'Can you suppose ill Language will prevail?'
    T: ['To the suppos'd author of the Answer to John Allen's Letter']
    ¶ No: 10 lines.
    Note: Part of the letter.

723. Feb. 1744 *Lon Mag* XIII, 95–97.
    'Thy charming lines, all pleasing, reach my hands.'
    T: 'The Vindication. An Heroic Epistle, in Answer to one receiv'd
    from her, June 2, 1743. On the Banks of the Al—a. To Miss
    Susanna Maria T—, of W—in C—.' ¶ No: 195 lines. ¶ A: 'E.
    Kimber.'

724. Feb. 1744 *Gent Mag* XIV, 99–100.
'Amidst these Io'Peans of the crowd.'
T: 'Epistle to Admiral Vernon, on his success in the West Indies, in imitation of Waller's style.' ¶ No: 69 lines. ¶ A: 'Caetera descent.'
Note: Line 5 suggests that the poem was written by someone who served under Vernon.

725. Feb. 1744 *Am Mag* I, 255.
'Descend, Urania, and inspire my verse.'
Note: A reprint of no. 721.

726. Feb. 1744 *Am Mag* I, 258–9.
'Tho' plagu'd with algebraic lectures.'
T: 'An Epistle from Cambridge.' ¶ No: 94 lines. ¶ A: [Edward Littleton.]
Note: Richardson, p. 54, n. 72, thought that this poem was American. The usual title is 'An Epistle to Henry Archer of Eton School.' Printed in Dodsley, VI, 290. Crum T2391. The *DNB* article on Littleton discusses the poem.

727. Feb. 1744 *Am Mag* I, 259.
'And is The Infant snacht away!'
T: 'On the Death of G—e B—r R—s, who died of a Quinsey, Feb. 13, 1743, 4. Aged 19 months.' ¶ No: 8 lines.

727A. Mar. 19, 1744 *NYWPB*, 1/1–2.
'Descend, Urania, and inpsire my verse.'
Note: A reprint of no. 721.

728. March 29, 1744 *PJ* #70, 1/1–2.
'Descend, Urania, and inspire my verse.'
Note: A reprint of no. 721.

729. March 1744 *Am Mag* I, 298.
'How shall I tune my Lyre! How shall I show.'
T: 'David's Elegy upon Saul and Jonathan. Paraphras'd, 1736.' ¶ No: 70 lines.

730. March 1744 *Lon Mag* XIII, 147–8.
'Ye fair, whose worth I so esteem.'
T: 'Fidenia*: Or, the Explanation.' ¶ A: E[dward] K[imber].
Note: *'A very beautiful Negro Girl.' 'Tune, Love's Goddess is a Myrtle Grove &c.' Kimber tells of his narrow escape from a shipwreck.

731. March 1744 *Lon Mag* XIII, 148.
'Adieu native plains, where blithsome I've rov'd.'
T: 'The Departure. *Tune*, Farewell to Lockaber.' ¶ No: 56 lines. ¶
A: E. K[imber].

732. March 1744 *Lon Mag* XIII, 148.
'Propitious gale! we had thy healing power!'
T: 'Written extempore in the Atlantick, upon approaching the Coast
of New York, after a six Weeks Voyage from England.' ¶ No: 13
lines. ¶ A: E[dward] K[imber].

733. April 1744 *Gent Mag* XIV, 218.
'To wed, or not wed—That is the question.'
T: 'The Batchelor's Soliloquy. In Imitation of a celebrated Speech
by Hamlet.' ¶ A: 'H.'
Note: Cf. nos. 1174, 1456, for similar imitations. Crum T3198.

734. April 1744 *Am Mag* I, 349.
'Whilst to relieve a generous Queen's Distress.'
T: 'We hear from *Annapolis-Royal* that a Play was acted the last
Winter for the Entertainment of the Officers and Ladies at that
Place, and that the following Lines were Part of the Prologue
compos'd and spoke on that Occasion.' ¶ No: 10 lines.

734A. June 11, 1744 *NYWPB* #73, 3/1.
'Much honoured Muse! accept this grateful Verse.'
T: 'On the Death of Henry Lane, Esq.' ¶ No: 14 lines. ¶ A: 'X.'

734B. June 25, 1744 *NYWPB* #75, 1/1.
'The Man in vertue's sacred paths sincere.'
T: 'XXII Ode of Horace, paraphrastically imitated.' ¶ No: 32 lines.
¶ A: 'P.' 'By a young Gentleman in New York.'

735. June 1744 *Am Mag* I, 430-1.
'Begin my Muse, but softly sing.'
T: 'Ode for St Cecilia Day. Or, on Musick.' ¶ No: 54 lines. ¶ A:
'Myrtillo,' [also] 'M.'

736. June 1744 *Am Mag* I, 431-2.
'Lovely Queen of soft Desires.'
T: 'On Sappho's Hymn to Venus attempted.' ¶ No: 35 lines. ¶ A:
'Myrtillo' [also] 'M.'

736A. July 9, 1744 *NYWPB*, #77, 1/1-2.
'The greatest Authors of our modern Age.'
T: 'To Mr. G[erahdu]s D[uyckinc]k, on his elaborate Performance,
for, or against, the Moravians or Bohemian Brethren.' ¶ No: 44
lines + 2 lines of Dutch. ¶ A: 'Gratias Esculpius.'

Note: Cf. no. 736B. This is a satire on Gerardus Duyckinck, *A Short Though True Account of the Establishment and Rise of the Church so called Moravian Brethren* (New York, 1744), Evans 5382.

736B. July 30, 1744 *NYWPB* #80, 1/1.
   'I've wrote a Book and fix'd my Name.'
   T: 'To Mister Gratius Esculapius, on his Observashons [!] upon my Performance against the Moraviens.' ¶ No: 56 lines. ¶ A: [Gerardus Duyckinck.]
   Note: Mock spelling—attack on Pope. See no. 736A. I have not been able to check the Duyckinck family genealogy, where no doubt a notice of Gerardus Duyckinck may be found.

737. July 1744 *Lon Mag* XIII, 355–7 & Aug., pp. 405–6.
   'Hail, much-lov'd man! forgive the aspiring Muse.'
   T: 'A Letter from a Son, in a distant Part of the World, March 2, 1743.' ¶ No: 192 lines. ¶ A: [Edward Kimber].
   Note: Lines describe various colonies. Index for 1744, under 'Kimber,' supplies identification.

738. July 1744 *Lon Mag* XIII, 358.
   'What pleasures more rejoice.'
   T: 'A Song. In a certain Military Retreat.' ¶ No: 20 lines. ¶ A: 'M. and C.' [Edward Kimber].
   Note: Attribution given in Index. 'Tune, Florimel.'

739. Aug. 16, 1744 *PG* #818.
   'Come deck, you drooping Nine, your Fav'rite's Herse.'
   T: 'To the Memory of Archibald Home, Esq. late Secretary of the Jerseys, etc.' ¶ No: 29 lines. ¶ A: 'By a Lady' [A. Coxe?]
   Note: Archibald Home, Deputy-Secretary and a member of the Council of New Jersey, who emigrated to America before 1733, was a productive poet. A manuscript volume of his 'Poems on Several Occasions,' which contained '15 pages of preliminary matter, 130 pages of Poems by Home, and 16 pages of Appendix, poems by Home and some of his friends,' was unfortunately burned in 1902. William Nelson, who owned the manuscript volume, reveals that 'A. Coxe,' a lady, wrote an elegy for him. William Nelson, *New Jersey Biographical and Genealogical Notes* [*Collections of* the New Jersey Historical Soc., v. 9] (Newark, 1916), pp. 131–133. Reprinted, see no. 745.

739A. Aug. 20, 1744 *NYWPB* #83, 1/1.
   'Envy be dumb, ye Criticks cease to carp.'

T: 'To Mr. F. J---y, on his surprizing Performance dispersed about the Streets in Print and Manuscript, also that inimitable Rhapsody in the New York Gazette, 978.' ¶ No: 32 lines. ¶ A: 'Antidotus Farewell.'

Note: *NYG* #976, 23 July 1744 and *NYG* #980, 20 Aug. 1744 are extant, but no issues between these two survive.

740. Aug. 1744 *Lon Mag* XIII, 406–7.
'I'll tell you, good sirs, what will make you all smile.'
T: 'A Ballad. Occasion'd by some attempts of a certain Colony, to be witty on a neighbouring corps of brave Gentlemen, by calling them Boys. Sic cecinere B.D.W.G.M.M.H.M.M.O.B.W.C.' ¶ No: 56 lines + refrain 'Derry down.' ¶ A: [Edward Kimber].
Note: Attribution in Index.

741. Aug. 1744 *Lon Mag* XII, 408.
'Alas! whilst aching pains declare.'
T: 'The Repentant Deboshee.' ¶ No: 48 lines. ¶ A: 'Indians' [E. Kimber].
Note: Attribution in index.

742. Aug. 1744 *Lon Mag* XIII, 408.
'Soft as the downy plumage of the dove.'
T: 'Acrostic.' ¶ A: 'Peregrinus Vespusianus' [i.e. E. Kimber].
Note: Spells out 'Susanna Anne LK.'

743. Aug. 1744 *Lon Mag* XIII, 408.
'Go, little bird, thy happy freedom prize.'
T: 'On sending a Carolina-Nightingale to Miss M—r.' ¶ No: 13 lines.

744. Aug. 1744 *Am Mag* I, 517–520.
'Friendship, thou sacred name, my muse inspire.'
T: 'Man's Happiness, the Contemplation of God and his Works, and the Practice of Virtue, In a Letter to a Friend.' ¶ No: 129 lines. ¶ A: 'Laelius.'

745. Aug. 1744 *Am Mag* I, 520–1.
'Come deck, you drooping Nine, your Fav'rite's Verse.'
Note: A reprint of no. 739.

746. Aug. 1744 *Am Mag* I, 523.
'Tho' sage Philosophers have said.'
T: 'The Paper-Mill. Inscrib'd to Mr. [William] Parks.' ¶ No: 64 lines. ¶ A: 'J[oseph] Dumbleton.'
Note: From the *VG*, July 26. Reprinted in the *Va. Mag. of Hist. and Biog.*, VII (1900), 442–444, and in Silverman, pp. 326–327.

747. Sept. 1744 *Lon Mag* XIII, 460.
   'Arise, and soar, my tow'ring soul.'
   T: 'A Pindaric Ode. To James Oglethorpe, Esq; in the Country. Written in the year 1728.' ¶ A: Rev. Samuel Wesley.
   Note: Perhaps reprinted from D. Lewis, *Miscellaneous Poems* (London, 1730), pp. 83–89 (Case 337 [2]).

748. Sept. 1744 *Lon Mag* XIII, 461.
   'Foul winds, foul weather vex'd us fore.'
   T: 'On making Foul-Island, after a bad Voyage, North about, from Charles-Town, South-Carolina, to England.' ¶ No: 4 lines. ¶ A: [E. Kimber.]
   Note: Attribution in Index.

749. Sept. 1744 *Lon Mag* XIII, 462.
   'Menedemus the stoic, once heartily jaded.'
   T: 'Epigram.' ¶ No: 12 lines. ¶ A: 'P. V. Democritus' [E. Kimber].
   Note: Attribution in index.

750. Sept. 1744 *Lon Mag* XIII, 462.
   'What soft'ning transports melt my soul.'
   T: 'Song. To a new Tune.' ¶ No: 32 lines. ¶ A: 'K.' [E. Kimber].
   Note: Dated '1743'. Attribution given in Index, under 'Kimber.'

751. Sept. 1744 *Am Mag* I, 560.
   'If, 'midst the Hurries of a Nuptial Day.'
   T: 'Verses, written by a young Gentleman to his Sister upon her Marriage.' ¶ No: 102 lines.

752. Sept. 1744 *Am Mag* I, 562–4.
   'When plastick nature moulds the wondrous clay.'
   T: 'An Epistle to Myrtillo.' ¶ No: 88 lines. ¶ A: 'Dorimond.'
   Note: Reprinted from the *London Mag.*, IX (July, 1740), 345. Richardson, p. 54, n. 71, thought that this poem was American.

753. Oct. 8, 1744 *BEP* #479, 1/1.
   'While you are boldly set in Truth's Defence.'
   T: 'To the Reverend Dr. Chauncy, On his late Piece, entitled, *Seasonable Thoughts on the State of Religion in New-England.* ¶ No: 78 lines.

754. Oct. 1744 *Lon Mag* XIII, 512.
   'You wish in vain, it cannot be.'
   T: 'In Answer to a Paragraph in a Letter from Charles-Town, South-Carolina, lately publish'd in the Papers, which hop'd the speedy Return of General Oglethorpe to that Part of the World.' ¶ No: 44 lines. ¶ A: 'By a Lady.'

755. Oct. 1744 *Am Mag* I, 602.
'Pursuant to your late command.'
T: 'To Miss W—t—n—ll, of Namptwich.' ¶ No: 196 lines. ¶ A:
'R. D.'
Note: Reprinted without acknowledgement from *The Lon Maga-*
zine, VI (March, 1737), 155–6.

756. Nov. 8, 1744 *AWM* ♯1296, 1/1–2.
'As once in Solyma, the sacred Town.'
T: 'A Panegyrick on Doctor John Kearsley. A Worthy Member of
Christ-Church in Philadelphia, a generous Benefactor, a zealous
Promoter, a constant Attendant, a prudent and skillful Manager
and Contriver of the Building, Beautifying and Compleating of
that Religious Edifice, and all its Ornaments.' ¶ No: 52 lines. ¶
A: [By a minister of Christ Church?]
Note: [3 lines from] 'Virg. Eclog. 5.'

757. Nov. 12, 1744 *SCG* ♯555, 2/2.
'Shall Wesley's Sons, o'er rule all human Kind.'
T: '... Lines, wrote when the Whitefieldian Farce was at its Height
in Charles-Town.' ¶ No: 34 lines. ¶ A: 'Homme-Rouge.'
Note: Reprinted, no. 768.

758. Nov. 1744 *Lon Mag* XIII, 563–4.
'Moments, wing'd with smiling pleasure.'
T: 'The Happy Pair; Or, the Departure, An Irregular Ode.' ¶ No:
135 lines. ¶ A: 'By Mr. Edward Kimber.'
Note: 'To Miss [Suzanna Lunn], July, 1744.' Identity of lady sup-
plied in Index for 1744 under 'Kimber.'

759. Nov. 1744 *Am Mag* I, 653.
'Accept, great shade, the Tribute of a lay.'
T: 'On the Death of Mr. Pope.' ¶ No: 32 lines. ¶ A: 'B. F.'
Note: Repr. without acknowledgement from *Lon Mag*, XIII (June
1744), 304.

760. Dec. 29, 1744 *PJ* ♯109.
'Father Divine! eternal One!'
T: 'Occasioned by a Recovery from a tedious Illness.' ¶ No: 39 lines.

761. Dec. 29, 1744 *PJ*.
'What will you then, requires a youthful Friend.'
T: 'The Wish.' ¶ No: 54 lines.
Note: Reprinted in the *Boston W. Mag.*, II (17 Mar. 1804), 84.

762. Dec. 29, 1744 *PJ* ♯109, 3/1.
'Happy that Man, that has per Ann.'
T: 'A Wish, Alamode de Crambo.' ¶ No: 24 lines. ¶ A: 'Eugenia.'

763. Dec. 29, 1744 *PJ* ∦109, 3/1.
'Come ye whose Souls harmonious sounds inspire.'
T: 'On the Death of Mr. Pope.' ¶ No: 36 lines.

764. Dec. 1744 *Am Mag* I, 698–701.
'Bright Hymen now the pleasing Knot has Ty'd.'
T: 'Advice to a young Lady just after her Marriage.' ¶ No: 68 lines.
¶ A: 'A. Z.'
Note: Dated 'Dec. 31, 1744.'

765. Dec. 1744 *Am Mag* I, 701.
'Another Sun!—'Tis true;—but not the Same.'
T: 'On the Device of the New Fire-Place, A Sun; with this Motto,
alter *idem*. i.e., A second Self; or, Another, the same.' ¶ No: 10
lines. ¶ A: 'By a Friend.'
Note: On Benjamin Franklin's stove.

1745

765A. Jan. 1, 1745 *NYWPB*.
'Two annual Courses Time has run.'
T: *The Yearly Verses of the Printer's Lad, who Carrieth about the
New York Weekly Post-Boy, to the Customers Thereof.*
Note: small broadside.

766. Jan. 1745 *Am Mag* II, 36.
'How hard my Lot! and ah! how cruel Fate!'
T: 'A Lady's Lamentation for the Loss of her Cat.' ¶ No: 108 lines.
Note: Poems on pets were a popular genre. Cf. Green on Byles' cat
(no. 280). See also 'On Belinda's Canary Bird: *Lon Mag* II (Feb.,
1733), 91; 'Celia's Lamentation for the death of her Sparrow,'
Lon Mag II (May, 1733), 257; 'On the death of a Young Lady's
Squirrel call'd Pug' *Lon Mag* II (July, 1733), 364; 'On a Lady's
drinking to her cat her admirer being by,' *Gent Mag* VIII (Oct.,
1738), 543; and 'On the Death of Cantorella Celia's Singing Bird'
(no. 775). Reprinted, nos. 1913 (28 lines only) 1917 (28 lines
only).

767. Jan. 14, 1745 *SCG* ∦564, 2/2.
'Fear not, you've conquer'd your undaunted Foes.'
T: [Acrostics on Frankland, Payne & Mitchel]. ¶ No: 21 lines. ¶ A:
'Demetrius.'

768. Feb. 5, 1744/5 *AWM* ∦1309, 4/1.
'Shall Wesley's Sons, o'er-rule all humane Kind.'
Note: A reprint of no. 757.

769. Feb. 26, 1744/5 *PJ* ≠118, 1/1–2/1; cont. Mar. 5, 1/1–2.
'Historic *Muse*, awake!—and from the shade.'
T: 'The Fatal-Conquest. A Poem. Occasioned by the Death of the brave Sir Richard Greenville, in the Year 1591, after sustaining, in the Revenge, an English Man of War, a Fight of 15 Hours against the Spanish Armada of 53 Sail.' ¶ No: 246 lines.

769A. Mar. 11, 1744/5 *NYWPB* ≠112, 3/2.
'When e'er the Eagle and the Lilly join.'
T: 'The following Prophecy of Johannes Lichtenberg, a Carthusian Monk, well versed in Astronomy, who lived about the year 1720, may perhaps divert some of your Readers, and for that End I have endeavoured to put it into an English Dress.' ¶ No: 16 lines with German.

769B. March 18, 1744/5 *NYWPB* ≠113, 1/2.
'Our Fathers left *Britannia's* fruitful Shore.'
T: 'Lines' ¶ No: 8 lines. ¶ A: 'By one of the Descendants of those Regicides that died in this Colony [Conn.]'
Note: Concludes an essay by 'Hezekiah W---t.' Reprinted, no. 771. Cf. no. 164.

770. Mar. 18, 1745 *SCG* ≠573, 2/1–2.
'To you *brave* Youth, who justly merit Praise.'
T: '... An Encomium in Praise ... of the brave Captain *Frankland* ...' ¶ No: 42 lines. ¶ A: 'Will English.'

771. Mar. 1745 *Am Mag* II, 123.
'Our Fathers left Britannia's fruitful Shore.'
Note: A reprint of no. 769B.

772. April 29, 1745 *NYEP* ≠23, 1/1–2.
'Gamsters atDice, oft get an empty Purse.'
T: 'On the Dice.' ¶ No: 52 lines. ¶ A: 'M. R.'

773. April 1745 *Am Mag* II, 169.
'The Nature's Master-piece, is form'd to please.'
T: 'A Character.' ¶ No: 44 lines.
Note: This same poet also wrote 'The Happy Man' (no. 774).

774. April 1745 *Am Mag* II, 170–2.
'O Hartopp! born of a Superior Race.'
T: 'The Happy Man. From the Latin of Dr. Watts, and written in Imitation of His Blank Verse.' ¶ No: 73 lines.
Note: By author of no. 773. This is a free translation of 'Votum sen Vita in Terris Beata ad verum dignissimum Johanem Hortoppium Bart. 1702'—Isaac Watts, *Horae Lyricae*, 1736, pp. 248–250.

775. April 1745 *Am Mag* II, 173–4.
'Shall Celia's fav'rite Bird lie dead.'
T: 'On the Death of Cantarella, *Celia's* Singing-Bird.' ¶ No: 56 lines.
Note: For the genre, see no. 766.

776. May 1745 *Am Mag* II, 217–222.
'High on the bright Expanse of azure Skies.'
T: 'The Palace of Fancy.' ¶ No: 246 lines.
Note: Reprinted without acknowledgement from *The London Magazine*, VI (Aug., 1737), 447–8; VI, 509–510 (Sept., 1737).

777. June 3, 1745 *BEP* ✳512, 1/1–2.
'I Sing Thy Praise, most famous Thomas.'
T: 'A Letter to the Rev. Mr. Thomas Foxcroft, containing an Encomium upon his learned Apology for Mr. Whitefield, in answer to a scurrilous Letter signed L. A.' ¶ No: 93 lines.

778. June 14, 1745 *MG*.
'Would you, my Fair, Triumphant lead along.'
T: 'To the LADIES of Maryland.' ¶ No: 45 lines. ¶ A: 'Juba.'
Note: Reprinted in Silverman, pp. 324–325; and in the *Mass Spy* Dec. 16, 1773, 4/1, crediting the *New London Gaz* as its source.

779. June 17, 1745 *SCG* ✳586, 2/1–2.
'And is Pope gone ?—Then mourn ye Britons! mourn.'
T: 'Verses, written extempore by a Native of this Place, on the Death of the great and celebrated Alexander Pope, Esq.' ¶ No: 44 lines. ¶ A: 'By a Native of this Place.'
Note: Sent in by 'Philagathus.' For 'Philagathus,' see also 858, 1050.

780. June 1745 *Scots Mag* VII, 275.
'Bless'd in himself, no dangers move.'
T: 'The Christian Hero. Partly an imitation of Horace's Integer vitae.' ¶ No: 36 lines.
Note: Cf. no. 1507.

780A. July 22, 1745 *NYWPB* ✳131, 1/1.
'When glorious Anne *Britannia's* Scepter sway'd.'
T: 'On the Taking of Cape-Breton.' ¶ No: 8 lines.
Note: Reprinted, nos. 781, 783, 786.

780B. July 25, 1745 *NYWPB* ✳131, 1/2.
'Britannia strove a Carthagene to gain.'
T: 'On the Taking of Cape-Breton.' ¶ No: 14 lines. ¶ A: 'By an Officer that went on the Expedition against Carthagena.'
Note: Reprinted, nos. 782, 784, 785.

780C. July 22, 1745 *NYWPB* #131, 1/2.
'To you, *Bostonians*, who have bravely fought.'
T: 'On the Taking of Cape-Breton.' ¶ No: 17 lines. ¶ A: 'By a Captain that uses the Coasting Trade to Boston.'

781. July 29, 1745 *BPB* #556.
'When glorious Anne Britannia's Scepter sway'd.'
Note: A reprint of no. 780A.

782. July 29, 1745 *BPB* #556.
'Britannia strove a Carthagene to gain.'
Note: A reprint of no. 780B.

783. July 29, 1745 *BEP* #520.
'When glorious Anne Britannia's Scepter sway'd.'
Note: A reprint of no. 780A.

784. July 29, 1745 *BEP* #520, 2/1.
'Britannia strove a *Carthagene* to gain.'
Note: A reprint of no. 780B.

785. July 1745 *Am Mag* II, 314–5.
'Britannia strove a *Carthagene* to gain.'
Note: A reprint of no. 780B.

786. July 1745 *Am Mag* II, 315.
'When glorious Anne Britannia's Scepter sway'd.'
Note: A reprint of no. 780A.

786A. Aug. 26, 1745 *NYWPB* #136, 1/1–2/1.
'As th' Eagle soaring in the lofty Skies.'
T: 'An Imitation of Horace, Lib. LV Ode IV &c. Humbly presented to the brave and worthy Commodore Warren, as the grateful Acknowledgment of his gallant and prosperous Achievement during this war &c.' ¶ No: 130 lines. ¶ A: 'By a Countryman of his.'
Note: Sept. 16, 1745, *NYWPB* #139, 4/2: 'The curious Reader is desired to correct the following Errors of the Press, in the Poem inscribed to Commodore *Warren*, in our *Post-Boy*, No 136. *Viz.* Col. 1, Line 3, *for*, his Prey, *read* the Prey; line 8, *for* timid, *read* tumid; line 14 from the bottom, *for* now, *read* then; line 2 from the bottom, *read* Resolves; page 2, col. 1, line 9, *read* guarding Care; and at the End should be the Date *New-York* Aug. 15, 1745.' Reprinted, no. 789.

787. Aug. 1745 *Am Mag* I, 358.
'The Persian King, when he his Troops survey'd.'
T: 'A Thought.' ¶ No: 10 lines. ¶ A: [By the author of no. 788].

788. Aug. 1745 *Am Mag* II, 358.
'See! lonly Wastes and barren Wilds proclaim.'
T: 'Isiah 35th Chap. *Paraphrased.*' ¶ No: 22 lines. ¶ A: [By the author of no. 787.]

789. Sept. 5, 1745 *AWM* ℔1339.
'As th' Eagle soaring in the lofty Skies.'
Note: A reprint of no. 786A.

789A. Sept. 9, 1745 *NYWPB* ℔138, 4/2.
'Proud France, why such excessive Joy.'
T: 'Lines made upon reading the King of France and Dauphin's Letters (in your Post-Boy) to the Queen and Dauphiness, concerning the Engagement at Fontenay.' ¶ No: 13 lines.
Note: Reprinted, no. 790.

790. Sept. 12, 1745 *AWM* ℔1340.
'Proud France, why such excessive Joy.'
Note: A reprint of no. 789A.

791. Sept. 30, 1745 *SCG* ℔601, 3/1.
'A Post there was where Wormwood knew.'
T: 'The Countrymen's *Lamentation.*' ¶ No: 20 lines.
Note: 'To the Tune of Johnny-O' A comment on the song is in *SCG*, Oct. 24, 3/1 by 'Charles Quaves.'

792. Oct. 7, 1745 *BPB* ℔566.
'When glorious Actions we would fain rehearse.'
T: 'On the Conquest of Cape-Breton.' ¶ No: 70 lines. ¶ A: 'By an honest Tar.' [Charles Hansford ?]
Note: Dated 'Williamsburg, in Va., Aug. 29.' On Hansford (c. 1685–1761), a Virginia poet, sailor and blacksmith, see James A. Servies and Carl R. Dolmetsch, eds., *The Poems of Charles Hansford* (Chapel Hill, N.C., 1961). Reprinted in J. A. Leo Lemay, 'A Poem, Probably by Charles Hansford,' *Va. Mag. of Hist. and Biog.*, LXXIV (1966), 445–447.

793. Nov. 8, 1745 *MG* ℔29.
'What Rake now doubts he has a Soul to save.'
T: 'Verses occassioned by Mr. Colley Cibber's Epitaph on Mr. Pope, in the Gentleman's Magazine for June, 1749.' ¶ No: 18 lines. ¶ A: 'Philo-Musus' [Dr. Adam Thomson.]
Note: A prefatory note says that this poem has been intended for the *Am Mag*. In a critical survey of contributions to the *Maryland Gazette*, Dr. Alexander Hamilton listed the poems of Thomson. When I published an edition of this essay in 1966, I mistakenly

thought that 'Philo-Musus' was the Rev. James Sterling. Since then I have completed this bibliography; and the information provided by Thomson's Philadelphia literary quarrel, particularly his essay in the *PG* 12 Sept. 1754, and the lead supplied by Seilhamer (see no. 713,), leave little doubt that the 'Philo Musus' publishing in Maryland and Pennsylvania in the 1740's and early 1750's is Thomson. See J. A. Leo Lemay, 'Hamilton's Literary History of the Maryland Gazette,' *Wm. and Mary Quart.*, XXIII (1966), 273–285.

794. Nov. 1745 *Am Mag* II, 507–509.
  'What! scale the Alps and stride the Glyceries!'
  T: 'a Fragment of an imaginary Converse with Clotho.' ¶ No: 30 lines. ¶ A: 'O. E.'

795. Dec. 12, 1745 *BNL* ⚹2277, 2/1.
  'Neptune and Mars in Council met.'
  T: 'On the Surrender of Louisbourg.' ¶ No: 32 lines. ¶ A: 'The following Lines were communicated to us by an Officer just arriv'd from Cape-Breton.'
  Note: Reprinted, nos. 796, 799.

796. Dec. 16, 1745 *BEP* ⚹540, 2/1–2.
  '*Neptune* and *Mars* in Council met.'
  Note: A reprint of no. 795.

797. Dec. 24, 1745 *PJ* ⚹167, 1/1–2.
  'Ye nymphs of *Salem*, who, with hallow'd lays.'
  T: 'Ode on Christmas-Day.' ¶ No: 48 lines.

798. Dec. 24, 1745 *MG*.
  'Attend ye Fair, Calliope the Song.'
  T: 'To The Ladies.' ¶ No: 134 lines. ¶ A: 'Eumolpus.'
  Note: Blank verse, poor.

799. Dec. 1745 *Am Mag* II, 559.
  '*Neptune* and *Mars* in Council met.'
  Note: A reprint of no. 1795.

1746

800. Jan. 1, 1746 *PJ*.
  'The French will grant that Shirley's schemes.'
  T: 'The New-Year's Verses, Of the Printer's Lad who carries about the Pennsylvania Journal to the Customers thereof.'

801. Jan. 11, 1745/6 *SCG* ⚹616, pp. 1 & 2.
'A Man of Wisdom may disguise.'
Note: A reprint of no. 640.

802. Jan. 14, 1745/6 *MG*.
'Shall brave New England's Glory fly.'
T: 'An ODE, In Honour of New-England, (on their important Conquest of Cape-Breton from the French).' ¶ No: 78 lines. ¶ A: 'Philo-Musus' [Dr. Adam Thomson].
Note: Prefatory note. 'The French are our natural Enemies, and Rivals in almost every Thing; but more particularly in settling the Northern Part of this vast Continent.' Thomson praises Governor William Shirley, Admiral Peter Warren, and William Pepperell. Reprinted, see no. 808.

803. Jan. 21, 1746 *MG*.
'Thou fondest Partner, of my Joy, my Grief.'
T: 'Essay, towards a Translation of the celebrated speech of the Emperor Adrian, to his Soul, when Dying.' ¶ No: 8 lines. ¶ A: 'Ignotus.'

804. Jan. 28, 1746 *MG*.
'She's gone, ah! gone, for evermore secure.'
T: 'On the Death of Miss Peggy Hill.' ¶ No: 47 lines. ¶ A: 'a young Muse'; 'Q. Z.'
Note: *MG* Fri. Sept. 27, 1745: 'Tuesday last died, in the bloom of Life at her Father's House near this City, Miss Margaret Hill, the only Daughter of Mr. Joseph Hill.'

805. Feb. 25, 1745/6 *PG* ⚹898.
'Go Trusty Wade, the War important Wage.'
T: 'A Point of War.' ¶ No: 22 lines.

806. Mar. 11, 1746 *BG* ⚹1252, 1/1–2.
'No brighter Colour paints the crimson Rose.'
T: 'Solomons Songs. Canto 2.' ¶ No: 74 lines. ¶ A: 'Philo-Muses.'
Note: 'Tho' the Author of the ensuing Translation is not so vain, as to imagine it will bear Reparation to the Publick for the Loss of the ingenious Mr. Adams's Paraphrase upon the whole Song, yet by inserting it in your Paper, you may give some Entertainment to several of your Customers; as you will some Encouragement to go on his Design, to your humble Servant, Philo-Muses.' Praise for the Rev. John Adams suggests that this poet may be Matthew Adams, who used the initials from the word *Musae* to sign his contributions to the 'Proteus Echo' essay series. On the other hand, the tone of this apologetic and hopeful preface makes it

seem like the work of a young poet, and this Boston 'Philo-Muses' continued publishing poetry after Matthew Adams' death. See nos. 811, 816, 1033, 1213, and 1955.

808. Mar. 25, 1746 *BG* #1254, 1/1–2/1.
'Shall brave New-England's Glory fly.'
Note: A reprint of no. 802.

809. Mar. 1746 *Am Mag*, III, 132–3.
'All bounteous Nature! in the varied Year.'
T: 'Spring.' ¶ No: 68 lines. ¶ A: 'Ruricola.'

810. April 1746 *Gent Mag*, XVI, 213–14.
'When faithless *Gallia*, proud of guilty pow'r.'
T: 'A Poetical Essay on the Reduction of Cape Breton, on June 17, 1745.' ¶ No: 186 lines.

811. May 6, 1746 *BG* #1260.
'On th' Euxine Shore, and rear'd by barb'rous Hands.'
T: 'On Ovid's Death. From the Latin of *Politian*,' ¶ No: 56 lines. ¶
A: 'Philo-Muses.'
Note: Cf. no. 806 for authorship.

812. May 8, 1746 *PG*.
'Shall Freedom, now, her care for *Britain* o'er.'
T: 'A Soliloquy.' ¶ No: 48 lines.

813. May 19, 1746 *SCG* #634, 1/1.
'Cain, the first Murd'rer, when from Eden driven.'
T: 'The Highlanders Pedigree.' ¶ No: 20 lines.

814. May 26, 1746 *SCG* #635, 1/1.
'In earliest Times when good old Saturn sway'd.'
T: 'The Golden Age.' ¶ No: 40 lines.

815. July 21, 1746 *NYEP* #87, 1/1–2/1.
'How do'st thou do, my Dear; you look as pale.'
T: 'A Dialogue, between a teasing Husband, and his vexatious tip-ling Wife.' ¶ No: 176 lines.
Note: Editor says that he is inserting the poem 'during this scarcity of news.'

815A. July 28, 1746 *NYWPB* #184, 3/2.
'No more, young Hero, roam about.'
T: 'To a young Officer.' ¶ No: 18 lines.

816. July 29, 1746 *BG* #1272, 1/1.
    'Night['s] sable Mantle o're the World is spread.'
    T: 'Solomon's Song. Canto 3.' ¶ No: 46 lines. ¶ A: 'Philo Muses.'
    Note: Manuscript notation on newspaper 'Mather Byles?' See no.
    806 for speculation on authorship.

817. July 1746 *Am Mag* III, 329.
    'Vain fears, and idle doubts, begone!'
    T: 'An Ode on Fortitude.' ¶ No: 42 lines.

818. Aug. 7, 1746 *PG*.
    'From Thomas Clemson ran away.'
    T: [advertisement for run-away.] ¶ No: 54 lines. ¶ A: 'Thomas
    Clemson.'

819. Aug. 28, 1746 *VG*.
    'God prosper long our noble King.'
    T: 'A Ballad, To the Tune of Chevy chase.' ¶ No: 96 lines. ¶ A:
    'Miss Jacobiton.'
    Note: This is similar to a ballad (with first line 'God prosper long
    our Government') attributed to Jonathan Swift. See Harold Wil-
    liams, *The Poems of Jonathan Swift*, III (Oxford, 1937), 1065. It is
    also similar to a New Year's Ode, which begins 'God prosper
    long our gracious King' in *The Poetical Works of John Gay*, ed. G.
    C. Faber (London, 1926), pp. 653–654. Cf. no. 1374. Crum G294
    gives the title 'An Ode for the New Year' and notes that it is
    satirically attributed to Colley Cibber.

820. Aug. 28, 1746 *VG*.
    'In Phedrus' Days, when Frogs could speak.'
    T: 'A Cap for the Hanover Cap-maker, who has got the Knack of
    Innocent Reservation.' ¶ No: 30 lines.

820A. Sept. 1, 1746 *NYWPB* #189, 3/2.
    'O *Stella* fair, whose cheeks bestows.'
    T: 'On a young Lady.' ¶ No: 15 lines.

820B. Sept. 8, 1746 *NYWPB* #190, 8/2.
    'Whilst savage Brutes, stirr'd up by *Gallic* Arts.'
    T: 'On the late Ravages committed by the skulking *French* Indians.'
    ¶ No: 12 lines. ¶ A: 'By a School-Master.'

821. Nov. 2, 1746 *BEP* #586, 2/2.
    'Whate're Men speak by this New light.'
    T: [Advertisement poetry.] ¶ No: 8 lines. ¶ A: [Ebenezer Morton?]
    Note: In advertisement for Ebenezer Morton, *More Last Words to
    these Churches* (Boston, 1746).

822. Nov. 24, 1746 *NYEP* ⚹105, 2/1–2.
'Once on a Time, as I have heard them say.'
T: 'a political Piece.' ¶ No: 45 lines. ¶ A: 'Z.'

823. Nov. 1746 *Gent Mag*, XVI, 609.
'Down by the brook which glides thro' yonder vale.'
T: 'Robin. A Pastoral Elegy.' ¶ No: 96 lines. ¶ A: Capt. John
Dobson.
Note: Capt. Dobson was Commander of the *Prince Rupert*, in the
Barbary Trade.

824. Nov. 1746 *Am Mag*, III, 518.
'How shall my feeble Muse attempt.'
T: 'An Hymn.' ¶ No: 62 lines. ¶ A: 'S. T.'

1747

825. Mar. 3, 1747 *MG* ⚹97.
'Old, toothless, pox'd, mischievous Hag of Night.'
T: 'An humble Address to that most venerable and antient Punk,
the Whore of Babylon! Translated from a French Original, by a
zealous Protestant.' ¶ No: 82 lines. ¶ A: 'P. Q. R. S. & T. W.'
[Rev. Hugh Jones?]
Note: *MG* for Feb. 24 said the piece had come to hand. The Rev.
Hugh Jones was currently quarreling with Maryland Catholics
(see *MG*, Dec. 2, 1746) and may be the author. Richard L. Mor-
ton's introduction to his edition of Jones' *The Present State of
Virginia* (Chapel Hill, N.C., 1956), supplements and corrects the
DAB account of Jones (1692–1760). Reprinted, see no. 828.

826. Mar. 17, 1747 *BG* ⚹1305, 1/1–2.
'Ye hostile Nations! let your Fury cease.'
T: 'A Persuasive to PEACE.' ¶ No: 36 lines.

827. Mar. 31, 1747 *MG*.
'The pow'rful Prince, by Lust of Empire driv'n.'
T: 'The Sixteenth Ode of Horace's Second Book Imitated, and in-
scribed to His Excellency Samuel Ogle, Esq.' ¶ No: 88 lines. ¶
A: [James Sterling].
Note: The subject, place of publication, and close similarity to no.
1507 suggest Sterling's authorship. Reprinted, see no. 830.

828. April 13, 1747 *NYEP* ⚹125.
'Old, toothless, pox'd, mischievous hag of night.'
Note: A reprint of no. 825.

829. April 20, 1747 *SCG* #679, 2/2.
     ''Tis sad for to tell, tho' known is full well.'
     T: [On 'the Duke's *Birth* and *Victory*']. ¶ No: 12 lines. ¶ A: By 'a
     lad but 12.'
     Note: Sent in by a 'Williamite' [as opposed to a *Jacobite*]. Local—
     mentions 'a certain honest merchant on the Bay.'

830. April 23, 1747 *PG* #958.
     'The pow'rful Prince, by Lust of Empire driv'n.'
     Note: A reprint of no. 827.

831. April 1747 *Lon Mag*, XVI, 188.
     'To *science* sacred, muse, exalt thy lays.'
     T: 'Philosophy. A Poem address'd to the Ladies who attend Mr.
     Booth's Lectures* in Dublin.'
     Note: *'On Physics and Experimental Philosophy. Our Mag. for
     Jan. 1746, p. 46.'

832. May 4, 1747 *NYEP* #128, 1/2.
     'There is a Thing which oft the Vulgar see.'
     T: 'Enigma.' ¶ No: 14 lines. ¶ A: 'J. T.'

833. May 4, 1747 *NYG* #224.
     'Sweet Nature smiles! and to the raptur'd Eyes.'
     T: 'An Epistolary Poem, address'd to Miss M—y W—n.' ¶ No: 56
     lines. ¶ A: 'Philoparthenos.'
     Note: [From *Gent Mag*—see no. 834]. Cf. nos. 834, 835, and 838.

834. May 11, 1747 *NYG* #225, 3/2.
     'In vain, fond Youth, dost thou attempt to move.'
     T: 'To Philoparthenos.' ¶ No: 8 lines.
     Note: 'The lines in your last, dedicated to a young Lady, are taken
     out of the Gentleman's Magazine for November, 1743.' Cf. no.
     833.

835. May 18, 1747 *NYG* #226, 3/2.
     'Qui Te cunque movit carmen dispandere tuum.'
     T: [On Philoparthenos.] ¶ No: 10 lines. ¶ A: 'Ephoros.'
     Note: Cf. no. 833.

836. May 25, 1747 *SCG* #684, 2/1.
     'Painter, display, in honour of the state.'
     T: 'Directions to the French King's Painter.' ¶ No: 20 lines.

837. May 25, 1747 *SCG* #684, 2/1–2.
     'Pass o'er this grave without concern.'
     T: 'An Epitaph on a Vice-A—l lately dead of the Gout.' ¶ No: 17
     lines.

838. June 1, 1747 *NYG* #228, 1/1.

'Objicis egregiis mihi quae convicia nugis?'

T: 'To Ephoros.' ¶ No: 12 lines. ¶ A: 'Anglicus Ouphanius.'

Note: Cf. no. 833.

839. June 1, 1747 *NYG* # 228, *Supp.*

'L[or]d have Mercy on us!—the Capital! the Capitol! is burnt down!'

T: 'The Speech Versyfied.' ¶ No: 79 lines. ¶ A: 'Ned. Type' [Benjamin Franklin].

Note: This is printed immediately after, and is a parody of 'The Speech of the Honourable Sir William Gooch, Baronet, His Majesty's Lieutenant Governor, and Commander in Chief, of the Colony and Dominion of *Virginia*: To the General Assembly, the 30th day of *March*, 1747.' Imitated by no. 843. Reprinted in *BEP*, June 8, 1747 (no. 840); in *MG*, June 16, 1747 (no. 842); in *William and Mary Quarterly*, 3rd ser., VII (1950), 270–274; and in *The Papers of Benjamin Franklin*, III, 135–140. The *BEP* reprinting (no. 840) notes 'From a Southern News Paper, dated May 4, 1747'—which perhaps suggests that this *NYG* printing (no. 839) may not have been the first, though it is the earliest extant printing; probably, however, this printing is the 'Southern' paper—from the *BEP* viewpoint.

840. June 8, 1747 *BEP* #617, 2/1–2.

'Lord have Mercy upon us!—the Capitol! the Capitol! is burnt down.'

Note: 'From a Southern News Paper, dated May 4, 1747.' A reprint of no. 839.

841. June 15, 1747 *SCG* #687, 1/2.

'Just in his youthful Prime and Bloom of Age.'

T: 'An Elegy, on the much lamented Death of the Rev. Mr. Robert Betham, who died May 31st, 1747, Aged 32 Years.' ¶ No: 30 lines.

Note: Betham's obituary appeared in the *SCG*, June 8. See no. 845 for an epitaph on Betham.

842. June 16, 1747 *MG Postscript.*

'L—D have Mercy on us!—the Capitol! the Capitol! is burned down.'

Note: A reprint of no. 839.

843. June 22, 1747 *NYEP*, p. 2.

'Hear me with patience while a motion is made.'

'A Prologue to the Corporation's Adress [sic] Spoken by A[lderma]n [Simon] J[ohn]st[o]n.' ¶ No: 81 lines.

Note: A burlesque of 'an Address and Petition To his Excellency the Governour To Ease this City of the Burthen of Keeping a Military Watch,' which was presented To Gov. George Clinton by Alderman Johnson on June 5. No. 844 is part of this burlesque. The speech is recorded in the *Minutes of the Common Council of the City of New York, 1675–1776*, V (New York, 1905), 195–7. This burlesque was probably inspired by Franklin's no. 839.

844. June 22, 1747 *NYEP*, p. 3.
'Who says we have not gained a mighty thing.'
T: 'The Epilogue Spoken by Jo[ri]s B[renckerhof]f.' ¶ No: 15 lines.
Note: See no. 843.

845. June 25, 1747 *SCG* ⚹688, 2/2–3/1.
'Whoe'er you be that on this ground may Tread.'
T: 'An Epitaph on the Reverend Mr. Robert Betham.' ¶ No: 24 lines.
Note: See no. 841 for Betham's elegy.

846. June 25, 1747 *SCG* ⚹ 688, 3/1.
'Oh! what alas, could give such Discontent.'
T: [Satire on strict observance of Sunday.] ¶ No: 12 lines. ¶ A: By a member of 'The Loyal Society.'
Note: Attack on puritanism in behavior; cf. the essays mocking Sundays in the *SCG* in January and February, 1747.

847. July 6, 1747 *SCG* ⚹ 690, 2/1.
'Wipe clean your Pen, my Friend and lay it by.'
T: 'To Mr. Richard Finch, Vindicator of Mr. Foster.' ¶ No: 32 lines. ¶ A: 'P. Q. R.'

848. July 7, 1747 *MG*.
'Once on a Time, an honest clown,'.
T: 'A Clown, his Son, and their Ass.' ¶ No: 46 lines.
Note: *Poor Richard* for 1743 (see *The Papers of Benjamin Franklin*, II, 373–374) contained a shorter version (26 lines) of this poem. See no. 1564 for another variant.

849. July 21, 1747 *MG*.
'One Evening, as I walked to take the Air.'
T: 'A Paradox.' ¶ No: 13 lines.
Note: Reprinted, no. 852.

850. July 28, 1747 *MG*.
'My Honey dear, now by my shoul, (excuse familiar Banter).'

T: 'Teague turn'd Planter.' ¶ No: 48 lines. ¶ A: 'Town Side' [Dr. Adam Thomson].

Note: An attack on 'A Planter,' John Webb, who wrote in June 23 & 30, 1747, issues of *MG*.—Thomson imitated Franklin's earlier satire on Webb: see no. 610. Dr. Alexander Hamilton, in his Literary History of the *MG* (see no. 793), revealed that Thomson was 'Town Side.'

851. Aug. 3, 1747 *NYEP* #141, p. 2.
'From envious Tales, and idle Life refrain.'
T: 'To the Officious Ladies of the Female Club.' ¶ No: 8 lines. ¶ A: 'Kursonus.'
Note: Cf. no. 862.

852. Aug. 3, 1747 *NYEP* #141, p. 2.
'One Evening, as I walk'd to take the air.'
Note: A reprint of no. 849.

853. Aug. 3, 1747 *SCG* #694, 2/1.
'When filial Words describe a Daughter's Grief.'
T: 'On her Father leaving desired her to forbid all young Men the House.' ¶ No: 34 lines. ¶ A: 'Carolina'; 'By a Young Lady.'

854. Aug. 6, 1747 *PG* #973.
'A God there is, the whole Creation tells.'
T: 'The Deity.' ¶ No: 38 lines.
Note: Typical scientific deism. Reprinted, no. 1578.

855. Aug. 31, 1747 *NYEP* #194, p. 1.
'As mornful *Philomel* the Groves supply.'
T: 'Being an intire Stranger, I take this Method of declaring my Mind to Miss S—r—h D—k—n.' ¶ No: 93 lines.
Note: 'Vera Copia.'

856. Aug. 31, 1747 *NYEP* #144, pp. 1–2.
'Quoth Simon to Thomas (and shew's him his Wife.)'
T: 'Simple Simon; or Who was to blame?' ¶ No: 32 lines.

857. Aug. 31, 1747 *SCG* #698.
'Hark! methought I heard the death-betok'ning knell.'
TL: 'On the Death of the Rev. Mr. Kenendy.' ¶ No: 30 lines. ¶ A: 'Omasius.'
Note: A good elegy. *SCG* Aug. 31: 'Last Saturday departed this Life, in the 27th Year of his Age, the Rev. Mr. *Thomas Kennedy*, Minister of the Scots Meeting house in this town.' See No. 860 for another elegy on Kennedy.

858. Aug. 31, 1747 *SCG* #698, 2/1-2.
'What Eye too many Tears can shed.'
T: 'Lines, occasioned by the Death of ... Mr. *John Bull,* who departed this life the 14th Instant, aged 21 years.' ¶ No: 40 lines. ¶ A: 'Philagathus.'
Note: Cf. no. 779 for 'Philagathus.'

859. Aug. 1747 *Gent Mag* XVII, 393.
'If the remembrance of whate'er was dear.'
T: 'An Epitaph in Barbadoes on the Wife of the Rev. Mr. Dudley Woodbridge.' ¶ No: 9 lines.
Note: Crum T987 gives the same first line for a poem entitled 'An Epitaph on a Grave Stone in Windsor Castle on Mrs. Isabella Denham of Windsor ...d. Nov. 25, 1748.'

860. Sept. 7, 1747 *SCG* #699, 2/2-3/1.
'How shall the muse in elegiac lay.'
T: 'On the Death of the Rev. Mr. Kennedy.' ¶ No: 56 lines. ¶ A: 'I—.'
Note: Contains attack on Whitefield—perhaps by the Rev. Alexander Garden? See no. 857 for another elegy on Kennedy.

861. Sept. 17, 1747 *PG.*
'They have a Right to write who understand.'
T: 'Jacob Taylor's Testimony in Favour of Poor Richard's Almanack.' ¶ No: 6 lines. ¶ A: Jacob Taylor.
Note: Reprinted, see no. 867, and *Franklin Papers,* III, 237. These are lines 3–8 of an 8–line poem in Jacob Taylor's almanac for 1745.

862. Oct. 12, 1747 *NYWJ* #721, 4/2.
'Long for an Answer have I staid.'
T: 'Lines to the same Officious Ladies.' ¶ No: 30 lines. ¶ A: 'Kursonus.'
Note: 'Several Ladies having taken the Verses address'd to the Officious Ladies of the Female Club, in Mr. De Forest's Paper, of the third of August [see no. 851], to be meant to them; if it has given offence to any of the said Ladies, I humbly ask their Pardon.'

863. Oct. 14, 1747 *MG.*
'Dick join'd in nuptial Conjugation.'
T: 'The Undecided Case.' ¶ No: 8 lines.

864. Oct. 14, 1747 *MG.*
'Virtue and Vice, Two mighty Powers.'
T: 'The Experiment. A Tale.' ¶ No: 96 lines.
Note: Against luxury.

865. Oct. 22, 1747 *PG*.
     'For Barclay's learn'd Apology is due.'
     T: 'The following Lines were wrote by a Gentleman in his *reading* Barclay's Apology (who before had entertained a mean Opinion of the People called Quakers, and their Principles) return'd with the same Book to a Friend who had lent it to him.' ¶ No: 20 lines. ¶ A: [Benjamin Franklin?]
     Note: See the *Franklin Papers*, III, 216. Cf. *PG* for Nov. 5, 1747, where a writer says that these lines have made him read Barclay. Benjamin Franklin printed the poem in an attempt to convince the moderate Quakers that self-defense was lawful. Cf. *Franklin Papers*, III, 183. The poem, like the *PG* newspaper essays of January 6, 1746/7, and November 19, 1747, and like Franklin's *Plain Truth* (published Nov. 17, 1747), was propaganda for Franklin's effort to organize armed forces in Pennsylvania.

866. Oct. 22, 1747 *PG*.
     'Two handsome chairs.'
     T: [Advertisement poetry.] ¶ No: 12 lines. ¶ A: 'Abraham Carpenter.'

867. Nov. 12, 1747 *PG*.
     'They have a Right to write who understand.'
     Note: A reprint of no. 861.

868. Nov. 16, 1747 *SCG* #709, 4/1–2.
     'When I am to chuse a Woman.'
     T: 'The choice of a Batchelor's Wife.' ¶ No: 78 lines.

869. Dec. 7, 1747 *BEP* #643, 2/1.
     'O when shall (long-lost) Honour guide the war.'
     T: 'Remarkables in *May*.' ¶ No: 14 lines. ¶ A: [Benjamin Franklin?]
     Note: 'From Poor Richard's Almanack for the Year 1748.' Reprinted in the *Franklin Papers*, III, 253.

870. Dec. 7, 1747 *BEP* #643, 2/2.
     'Luke, on his dying Bed, embrac'd his Wife.'
     T: 'From Poor Richard's Almanack for 1748.' ¶ No: 8 lines. ¶ A: [Benjamin Franklin?]
     Note: Reprinted in the *Franklin Papers*, III, 248.

871. Dec. 7, 1747 *BEP* #643.
     'Don't after foreign Food and Cloathing roam.'
     T: 'From Poor Richard's Almanack for ... 1748.' ¶ No: 8 lines. ¶ A: [Benjamin Franklin?]
     Note: Reprinted in the *Franklin Papers*, III, 249.

872. Dec. 21, 1747 *NYEP* #159, p. 1.
  'It must be so—Milton thou reasons't well.'
  T: 'Act V. Scene I of Cato Imitated.' ¶ No: 30 lines. ¶ A: 'Horatio.'
  Note: An imitation of Addison's *Cato.* Cf. nos. 1009, 1923A.

873. Dec. 21, 1747 *NYEP* #159, p. 1.
  'Lull'd in pleasing Sleep old Cornell lies.'
  T: 'The Miser's Dream.' ¶ No: 24 lines.

1748

874. Feb. 8, 1748 *BEP* #652, 1/2–2/2.
  'Rais'd on a Throne of Block-work see him sit.'
  T: 'Character of a Country Justice, called Clodpate.'
  Note: A reprint of no. 42.

875. Feb. 15, 1747/8 *NYG* #265, p. 1.
  'Immortal Chew, first set our *Quakers* right.'
  T: [Attack on Quakers.] ¶ No: 19 lines.
  Note: Attack also on Samuel Chew. See reply by Michael Lightfoot
    —*NYG* Feb. 24.

876. Feb. 24, 1748 *MG*, pp. 1 & 2.
  'Well sung the Bard to Critics, Wits and Beaus.'
  T: 'Epistle to a Friend.' ¶ No: 239 lines. ¶ A: 'Philo-Musaeus' [Dr.
    Adam Thomson].
  Note: In the prefatory letter, Thomson hopes that the poem will
    help 'promote The Design of establishing better Opportunities
    for Education in the Country.' In the poem, he attacks the inade-
    quate training and ability of colonial doctors, lawyers, and min-
    isters; but praises Drs. John and Alexander Hamilton; lawyers
    Edmund Jenings, Daniel Dulany the Elder, Henry Darnell III,
    Stephen Bordley, and James Calder; and ministers John Gordon,
    Henry Addison, John Eversfield, Jacob Henderson, John Lang,
    and James Sterling. See reply by 'Philo-Kalus,' *MG*, Mar. 30,
    1748. Cf. no. 879.

877. Mar. 7, 1747/8 *NYWJ* #742.
  'Rais'd on a Throne of Block work see him sit.'
  T: 'Character of a Country Justice, called Clodpate.'
  Note: A reprint of no. 42.

878. Mar. 21, 1747/8 *NYG* #270, 4/1.
  'Mars, O God of War, why hast thou.'
  T: 'The Lamentation of Lewis the Beloved of his People, for the
    Loss of his Ships.' ¶ No: 19 lines.
  Note: Free verse.

879. May 4, 1748 *MG*, p. 4.
'The Parson says, my Verse I stole.'
T: 'An Epigram, Occasioned by the Letter signed Philo-Kalus.' ¶
No: 12 lines. ¶ A: 'Philo-Musaeus' [Dr. Adam Thomson].
Note: 'a certain Reverend Gentleman, noted for his Gravity, as I am
well inform'd, in a public Company, threatened to expose the
Verses, much in the same Manner as is performed in the aforesaid
elegant Epistle.' 'Philo-Kalus' [Rev. Theophilus Swift] had been
provoked by no. 876 and his 'elegant Epistle' had appeared in the
MG for Mar. 30, 1748. Thomson ('Philo-Musaeus') said that
Swift's lines on the subject 'may be sung to the Tune of the hun-
dred and nineteenth Psalm. The Poetical Epistle, I am told, was
read to a Congregation after Divine Service, and condemn'd by
the Parson for the sake of an ill placed Compliment, which he
conscientiously judged to be ironical.'

880. May 11, 1748 *SCG* #734, 2/1–2.
'Oh death tremendous! inexorable king.'
T: 'on the much lamented Death of Benjamin Godin, Esq.' ¶ No: 32
lines. ¶ A: 'C. E. F.'
Note: Godin had lived in Carolina for 45 years.

881. May 18, 1748 *MG*, pp. 1–2.
'Now while the Sun revolving feasts each sense.'
T: 'An Epithalamium on the late Marriage of the Honourable Bene-
dict Calvert, Esq.; with the agreeable young Lady, of your City,
his Kinswoman.' ¶ No: 116 lines. ¶ A: [James Sterling.]
Note: April 27, 1748 *MG*: 'Last Thursday [April 1] the Honourable
Benedict Calvert, Esq.; Collector of his Majesty's Customs for
Patuxent District, &c. was married to Miss Elizabeth Calvert,
only surviving Daughter of the late Honourable Charles Calvert,
Esq.; deceased, formerly Governor of this Province.' The poem
is dated from 'Kent County, April 29, 1748,' thus suggesting
Sterling's authorship.

882. June 8, 1748 *MG*.
'Prussia's proud Prince, the Story goes.'
T: 'Satyr upon the Prussian Flag.' ¶ No: 24 lines.
Note: Pretty good scurrilous doggerel; probably not local.

883. July 11, 1748 *NYG* #286.
'Of all the Beauty that e're cround the Land.'
T: 'To Miss A— S—.' ¶ No: 33 lines. ¶ A: 'P— G—.'

884. July 18, 1748 *NYG* #287, 1/1–3.
'The gloomy Horrors all around.'
T: 'A Night Piece.' ¶ No: 98 lines. ¶ A: 'A. B.'

885. July 1748 *Universal Mag*, III, 21.
  'Both man and chylde is glad to here tell.'
  T: 'A newe Balade made of Thomas Crumwell, called trotle on sway.'

886. Sept. 1, 1748 *PG*.
  'While scarce a Day but fresh Alarms.'
  T: 'An Ode, humbly inscribed to the Associators of Pennsylvania.' ¶ No: 162 lines. ¶ A: 'Philomusaeus' [Dr. Adam Thomson].
  Note: With prefatory note. Contains references to Benjamin Franklin, organizer of the Associators.

887. Sept. 12, 1748 *SCG* #752, 1/2–2/1.
  'What Words, what sense sufficient can express.'
  T: 'Lines' [on the Death of William Hovel Hill] 'who died on the 4th Instant.' ¶ No: 40 lines.
  Note: This seems to be an adaptation of Sir Francis Fane's 'On the Penitent Death of the Earl of Rochester ... 1680.' On Fane (d. 1689?), see *CBEL*, II, 422. Crum W795.

888. Oct. 10, 1748 *IA* #41.
  'Have you not seen at Country Wake.'
  T: [On France and England making peace.] ¶ No: 16 lines.

889. Oct. 31, 1748 *IA* #44.
  'Three learned Gothicks, in their furious Zeal.'
  T: 'An Epigram, translated from the Latin.' ¶ No: 8 lines.

890. Oct. 31, 1748 *IA* #44.
  'Seek you to know what keeps the mind.'
  T: 'The Ingredients of Contentment.' ¶ No: 22 lines.
  Note: Reprinted, no. 913.

891. Nov. 7, 1748 *IA* #45.
  'As nigh a river's silver stream.'
  T: 'The Doubtful Lover.' ¶ No: 40 lines.

892. Nov. 28, 1748 *IA* #48.
  'Calmly repos'd upon a pleasant Green.'
  T: 'A Philosophical Contemplation.' ¶ No: 52 lines. ¶ A: 'Phylander.'
  Note: Reprinted, no. 1021.

893. Dec. 1, 1748 *PJ* #315, 1/1.
  'Adventus vester cunctis gratissimus hic est.'
  T: 'Emenentissimo viro Jocobo Hamilton, Armigero, Provinciae Pensilvaninsis in America, Gubernatori.' ¶ No: 30 lines. ¶ A: 'J. F.' [Aaron Burr, Sr. ?].

Note: Dated 'Pridie calendas Decembris, Anno 1748.' 'J. F.' used
the abbreviated title 'S.P.D.' He is evidently the same author who
contributed 'Dignissime Domine' to the *PG*, May 5, 1748; see
the *Franklin Papers*, III, 286–287. For Burr (1716–1757), father of
Vice-President Aaron Burr, see Franklin B. Dexter, *Biographical
Sketches of the Graduates of Yale*, I (New York, 1885), 530–534.

894. Dec. 12, 1748 *IA* ✳50.
'And why, my friend, these melting tears.'
T: 'A Poem on the Death of a young child.' ¶ No: 24 lines.
Note: Reprinted in *The Rural Repository*, XIV (Jan. 26, 1838), 128,
under the title 'To Mourning Friends.'

895. Dec. 28, 1748 *MG*.
'Why, Celia, is your spreading waist.'
T: 'A Fable, The Poet and his Patron.' ¶ No: 82 lines.

1749

896. Jan. 3, 1748–9 *PJ* ✳320.
'No more the Morn, with tepid rays.'
T: 'Winter. An Ode.' ¶ No: 36 lines. ¶ A: [Dr. John Hawkesworth.]
Note: Formerly attributed to Samuel Johnson, this poem is actually
by Hawkesworth, an English poet who generally compiled the
poetry section of the *Gentleman's Mag*, where this poem first ap-
peared in Dec., 1747, p. 588. See David Nichol Smith and Ed-
ward L. McAdam, *The Poems of Samuel Johnson* (Oxford, 1941),
p. 397.

897. Jan. 4, 1749 *MG*.
'Great God! whose Power o'er Heav'n and Earth presides.'
T: 'Hymn to the Supreme Being.' ¶ No: 26 lines.

899. Jan. 9, 1748/9 *IA*.
'Charmer of a lonesome hour!'
T: 'The Pipe.' ¶ No: 16 lines.

900. Jan. 9, 1748/9 *IA* ✳54.
'Now gloomy Winter shews his hoary head.'
T: 'On Winter.' ¶ No: 32 lines.
Note: Reprinted in the *Columbian Mag.*, I (Dec. 1798), 334.

901. Jan. 9, 1748/9 *IA* ✳54.
'Since Polly, you ev'ry Charm possess.'
T: 'Advice to Polly.' ¶ No: 12 lines.

902. Jan. 9, 1748/9 *IA* #54.
'*Thomas* loves *Mary* passing well,'.
T: 'The Perplex'd Lovers.' ¶ No: 32 lines.

903. Jan. 9, 1748/9 *NYG* #312, 1/2.
'In ancient Ages Characters Men found,'
T: 'Solution to the Aenigma inserted in our last.' ¶ No: 30 lines. ¶
A: 'By an inhabitant of New York.'

904. Jan. 11, 1749 *MG*.
'Love! thou divinest good below.'
T: 'A Fable. The Lawyer and Justice.' ¶ No: 118 lines.
Note: The poem praises Lord Chancellor Hardwick.

905. Jan. 16, 1748/9 *IA* #55.
'Vast Happiness enjoy thy gay Allies!'
T: 'Virtue addressing herself to Vice.' ¶ No: 34 lines.

906. Jan. 16, 1748/9 *NYG* #313, 1/2.
'In a thick Shade, the Owl, the Bat.'
T: 'A Burger to the late petty Scriblers, sends A Fable.' ¶ No: 17
lines.
Note: A reprint of no. 139.

907. Jan. 16, 1748/9 *NYG* #313, 4/2.
'*Katharine* is sometimes called *Kate*.'
T: —. ¶ No: 16 lines. ¶ A: 'I.S.'
Note: Dated 'Boston, Dec. 27th, 1748.'

908. Jan. 17, 1748/9 *PJ* #322.
'Thro' what romantick scenes does *Fancy* stray.'
T: 'On Dreams.' ¶ No: 96 lines.
Note: Reprinted, see nos. 915, 925.

909. Jan. 25, 1749 *MG*.
'Duty demands, the parent's voice.'
T: 'A Fable. The Wolf, the Sheep, and the Lamb.' ¶ No: 104 lines.
Note: Reprinted, no. 932.

910. Jan. 30, 1748/9 *NYWJ* #789, 1/2.
'As we appear unto Beholders.'
T: 'A Late Petition and Address poetically imitated.' ¶ No: 65 lines.
¶ A: 'Your Humble Trouts.'

911. Jan. 1749 *Gent Mag*, XIX, 38.
'Sylvius! let *Reason* rule thy breast.'
T: 'To Sylvius, on his Address to Lavinia.' ¶ No: 24 lines. ¶ A:
'Bostoniensis.'

912. Feb. 1, 1749 *MG*.
'Sixteen, d'ye say? Nay then tis time.'
T: 'A Fable. Hymen, and Death.' ¶ No: 52 lines.

913. Feb. 1, 1749 *MG*.
'Seek you to know what keeps the mind.'
T: 'The Ingredients of Contentment.'
Note: A reprint of no. 890.

914. Feb. 6, 1748/9 *NYG* #316, 1/1.
'Wou'd you pass thro' Life with Pleasures.'
T: 'The Tenth Ode of Horace's 2d Book, Paraphras'd.' ¶ No: 56
lines.
Note: On Gov. James Hamilton of Penna.

915. Feb. 20, 1749 *BEP* #706, 1/1-2.
'Thro' what romantick scenes does *Fancy* stray.'
Note: A reprint of no. 908.

916. Feb. 20, 1748/9 *NYG* #318, 1/2.
'Nor wings, nor feet, unto my share have fell.'
T: 'A Riddle.' ¶ No: 14 lines.

917. Feb. 28, 1748/9 *PG* #1055.
'As late I mus'd on fortune's ebb and flow.'
T: 'Luxury and Want, A Vision.' ¶ No: 64 lines.

918. Feb. 28, 1748/9 *PG* #1055.
'Not all that parent earth can give.'
T: 'Seeking for Happiness.' ¶ No: 33 lines.
Note: Crum N343.

919. Feb. 28, 1748/9 *PG* #1055.
'A Monarch in my rustic bower.'
T: 'The Hermit's Empire. A Sapphic Ode.' ¶ No: 27 lines.
Note: Reprinted, no. 1905 (in 24 lines).

920. Feb. 28, 1748/9 *PG* #1055.
'He's not the happy man, to whom is giv'n.'
T: 'The Happy Man.' ¶ No: 26 lines.
Note: Printed in Dodsley's *Collection of Poems* III (London, 1748),
321.

921. Feb. 28, 1748/9 *PG* #1055.
'Grant me, kind heav'n! the man that's brave.'
T: 'The Lady's Choice. An Ode.' ¶ No: 16 lines.
Note: Reprinted, no. 926.

922. Feb. 28, 1748/9 *PG* #1055.
  'To thee, O Lord, whose penetrating eye.'
  T: 'The Prayer of Henry IV. King of France Paraphras'd.' ¶ No: 27
  lines.

923. Mar. 6, 1749 *NYEP* #198, p. 1.
  'Long e'er the Sun usurp'd with flaming Light.'
  T: 'Aenigma.' ¶ No: 22 lines.

924. Mar. 6, 1749 *BEP* #708.
  'Ye Wise! instruct me to endure.'
  T: ['On Censure.'] ¶ No: 30 lines. ¶ A: [Jonathan Swift.]
  Note: 'From the *NYG*, Jan. 23, 1748-9' (not extant). See Harold
  Williams, *The Poems of Jonathan Swift*, II (Oxford, 1958), 413.
  Reprinted, no. 2017.

925. Mar. 13, 1749 *NYEP* #199, pp. 2-3.
  'Thro' what romantick Scenes doth Fancy stray.'
  Note: A reprint of no. 908.

926. Mar. 13, 1749 *NYEP* #199, p. 3.
  'Grant me, kind heav'n! The man that's brave.'
  Note: A reprint of no. 921.

927. Mar. 20, 1749 *SCG* #776, 1/1-2.
  'The Muse an Ode select prepares.'
  T: 'Ode for St. Patric's Day. Humbly inscrib'd to the President and
  Members of the Irish Society.' ¶ No: 64 lines. ¶ A: 'Joseph
  Dumbleton.'

928. Mar. 20, 1749 *SCG* #776, *Postscript*, 1/1.
  'Great Spirit hail!—Confusion's angry Sire,'.'
  T: 'A Rhapsody on Rum.' ¶ No: 28 lines. ¶ A: 'J. Dumbleton.'
  Note: Reprinted, no. 942; a longer version (53 lines) appeared in
  the *Virginia Gazette* (not extant) and was reprinted, see nos. 943,
  945, and 946. Reprinted in the *Cincinnati Literary Gazette*, XI,
  no. 6 (Aug. 7, 1824). The shorter version is reprinted in Silver-
  man, pp. 327-328.

929. Mar. 27, 1749 *NYG* #323, pp. 1 & 2.
  'Two sparks were earnest in Debate.'
  T: '[From the Virginia Gazette.] The Wager. A Tale.' ¶ No: 274
  lines. ¶ A: '(By a Gentleman of Virginia).' [William Dawson?]
  Note: Not extant in the *VG*. For a shorter reprint, see no. 1615,
  where the poem is called a 'Sequal to the Pig' (i.e., a sequel to no.
  485).

930. April 3, 1749 *NYEP* #202, 1/1.
'If Marriage gives a Happiness to Life.'
T: 'The Batchelors Wish.' ¶ No: 16 lines.

931. April 3, 1749 *NYEP* #202, 2/1.
'A Dog impleads a Sheep, pretends a Debt.'
T: 'A Fable, The Dog and Sheep.' ¶ No: 16 lines.

932. April 10, 1749 *NYEP* #203, 2/1–3/1.
'Duty demands the parent's voice.'
Note: A reprint of no. 909.

933. May 11, 1749 *BNL* #2447, 2/1.
'What gloomy Star beclouds this Western clime!'
T: 'A short Hint by Way of Lamentation on restoring Cape-Breton
to the French.' ¶ No: 34 lines. ¶ A: 'S. N.' [Samuel Niles ?]
Note: On the Rev. Samuel Niles, see the *DAB*.

934. May 22, 1749 *IA* #73.
'Thy Funeral Honours weeping Friends have paid.'
T: 'To the Memory of the Rev. Dr. Watts.' ¶ No: 38 lines. ¶ A:
'Moses Browne.'
Note: Because of Isaac Watts' numerous connections with America,
I have included this elegy. Browne was a prolific English poet.

935. June 12, 1749 *IA* #76.
'Thou'rt gone, dear Prop of my declining years.'
T: 'By a Lady on the Loss of her Son at Sea.' ¶ No: 61 lines. ¶ A:
'By a Lady.'
Note: Good verse.

936. June 26, 1749 *IA* #78.
'The hostile Fleet, Brave Warren! strait ingage.'
T: 'On the Motto under the Arms of The Honourable Sir Peter
Warren's Chariot.' ¶ No: 31 lines.
Note: 'Boston, June 24. I have attempted the Translation of the
Latin Verses which appeared in your No. 76 [June 12, 1749], and
now submit it to the Correction of your Readers.'

937. June 26, 1749 *IA* #78.
'The fiercest Animals that range the Wood.'
T: 'On the Supporters of the Arms of the Hon. Sir Peter Warren.
Two Sailors with drawn Hangers.' ¶ No: 16 lines.
Note: With prefatory note.

938. June 29, 1749 *PJ* #345, 1/1–2.
'From earth remov'd, in ev'ry virtue warm.'

T: 'On the Death of the Reverend Dr. Watts.' ¶ No: 82 lines. ¶ A: 'B. Sowden.'

Note: I have not been able to identify Sowden.

939. July 3, 1749 *IA* ⋕79.
'Panting for Air beneath the scorching Sun.'
T: 'On a Thunder Storm.' ¶ No: 20 lines.

940. July 10, 1749 *NYWJ* ⋕ 812, 1/2.
'As it is the Fashion in quiet times.'
T: [Riddle.] ¶ No: 24 lines.

941. Aug. 24, 1749 *PJ* ⋕353, 1/1.
'Within this doleful tomb, at length there lies interr'd.'
T: 'An Epitaph on the late worthy Gentleman, Thomas Applewhaite, Esq.; of Barbados, spoken Extempore, by a Stranger at his Funeral on hearing his Character.' ¶ No: 16 lines.
Note: Cf. no. 949. Reprinted in *IA*, Sept. 4, 1749.

942. Sept. 1749 *Gent Mag*, XIX, 424.
'Great spirit, hail!—confusion's angry fire.'
Note: Dated 'Carolina, J. Dumbleton.' A reprint of no. 928.

943. Oct. 26, 1749 *PG* ⋕1089.
'Great spirit hail!—Confusion's angry fire;'.
¶ No: 53 lines.
Note: 'From the Virginia Gazette.' '"Nec prius est extincta situs, quam vita bibendo." Ovid, Met. 1. 7.' An expanded version of no. 928.

944. Oct. 30, 1749 *NYG* ⋕354, 1/2.
'Nor Form nor Substance in my Being share.'
T: 'A Riddle.' ¶ No: 44 lines.

945. Nov. 1, 1749 *MG*, pp. 3–4.
'Great Spirit, hail!—confusion's angry fire.'
Note: 'From the Virginia Gazette.' An expanded version of no. 928.

946. Nov. 7, 1749 *BG* ⋕1548, 1/1.
'Great spirit hail!—Confusion's angry fire.'
Note: 'From the Virginia Gazette.' An expanded version of no. 928.

947. Nov. 8, 1749 *MG*.
'Miss Molly, a fam'd toast, was fair and young.'
T: 'The Specific: or, A Cordial for the Ladies.' ¶ No: 96 lines.

948. Nov. 21, 1749 *BG* ⋕1550, 1/1.
'Great Gooch! The Muse.'

T: 'To the Hon. Sir William Gooch, Bart. Governor of Virginia.' ¶
No: 44 lines.
Note: '(Occasion'd by His leaving the Colony).' This is probably reprinted from a no-longer extant *VG*.

949. Nov. 1749 *Lon Mag*, XVIII, 525.
'When his immortal part by heaven.'
T: 'An Epitaph design'd for the Honourable Thomas Applewhait,
Esq.; one of the Members of his Majesty's Council in Barbadoes,
who died there June 14, 1749.' ¶ No: 12 lines.
Note: 'The following Epitaph and Epigrams from Correspondents
in one of the Sugar Colonies.' Cf. no. 941.

950. Nov. 1749 *Lon Mag*, XVIII, 525.
'Rufus by nature form'd unfit.'
T: 'Epigram.' ¶ No: 8 lines.
Note: From the 'Sugar Colonies.' On a local minister. Cf. no. 951.

951. Nov. 1749 *Lon Mag*, XVIII, 525.
'In the desk or the pulpit, when Rufus appears.'
T: 'Another' [Epigram]. ¶ No: 6 lines.
Note: From the 'Sugar Colonies.' On a local minister. Cf. no. 950.

952. Dec. 25, 1749 *NYG* #362, 3/1.
'Inspiring Phoebus! warm my friendly Mind.'
T: [Epithalamium.] ¶ No: 12 lines. ¶ A: 'Philogamos.'
Note: 'B—lay' was just married. Cf. no. 954.

1750

953. Jan. 1, 1750 *NYEP* #241, 2/2.
'If 'mid the Joys that crown thy happy choice.'
T: 'To Mr. — on his late Marriage.' ¶ No: 58 lines.

954. Jan. 1, 1749/50 *NYG* #363.
'Since B—lay's Praise, the Poet has proclaim'd.'
T: [on 'A—ty's marriage]. ¶ No: 8 lines.
Note: Cf. no. 952.

955. Jan. 8, 1750 *SCG* #817, 1/1–2/1.
'In fair *Northumberland*, I trow.'
T: 'The Northern Miracle. A Tale.' ¶ No: 127 lines. ¶ A: 'J.
Dumbleton.'

956. Jan. 9, 1750 *BG* #1557, 2/3.
'What Happiness has Man, on Earth, to prove.'
T: [Epithalamion.] ¶ No: 22 lines.

Note: 'Last Thursday Evening [Jan. 4] was married at *Cambridge*, Mr. Benjamin Brandon, A. M. Merchant of this Town, to Miss *Elizabeth Foxcraft*, second Dau'ter of the Hon. Francis Foxcraft, Esq.'

957. Jan. 25, 1750 *BNL* #2490, 1/2.
'Illustrious George! By Heav'n's Discretion chose.'
T: 'Address to his Majesty, on the Settling of Nova Scotia.' ¶ No: 44 lines.
Note: Included in letter 'from a Person at Chebucta [N. S.], to his Friend in London.'

958. Feb. 1, 1750 *BNL* #2491, 1/1–2.
'Hail Brother Trade! What brought you here.'
T: 'A Touch of the Times.' ¶ No: 100 lines. ¶ A: 'C. B.'
Note: 'A Dialogue between Politicus, a B[*osto*]n Merchant, and Honestus, a Country Trader, and a quondam good Customer to Politicus.' The poem celebrates the death of 'Old Tenor' (paper money). For excerpts from the poem, and for an examination of the general background, see Herman J. Belz, 'Currency Reform in Colonial Massachusetts, 1749–1750,' *Essex Institute Historical Collections*, CIII (1967), 66–84, esp. p. 80.

959. Feb. 5, 1750 *BEP* #756.
'If a lawful Excuse, I can plead for my Muse.'
T: 'The Poor Man's Reflection on the approaching Dollars. Inscrib'd to the Rich.' ¶ No: 48 lines. ¶ A: 'Philanthropos.'
Note: Cf. no. 958. Reprinted, see no. 962.

960. Feb. 19, 1749/50 *NYWJ* #844, 4/1.
'My Brothers Uncle now I am.'
T: 'On a late Marriage at Nantucket.' ¶ No: 12 lines.
Note: 'I'm my own grand-paw' genre.

961. Feb. 26, 1750 *BPB* #795.
'In ev'ry Climate, Age and State.'
T: 'Lines were wrote just after the arrival of the money granted us by Parliament.' ¶ No: 36 lines.
Note: Reprinted, see no. 966.

962. Feb. 27, 1749/50 *NYWJ* #845, 4/1.
'If a lawful Excuse, I can plead, for my Muse.'
Note: Reprint of no. 959.

963. Feb. 1750 *Gent Mag*, XX, 84.
'Let's away to New Scotland, where Plenty sits queen.'
T: 'Nova Scotia. A New Ballad.' ¶ No: 16 lines.
Note: Only a portion of the poem is reprinted from the *Weekly Entertainer*. Reprinted, see no. 973.

964. Mar. 1, 1750 *BNL* #2495, 2/2.
'At Will, while *Fortune* turns the wheel.'
T: 'The Lottery.' ¶ No: 10 lines.

965. Mar. 5, 1749/50 *NYG* #372.
'Come, see this Edifice in Ruin lye.'
T: 'Lines on the Loss of the Charity School.' ¶ No: 29 lines. ¶ A: 'W.'

966. April 2, 1750 *NYWJ* #849, 4/1.
'In ev'ry Climate, Age and State.'
Note: A reprint of 961.

967. April 3, 1750 *BG* #1568, 1/3.
'The Loom, the Comb, the Spinning Wheel.'
T: ['An Almanac Observation—August 1702.'] ¶ No: 28 lines.
Note: 'The following honest Observation of one of our Country Men, were Published among us in the Year 1702. ...' On New England trade. Reprinted, see no. 1147, where a fuller title is given.

968. April 20, 1750 *NYWJ* #869.
'Argo, that ship renown'd of ancient Greece.'
T: 'On the Launching of the British Buss, (or Vessel) built for the Herring Fishery.' ¶ No: 22 lines.

969. April 23, 1750 *BEP* #767, 4/2.
'As many People now-a-days.'
T: 'Dream.' ¶ No: 38 lines. ¶ A: 'V. D.' [Joseph Green].
Note: Cf., *BEP*, May 27, 1754; BEP May 12, 1755. Reprinted, see no. 970. Green seems to satirize a recent theatrical performance. Subsequent repetition of the pseudonym 'V. D.' reveals that the author is Green. Cf. nos. 975, 976, 990, and 997.

970. May 9, 1750 *NYWJ* #854, 4/1.
'As many People now-a-days.'
Note: A reprint of no. 969.

971. May 1750 *Lon Mag*, XIX, 197.
'Lo! from your solitary, sad recess.'
T: 'A Monody, as a Tribute to the Memory of a most tender Mother, the Hon. Mrs. Hannah Lee, late excellent Wife of the Hon. Thomas Lee, Esq.; President of his Majesty's Council, and Commander in Chief in Virginia.' ¶ No: 29 lines. ¶ A: [Philip Ludwell Lee.]
Note: Poor verse. For authorship, see Burton J. Hendrick, *The Lees of Virginia* (New York, 1935), p. 88.

972. June 4, 1750 *NYWJ* #858, 4/1.
'In this judicious Piece, the Work of Years.'
T: 'On Reading the Rev. Mr. Grove's System of Moral Philosophy.'
¶ A: 'J. H.'
Note: Crum I1567. On Henry Grove (1684–1738), see the account in Caroline Robbins, *The Eighteenth-Century Commonwealthman* (Cambridge, Mass., 1959), pp. 251–254.

973. June 18, 1750 *NYEP* #265, 3/1.
'Let's away to New-Scotland, where plenty sits queen.'
T: 'Nova-Scotia.' (Part of a new Ballad. To the Tune of John and the Abbott of Canterbury.)
Note: A reprint of no. 963.

974. June 18, 1750 *NYWJ* #863, 3/2.
'What vain conceit mistaken mortal fires.'
T: 'On the universality and impartiality of Death. To Gripus.' ¶ A: 'T. S.'

975. July 30, 1750 *BPB* #816.
'You're so choice of your wine.'
T: 'To V. D.' [Joseph Green]. ¶ No: 42 lines. ¶ A: 'H—k.'
Note: Dated 'July 26th 1750 by H—k'; mentions [Mather] B[yles]. MS copy in Smith-Carter Papers, Mass. Hist. Soc.; another MS poem 'To V. D.' is in Smith-Carter Papers, which apologizes to 'V. D.': first line 'You take amiss, I understand.' For Green's reply, see no. 976. Cf. nos. 969, 976. I have not yet been able to identify 'H—k.'

976. July 31, 1750 *BG* #1585, 1/3.
'The Poet is mad.'
T: 'To the POET in the Post Boy, in his own Style.' ¶ No: 24 lines.
¶ A: 'J. G—ne' [Joseph Greene].
Note: A contemporary manuscript hand added *ree*, thus identifying the author as Joseph Green[e]. A reply to no. 975. The author of no. 975 apologized, see note to no. 975.

977. July 1750 *Gent Mag*, XX, 324.
'Accept, Dear Ma'am, the fabled lay.'
T: 'And Please the PIGS, A Tale. Address'd to a Lady of Jamaica, occasion'd by a late Incident there.' ¶ No: 96 lines. ¶ A: 'Porcus.' [Rev. John Rhudde].
Note: Dated 'Jamaica, Parish of St. Mary.' Rhudde was currently Rector of St. Mary's: see no. 1221.

978. Sept. 24, 1750 *NYWJ* #874, 1/1–2/1.
'Great Blest Master-Printer come.'

T: 'A Contemplation upon the Mystery of Man's Regeneration, in Allusion to the Mystery of Printing.' ¶ No: 112 lines.

Note: On Jan. 24, 1750, the *MG* printed an essay on the mysteries of printing, signed 'Nic. Turntype,' which is really a satire on the ceremonies and 'mysteries' of religion. The essay was reprinted in the *NYWJ* for Mar. 5, 1750, and evidently inspired the above poem.

979. Oct. 8, 1750 *NYWJ* #876, 1/1–2.
'Scarce in an Age one Twigg of Laurel grows.'
T: [Attack on James Porterfield.] ¶ No: 42 lines. ¶ A: [William Smith, Jr.]
Note: Sent in by–'M.' Refers to 'Cottylo,' who is 'A Muse of Mr. P[*orterfiel*]d's Invention, see his *Breeches*, Pag. 15, ult.' This is probably by the author who wrote *Some Critical Observations upon a late Poem, entitled, The Breeches, written by James Porterfield, A. B.* (New York, 1750); Evans 6611. See Porterfield's reply, no. 980. According to Beverley McAnear, William Smith, Jr., of New York, wrote *Some Critical Observations*: 'American Imprints Concerning King's College,' *Papers of the Bibliographical Society of America*, XLIV (1950), 306–307n.

980. Oct. 8, 1750 *NYWJ* #876, 1/2–2/1.
'Ye paulty scriblers of a foggy clime.'
T: [Attack on C—] [c–m–n–s?] ¶ No: 55 lines. ¶ A: 'J. P.' [James Porterfield].
Note: 'What right have ye to that auspicious name?/No more than A–s–q has to that of Doctor,/Or S–m–t to that of councillor or proctor,/No more than C–o–l–y to a physician;/No more than C–m–n–s to that of saint.' For the background, see no. 979. *Some Critical Observations* (see no. 979) reveals that Porterfield was an Irishman who had recently come to New York, that he had previously published a poem entitled *The Petticoat*, and that his poem, *The Breeches* (New York, 1749—no copy known) satirized the governor and principal officers in Jamaica.

981. Oct. 22, 1750 *NYEP* # 283, 3/1.
'When Life hath fail'd one; (and Life's but a Bubble!).'
T: 'An Epitaph, Upon *Thomas Turny* late Sweeper of Yale-College in New-Haven.' ¶ No: 12 lines.
Note: An imitation of no. 202. Reprinted, see no. 986.

982. Oct. 22, 1750 *NYWJ* #878, 1/2.
'Early, this morn, I went to bed.'
No: 36 lines. ¶ A: 'R. D.'
Note: Sent in by 'X.' Cf. no. 657.

983. Oct. 25, 1750 *BNL* #2528, 2/1.
'Shall boastful Pomp, the high imperial Name.'
T: 'Lines to the Memory of the brave and much lamented Capts. Barthlo and How.' ¶ No: 34 lines. ¶ A: 'Philopatria.'
Note: On Capt. Edward How, see L. H. Gipson, *British Empire*, V, 196.

984. Oct. 1750 *Lon Mag*, XIX, 472.
'While Britain complains of neutrality broke.'
T: 'Crambo Verses.' ¶ No: 16 lines.
Note: From the West Indies.

985. Nov. 2, 1750 *BNL* #2529, 2/1.
'The wish'd Supports of Wealth are vain.'
T: From Martial: '*Callidus effracta Nummos fur auferat Arca.* Imitated.' ¶ No: 18 lines.
Note: Dated 'Boston, October 30, 1750.'

986. Nov. 19, 1750 *BEP* #797, 2/1.
'When Life hath fail'd one; (and Life's but a Bubble!).'
Note: A reprint of 981.

987. Nov. 1750 *Scots Mag*, XII, 519–520.
'Ye lovely maids! whose yet unpractis'd hearts.'
T: 'The Art of Coquetery.' ¶ A: 'By *Mrs*. Charlotte Lennox.'

988. Nov. 1750 *Universal Mag*, VII, 232.
'A Trout, the plumpest in the Tide.'
T: 'The Trout, a Fable.' ¶ No: 28 lines. ¶ A: 'S[amuel] Boyce.'
Note: Reprinted, see no. 1117. Copied in Benjamin Wadsworth's Commonplace Book (Harvard MS: Am 967), p. 3. Boyce was a well-known English poet. See *CBEL*, II, 354.

989. Dec. 31, 1750 *NYG*.
'To wish you Happy thro' the coming Year.'
T: 'The Yearly Verses of the Printer's Lads, who carry the NY Gazette reviv'd ...'

1751

990. Jan. 7, 1751 *BEP* #804, 1/1.
'Pray Master CLIO now take care.'
T: 'To Mr. CLIO, at North-Hampton, in Defence of Masonry.' ¶ No: 70 lines. ¶ A: 'A M–s–n.' [Joseph Green?]
Note: Dated 'Boston, Jan. 1, 1750–1.' A scurrilous cartoon (the first illustration to accompany a newspaper poem) prefaces the poem.

A satire on masonry. Contemporary manuscript copies of no. 990 and no. 997 are in the Am. Antiq. Soc. copy of Joseph Green, *Entertainment for a Winter's Evening* (Boston [1750]). Although Joseph Green directly denied writing this satire in a notice in the *BPB*, January 14, 1751, the reply by 'Clio' (see no. 997) attributed it to him. Cf. no. 1041.

991. Jan. 7, 1750–1 *NYG* #416, 1/2.
'To day Man's dress'd in gold and silver bright.'
T: 'The difference between Today and Tomorrow.' ¶ No: 20 lines.
Note: Reprinted, see nos. 998, 999, 1004. Crum T2930.

992. Jan. 9, 1751 *MG*.
'Geron, a jovial Monk, a Tipling Blade.'
T: 'Old Geron and his Maid Margery; or, the Leak discover'd. A Tale.' ¶ No: 41 lines.

993. Jan. 14, 1750–1 *NYG* #417, 1/1.
'Though long extinguish'd the poetic Fire.'
T: 'On the Marriage of the Rev'd Mr. Cumming to Mrs. Dubois.' ¶ No: 52 lines.

994. Jan. 16, 1751 *MG*.
'Of two Battalions set in Rank and File.'
T: 'The Table-Battle; or, the Canonical Gamesters. A Tragi-Comic Tale.' ¶ No: 214 lines.

995. Jan. 16, 1751 *MG*.
'The Members of the *ancient* Tuesday Club.'
T: '*LUGUBRIS CANTUS*. In imitation of *Spencer*, Author of *The Fairy Queen*.' ¶ No: 48 lines. ¶ A: [Jonas Green, Dr. Alexander Hamilton, *et al.*]
Note: Prefatory note: 'We hope our Readers will not be displeased with the following mournful, composed last Night in the ancient Tuesday Club in this City, bewailing the present lamentable Indisposition of their worthy President.' Dr. Alexander Hamilton noted that this poem was by the 'conjoint muses' of the Tuesday Club.

996. Jan. 23, 1751 *MG*.
'What happy Hours the Man enjoys.'
T: [Retirement theme.] ¶ No: 40 lines.
Note: Reprinted, see no. 1017.

997. Jan. 24, 1751 *BNL* #5346, 2/1.
'When Masons write in Masons Praise.'
T: To 'Mr. Vini Doctor.' [i.e., to Joseph Green.] ¶ No: 12 lines. ¶ A: 'Clio.'
Note: Dated 'Northampton, Jan. 21st, 1750, 1.' A reply to no. 990.

998. Jan. 29, 1750–1 *PG* #1155.
'Today Man's dress'd in gold and silver bright.'
Note: A reprint of 991.

999. Jan. 29, 1750/1 *PJ* #428.
'Today man's dress'd in gold and silver bright.'
Note: A reprint of 991.

1000. Feb. 4, 1750/1 *NYWJ* #1011, 2/2–3/2.
'Of publick use I am, by nature free.'
T: 'Enigma.' ¶ No: 38 lines. ¶ A: 'S. H.'

1001. Feb. 7, 1750/1 *VG*.
'Active Spark of heav'nly Fire.'
No: 52 lines.
Note: Local, sent with letter.

1002. Feb. 14, 1750/1 *VG*.
'Love, the most fav'rite Gift design'd.'
T: 'Love and Honour.' ¶ No: 92 lines. ¶ A: 'By a Gentleman of
Virginia' [William Dawson?].
Note: Although Dawson used the pseudonym 'A Gentleman of
Virginia,' cf. no. 1042.

1003. Feb. 18, 1751 *NYEP* #200, 1/1.
'A Pipe of strong and sparkling Wine.'
T: 'A Fable.' ¶ No: 52 lines. ¶ A: 'Withers Secundus.'
Note: An imitation of George Withers.

1004. Feb. 20, 1751 *MG*.
'To Day Man's dress'd in Gold and Silver bright.'
Note: A reprint of 991.

1005. Feb. 26, 1750/1 *PJ* #432.
'Harmonious maids, assist my artless flame.'
T: 'The Hermit.' ¶ No: 22 lines.

1006. Feb. 26, 1750/1 *PJ* #432.
'Whilst anxious mortals strive in vain.'
T: 'No True Felicity below.' ¶ No: 54 lines.

1007. Feb. 1751 *Gent Mag*, XXI, 86.
'Insatiate fiend! Thy purple daughter cease.'
T: 'On the Smallpox.' ¶ No: 94 lines.
Note: 'Norwich, February 20.' Quotes Pope.

1008. Mar. 4, 1751 *NYEP* #202, 1/1–2.
'Friend, when a rival Poem you peruse.'

T: 'To the Critic.' ¶ No: 74 lines. ¶ A: 'D. H.'
Note: 'The Critic' is Rev. Aaron Burr, Pres. of Princeton. The
author seems to be a student there.

1009. Mar. 4, 1751 *SCG* ♯877, 1/2.
'It must be so—Milton, thou reas'nest well.'
T: 'The Maid's Soliloquy.' ¶ No: 30 lines. ¶ A: 'a Lady in this
Province.'
Note: Cf. nos. 872, 1923A.

1010. Mar. 5, 1751 *BG* ♯ 1616, 1/1.
'If ever I should change my State of Life.'
T: 'The Choice.' ¶ No: 42 lines. ¶ A: 'Philander' ['a young and
rising genius'].
Note: Dated 'Feb. 12, 1750.'

1011. Mar. 7, 1750/1 *VG*.
'From dear Chloe, I stole two Kisses in Play.'
T: ['Epigram on the Ladies.'] ¶ No: 4 lines. ¶ A: 'T. T.'
Note: Cf. 1015, from where I have taken the title. 'T. T.' is also the
author of 1013, where he reveals that he has just come from
England. He is very probably the 'Dr. T. T.' who wrote no. 1125,
and I speculate there that he may be Dr. Thomas Thornton. Cf.
nos. 1015, 1018.

1012. Mar. 7, 1750/1 *VG*.
'Sing, O my Muse (as well you may).'
T: 'Homeri Ilias, Lib 1.' ¶ No: 118 lines. ¶ A: 'Philomeros.'
Note: Local.

1013. Mar. 7, 1750/1 *VG*.
'The Moon grows red, pale, big, and walks by Night.'
T: 'The Moon is a Woman. Translated.' ¶ No: 4 lines (with the
Latin). ¶ A: 'T. T.'
Note: Dated 'York, March 4th, 1750–1.' Prefatory note: 'Saturday
I arrived here from England, and beyond all Expectation my In-
tellectual Appetite was as elegantly feasted by your last Paper, as
my Corporal was by Mr. J. Mitchell.' This probably refers to Dr.
John Mitchell (d. 1768), for whom, see the *DAB*. For 'T. T.',
see no. 1011.

1014. Mar. 7, 1750/1 *VG*.
'Ye Britons be merry, because you've grown wise.'
T: 'A New Ballad on the British Herring Fishery.' ¶ No: 60 lines.
Note: Crum Y11.

1015. Mar. 14, 1750/1 *VG*.
'When Daphne o'er the Meadows fled.'

T: 'Daphne. To Dr. T. T. occasioned by his Epigram on the Ladies, *supposed* to be written after a Dissappointment.' ¶ No: 12 lines.
Note: This probably refers to no. 1011, but may refer to no. 1013.

1017. Mar. 26, 1751 *BG* #1619, 1/1–2.
'What happy Hours the Man enjoys.'
Note: A reprint of no. 996.

1018. Mar. 28, 1751 *VG*.
'Since Worms your Study wholly now engage.'
T: 'Epistle to Dr. — in Williamsburg, sent with De Gol's disserta-
tion on Worms, when the Author was sick.' ¶ No: 62 lines.
Note: Probably addressed to Dr. T. T. (Cf. nos. 1011, 1013, and
1015).

1019. April 8, 1751 *SCG* #882, 1/1–2.
'Shine thou bright Sun, with a distinguish'd Ray.'
T: [Religious verse]. ¶ No: 84 lines.

1020. April 9, 1752 *MG*.
'It was, as learn'd Traditions say.'
T: 'The Sparrow and the Dove. A Fable.' ¶ No: 378 lines.

1021. April 15, 1751 *SCG* #883, 1/1.
'Calmly repos'd upon a pleasant Green.'
Note: Prefatory note by 'F— S—.' A reprint of no. 892.

1022. April 18, 1751 *VG*.
'Exalted Muse, in mystic lays.'
T: 'An Ode' [on Masons]. ¶ No: 24 lines. ¶ A: 'N. S.'
Note: Dated 'Williamsburg, April 5, 1751.' Prefatory letter prais-
ing masons. This masonic poem has been reprinted by Lyon G.
Tyler, 'Williamsburg Lodge of Masons,' *William and Mary
Quart.*, 1st ser., I (1892), 3; and by George Eldridge Kidd, *Early
Freemasonry in Williamsburg, Virginia* (Richmond, 1957), pp. 1–3.

1023. April 18, 1751 *VG*.
'Soft Babe! sweet Image of a harmless Mind.'
T: 'Verses wrote by a Gentleman just before his going to Prison on
seeing his Child asleep in its Cradle.' ¶ No: 57 lines.
Note: Reprinted, no. 1124, and reprinted in the *Gazette of the U.S.*,
II (May, 1790), 672.

1024. April 23, 1752 *MG*.
'The Man, who seeks to win the Fair.'
T: 'The Panther, the Horse, and other Beasts. A Fable.' ¶ No: 120
lines.

1025. April 25, 1751 *VG.*
    'With Heart untouch'd, and Look serene.'
    T: 'Love without Sight.'

1026. May 6, 1751 *SCG* #886, 1/1.
    'Apollo's Sons, whene'er the Wealthy die.'
    T: 'To the Memory of a much lov'd Friend Mrs. Hannah Dale
    (Relict of Doctor Dale) who died the 9th of April, 1751, aged 29
    Years.' ¶ No: 48 lines. ¶ A: 'H— S—.'
    Note: '(written by a Lady of her Acquaintance).' The widow of Dr.
    Thomas Dale. See no. 1029 for a more correct version.

1027. May 6, 1751 *SCG* #886, 1/2.
    'Fairest Nymph where all are fair.'
    T: 'To Miss M— C—.' ¶ No: 32 lines. ¶ A: 'A. B.'

1028. May 6, 1751 *SCG* #886, 2/1.
    'When *Pharoah's* Pride brought down on Egypt's Land.'
    T: 'To the Printer.' ¶ No: 12 lines. ¶ A: 'K. X.'

1029. May 13, 1751 *SCG* #887, 3/1–2.
    'Apollo's Sons, whene'er the Wealthy die.'
    T: 'The Verses upon Mrs. Dale's Death, inserted in our last, having
    been very much varied from the Original, by the Gentleman who
    delivered the copy to the Printer, the Lady who wrote them is ap-
    prehensive her Intention and Meaning are perverted from a true
    copy, Viz.' ¶ No: 50 lines. ¶ A: 'H— S—.'
    Note: Corrected version of no. 1026.

1030. May 16, 1751 *VG.*
    'I sicken at the Nonsense of the Croud.'
    T: 'Modern Conversation.' ¶ No: 39 lines. ¶ A: 'Miso-Ochlos.'
    Note: 'The following well-merited, tho' poorly written Burlesque.'

1031. May 20, 1751 *NYEP* #213, 3/1–2.
    'Britain, lament! How great thy Cause of Woe.'
    T: 'An Elegy, on the Death of His Royal Highness Frederick Lewis,
    Prince of Wales; Who departed this Life on Wednesday, March
    20, 1751, about eleven at Night.' ¶ No: 33 lines.

1032. May 30, 1751 *VG.*
    'Old Battle-array, big with Horror is fled.'
    T: 'A Pipe of Tobacco: A New Year's Ode.' ¶ No: 36 lines. ¶ A:
    [Isaac H. Browne.]
    Note: Printed in Dodsley, II, 280.

1033. June 18, 1751 *BG* #1631, 1/1.
    'While grov'ling *Bards* presume to sing.'

T: 'Casimire Lyric. Lib 4. Ode 7. Jessea quisquis reddere **Carmina** Audit &c.' ¶ No: 64 lines. ¶ A: 'Philo Muses.'

1034. June 24, 1751 *BPB* ✳861.
'While Zephyr softly waves his Wings.'
T: 'Summer From the Italian of Vivaldi's Seasons.' ¶ No: 14 lines.
Note: Cf. no. 1088.

1035. July 4, 1751 *VG*.
'Now when the War of Elements is o'er.'
T: ['A Description of a Storm, May 9, 1751.'] ¶ No: 128 lines. ¶ A:
[Samuel Davies.]
Note: Dated 'Hanover, May 10, 1751.' Reprinted in Samuel Davies,
Miscellaneous Poems (Williamsburg, 1752), pp. 127–131, and in
Richard Beale Davis, ed., *Collected Poems of Samuel Davies*
(Gainesville, Fla., 1968), pp. 127–131.

1036. July 8, 1751 *NYG* ✳442, 1/1.
'How shall the Muse find Language to express.'
T: 'Upon the Death of the Late Mr. — — of blessed Memory.' ¶
No: 65 lines. ¶ A: 'A. B.'
Note: The subject of poem was a political leader.

1037. July 9, 1751 *BG* ✳1634, 2/1.
'Thrice happy were the Golden Days.'
T: The Spouse of Christ returning to her first Love. An Hymn. ¶
No: 36 lines. ¶ A: 'Compos'd (as 'tis tho't) by a Lady in New
England.'

1038. July 18, 1751 *PJ* ✳452, 2/2.
'That *Sawney* might kill two Birds with one Stone.'
T: 'On reading a vile Piece of Scurrility in a late Performance, en-
titled, *A Defence of Dr. Thomson.*' ¶ No: 3 lines.
Note: An attack on Dr. Alexander Hamilton, cf. no. 1039.

1039. July 18, 1751 *PJ* ✳452, 2/2.
'That your Work does abound.'
T: 'To Dr. Hamilton, on his Defence of Dr. Thomson.' ¶ No: 6
lines.
Note: Cf. no. 1038.

1040. July 29, 1751 *NYEP* ✳223, 3/2.
'Here lies, and here's likely to lie, after all the Trouble.'
T: 'On Col—l P—d—ns Lottery.' ¶ No: 12 lines.

1041. Aug. 22, 1751 *BNL* ✳2565, 1/1.
'When first from Nothing at th' Almighty's Call.'

T: 'An address to the Masons at Hallifax.' ¶ No: 63 lines. ¶ A: 'Clio. By a Brother.'

Note: Dated 'Northampton, Aug. 16, 1751.' Cf. nos. 990 and 997.

1042. Aug. 24, 1751 *VG*.

'To You, whose comprehensive Mind.'

T: 'Modern Infidelity: On the Principles of Atheism Exposed and Refuted. A Poem. Inscribed to a Friend.' ¶ No: 284 lines. ¶ A: 'By a Gentleman of Virginia, lately deceas'd.'

Note: Since William Dawson did not die until July 20, 1752 (see the *VG* July 24, 1752), this poem cannot be by him and casts doubt upon the identification of other poems by 'a Gentleman of Virginia' as Dawson's.

1043. Aug. 26, 1751 *BEP* ♯836, 1/2–2/1.

'For you, dear Sir, the Muse unus'd to sing.'

T: 'A Consolatory Letter to a near Relative, on the Death of his Agreeable Consort, July 22, 1751.' ¶ No: 37 lines. ¶ A: [Rev. John Adams.]

Note: Dated 'Annapolis-Royal.' 'Martha' was the woman's name. Reprinted from John Adam's *Poems* (Boston, 1745), pp. 88–94; Evans 5527.

1044. Sept. 16, 1751 *NYG* ♯452, 1/1.

'Fame is a publick Mistress none enjoys.'

T: 'To Philanthropos.' ¶ No: 8 lines.

Note: 'Philanthropos' also has an article in the *NYG* for Sept. 2.

1045. Sept. 16, 1751 *SCG* ♯905, 2/1.

'My good old friend! accept from me.'

T: 'Receipt for an Asthima.' ¶ No: 52 lines.

1046. Sept. 23, 1751 *BEP* ♯841, 2/1.

'First lay some Onions to keep the Pork from burning.'

T: 'Directions for making a Chouder.' ¶ No: 14 lines.

Note: Reprinted, see no. 1048.

1047. Sept. 23, 1751 *SCG* ♯906, 1/1–2.

'Beneath an aged *holm* [!]; whose arms had made.'

T: 'Pastoral Elegy, on a young Gentleman lately deceased.' ¶ No: 79 lines.

Note: In the *SCG* for Oct. 3, there are several corrections of this printing.

1048. Sept. 30, 1751 *NYEP* ♯232, 3/2.

'First lay some Onions to keep the Pork from burning.'

Note: A reprint of 1046.

1049. Oct. 3, 1751 *SCG* ⚹907, 2/1.
  'Port Royal plains, let ever balmy dew.'
  T: 'Epitaph.' ¶ No: 14 lines. ¶ A: 'Port Royal.'

1050. Oct. 7, 1751 *SCG* ⚹908, 2/1–2.
  'Who can describe the horrors of that night.'
  T: 'Distress & Deliverance, Sept. 16, 1751.' ¶ No: 40 lines. ¶ A:
    'Philagathus.'
  Note: Accompanies a news note about the distress of the ship *Great
    Britain*, Captain James Hume. Although part of the page of the
    SCG is missing, the poem is complete in the reprint, no. 1064A.
    For 'Philagathus,' see no. 779.

1051. Oct. 14, 1751 *NYG* ⚹456, 1/2.
  'A Gentleman of a spotless Character.'
  T: 'Sacred to the Memory of the Rev. Gualterius Dubois.' ¶ No: 71
    lines [prose epitaph].
  Note: Reprinted, see nos. 1052, 1576.

1052. Oct. 24, 1751 *BNL* ⚹2574, 1/2.
  'A Gentleman of a spotless Character.'
  Note: A reprint of no. 1051.

1053. Oct. 1751 *Universal Mag*, XXIX, 214.
  'When zephyrs gently curl the azure main.'
  T: 'Idyllium V. of Moschus: The Choice.' ¶ No: 12 lines.

1054. Dec. 17, 1751 *PJ* ⚹474, 1/1–2.
  'Thrice happy he, whom providence has plac'd.'
  T: 'On a Country Life.' ¶ No: 84 lines.

1752

1055. Jan. 2, 1751/2 *VG*.
  'The Beau, with his delicate Womanish Face.'
  T: 'Chloe's Choice. A new Song.' ¶ No: 16 lines.

1056. Jan. 17, 1751/2 *VG*.
  'Now had the Son of Jove mature, attain'd.'
  T: 'The Choice of Hercules.' ¶ No: 270 lines. ¶ A: [Robert Lowth.]
  Note: From Xenophon, *Memorable things of Socrates* ... 'here cloath'd
    in a new Dress by a very eminent Hand ...' Printed in Dodsley,
    III, 7.

1057. Jan. 23, 1752 *BNL* ⚹2587, 2/2.
  'Come from the House of Grief, let us my Friend.'

T: [Elegy of Mrs. Catharine (née Dudley) Dummer, widow of William Dummer.] ¶ No: 34 lines.

Note: Dated 'Boston, Jan. 20, 1752.'

1058. Jan. 30, 1751/2 *VG.*
'While thro' Life's Thorney Road I go.'
T: 'The Journey of Life.' ¶ No: 32 lines.

1059. Jan. 1752 *Lon Mag,* XXI, 40.
'Is Lee snatch'd from us ? Is his soul then fled ?'
T: 'An Elegiack Monody: Upon hearing of the Death of the Hon. Thomas Lee, Esq.; Commander in Chief and President of his Majesty's Council in Virginia. By an acquaintance lately come over from thence.' ¶ No: 38 lines. ¶ A: [Edward Kimber ?]

1060. Feb. 10, 1752 *NYG* #473, p. 2.
'It must be so—*Machiavel* reasons well.'
T: 'A Political Soliloquy. An imitation of Mr. Addison's Cato. Occasioned by the present Party Animosities.' ¶ No: 62 lines. ¶ A: 'By an impartial Hand.'

1061. Feb. 17, 1752 *NYG* #474, 1/2–3.
'Come on ye Critics, find one Fault who dare.'
T: 'To the most profound Genius, The Author of the incomprable incomprehensible What-d'ye-call-it, said to have been lately acted at the New Zale van Clajapham, in the Out Ward of the City of New-York; and part of it actually publish'd in the New York Gazette: Feb. 3, 1752.' ¶ No: 89 lines. ¶ A: [Charles Sackville, Earl of Dorset.]

Note: The first fourteen lines are from Dorset's 'Satire on Edward Howard's *British Princes,* 1669.' On Sackville (1638–1706), see *CBEL,* II, 280, and David M. Vieth, *Attribution in Restoration Poetry* (New Haven, 1963), pp. 252, 442. Crum C569. An enjoyable local satire, echoing Pope's *Dunciad!*

1062. Mar. 10, 1751/2 *PG.*
'Along the Road, as , in an open Chair.'
T: 'The Open Chair, On meeting a fine old Gentleman, and a very fair young Lady, his Daughter, in the Road, in a hard Frost.' ¶ No: 12 lines. ¶ A: 'T. P.' (sent in with 2 other poems, by 'T. P.'). [Provost William Smith ?]

Note: 'The Frost seems going off; I wish you Joy of its Departure, for I fancy you have been somewhat scarce of Occurrences by it. I have lately met with these Epigrams, which I send you, which seem, partly at least owing to the Frost. *We* have had *Lapland* Odes, and there is a Song on the feather'd Snow descending, but these Pieces look to have a new Turn, and may pass, especially in a Dearth of New, for an *American* curiosity; if you think, so they are at your Service for the Publick, and perhaps I may send you e'er long some other Pieces of the same Writer's.' Dated February 15, 1752. Cf. nos. 1063 & 1064. Reprinted, see no. 1065. Since Provost William Smith wrote no. 1068 (which was also sent in by 'T. P.'), he is probably the author of these three poems (nos. 1062, 1063, 1064). This surmise gains some support from the *NYG*'s reprinting of these poems, for the *NYG* was currently publishing Smith's works.

1063. Mar. 10, 1751/2 *PG* ♯1213.
'In other Lands, oft Times their airing Fair.'
T: 'The Caution.' ¶ No: 12 lines. ¶ A: 'T. P.' [Provost William Smith?]
Note: Cf. no. 1062. Reprinted, no. 1066.

1064. Mar. 10, 1751/2 *PG*.
'Lucinda, what d'you call this frosty Jaunt.'
T: 'To Lucinda.' ¶ No: 6 lines. ¶ A: 'T. P.' [Provost William Smith?]
Note: Cf. no. 1062. Reprinted, see no. 1067.

1064A. Mar. 16, 1752 *BEP* ♯865, 2/1.
'Who can describe the horrors of that night.'
Note: A reprint of no. 1050.

1065. Mar. 16, 1752 *NYG* ♯478, 2/2.
'Along the Road, as in an open Chair.'
Note: A reprint of 1062.

1066. Mar. 16, 1752 *NYG* ♯478, 2/2.
'In other Lands, oft Times their airing Fair.'
Note: A reprint of 1063.

1067. Mar. 16, 1752 *NYG* ♯478, 2/2.
'Lucinda, what d'you call this frosty Jaunt.'
Note: A reprint of 1064.

1068. Mar. 24, 1751/2 *PG* ♯1215.
'Some Birds (it is no News to tell).'
T: 'The Mock Bird and Red Bird; A Fable.' ¶ No: 60 lines. ¶ A: [Provost William Smith.]
Note: Sent in with a long letter, dated Feb. 22, 1752, by 'T. P.,' who calls the poem 'an American Fable.' Sabin 84624 attributes the poem to Smith, who signed at least one of his publications 'by the author of the American Fables.' See no. 1129. Reprinted, nos. 1070, 1071.

1069. Mar. 30, 1752 *NYG* #480, 3/1.
'If Aught, fair Maid: could add new Grace.'
T: 'An extempore Ode on the modest Behaviour and agreeable Con-
fession of a young Pair during the Solemnizing of their Marriage.'
¶ No: 28 lines. ¶ A: [Provost William Smith?]
Note: Dated 'Hampstead Plains, March 26, 1752.' On the 'marriage
of Mr. David Algeo, Merchant, in New York, and Miss Polly
Martin, Daughter to *Josiah Martin*, Esq.; of *Queens* County.'
William Smith, future Provost of the Philadelphia Academy, was
at this time a tutor to Josiah Martin's sons.

1070. April 6, 1752 *NYG* #481, 1/1–3.
'Some Birds, (it is not News to tell.)'
Note: A reprint of 1068.

1071. April 13, 1752 *BPB* #903, 1/1.
'Some Birds, (it is no News to tell).'
Note: 'From the *PG*, 24' with essay, A reprint of 1068.

1072. April 16, 1752 *PG* #1218.
'Hark—how the Groves and Woods resound.'
T: 'On the Spring.' ¶ No: 32 lines. ¶ A: 'T. B.'
Note: Cf. 1082.

1072A. April 17, 1752 *VG*, 2/1–2.
'That your Petitioner was born, and bred at Home in *Scotland*, a
Presbyterian true Blue.'
T: 'To their H[onour]s.' ¶ No: 43 lines. ¶ A: [Rev. John Robertson?]
Note: This is a travesty of an imagined speech by the Rev. Samuel
Davies before the General Court of Virginia. On Robertson and
his quarrel with Davies, see Craig Gilborn, 'Samuel Davies'
Sacred Muse,' *Jo. of Presbyterian Hist.*, XLI (1963), 63–79. Cf.
nos. 1077, 1079, 1080, 1085.

1073. April 30, 1752 *PG* #7220.
'Tis not yet Day, and sure it must be nigh.'
T: 'On Light.' ¶ No: 76 lines.
Note: Religious, but good.

1074. May 7, 1752 *PJ* #444, 3/1.
'A Wretch who Triumphs o'er her Neighbours Woe.'
T: 'A Character of a very sower looking, ill-natur'd Woman, who
was very busy in promoting an intended Insult to the Ladies.' ¶
No: 26 lines.

1075. May 11, 1752 *MG* #486, 1/1–3.
'Dear Charmers! with melodious Strains.'

T: 'Vernal Advice, Or, An Anacreontic Ballad, for the Month of May, Address'd to the Ladies.' ¶ No: 112 lines. ¶ A: 'Strephon.'

Note: Dated 'Queens County, May 1, 1752,' with a good essay.

1076. May 11, 1752 *NYG* ⋕486, 2/1–3.

'Trees once could speak, some Authors say.'

T: 'Peach-Tree: An American Fable.' ¶ No: 78 lines. ¶ A: [*Provost* William Smith.]

Note: Cf. No. 1129 for authorship.

1077. May 15, 1752 *VG*.

'Critics in Verse, as Squibs on Triumphs waif.'

T: 'To the Virginia Zoilus, alias Walter Dymocke.' ¶ No: 6 lines. ¶ A: [By Rev. Samuel Davies?]

Note: Dated 'April 30, 1752.' 'Dymocke' was a pseudonym for Rev. John Robertson; see Gilborn (no. 1072A).

1078. May 22, 1752 *VG*.

'Here lie I fix'd in Earth full low.'

T: 'Epitaph on William Waugh.' ¶ No: 24 lines.

1079. May 29, 1752 *VG*.

'Admitting that you have been arch.'

T: 'A Reply to Dymocke's full and complete Answerer, by an Unknown Friend of Dymocke's.' ¶ No: 36 lines.

Note: Dated 'May 22, 1752, being Friday.' Against the Rev. Samuel Davies, cf. no. 1072A.

1080. June 25, 1752 *VG*.

'Each Critic, come! your Squib provide.'

T: 'On the humble Demand of a Triumph by Dymocke's short, full, and complete Answer.' ¶ No: 16 lines.

Note: Cf. no. 1072A. On the Samuel Davies-John Robertson quarrel.

1081. June 1752 *Gent Mag*, XXII, 281.

'One lovely Maid alone my thoughts employs.'

T: 'The fifth Elegy of Joannes Secundus's first Book, intitled Julia, imitated.' ¶ No: 96 lines. ¶ A: 'Britanno-Americanus' [Dr. Adam Thomson].

Note: Dated 'North America, March 20.' The attribution to Thomson is made in the *PG*, Sept. 12, 1754. Reprinted, see no. 1093.

1082. July 9, 1752 *PG* ⋕1230.

'Now the full Harvest of the golden Year.'

T: 'On the Harvest.' ¶ No: 40 lines. ¶ A: 'T. B.'

Note: Religious. Cf. 1072. Reprinted, see no. 1083.

1083. July 21, 1752 *BG* #1688.
   'Now the full Harvest of the golden Year.'
   Note: A reprint of 1082.

1084. Aug. 10, 1752 *NYG* # 499, 2/2.
   'Escap'd from the fleeting *Joys*, from certain *Strife*.'
   T: 'Epitaph, on Miss Philipse.' ¶ No: 21 lines. ¶ A: [Provost William Smith.] Note: Attribution is in A. F. Gegenheimer, *William Smith* (Philadelphia, 1943), p. 7.

1085. Aug. 14, 1752 *VG*.
   'O Walter! Thou for great Atchievments born!'
   T: 'Elegy on Walter Dymocke.' ¶ No: 102 lines. ¶ A: [Samuel Davies?]
   Note: Cf. no. 1072A. This is a mock elegy on the Rev. John Robertson.

1086. Aug. 31, 1752 *BEP* #889, 2/1.
   'Tho' for a while the Wretch escapes.'
   ¶ No: 28 lines. ¶ A: 'S. C.'
   Note: Dated 'Boston, Aug. 24, 1752.' Supposedly from a mistreated woman.

1087. Sept. 22, 1752 *VG*.
   'O! For the Tuneful Voice of Eloquence.'
   T: 'Prologue.' ¶ No: 46 lines. ¶ A: [John Singleton.]
   Note: 'On *Friday* last [Sept 15] The Company of Comedians from England, open'd in the Theatre in this City, when *The Merchant of Venice*, and the *Anatomist*, were perform'd, before a numerous and polite audience, with great Applause; the following Prologue, suitable to the Occasion, was spoken by Mr. [William] Rigby.' Reprinted in Paul L. Ford, *Washington and the Theatre* (New York, 1899), pp. 12–14, who notes, 'This should not be confused with the apocryphal one printed by Dunlap (I, 17) as given by Holland, and from that source frequently reprinted in other books.' See no. 1184 for the 'apocryphal' prologue. John Singleton was an actor with the Hallam Company, playing Gratiano in *The Merchant of Venice. VG* Aug. 28, 1752. He aslo gave violin lessons in Williamsburg and evidently is the author of *A General Description of the West Indian Islands* (Barbadoes, 1767; revised editions printed in London, 1776, 1777).

1088. Sept. 25, 1752 *BEP* #891, 2/1.
   'Now the *Summer's* sultry Beams.'
   T: 'Summer. From the Italian of Vivaldi's Seasons.' ¶ No: 20 lines.
   Note: Dated 'Boston, September 25, 1752.' Cf. no. 1034.

1089. Sept. 30, 1752 *HG* #27.
'Well, what a busy world is this!'
T: 'All things are full of Labour. Eccles. i. 8.' ¶ No: 28 lines. ¶ A: 'Aishmella.'
Note: Reprinted in the *Royal Am. Mag.*, I (June, 1774), 232.

1090. Oct. 6, 1752 *VG*.
'Might I, like others, make Request.'
T: 'The Choice.' ¶ No: 46 lines.
Note: On contentment. Reprinted, see nos. 1095, 1105, 1114, 1119.

1091. Oct. 23, 1752 3/1. *NYG*.
'As late I stray'd on H[a]m[stea]d's lonesome Plain.'
T: 'On the Death of a late valorous and noble Knight [Sir Peter Warren]: (In Imitation of Waller's Thrysis and Galatea.)' ¶ No: 68 lines. ¶ A: [Provost William Smith.]
Note: The advertisement, printed just below the poem reveals the author: 'To-morrow will be published, and to be sold at the New Printing-Office in Beaver-Street. (Price One Shilling.) By the Author of the above Pastoral. 'Some Thoughts on Education: with Reasons for erecting a College in this Provence, and fixing the same at the City of *New York*—The whole concluding with a POEM, being a serious Address to the House of Representatives.' Evans 6935. Sabin 84672. Reprinted, see nos. 1092 and 1111.

1092. Oct. 26, 1752 *PJ* #517, 1/1–2.
'As late I stray'd on H–m—d's lonesome Plain.'
Note: A reprint of no. 1091.

1093. Nov. 2, 1752 *PG* #1245.
'One lovely Maid alone my Thoughts employs.'
Note: A reprint of no. 1081.

1094. Nov. 6, 1752 *NYG* #510.
'Early, O *Strephon*, to our Cost, we know.'
T: 'A Pastoral Elegy, On the Death of Admiral Warren.' ¶ No: 100 lines. ¶ A: 'Hibernicus,' and 'N. L.'

1095. Nov. 16, 1752 *MG*.
'Might I, like others, make Request.'
Note: A reprint of no. 1090.

1096. Nov. 20, 1752 *NYM*, 3/2.
'Hail! Great good Man, hail! Patron of the Poor.'
T: 'To J[ohn] W[att]s, Esq.; on his giving a large Sum of Money to relieve the distressed and indigent Inhabitants of this City.' ¶ No: 22 lines. ¶ A: 'A Lover of Benevolence.'

Note: Reprinted, no. 1108, where the name John Watts is spelled out.

1097. Nov. 20, 1752 *SCG* #962, 1/3–2/1.
'Ye good people all, who of cordage have need.'
T: [Burlesque of advertisement.] ¶ No: 40 lines.
Note: Advertisement of James Reid burlesqued [it may be sung to the Tune of 'A Cobler there was']. Cf. nos. 514–515 for a poetic advertisement by Reid, and a satire on it.

1098. Dec. 4, 1752 *NYM*, 3/1.
'A British Admiral, of late, assign'd.'
T: 'On the Death of Sir Peter Warren.' ¶ No: 32 lines.

1099. Dec. 11, 1752 *BPB* #936.
'The bleak North-west with nipping rigour reigns.'
T: 'Description of a Winter's Morning.' ¶ No: 20 lines.

1100. Dec. 11, 1752 *BPB* #936.
'To-Morrow didst thou say?'
T: 'To-Morrow.' ¶ No: 34 lines. ¶ A: [Nathaniel Cotton.]
Note: Reprinted see no. 1106. See accompanying poem, no. 1101. Refers to Milton's 'L'Allegro.' Printed in Dodlsey, IV, 255. On Cotton (1705–1788), see *CBEL*, II, 314.

1101. Dec. 11, 1752 *BPB* #936.
'Well-Yesterday is pass'd, and cannot be.'
T: 'Yesterday.' ¶ No: 37 lines. ¶ A: [Nathaniel Cotton.]
Note: Cf. no. 1100. Reprinted, see no. 1107.

1102. Dec. 11, 1752 *NYM*, 2/1.
'If Human Life, in prosp'rous Station plac'd.'
T: 'The Hurricane. Some Verses occasioned by the late Calamities of South-Carolina.' ¶ No: 66 lines. ¶ A: ['Sylvio.']
Note: 'To Sylvio' in the *NYM*, Dec. 18, 1752, 1/1–2, criticizes the poem, pointing out its borrowings (see no. 1103). Reprinted, see nos. 1104, 1112, 1115, 1121.

1103. Dec. 18, 1752 *NYM*, 1/2.
'If Virtue by Success declines.'
T: 'To Hercinia.' ¶ No: 12 lines. ¶ A: Gracian.
Note: Points out that no. 1102 borrows from Gracian. This translation of a poem by Gracian is contained in an essay, entitled 'To Sylvio,' which indicates the borrowings (especially from Gracian) by the author of no. 1102.

1104. Dec. 19, 1752 *PJ* #524, 2/1–2.
'If human Life, in prosp'rous Station plac'd.'
Note: A reprint of 1102.

1105. Dec. 19, 1752 *PJ* ⚹524.
'Might I, like others, make Request.'
Note: A reprint from 1090.

1106. Dec. 22, 1752 *VG.*
'To-morrow didst thou say ?'
Note: A reprint of no. 1100.

1107. Dec. 22, 1752 *VG.*
'Well—*Yesterday* is pass'd, and cannot be.'
Note: A reprint of no. 1101.

1108. Dec. 23, 1752 *HG* ⚹39.
Hail! Great good Man hail! Patron of the Poor.'
Note: A reprint of no. 1096.

1109. Dec. 25, 1752 *NYG* ⚹517, 3/1.
'Awake, my Soul, your Halelujahs sing.'
T: 'Christmas Morn.' ¶ No: 22 lines.

1110. Dec. 29, 1752 *VG.*
'This Earth, the Sun, and yonder Stars of Light.'
T: 'An Ode, for the first of January.' ¶ No: 24 lines.

1111. Dec. 30, 1752 *HG* ⚹40.
'As late I stray'd on *H—m—d's* lonesome Plain.'
Note: A reprint of no. 1091.

1753

1112. Jan. 1, 1753 *BPB* ⚹939, 2/1.
'If human Life, in prosp'rous Station plac'd.'
Note: A reprint of no. 1102.

1113. Jan. 1, 1753 *NYG* ⚹518, 2/3.
'The bleak North-west with nipping rigour reigns.'
T: 'A Description of a Winter's Morning.' ¶ No: 20 lines.
Note: Reprinted, see no. 1116.

1114. Jan. 4, 1753 *BNL* ⚹2635, 1/1.
'Might I, like others, make Request.'
Note: A reprint of no. 1090.

1115. Jan. 8, 1753 *SCG* ⚹969, 1/3–2/1.
'If human life, in prosp'rous station plac'd.'
Note: 'From the New York Mercury, Dec. 11, 1752.' A reprint of
no. 1102.

1116. Jan. 9, 1753 *PJ* #527, 2/1.
'The bleak North-west with nipping rigour reigns.'
Note: A reprint of no. 113.

1117. Jan. 11, 1753 *MG*.
'A Trout, the plumpest in the Tide.'
Note: A reprint of no. 988.

1118. Feb. 1, 1753 *MG*.
'Hail sacred art! thou Gift of Heaven, designed.'
Note: A reprint of no. 95.

1119. Feb. 3, 1752/3 *HG*, pp. 1–2.
'Might I, like others, make Request.'
Note: A reprint of no. 1090.

1120. Mar. 5, 1752/3 *NYG* #527, 1/1–3.
'Some Husbands on a Winter's Day.'
T: 'The Obedient Wives. A Tale.'
Note: A reprint of no. 485.

1121. Mar. 10, 1752/3 *HG* #50, 2/2.
'If human Life in prosp'rous Station plac'd.'
Note: A reprint of no. 1102.

1122. Mar. 12, 1753 *NYG* #528, 2/2.
'Hail sacred Art: thou Gift of Heaven, designed.'
Note: A reprint of no. 95.

1123. Mar. 12, 1753 *NYG* #528, 3/1.
'Dumb Betty is now much thought on by the Town.'
T: 'Dumb Betty, a *New* York Song.' ¶ No: 32 lines. ¶ A: [Provost
William Smith?] Note: A note to the poem puffs Smith's recent
publications.

1124. Mar. 13, 1753 *BG* #11, 2/2.
'Soft Babe! sweet Image of a harmless mind.'
Note: A reprint of no. 1023.

1125. Mar. 15, 1753 *MG*.
'Behold the wond'rous Power of Art.'
T: 'Extempore: On seeing Mr. Wollaston's Pictures, in Annapolis.'
¶ No: 12 lines. ¶ A: 'By Dr. T. T.'
Note: Reprinted on p. 140 in George C. Groce, 'John Wollaston
(fl. 1736–1767): A Cosmopolitan painter in the British Colonies,'
Art Quarterly, XV (1952), 132–149, where it is mistakenly sup-
posed that the author was 'connected in some way with St. John's
College at Annapolis.' John Wollaston was painting in Philadel-

phia at this time. Dr. T. T. may be the **Dr. Thomas Thornton**
who was invited as a stranger to the Annapolis Tuesday Club on
Jan. 22^{d}, 1754.

1126. Mar. 17, 1752/3 *HG* ⋕51, 2/2.
'To be or not to be; that is the question.'
T: 'Socrates on Death.' ¶ No: 42 lines.

1127. Mar. 22, 1753 *MG*.
'As whilom roving o'er the lonely Plain.'
T: 'A Poem, Sacred to the Memory of Miss Margaret Lawson, Miss
Elizabeth Lawson, Miss Dorothy Lawson, and Miss Elizabeth
Read.' ¶ No: 110 lines. ¶ A: 'T. Cradock.'
Note: On the Reverend Thomas Cradock (1718 ?–1770), see Nelson
Waite Rightmyer, *Maryland's Established Church* (Baltimore
1956), pp. 177–178. Notice of the death of the girls appeared in
the *MG* Dec. 28, 1752.

1128. Mar. 26, 1753 *BPB* ⋕951.
'Hail sacred Art! Thou Gift of Heaven, designed.'
Note: A reprint of no. 95.

1129. April 16, 1753 *NYG* ⋕533, 1/1–3.
'When fair Intention has been slighted.'
T: 'The Birds of different Feather, An American Fable.' ¶ No: 132
lines. ¶ A: [William Smith].
Note: Provost William Smith's authorship is revealed by his *Indian
Songs* (New York, 1752), which are described as 'By the Author
of the American Fables.' Cf. no. 1076.

1130. May 7, 1753 *NYM*, 1/1.
'Freed from the tyrant Rage of Winter's sway.'
T: 'An Address to May.' ¶ No: 58 lines. ¶ A: 'Castalio.'
Note: Contains a reference to Long Island, N.Y.

1131. May 7, 1753 *SCG* ⋕986, 1/2.
'The number of our years (Sir) I nearly—.'
T: 'A Problem.' ¶ No: 6 lines ?—some are missing.
Note: Cf. nos. 1132, 1134.

1132. May 14, 1753 *SCG* ⋕987, 2/1.
'A Country Spark, addressing charming She.'
T: 'A Problem.' ¶ No: 14 lines.
Note: Cf. no. 1131.

1133. May 14, 1753 *NYG* ⋕537, 2/1.
'Berkley, farewell,—on Earth an honour'd **Name**.'

T: 'On the sudden Death of Doctor Berkley, late Bishop of Cloyne, at Oxford.' ¶ No: 42 lines. ¶ A: [Provost William Smith?] Note: The poem commends Smith's *Mirania* (New York, 1753).

1134. May 14, 1753 *SCG* #987, 2/1.
'The Age of the fortunate Man is your last.'
T: [Answer to 'A Problem.'] ¶ No: 6 lines.
Note: Cf. no. 1131.

1135. May 1753 *Gent Mag*, XXIII, 240–1.
'At length our fine winter for spring has made way.'
T: 'Hor. B. I. Ode IV Imitated. By a Friend, (whom Providence protect) now residing in South Carolina, ... To John Cordes, Esq. ¶ No: 24 lines. ¶ A: 'C. W.' [Charles Woodmason].
Note: Dated 'Charles Town, March 26, 1753.' Reprinted in Silverman, p. 337; and in Claude E. Jones, 'Charles Woodmason as a Poet, *S. C. Hist. Mag.*, LIX (1958), 191.

1136. May 1753 *Gent Mag*, XXIII, 241.
'With quick vibrations of aetherial flame.'
T: 'The XXVIII Chapter of Job paraphrased.' ¶ No: 116 lines. ¶ A: [By Charles Woodmason?].
Note: This is printed between 2 of Woodmason's poems.

1137. May 1753 *Gent Mag*, XXIII, 242.
'The price of rice, or talk on "*Change.*" '
T: 'Hor. B. II, Ode II. Imitated.' ¶ No: 30 lines. ¶ A: 'By C. W.' [Charles Woodmason].
Note: 'To Mr. J. B. at Wathos, in Carolina.'

1138. June 4, 1753 *NYM*, 2/1.
'All on that Main, the verdant Trees abound.'
T: [An extract from Morrel's *New England* (London, 1625).] ¶ No: 22 lines. ¶ A: 'William Morrel.'

1139. July 2, 1753 *NYM*, 1/2–3.
'And did the Omnipotent, Eternal Mind.'
T: 'Man more Happy than Brutes.' ¶ No: 167 lines.

1140. July 5, 1753 *PG* #1280.
'Whene'er thro' Nature's boundless Works I stray.'
T: 'On the surprizing Scenes of the Creation.' ¶ No: 46 lines.
Note: Dated 'Phila., July, 1753.' Pretty good—scientific deism.

1140A. July 7, 1753 *NCG*, 3/2–4/1.
'How every [da]y unworthy of thy love.'
T: 'A Hymn to the Supreme.' ¶ No: 88 lines.

1141. July 16, 1753 *NYM* #49, 1/3.
    'Goddess! Presiding o'er the Plains.'
    T: 'Ode to Health.' ¶ No: 62 lines. ¶ A: ['Cynthio'?]—pseudonym
      signed to the accompanying poem.
    Note: See no. 1142.

1142. July 16, 1753 *NYM*.
    'Each Creature's link'd to that below it.'
    T: 'On Woman.' ¶ No: 10 lines. ¶ A: 'Cynthio.'
    Note: See no. 1141. Reprinted, see no. 1159.

1143. July 23, 1753 *NYM*, 1/3.
    'Celestial Maid, whom endless Smiles adorn.'
    T: 'An Address to Contentment.' ¶ No: 26 lines.
    Note: Cf. no. 1156, 1158.

1143A. July 30, 1753 *NYM*, 3/1.
    'Accept, O Lloyd, the Tribute of a Muse.'
    T: 'Soteria Lloydiana. To Henry Lloyd, Esq.; on his Recovery from
      a dangerous Cancer.' ¶ No: 29 lines. ¶ A: 'Ja. Lysaght.'

1144. July 1753 *Gent Mag* XXIII, 337–8.
    'While you, my friend, indulg'd in each desire.'
    T: 'C. W. in Carolina to E. J. at Gosport.' ¶ No: 128 lines. ¶ A: 'C.
      W.' [Charles Woodmason].
    Note: Repr. by Hennig Cohen, 'A Colonial Topographical Poem,'
      Names, I (Dec., 1953), 252–258; and by Silverman, pp. 333–336.

1145. July 1753 *Lon Mag*, XXII, 336.
    'Vice admiral Vernon!--Ipswich!--Suffolk!--how!'.
    T: 'Extempore. Occasioned by Reading in the Papers that Mr.
      Vernon had a Flag given him, after many Years Retirement, near
      Ipswich in Suffolk; and was about being sent with a Squadron to
      the West Indies. Written in the Year 1739.' ¶ No: 10 lines. ¶ A:
      'J. Rhudde, Late Chaplain in the royal navy of Great-Britain, and
      rector of St. Mary's Jamaica; now vicar of Portersham, Dorset.'

1146. Aug. 9, 1753 *PG* #1285.
    'When fam'd Apellos drew the beuteous Face.'
    T: 'To the Painter, on seeing the Picture of a Lady, which he lately
      drew.' ¶ No: 24 lines.
    Note: Dated 'Philad., August 1753.' Competent verse. The most
      likely artist to have been the subject of this poem was John
      Wollaston.

1147. Aug. 16, 1753 *BNL* #2667, 1/2.
    'The Loom, the Comb, and the spinning Wheel.'

T: 'Observations, August 1702' ['an Almanack Observation. .']. ¶
A: Sent in by 'D. V.'
Note: A reprint of no. 967. That 'D. V.' is the reverse of Joseph
Green's pseudonym, 'V. D.,' may be of some significance.

1148. Aug. 16, 1753 *PJ* #558, 1/3–2/1.
'When General Mathew pass'd this mortal Bound.'
T: 'The following Lines were wrote at St. Christophers on the Ar-
rival of his Excellency George Thomas Esq.; at Antigua.' ¶ No:
59 lines.
Note: Cf. no. 1441. Reprinted, nos. 1150, 1176.

1149. Aug. 21, 1753 *BG* #34, pp. 1 & 2.
'Happy the Maid, whose Body pure and chaste.'
T: 'Advise to the Fair Sex.' ¶ No: 117 lines.
Note: Reprinted (in 106 lines), no. 1175.

1150. August 28, 1753 *BG* #35, 1/1–2.
'When General Mathew pass'd this mortal Bound.'
Note: A reprint of no. 1148.

1151. August 1753 *Gent Mag*, XXIII, 372.
'Rome shall lament her ancient Fame declin'd/and Philadelphia be
the Athens of mankind.'
¶ No: 2 lines. ¶ A: 'George Webb.'
Note: This couplet is quoted in the conclusion of an article entitled
'A Comparative View of Philadelphia, Boston and New York.'
The attribution identifies Webb as the author of the excellent
poem in Titan Leeds, *The American Almanac for 1730* (Philadel-
phia, 1729). The two lines above are lines 29–30 in Leeds, ex-
cepting that *Rome* has been substituted for *Europe. Translatio*
Theme.

1153. Sept. 3, 1753 *NYM*, 1/3.
'Glory is not half so fair.'
T: 'On Virtue.' ¶ No: 8 lines.

1154. Sept. 17, 1753 *SCG* #1005, 2/1.
'A Worthy merchant in wealth did so abound.'
T: 'An Algebraic Question.' ¶ No: 12 lines. ¶ A: 'S. J.'
Note: Cf. no. 1155.

1155. Sept. 24, 1753 *SCG*, 3/1.
'There is a man that most does know.'
¶ No: 14 lines. ¶ A: 'Michael Tonge.'
Note: Cf. no. 1154.

1156. Oct. 1, 1753 *NYM*, 1/3.
'Enamour'd Bards! your moving Strains.'
T: 'Contentment to her Supplicants.' ¶ No: 36 lines.
Note: Reply to no. 1143.

1157. Oct. 4, 1753 *MG*.
'Houses, Churches, mix'd together.'
T: 'A Description of London.' ¶ No: 24 lines. ¶ A: [John Banks].
Note: On John Banks (1709–1751), see the *DNB*. The poem is
found in his *Miscellaneous Works, in Verse and Prose of Mr. John
Bancks* I (London, 1739), 337–8. Banks' poem was later imitated
by a Captain Martin, 'Captain of a Man of War.' See Kenneth
Silverman, 'Two Unpublished Colonial Verses,' *Bull. of the N. Y.
Public Lib.*, LXXI (1967), 61–63, for Martin's 'A Description
of Charles Town in 1769.'

1158. Oct. 8, 1753 *NYM*, 1/3.
'Descend, Contentment! from thy seat above.'
T: 'An Address to Contentment.' ¶ No: 20 lines.
Note: Cf. no. 1143.

1159. Nov. 1, 1753 *MG*.
'Each Creature's link'd to that below it.'
Note: A reprint of no. 1142.

1160. Nov. 22, 1753 *PG* ⚡1300.
'My artless Strains disclaim the tuneful Nine.'
T: 'Verses sacred to the Memory of Mr. R–b–T T—te, Student of
the Academy, a Youth of uncommon Strength of Genius, Probity
of Manners, and Sweetness of Temper, who departed this Life in
the fourteenth Year of his Age, November 13, 1753.' ¶ No: 76
lines.
Note: The subject was Robert Tuite, who entered the Academy in
1751.

1161. Dec. 6, 1753 *MG*.
'Accept, dear Jens, this humble Chair.'
T: 'To an Infant with his Nursing Chair. Written Extempore, and
sent home in the Twigs.' ¶ No: 30 lines.

1162. Dec. 24, 1753 *NYM*, 2/1.
'So farewell to the little Good you bear me!'
T: 'The Vicissitudes of Life.' ¶ No: 22 lines.
Note: An imitation of Shakespeare's King Henry VIII.

1163. Dec. 24, 1753 *SCG* ⚡1019, 1/1–2.
'As *Damon* one Day with his fair One was sate.'

T: 'Song by the Humourist.' ¶ No: 20 lines. ¶ A: 'Humourist.'

Note: For a discussion of the Humourists' writings, see Hennig Cohen, *The South Carolina Gazette, 1732–1775* (Columbia, S. C., 1953), pp. 225–228. Cf. no. 1181.

1164. *Gent Mag* 1753, XXIII, preface [after Dec., 1753].

'Again the pictur'd page displays.'

T: 'To Mr. Urban on completing the Twenty-Third Volume of his Magazine. Alluding to the Frontispiece.'

Note: Includes complimentary verses to Benjamin Franklin.

1165. Dec. 1753 *London Mag*, XXII, 577.

'Oh little Scug! lie gently, earth.'

T: 'On the Death of a Lady's Squirrel.'

Note: Cf. Benjamin Franklin's epitaph sent to Georgiana Shipley, in his letter of Sept. 26, 1772, on an American squirrel. Smyth, *The Writings of Benjamin Franklin*, V, 438–9.

1754

1166. Jan. 1, 1754 *BG* ✳53, 2/1–2.

'Sylvia! with the Wheel I send.'

T: 'To a young Lady with a Spinning Wheel.' ¶ No: 20 lines.

1167. Jan. 1, 1754 *BG* ✳53, 2/2.

'How bless'd her State! in Innocence array'd.'

T: To the Memory of a dear Daughter, who died aged three Years.' ¶ No: 31 lines.

1168. Jan. 1, 1754 *BG* ✳53, 2/2.

'The Rose's Age is but a Day.'

T: 'The Rose.' ¶ No: 4 lines.

Note: Cf. Freneau's 'The Wild Honeysuckle.' Crum T1259.

1168A. Jan. 1, 1754 *SCG* ✳1020, 1/2.

T: 'Verses written in a young Lady's Almanack for the Year 1754.' ¶ No: 6 or 8 lines.

Note: First 4 or 6 lines missing.

1169. Jan. 3, 1754 *NG*.

'Alas, how frail is Man! ah hapless Race!'

T: 'Reflections on an Instance of Human Frailty.' ¶ No: 48 lines.

Note: The instance was evidently adultery.

1170. Jan. 15, 1754 *SCG* ✳1022, 1/3.

'Law, Physics, and Divinity.'

T: 'The Triple Plea.' ¶ No: 32 lines.

Note: Crum L80 dates the poem 1681.

1171. Jan. 21, 1754 *NYM*, 1/2–3.
'Mysterious Inmate of this Breast.'
T: 'A Soliloquy.' ¶ No: 48 lines.

1172. Jan. 31, 1754 *MG* #456.
'Hail wedded Love! mysterious Law! true Source of human Off-
spring.'
T: 'The Maid's Soliloquy, An Imitation of that Made by Mr. Addi-
son's Cato.' ¶ No: 32 lines.
Note: Reprinted from the *Scots Mag* which in turn, reprinted it
'From the Antigua Gazette.'

1173. Jan. 1754 *Lon Mag*, XXIII, 39–40.
'In life too far advanc'd to taste again.'
T: 'On Reading Mr. Hervey's Meditations, in the West-Indies.' ¶
No: 42 lines. ¶ A: 'N. N.'
Note: Dated: 'Barbadoes, Oct. 25, 1753.'

1174. Feb. 2, 1753/4 *HG* #97.
'To wed or not to wed—that is the Question.'
T: 'From the Gentleman's Magazine.' ¶ No: 31 lines.
Note: Cf. no. 733.

1175. Feb. 9, 1753/4 *HG* #98.
'Happy the Maid, whose Body Pure and chaste.'
No: 106 lines.
Note: A reprint of no. 1149.

1176. Feb. 9, 1753/4 *HG* #98, 1/2–2/1.
'When General Matthew pass'd this mortal Bound.'
Note: A reprint of no. 1148.

1177. Feb. 23, 1753/4 *HG* #100, 2/2–3.
'Almighty Archer of the Skies!'
T: 'A Touch on the Times: Or, Honora's Address to Cupid.' ¶ No:
71 lines. ¶ A: 'R. T.'

1178. Feb. 1754 *Gent Mag* XXIV, 88.
'Let others muse on sublunary things.'
T: 'To Benjamin Franklin Esq.; of Philadelphia, on his Experiments
and Discoveries in Electricity. (See the Frontispiece, and Verses
perfixed [!] to Vol. xxiii).' ¶ No: 78 lines. ¶ A: 'C. W.' [Charles
Woodmason].
Note: Dated 'Cooper River, S. Carolina, Sept. 20, 1753.' Reprinted,
see nos. 1194, 1195, and 1197; *The Franklin Papers*, V, 59–62;
and Silverman, pp. 337–339.

1179. Feb. 1754 *Gent Mag* XXIV, 88.
'When, *Lydia*, you, the manly charms.'
T: 'Hor. Ode 13, Book 1, Translated.' ¶ No: 24 lines.
Note: Perhaps by Woodmason? Cf. no. 1178.

1180. Mar. 19, 1754 *SCG* ⚹1031, 1/1–2.
'When now no more the summer's scorching sun.'
T: 'The Temple of Happiness. An Allegorical Poem.' ¶ No: 94
lines [to be continued].
Note: Dated 'March 8, 1754.' An editorial note thanks the author in
the *SCG*, Mar. 12, 1754, 3/1.

1181. Mar. 26, 1754 *SCG* ⚹1032, 1/1.
'The lazy man as yet undrest.'
T: 'The Rising Beauty. A Song.' ¶ No: 24 lines. ¶ A: 'Humourist.'
Note: In Humourist, No. XIII, an essay serial that began in *SCG*
⚹1021, Jan. 1, 1754. On the 'Humourist,' see no. 1163.

1183. Mar. 1754 *Gent Mag*, XXIV, 137.
'Sweet bird! whose fate and mine agree.'
T: 'Ode, To a Virginia Nightingale, who was cured of a Fit in the
Boson of a young Lady, who afterwards nursed the Author in a
dangerous Illness.' ¶ No: 18 lines. ¶ A: 'Herbert Trueman.'
Note: Ugh!

1184. April 25, 1754 *PG* ⚹1322, 2/2.
'To this New World, from fam'd Britannia's Shore.'
T: 'Prologue.' ¶ No: 36 lines. ¶ A: [Dr. Adam Thomson].
Note: 'On Monday, the 15th of this inst. April, the Company of
Comedians from *London*, opened the New Theatre, in Water-
street; when the Fair Penitent, and Miss in her Teens, were per-
form'd before a numerous and polite Audience, with universal
Applause.
'The following *Prologue* and *Epilogue*, suitable to the Occasion,
were spoken by Mr. Rigby, and Mrs. Hallam.' See *PG* Mar. 26,
1754, for the fight over production of plays in Philadelphia. This
prologue is frequently attributed to John Singleton, (cf. above no.
1087). See, for example, George O. Seilhamer, *History of the
American Theater Before the American Revolution* (Philadelphia,
1888), p. 41. Reprinted, nos. 1199, 1542 (revised), and 1847
further revised).

1185. April 25, 1754 *PG* ⚹1322, 2/2–3.
'Much has been said in this reforming Age.'
T: 'Epilogue.' ¶ No: 27 lines. ¶ A: [Dr. Adam Thomson].
Note: See note to 1184. Reprinted, nos. 1200, 1543 (extensively re-
vised and enlarged), and no. 1848 (with further revisions).

1186. May 14, 1754 *SCG* #1039, 1/1–2.
  'In answer to the widow's letter.'
  T: 'To the Printer.' ¶ No: 100 lines.
  Note: The widow's letter appeared in *SCG* May 3.

1187. May 27, 1754 *BEP* #978.
  'Ye cruel Winds that blow from North to East.'
  T: 'On some fine Peach Trees being kill'd by the late cold Easterly
  Winds.' ¶ No: 30 lines. ¶ A: 'V. D.' [Joseph Green].
  Note: Dated 'Boston, May 17, 1754.' Reprinted, see no. 1188.
  Copied in 'Miscellaneous Extracts' (Harvard MS Am 505) pp.
  85–87.

1188. June 3, 1754 *NYG* #592.
  'Ye cruel Winds that blow from North to East.'
  Note: A reprint of no. 1187.

1189. June 13, 1754 *BNL* #2710, 1/1.
  'Pergis extremas, bone Dux, in oras,'
  T: 'Ad Virum ornatissimum Gulielmam Shirely, Armigerum, Pro-
  vinciae Massachusittenis Gubernatorem, Iter in orientales Novae-
  Angliae Partes parantem.' ¶ No: 20 lines. ¶ A: ['Johann: Bever-
  idge.']
  Note: The author, and a slightly different title, are given in the re-
  print, no. 1488. Reprinted in Beveridge, *Epistolae Familiares*
  (Philadelphia, 1765), pp. 25–26.

1190. June 20, 1754 *PG* #1330.
  'Our humble *Prologue* means not to engage.'
  T: ['Prologue']. ¶ No: 44 lines. ¶ A: [Provost William Smith?]
  Note: 'Last Evening, at the New Theatre in Water-Street, the *Care-
  less Husband*, and *Harlequin Collector*, were acted before a very
  crowded and polite Audience, for the Benefit of the *Charity Chil-
  dren* belonging to the Academy of this City; on which Occasion
  the following Prologue was spoken by Mr. Rigby. Reprinted, see
  nos. 1192, 1219. Reprinted in Oral Coad and Edward Mims, Jr.,
  The American Stage (New York, 1929), p. 18; and from there re-
  printed in Johnston (see no. 344), pp. 36–37.

1191. June 20, 1754 *PJ* #602, 1/1.
  'What is this fleeting Life of Man?'
  T: 'On the Vanity and Vicissitudes of Human Life.' ¶ No: 48 lines.

1192. June 24, 1754 *NYG* #595, 2/3–3/1.
  'Our humble Prologue means not to engage.'
  Note: A reprint of no. 1190.

1193. June 27, 1754 *PG* ⚏1331, 2/2–3.
'Oft thankless Slaves for Favours humbly ask.'
No: 48 lines. ¶ A: [Dr. Adam Thomson].
Note: 'On Monday Night last the Provok'd Husband, with Miss in her Teens, were acted at the New Theatre in Water-street, when the following Farewell Epilogue was spoken by Mrs. Hallam.' Thomson's authorship is proven by his defense in the *PG*, Sept. 12, 1754. See the burlesque on this poem, no. 1201.

1194. June 1754 *Scotts Mag*, XVI, 275.
'Let others muse on sublunary things.'
Note: A reprint of no. 1178.

1195. July 1, 1754 *BPB* ⚏1006, 1/1.
'Let others muse on sublunary things.'
Note: A reprint of no. 1178.

1196. July 8, 1754 *NYM*, 1/1–3.
'Come hither, *Friend*, who like with me to rove.'
T: 'De Arte Poetica.' ¶ No: 170 lines. ¶ A: 'Philo-Musus.'
Note: Dr. Adam Thomson in *PG* Sept. 12, 1754 says he did not write this poem.

1197. July 15, 1754 *NYG* ⚏589, 1/1–2.
'Let others muse on sublunary things.'
Note: A reprint of no. 1178.

1198. July 1754 *Scots Mag*, XVI, 337.
'In vain alas! (do lazy mortals cry).'
T: 'The Inquiry.'
Note: Cf. Benjamin Franklin on oyster at the one end of the Chain of Being. Excellent cosmological poetry.

1199. July 1754 *Gent Mag*, XXIV, 331–2.
'To this new world, from fam'd Britannia's shore.'
Note: A reprint of no. 1184.

1200. July 1754 *Gent Mag*, XXIV, 332.
'Much has been said in this reforming age.'
Note: A reprint of no. 1185.

1201. Aug. 15, 1754 *PG* ⚏1338.
'Let thankless Slaves for Favours humbly *ask*.'
T: 'Buckram the Journeyman Taylor's Love-letter To his Sweetheart Sue, in which the Humour of our last cold chiming Epilogue is exactly copied, and its particular Beauties either Transcribed or imitated.' ¶ No: 34 lines. ¶ A: 'Buckram' [David James Dove?]

Note: A burlesque of no. 1193. Dr. Adam Thomson's reply, *PG*, Sept. 12, 1754, 2/3–3/1, reveals that the author of this burlesque was a schoolteacher well known for his strict discipline. This points at David James Dove, schoolmaster and satirical poet of Philadelphia and Germantown.

1202. Aug. 22, 1754, *MG*.
'Six Bottles of Wine, right old, good and clear.'
T: 'Memorandum for a Seine-Hauling, in Severn River, near a delightful Spring at the foot of Constitution Hill.' ¶ No: 22 lines. ¶ A: [Jonas Green].
Note: Dated 'Annapolis, Aug. 20, 1754.' Reprinted in *Md Hist Mag*, LII (1957), 251. An imitation of the style of Matthew Prior, cf. no. 1381. Dr. Alexander Hamilton in his 'History of the Tuesday Club,' The Johns Hopkins University Library, points at Green as the author.

1203. Aug. 1754 *Scots Mag*, XVI, 372.
'Ye deities who rule the deep.'
T: 'Horace, book I. Ode 3 imitated.' ¶ No: 42 lines. ¶ A: 'C. W.' [Charles Woodmason].
Note: The initials and American references indicate Woodmason's authorship. Reprinted, no. 1204.

1204. Aug. 1754 *Gent Mag*, XXIV, 381.
'Ye deities who rule the deep.'
Note: A reprint of no. 1203.

1205. Sept. 5, 1754 *PG* #1341.
'All gracious Heaven, how intricate thy ways!'
T: 'Verses, on the Death of a hopeful Student &c.' ¶ No: 18 lines. ¶ A: 'By a young Gentleman of the Academy.'
Note: On the death of William Thomas Martin, d. Aug. 28, 1754; obit in *PG*, Sept. 5. This poem is not one of those included in William Smith's sermon on Martin's death: *Personal Affliction and Frequent Reflection* (Phila., 1754). Reprinted, see nos. 1206, 1207, 1212.

1206. Sept. 9, 1754 *NYM*.
'All gracious Heaven, how intricate thy Ways!'
Note: A reprint of no. 1205.

1207. Sept. 9, 1754 *NYG* #606, 3/1.
'All gracious Heaven, how intricate thy Ways!'
Note: A reprint of no. 1205.

1208. Sept. 12, 1754 *BNL* #2723, 2/1.
'Grassante bello protegis Accadam.'
T: 'Ad Illustrissimum Ac vera vertute et Insigni doctrina orna-
tisseraum virum Gulielmum Shirley, Armigerum, Provinciae
Massachusettenis Gubernatorem, &c. Post reditum suum a Con-
ventu cum Indis orientalibas habito apud Falmouth, 1754.' ¶ No:
56 lines. ¶ A: 'Jo Beveridge.'
Note: For a translation, see no. 1213. Reprinted, no. 1214. Re-
printed in Beveridge, *Epistolae Familiares* (Philadelphia, 1765),
pp. 26–28.

1209. Sept. 12, 1754 *SCG* #1056, 1/1.
'Too fond of what the martial harvests yield.'
T: 'To the Memory of Lieut. Peter Mercier, Esq; who fell in the
late Battle near Ohio River in Virginia, July 3^d, 1754.' ¶ No: 38
lines. ¶ A: 'M. W.'
Note: Dated 'Charles-Town, Aug. 31, 1754.' Reprinted in McCarty
I, 301–302 (from no. 1218), in A. S. Salley, *The Independent
Company from South Carolina at Great Meadows* (Columbia, S. C.,
1932), p. 14. Reprinted, see no. 1218.

1210. Sept. 19, 1754 *BNL* #2724, 2/1.
'Dum diu Eois retineris oris.'
T: 'Ad clarissimum Virum Gulielmum Shirley, Provinciae Massa-
chusittensis Praefectium, ab Oris Nov-Angliae Orientalibus nobis
jam tandem redditum.' ¶ No: 36 lines.

1211. Sept. 19, 1754 *MG.*
'Over the Hills with Heart we go.'
T: 'A Recruiting Song, for the Maryland Independent Company
(By an Officer of the Company).' ¶ No: 64 lines. ¶ A: 'Officer of
the Maryland Independent Co.' [Lt. John Bacon?].
Note: John Bacon, son of the Rev. Thomas Bacon, left Annapolis
with a 'Second party of Capt. [John] Dagworthy's Company,' *MG*
Oct. 3, 1754. The *MG* for April 8, 1756 reported that he had
been killed and scalped. Reprinted, no. 1251.

1212. Sept. 26, 1754 *MG.*
'All gracious Heaven, how intricate thy Ways!'
Note: A reprint of no. 1205.

1213. Sept. 26, 1754 *BNL* #2725, 2/1–3.
'Great Leader of our martial Band.'
T: 'To the most illustrious in real Virtue and polite Literature Wil-
liam Shirley, Esq; Governor of the Province of the Massachu-

setts, &c. On his Return from a Treaty with the Eastern Indians at Falmouth, 1754.' ¶ No: 84 lines. ¶ A: 'Philo Muses.'
Note: A translation of no. 1208. Dated 'Sept. 16, 1754.'

1214. Oct. 3, 1754 *BNL* ⚹2726, 2/1.
'Grassante bello protegis Accadam.'
Note: A reprint of no. 1208, so that readers could compare it with the accompanying English translations (nos. 1213 and 1215).

1215. Oct. 3, 1754 *BNL* ⚹2726, 2/2.
'Shirley, whilst War it's Desolation spreads.'
T: English Translation 'of Mr. Beveridge's Latin Ode ...' ¶ No: 53 lines.
Note: Cf. nos. 1208 and 1214.

1217. Oct. 21, 1754 *BEP* ⚹999, 1/2.
'When Whitefield comes, 'Tis fair: A Fog ensues.'
T: 'On the Fog at the Close of Mr. Whitefields preaching here.' ¶ No: 13 lines.

1218. Oct. 31, 1754 *PG* ⚹1249.
'Too fond of what the Martial Harvests yield.'
Note: A reprint of no. 1209.

1219. Oct. 1754 *Lon Mag*, XXIII, 471.
'Our humble prologue means not to engage.'
Note: Reprint of no. 1190.

1220. Oct. 1754 *Lon Mag*, XXIII, 472.
'A Kid, an heifer, and a lambkin mild.'
T: 'An Imitation of a Fable in *Phaedrus*, Adapted to the Times.' ¶ No: 22 lines.
Note: A satire on French ambitions in America. Reprinted, no. 1231.

1221. Oct. 1754 *Gent Mag* XXIV, 447.
'Thou source of all that's great and good!'
T: 'Hymn. On returning from a Mission to America By the Rev. Mr. John Rhudde, late Chaplain of the Oxford, and Rector of St. Mary's, Jamaica; now rector of Portersham, Dorset.' ¶ No: 48 lines. ¶ A: John Rhudde.

1222. Nov. 19, 1754 *PG* ⚹1351.
'She come! she comes! ye Nine, strike every String.'
T: 'Prologue to Philosophical Exercises at Philadelphia, November 12, 1754, spoken by Mr. Jacob Duché.' ¶ No: 54 lines. ¶ A: [Jacob Duché and Provost William Smith].
Note: Reprinted, see nos. 1227, 1229, 1239 (where the authorship is given).

1223. Nov. 14, 1754 *PG* #1351.
  'Ladies! There's something happen'd now so queer.'
  T: 'Epilogue to the same [see 'Prologue' same date] Spoken by
    Master Billy Hamilton. ¶ No: 32 lines. ¶ A: [Provost William
    Smith].
  Note: Reprinted, see nos. 1228, 1230, 1240.

1224. Nov. 14, 1754 *SCG*, 4/1.
  'Dear Nymph! in vain has Ramsay shewn his Art.'
  T: [To a girl]. ¶ No: 8 lines. ¶ A: 'Eugenius.'

1225. Nov. 16, 1754 *HG* #135.
  'Arise my Muse, salute the dawning Day.'
  T: 'On the Anniversary of His Brittannick Majesty's Birth-Day.' ¶
    No: 34 lines.
  Note: With an account of the celebration in Halifax.

1226. Nov. 21, 1754 *BNL* #2733, 1/1–2.
  'Gallica cum rabris Europam Marte nefando.'
  T: 'Ad Noblissimum Virum Georgium Montague Dunk, Comitem
    de Halifax, Provinciarum, quae sunt ditionis Britannicae in
    America, Praefectum, &c.' ¶ No: 97 lines. ¶ A: [John Beveridge].
  Note: Dated 'Falmouth, New-Angloran, Novr 1, 1754.' Reprinted,
    no. 1257. Reprinted in Beveridge, *Epistolae Familiares* (Philadel-
    phia, 1765), pp. 35–38.

1227. Nov. 25, 1754 *NYG* #617, 2/2.
  'She comes! she comes! ye Nine, strike every String.'
  Note: A reprint of no. 1222.

1228. Nov. 25, 1754 *NYG* #617, 2/2–3.
  'Ladies! there's something happen'd now so queer.'
  Note: A reprint of no. 1223.

1229. Nov. 28, 1754 *MG*.
  'She comes! she comes! ye Nine, strike every String.'
  Note: A reprint of no. 1222.

1230. Nov. 28, 1754 *MG*.
  'Ladies! there's something happen'd now so queer.'
  Note: A reprint of no. 1223.

1231. Nov. 1754 *Scots Mag*, XVI, 535–6.
  'A Kid, an heifer, and a lambkin mild.'
  Note: A reprint of no. 1220.

1232. Dec. 5, 1754 *PG* #1354.
  'Once more I seek the Cypress-shade.'

T: 'Ode to the memory of Charles Willing, Esq.' ¶ No: 48 lines.
Note: Charles Willing, Mayor of Phila. died 'last Saturday.' There
is also an 'Epitaph' of 6 lines, and a 'Moral' of 8 lines.

1233. Dec. 12, 1754 *MG*, p. 2.
'The Muse that us'd in Silvan Strains to sing.'
T: 'A Poem, Occasioned by his Majesty's most gracious Benevo-
lence to his British Colonies in America, lately invaded by the
French.' ¶ No: 96 lines. ¶ A: [James Sterling].
Note: Accompanying letter mentions 'a Coalition of the British
Colonies, and to that Union, which is, at this Time, so desirable.'
The suggestion of colonial union and the references in lines 84–85
to conversation and friendship with Gov. Horatio Sharpe strong-
ly suggest Sterling's authorship. Reprinted, nos. 1234, 1236,
1241, 1242.

1755

1234. Jan. 14, 1755 *PJ* ₦632, 1/1.
'The Muse that us'd in Silvan Strains to sing.'
Note: A reprint of no. 1233.

1235. Jan. 14, 1755 *PJ* ₦632, 2/1.
'Come, ye great spirits, Cavendish, Raleigh, Blake!'
T: [On the French and Indian War.] ¶ No: 13 lines.
Note: Verses concluding an essay surveying the history of French
advances in North America.

1236. Jan. 14, 1755 *PG* ₦1360.
'The Muse that us'd in silvan Strains to sing.'
Note: A reprint of no. 1233.

1237. Jan. 1755 *Scots Mag*, XVII, 43.
'Go, gentle youth! to distant climes repair.'
T: 'To William Lyttelton, Esq.; youngest brother to Sir George
Lyttelton, on his being appointed Governor of South-Carolina.' ¶
No: 28 lines.
Note: Dated 'Bewdley, Jan. 15, 1755.' Reprinted, nos. 1238, 1250.
Cf. no. 1252. For another poem possibly by the same author, see
no. 1252.

1238. Jan. 1755 *London Mag* XXIV, 38.
'Go, gentle youth! to distant climes repair.'
Note: A reprint of no. 1237.

1239. Jan. 1755 *Gent Mag* XXV, 36.
    ' "She comes! she comes! ye Nine strike ev'ry string." '
    T: 'Prologue to Philosophical Exercises at Philadelphia, Nov. 12, 1754. Spoken [and written by] Mr. Jacob Duché.'
    Note: Accompanying note says that Duché wrote the prologue, except for the lines within quotations. A reprint of no. 1222.

1240. Jan. 1755 *Gent Mag* XXV, 36–7.
    'Ladies! there is something happened now so queer.'
    Note: A reprint of no. 1223.

1241. Feb. 3, 1755 *NYG* #627, 1/1–2.
    'The Muse that us'd in silver Strains to sing.'
    Note: A reprint of no. 1233.

1242. Feb. 11, 1755 *BG* #111, 2/1–2.
    'The Muse That us'd in Silvan Strains to sing.'
    Note: A reprint of no. 1233.

1243. Mar. 1, 1755 *HG* #150, 2/1.
    'Pure was this Lady, and the fairest Dame.'
    T: 'Acrostick on a Lady [Prudence Cooke] lately Deceased.' ¶ No: 15 lines. ¶ A: 'M. M.'
    Note: Cf. no. 1244.

1244. Mar. 1, 1755 *HG* #150, 2/2.
    'Weep weep *Accadie*, weep, if all that's dear.'
    T: 'On the much lamented Death of Mrs. Cooke.' ¶ No: 16 lines.
    Note: Cf. no. 1243.

1245. Mar. 3, 1755 *NYM*.
    'Shou'd it e'er be my Lot, with a Husband to live.'
    T: 'To Amyrillis. Rules for taking a Husband.' ¶ No: 28 lines.

1246. Mar. 10, 1755 *NYG* #632, 2/2.
    'The World's great Lord commands the *Dove* to fly.'
    T: 'A Thought arising from the Similitude of the Name Columbus, with the Latin Name of a Dove, which is also Columbus, That Bird being the first Discoverer of the New World after the Flood, as Columbus was of America.' ¶ No: 33 lines.
    Note: Reprinted, no. 1248.

1247. Mar. 17, 1755 *NYM*.
    'A Bag-wig of a jauntee air.'
    T: 'The Bag-Wig and the Tobacco-Pipe, A Fable.' ¶ No: 54 lines.

1248. Mar. 21, 1755 *BNL* #2750, 1/2.
    'The World's great Lord commands the *Dove* to fly.'
    Note: A reprint of no. 1246.

1249. Mar. 27, 1755 *The Instructor* I, ₦4, 13–14.
'While Faction lifts her impious Hand.'
T: 'An Ode: Suitable for the present Times.' ¶ No: 36 lines.

1250. Mar. 27, 1755 *SCG* ₦1083, 1/1.
'Go, gentle Youth! to distant Climes repair.'
Note: A reprint of no. 1237.

1251. Mar. 1755 *Scots Mag* XVII, 139–40.
'Over the hills with heart we go.'
Note: A reprint of no. 1211.

1252. Mar. 1755 *Scots Mag* XVII, 140.
'The *British* lion from his slumber wakes.'
T: 'On the present Vigorous Preparations for a French war.' ¶ No: 34 lines. ¶ A: 'Britannicus.'
Note: Dated 'Bewdley, March 17.' 'The same brave spirit too that reigns at home/Inspires her sons beyond th' Atlantic fame;/There she beholds a race of heroes rise,/T' assert her fame beneath *Columbian* skies.' Perhaps by the same author as no. 1237.

1253. Apr. 1, 1755 *BG* ₦118.
''Tis come! attend thou blest seraphick throng.'
T: 'Christus Ascendens. A Poem.' ¶ No: 64 lines.
Note: 'wrote and sent by a Son to his Father in Boston.'

1254. Apr. 17, 1755 *The Instructor* I, 28.
'The Man, whose Heart from Vice is clear.'
T: 'The Pious Sailor. A sacred Ode.' ¶ No: 24 lines.

1255. May 12, 1755 *BEP* ₦1029, 2/1.
'The Man that wou'd in Health his Life prolong.'
T: 'On the present Expedition.' ¶ No: 48 lines. ¶ A: 'V. D.' [Joseph Green].
Note: See *BEP*, May 27, 1754; *BEP*, Apr. 23, 1750.

1256. May 15, 1755 *PJ* ₦649.
''Tis strange, what diff'rent thoughts inspire.'
T: 'Possession and Desire.' ¶ No: 58 lines. ¶ A: [Jonathan Swift.]
Note: See Harold Williams, *The Poems of Jonathan Swift*, II (Oxford, 1958), 411.

1257. May 1755 *Gent Mag* XXV, 228.
'Gallica cum rabies Europam Marte nefando.'
Note: A reprint of no. 1226.

1258. June 2, 1755 *BG* ₦9.
'My son, th' Instruction that my Words impart.'
T: [Advice to a son.] ¶ No: 62 lines. ¶ A: 'W. K.'
Note: A revised reprint of no. 205.

1259. June 5, 1755 *BNL* #2761, 1/2.
   'Rise, *Britons!* rise, with all your father's might.'
   T: 'On the present State of Affairs.' ¶ No: 30 lines.
   Note: Crum R227 has the title 'Lines writ in the War with France,
      1756.'

1260. June 9, 1755 *BG* #10, 1/1.
   'Too long Britania! gentle to her Foes.'
   T: 'On the Prospect of a War.' ¶ No: 64 lines. ¶ A: 'From a young
      Genius.'
   Note: Reprinted, nos. 1261, 1265.

1261. June 21, 1755 *CG* #11, 1/1–2.
   'Too long *Britannia!* gentle to her Foes.'
   Note: A reprint of no. 1260.

1262. July 3, 1755 *SCG* #1097, 1/1.
   'The Doctors in *Charles-Town* have lately agreed.'
   T: 'A Song.' ¶ No: 16 lines + refrain 'Derry down.' ¶ A: 'O. O.'
   Note: Cf. no. 1263.

1263. July 3, 1755 *SCG* #1097, 1/1.
   'When sad Distempers rage, then Doctors strive.'
   T: [Satire on Charleston doctors.] ¶ No: 12 lines.
   Note: Cf. no. 1262.

1264. July 17, 1755 *PG* #1386.
   'A wak'ning Thought! Must Time expire indeed.'
   T: 'Reflections on the General Conflagration.' ¶ No: 18 lines. ¶ A:
      'Rusticus.'
   Note: Ugh! 'Dated Kingwood, July 1755.'

1265. Aug. 7, 1755 *PG* #1389.
   'Too long Britannia! gentle to her Foes.'
   Note: A reprint of no. 1260.

1266. Aug. 11, 1755 *BG* #19, 3/3.
   'Ecce Viator adest ah me! quam pallidus ore.'
   T: 'Questus de Ohio.' ¶ No: 26 lines. ¶ A: 'C. B.'
   Note: In *BG*, Aug. 18, 1755, 'P. M.' criticizes this poem. See no.
      1267, for the first of a series of exchanges between 'C. B.' and
      'P. M.'; cf. nos. 1272, 1273, 1275, 1280, 1281. Translated, see no.
      1279.

1267. Aug. 25, 1755 *BG* #21.
   'At Tu iterium Trucidas P. M. sarcasticé cantat.'
   T: 'A Touch on the Times, To improve P. M.'s sarcastical Genius.'
      ¶ No: 13 lines. ¶ A: 'C. B.'
   Note: See no. 1266. Cf. no. 1272.

1268. Aug. 1755 *Scots Mag* XVII, 395.
'Beneath some Indian shrub, if chance you spy.'
T: 'On the death of Gen. [Edward] Braddock.' ¶ No: 10 lines.
Note: For a fuller title, see no. 1270. Reprinted in Winthrop Sargent, *History of an Expedition* (Philadelphia, 1855), p. 415, and in Lee McCardall, *Ill-Starred General* (Pittsburgh, 1958), p. 269.

1269. Aug. 1755 *Gent Mag* XXV, 372.
'Hail King supreme! all wise and good.'
T: 'Hymn in the Country.' ¶ No: 32 lines. ¶ A: 'By a Youth of Fifteen.' 'Americanus.'
Note: Ugh.

1270. Aug. 1755 *Gent Mag* XXV, 383.
'Beneath some *Indian* shrub, if chance you spy.'
T: 'On the Death of Gen. Braddock, said to be slain in an Ambuscade, by the French and Indians, on the Banks of the Ohio, July 9, 1755.'
Note: A reprint of no. 1268.

1271. Aug. 1755 *Universal Mag* XVII, 81.
'In the first place, reverse what all schoolmasters use.'
T: 'A Rebus.' ¶ No: 6 lines. ¶ A: 'Kingstonianus.'

1272. Sept. 1, 1755 *BG* ⚹22, 3/2.
'Whoever picks your Bone will swear.'
T: 'Mirisico Dichonum Divenatori, Dom° C. B.' ¶ No: 19 lines in Latin & English. ¶ A: 'P. M.'
Note: Cf. nos. 1266, 1267, and 1273.

1273. Sept. 8, 1755 *BG* ⚹23, 3/3.
'Quickquid in buccam venerit, effutit.'
T: 'Dom°. P. M.' ¶ A: 'C. B.'
Note: Cf. nos. 1266, 1267, and 1272.

1274. Sept. 8, 1755 *NYM*, 3/1–2.
'E're while from eastern shores, well-pleas'd we heard.'
T: [On the French and Indian war.] ¶ No: 86 lines. ¶ A: 'Elegiacus' [Benjamin Young Prime].
Note: Reprinted, no. 1277. Reprinted in Prime's *Patriot Muse* (London, 1764), pp. 9–11. For accounts of Prime, see C. Webster Wheelock, 'Benjamin Young Prime, class of 1751, Poet-Physician,' *Princeton U. Lib. Chron.*, XXIX (1968), 129–135; and 'The Poet Benjamin Prime (1733–1791), *Am. Lit.*, XL (1969), 495–471.

1275. Sept. 15, 1755 *BG* #24, 2/2.
   'Sit licet in Satyra P. M. nimis acer & ardens.'
   T: [Reply to C. B.] ¶ No: 20 lines in Latin & English. ¶ A: 'P. M.'
   Note: Cf. no. 1266.

1276. Sept. 15, 1755 *BG* #24, 2/2.
   'While Caelia here each raptur'd Lover spies.'
   T: 'On the Picture of a young Lady drawn in the Picture of Diana.'
   ¶ No: 12 lines.

1277. Sept. 18, 1755 *BNL* #2766, 3/1.
   'Ere while from eastern shores, well pleas'd we heard.'
   Note: A reprint of no. 1274.

1278. Sept. 22, 1755 *BG* #25 *Supp.*
   'Why do the Heathen Rage, or Why.'
   T: 'The following VERSE, on the present Expedition against
   C[*row*]n P[*oin*]t, was wrote in the camp at the Falls.' ¶ No: 48
   lines. ¶ A: 'By a Sergeant-Major of the Regiment of Rhode-
   Island, August 1, 1755.'

1279. Sept. 22, 1755 *BG* #26 *Supp*, 2/1.
   'Lo, the swift Courier hov'ring on the Eye!'
   T: 'A Monody on the Defeat at Ohio.' ¶ No: 36 lines. ¶ A: 'N. H.'
   Note: This is a translation of no. 1266. 'As the ungenerous and
   causeless Criticising of Mr. P. M. have produced a literary Con-
   test; for the sake of the Illiterate I have here translated the Com-
   position which was the first subject of his sarcastical Genius.'

1280. Sept. 22, 1755 *BG* #25 *Supp*, 2/2.
   'Asseris in Satyra atroci te velle Magistrum.'
   T: 'Dom° P. M.' ¶ No: 6 lines in Latin & English. ¶ A: 'C. B.'
   Note: Cf. no. 1266.

1281. Sept. 22, 1755 *BG* #25 *Supp*, 2/2.
   'Hold, Censure hold! a Timrous Virgin spare.'
   T: 'In Answer to the Epigram (in No. 23) on the Representative
   Goddess.' ¶ No: 8 lines. ¶ A: 'N. H.'
   Note: Cf. no. 1266.

1282. Sept. 22, 1755 *NYG* #661, 3/2.
   'Feeble and tuneless are my native Lays.'
   T: [Praise of Sir Charles Hardy.] ¶ No: 38 lines.
   Note: Welcoming verse for Sir Charles Hardy, Gov. of N. Y.

1283. Sept. 29, 1755 *NYM*, 2/2.
   'There curst Canadia's motley-savage Herd.'
   T: 'on The Bravery of our Commanders ... on the Banks of Lake-
   George.' ¶ No: 20 lines. ¶ A: [Benjamin Young Prime?]

Note: Spoken 'at the public Commencement, held at Newark.' Reprinted nos. 1285, 1286, 1293. Prime, who graduated in 1751 from Princeton, was writing similar poetry, returned to Princeton to be a tutor at about this time, and published in the *NYM* (cf. no. 1274).

1284. Sept. 1755 *Gent Mag* XXV, 421.
'Ah! *Braddock* why did you persuade.'
T: 'Apology for the Men who deserted Gen. Braddock, when surprized by the ambuscade.' ¶ No: 6 lines.
Note: Reprinted in Sargent (see no. 1268), p. 416, and in McCardall (see no. 1268), p. 269.

1285. Oct. 4, 1755 *CG* #26.
'There Canada's curst motly savage Herd,'
T: 'In a Latin Oration pronounced at the Commencement lately at Newark in New Jersey, the following English Lines were introduced on the late Defeat of the French at Lake George.'
Note: A reprint of no. 1283.

1286. Oct. 13, 1755 *BG* #28, 2/2.
'There curst Canadia's motely savage Herd,'
Note: A reprint of no. 1283.

1287. Oct. 16, 1755 *SCG*, 3/1.
'Who don't remember the last Hurricane.'
T: [Verse in advertisement.] ¶ No: 8 lines. ¶ A: 'John Wood.'

1288. Oct. 1755 *Scots Mag* XVII, 488.
'Then 'tis decreed—the vain exulting *Gaul*.'
T: 'Verses on Gen. Braddock's defeat.' ¶ No: 60 lines.
Note: For the source, and a fuller title, see no. 1289. Reprinted, nos. 1289, 1290, 1292. Reprinted in McCarty, III, 5–7. Davis (see no. 1035), suggests that this poem may be by Samuel Davies, pp. 219–221.

1289. Nov. 10, 1755 *NYM*, 4/2.
'Then 'tis decreed—the vain exulting Gaul.'
T: 'Verses occasion'd by the melancholly News of the British Forces being defeated and General Braddock slain, on the banks of the River Ohio.'
Note: 'From the Bristol Journal, of September the 13th, 1755.' A reprint of no. 1288.

1290. Nov. 10, 1755 *NYG* #668.
'Then 'Tis decreed—the vain exulting Gaul.'
Note: A reprint of no. 1288.

1291. Nov. 17, 1755 *NYG* #669, 1/1–2.
 'He is not form'd for Arms, the Soldier's Pride.'
 T: 'On Martial Virtue.' ¶ No: 50 lines.

1292. Nov. 22, 1755 *CG* #33, 1/1–2.
 'Then 'Tis decreed—The vain exulting Gaul.'
 Note: A reprint of no. 1288.

1293. Nov. 28, 1755 *VG*.
 'There curst Canadia's motely savage Herd.'
 Note: A reprint of no. 1283.

1294. Dec. 15, 1755 *NYG* #673, 3/2.
 'With ev'ry Patriot Virtue crown'd.'
 T: 'To Major General [William] Johnson.' ¶ No: 20 lines. ¶ A: 'A. d. C.'

1295. Dec. 1755 *Scots Mag* XVII, 599–600.
 'Hendrick, bold Sachem of the Mohawk race!'
 T: 'On the Death of old Hendrick, Sachem of the Mohawks.' ¶ No: 14 lines. ¶ A: 'W. Rider.'
 Note: Partially reprinted, no. 1332. William Rider (1723–1785) was a minor English author.

1756

1296. Jan. 1, 1756 *PJ* #682, 1/1.
 'In the Almighty's Pow'r how great is Man.'
 T: 'On that matchless Pile of Art, called, the Microcosm Or the World, in Mineature, Inscribed, to the ingenious Inventor and Builder thereof. Mr. Henry Bridges.'
 Note: Like nos. 1297 and 1298, this poem is in effect an advertisement for Bridges, who was currently exhibiting in Philadelphia. Reprinted, no. 1301.

1297. Jan. 22, 1756 *PG* #1413, 3/2.
 'To sooth the Soul by tender strokes of art.'
 T: 'A Parody on Pope's Prologue to Cato. Addressed to Mr. Henry Bridges, Constructor of that elaborate Piece of Mechanism, the Microcosm.' ¶ No: 36 lines.
 Note: Cf. no. 1296. Reprinted, no. 1302, 1319.

1298. Jan. 22, 1756 *PJ* #685.
 'Bridges! whene'er thy Little World we view.'
 T: 'On seeing the Microcosm at the King's Theatre in the Hay-Market London 1751.'
 Note: Cf. no. 1296. Reprinted, nos. 1305, 1321.

1299. Feb. 16, 1756 *NYM* #184, 1/1–2.
'War, mournful War, I sing my Country's Woe.'
T: 'Lines ... Reflections on the State of our Country, and also on the Bravery of some of our Commanders.' ¶ No: 131 lines. ¶ A: 'Respublica.'
Note: Mentions Admiral Boscawen; General Edward Braddock; William Johnson; Phineas Lyman.

1300. Feb. 1756 *Lon Mag* XXV, 85–6.
'From climes where hot Phoebus is scorching my skin.'
T: 'To Chloe, with a Present of Sweetmeats.' ¶ No: 22 lines. ¶ A: 'F—'
Note: Dated 'Antiqua, Dec., 1755.'

1301. Mar. 1, 1756 *NYM* #186, 1/1.
'In the Almight's Pow'r, how great is Man!'
Note: A reprint of no. 1296.

1302. Mar. 8, 1756 *NYG* #686, 2/3.
'To sooth the Soul by tender Strokes of Art.'
Note: A reprint of no. 1297.

1303. Mar. 11, 1756 *SCG*, 2/1.
'Assist, ye greater Bards assist.'
T: 'On Miss Dolly S—.' ¶ No: 28 lines.

1304. Mar. 15, 1756 *BG* #50, 1/3.
'Artful Painter, by this Plan.'
T: 'The Petition.' ¶ No: 26 lines.
Note: Reprinted, no. 1310.

1305. Mar. 15, 1756 *NYG* #687, 2/2.
'Bridges! whene'er thy *Little World* we view.'
Note: A reprint of no. 1298.

1306. Mar. 20, 1756 *CG* #50, 2/2.
'How welcome this, when fill'd with Fear.'
T: 'Sudden Reflections, upon hearing of the valiant Conduct and remarkable Success of the Provincial Forces, in their late Engagement with the French, at Lake George.' ¶ No: 55 lines.
Note: Dated 'Sept. 13, 1755.'

1307. Mar. 25, 1756 *MG*.
'Fair as the dawning Light! auspicious Guest.'
T: 'Chearfulness.' ¶ No: 50 lines.
Note: Crum F26.

1308. Mar. 25, 1756 *MG.*
'How vain is Man! How fluttering are his Joys!'
T: 'Reflections on the Uncertainty of wordly Enjoyments.' ¶ No: 36
lines.

1309. Mar. 25, 1756 *MG.*
'Should the whole Earth of growing Numbers stand.'
T: 'A Father's advice to his Son, on the important Subject of Eter-
nity.' ¶ No: 12 lines.

1310. Mar. 29, 1756 *NYM* ⚭190, 1/1–2.
'Artful Painter by this Plan.'
Note: A reprint of no. 1304.

1311. Apr. 3, 1756 *CG* ⚭52, 3/2.
'All hail, ye great *Preservers* of our Land!'
T: [On English Success in war.] ¶ No: 45 lines. ¶ A: 'B—'

1312. Apr. 24, 1756 *CG* ⚭55.
'And live we yet by Power Divine?'
T: [Religious verse.] ¶ No: 28 lines.

1313. Apr. 26, 1756 *BG* ⚭56, 3/2.
'Vital Spark of heavenly Flame.'
T: 'The lying Christian to his Soul.' ¶ No: 18 lines. ¶ A: [Alexander
Pope.]
Note: Printed in Norman Ault and John Butt, *Minor Poems* (Ox-
ford, 1954), p. 94. Crum V67.

1314. Apr. 1756 *Lon Mag* XXV, 189.
'No more I'll paint in soft descriptive strain.'
T: 'On the present State of America, and General Braddock's De-
feat.' ¶ No: 59 lines. ¶ A: ['by an English Lady in America.']
Note: For a reprint under a different title, see no. 1315.

1315. Apr. 1756 *Scots Mag* XVIII, 180.
'No more I'll paint, in soft descriptive strains.'
T: 'Verses written by an English Lady in America, in the year 1755.'
Note: A reprint of no. 1314.

1316. May 8, 1756 *CG* ⚭57, 4/2.
'Whereas *John Perkins*, of *North-Amity*, instead of his *own* Name.'
T: [Doggerel.] ¶ No: 10 lines. ¶ A: Signed by John Orsborn and
James Sherman.
Note: Dated 'April 27, 1756.'

1317. May 17, 1756 *NYM* ⚭197, 1/1.
'Ah me! What horrid Noise is this! Tis sure.'

T: 'The Soliloquy of an Impenitent wak'd by the Earthquake.' ¶ No:
64 lines.
Note: For a companion piece, see no. 1318.

1318. May 17, 1756 *NYM* ✻197, 1/1–2.
'What shocking Sound has roused me thus from Sleep.'
T: 'The Soliloquy of a true Christian wak'd by the Earthquake.' ¶
No: 44 lines.
Note: Cf. no. 1317. Reprinted, no. 1382.

1319. May 24, 1756 *BG* ✻60, 3/2.
'To sooth the Soul by tender Strokes of Art.'
Note: A reprint of no. 1297.

1320. May 29, 1756 *CG* ✻60, 4/2.
'Free is my Heart, and just my Cause.'
T: 'The Soldiers Soliloquy.' ¶ No: 32 lines. ¶ A: 'D—'
Note: Mentions 'heroic' John Winslow and 'brave' Phineas Lyman.
Reprinted, no. 1323.

1321. May 31, 1756 *BG* ✻61, 3/2.
'Bridges! when'er Little World we view.'
Note: A reprint of no. 1298.

1322. June 5, 1756 *SCG*, p. 7.
'Be all thy Labours, all thy Cares pursu'd.'
T: [lines praising William Henry Lyttelton, new Gov.] ¶ No: 6
lines.
Note: This may be the last 6 lines of a longer poem. Dated 'Charles-
town, June 3.' Reprinted, no. 1325.

1323. June 7, 1756 *NYM* ✻200.
'Free is my Heart, and just my Cause.'
Note: A reprint of no. 1320.

1324. June 24, 1756 *BNL* ✻2816, 2/1.
'Friends! Countrymen! or, if a nobler Name.'
T: [Verses rousing Americans to fight.] ¶ No: 17 lines. ¶ A: [Rev.
James Maury?]
Note: The poem is reprinted from a no-longer extant issue of 'the
Virginia Gazette, April 30.' These verses preface the first num-
ber of an essay series, 'The Virginia Centinel, No. 1.' The essay
mentions that 'acceptable and popular Officer ... Col. Washing-
ton.' Other numbers of the essay series reprinted from the *VG*
reveal that the author was a minister who corresponded with
ministers in France, had a parish on the Virginia frontier, and
was unusually familiar with details of the Huguenot persecution

and emigration. This information, coupled with the similarity of proposals by the Rev. James Maury to the contents of proposals by the 'Virginia Centinel,' suggests Maury's authorship. See Maury's proposals to the Hon. Philip Ludwell, *Va. Mag. of Hist. and Biog.*, XIX (1911), 292–304. (An incomplete draft of this letter was published in Ann Maury, *Memoirs of a Huguenot Family* [New York, N. Y.], pp. 431–442.) See also Worthington C. Ford, 'Washington and "Centinel X," ' *Pa. Mag. of Hist. and Biog.*, XX (1898), 436–451. Reprinted, no. 1330. Cf. no. 1367. Although this number of the 'Virginia Centinel' was also copied in the *NYG* June 14, the *CG* June 26, and the *BEP* June 28, none of these reprinted the poem.

1325. July 1, 1756 *PG* #1426.
'Be all Thy Labours, all Thy Cares pursu'd.'
Note: A reprint of no. 1322.

1326. July 15, 1756 *PG* #1438.
'Draw near ye Youths in whom soft Sorrows Dwell.'
T: 'To the Memory of' William Willcocks. ¶ No: 21 lines. ¶ A: 'By a Fellow-Student.' [Francis Hopkinson.']
Note: The poem follows an obituary notice: 'On the 28th of last Month died Mr. William Willcocks, Son of Robert Willcocks, Esq., of Kent, upon Delaware, in the 15th Year of his Age.' Cf. no. 1327. Reprinted in Hopkinson's *Miscellaneous Essays*, III, pt. 2 (Philadelphia, 1792), p. 10.

1327. July 15, 1756 *PG* #1438.
'Now hostile Fury every Breast inspires.'
T: [Elegy on William Willcocks.] ¶ No: 36 lines. ¶ A: 'by another Hand.'
Note: Cf. no. 1326.

1328. July 22, 1756 *PJ* #711, 2/2.
'Relentless Death! still shall Thy rugged hand.'
T: 'Verses occasioned by the Death of Mr. John R. Bayard.' ¶ No: 38 lines. ¶ A: By 'a young Gentleman in the Country.'
Note: Bayard died July 15, 1756.

1329. Aug. 2, 1756 *NYM* #208, 1/1–2.
'Hail Britains, who, in western Regions dwell!'
T: A 'poetical Essay upon the Arrival of the Earl of Loudon.' ¶ No: 29 lines.
Note: Cf. no. 1331.

1330. Aug. 12, 1756 *MG* pp. 1 & 2.
'Friends, Countrymen! or, if a nobler Name.'

Note: A reprint of no. 1324. There are 2 Va. Centinel essays in the *MG* of this date.

1331. Aug. 16, 1756 *NYM* #210, 1/1–2.
'In Transport rise, ye Sons of Britain, rise.'
T: 'On the Arrival of his Excellency John Earl of Loudon, Commander in Chief of his Majesty's Forces in North America.' ¶ No: 100 lines. ¶ A: 'Americanus.'
Note: Cf. no. 1329.

1332. Sept. 6, 1756 *NYM* #213, 1/3.
'Hendrick, bold Sachem of the Mohawk Race!'
Note: A partial (10 lines) reprint of no. 1295.

1333. Sept. 23, 1756 *SCG*, 3/1.
'Dear Sir, 'tis with pleasure the following I write.'
T: 'A late Epistle to Mr. C[*levelan*]d, or A[*dmiral*] B[*yng*]g's Letter versified.' ¶ No: 30 lines. ¶ A: 'B[*yn*]g'
Note: A satire on the cowardice of Admiral Byng. See Byng's letter, dated May 25, 1756, printed in *SCG*, Sept. 16, 1756, 1/1: 'Extract of a Letter from Admiral Byng to Mr. Cleveland, Secretary of the Admiralty.' Cf. no. 1334.

1334. Sept. 23, 1756 *SCG*, 3/1.
'If you believe what Frenchmen say.'
T: 'On a certain most Admirable Admiral.' ¶ No: 10 lines.
Note: Another satire on Byng. Cf. no. 1333.

1335. Sept. 30, 1756 *PJ* #721, 1/1.
'Still shall the Tyrant Scourge of Gaul.'
T: 'Ode to the Inhabitants of Pennsylvania.' ¶ No: 60 lines. ¶ A: 'Eugenio.'
Note: This war poetry mentions Braddock and Peter Schuyler, and praises the Earl of Loudon and John Armstrong, as well as Pennsylvania's Governor William Denny. Printed also in *PG* (no. 1336). Reprinted, nos. 1339, 1342. Reprinted in McCarty, I, 339–341; in Duyckinck, I, 448; and in Stevenson, pp. 114–115.

1336. Sept. 30, 1756 *PG* #1449, 1/1.
'Still shall the Tyrant Scourge of Gaul.'
Note: See no. 1335.

1337. Oct. 4, 1756 *NYG* #716, 3/2.
'How kind has Heav'n adorn'd this happy Land.'
T: 'On the Times.' ¶ No: 16 lines.
Note: Several lines echo Joseph Addison's 'Letter from Italy.' Reprinted, nos. 1338, 1341, 1343.

1338. Oct. 9, 1756 *CG* #79, 3/2.
'How kind has Heav'n adorn'd this happy Land.'
Note: A reprint of no. 1337.

1339. Oct. 23, 1756 *CG* #81, 1/1–2.
'Still shall the Tyrant Scourge of Gaul.'
Note: A reprint of no. 1335.

1340. Oct. 25, 1756 *NYG* #719, 3/1.
'All Night invoking sleep's balsamic Dew.'
T: 'A Complaint to the God of Sleep.' ¶ No: 14 lines. ¶ A: 'By a
Lady.'

1341. Oct. 28, 1756 *NHG* #4.
'How kind has Heav'n adorn'd this happy Land.'
Note: A reprint of no. 1337.

1342. Oct. 28, 1756 *NHG* #4.
'Still shall the Tyrant Scourge of Gaul.'
Note: A reprint of no. 1335.

1343. Nov. 4, 1756 *MG*.
'How kind has Heav'n adorn'd this happy Land.'
Note: A reprint of no. 1337.

1344. Dec. 2, 1756 *NHG* #9.
'Minorca's gone! Oswego too is lost!'
T: [From the advertisement for *Ames's Almanack* for 1757.] ¶ No:
8 lines. ¶ A: [Nathaniel Ames.]
Note: Reprinted in Samuel Briggs, *The Essays, Humor, and Poems
of Nathaniel Ames* (Cleveland, Ohio), p. 274.

1345. Dec. 13, 1756 *NYG* #726, 1/1.
'An humble Muse resumes the plaintive Strain.'
T: 'To the Memory of the late Rev. William Johnson.' ¶ No: 74
lines.
Note: Rev. William Johnson (1731–1756) son of the Rev. Samuel
Johnson, President of King's College, died in London shortly
after being ordained. See Weis, *Middle Colonies*, p. 247.

1346. Dec. 16, 1756 *SCG*, 2/1.
'Fair Carolina, now doth much lament.'
T: 'An Elegy On the much lamented Loss of Col. Hyrne's Lady.' ¶
No: 28 lines.
Note: Probably on Mrs. Henry Hyrne.

1757

1347. Jan. 20, 1757 *PG* #1465, 1/2.
   'Peace with your Fiddling there—It shall be spoke.'
   T: 'An occasional Prologue for the young Gentlemen of the College
      of Philadelphia, who, for their Improvement in Oratory, acted
      Alfred, in January, 1757.' ¶ No: 54 lines. ¶ A: [William Smith.]
   Note: 'Spoken by W. Hamilton, entering hastily and interrupting
      the Music.' Reprinted, nos. 1348, 1357, 1363, 1368 (where the
      attribution is given). Cf. no. 1349.

1348. Jan. 27, 1757 *PJ* #738, 1/2.
   'Peace with your Fiddling There—It shall be spoke.'
   Note: A reprint of no. 1347.

1349. Jan. 27, 1757 *PJ* #738, 1/3.
   'To rouse the slumbring *Virtue* of the Free.'
   T: 'Occasional Epilogue for the same.' ¶ No: 45 lines. ¶ A: [Pro-
      vost William Smith.]
   Note: 'Spoken by Mr. Duche jun. who acted Alfred.' Cf. no. 1347.
      Reprinted, nos. 1350, 1358, 1359, 1369 (where the attribution is
      given).

1350. Feb. 10, 1757 *PG* #1468, 1/2.
   'To rouse the slumb'ring Virtue of the Free.'
   Note: A reprint of no. 1349.

1351. Feb. 10, 1757 *PG* #1468.
   'To Thee, sweet *Harmonist*, in grateful Lays.'
   T: 'To Miss Hopkinson, on her excellent Performance of the vocal
      Parts in an Oratorical Exercise at the College of Philadelphia.' ¶
      No: 34 lines. ¶ A: 'J. Duché.'
   Note: Dated 'Philadelphia, Jan. 18, 1757.' Reprinted, nos. 1360,
      1370. Reprinted in the *Universal Magazine*, VIII (Mar. 1792),
      198.

1352. Feb. 10, 1757 *PG* #1468.
   'The pleasing Task be mine, sweet Maid!'
   T: 'To Miss Lawrence, for her kind Assistance on the same Occa-
      sion.' ¶ No: 20 lines. ¶ A: 'F. Hopkinson.'
   Note: Dated 'Phila. Feb. 1, 1757.' Reprinted, nos. 1361, 1371.
      George Everett Hastings, *The Life and Works of Francis Hopkin-
      son* (Chicago, 1926), p. 55, mentions this poem. Reprinted in
      Hopkinson's *Miscellaneous Essays*, III, pt. 2 (Philadelphia, 1792),
      pp. 8–9.

1353. Feb. 24, 1757 *SCG* №1184, 1/1.
'Oh! why is British Virtue at a Stand?'
T: [Urging military preparedness.] ¶ No: 24 lines.
Note: Reprinted, nos. 1362, 1365, 1372.

1354. Feb. 1757 *Scots Mag* XIX, 75–6.
'Long had a mungrel *French* and *Indian* brood.'
T: 'Extract from a poem on the barbarities of the French, and their
savage allies and proselytes, on the frontiers of Virginia.' ¶ No:
86 lines. ¶ A: 'By Sam. Davies, A. M.'
Note: For another printing, see no. 1355. Reprinted, nos. 1401,
1406. Reprinted in Davis (see no. 1035), pp. 170–172.

1355. Feb. 1757 *Gent Mag* XXVII, 83.
'Long had a mungrel French and Indian brood.'
Note: For another printing, see no. 1354.

1356. Feb. 1757 *Gent Mag* XXVII, 83.
'Welcome, pretty harmless creature.'
T: 'To a Robin Red-breast that lodg'd in my House.' ¶ No: 16 lines.

1357. Mar. 7, 1757 *NYM* №239, 1/2–3.
'Peace with your Fiddling there—It shall be spoke.'
Note: A reprint of no. 1347.

1358. Mar. 7, 1757 *NYM* №239, 1/3.
'To rouse the slumbering Virtue of the Free.'
Note: A reprint of no. 1349.

1359. Mar. 18, 1757 *NHG* №24.
'To rouse the slumb'ring *Virtue* of the Free.'
Note: A reprint of no. 1349.

1360. Mar. 18, 1757 *NHG* №24.
'To Thee, sweet Harmonist, in grateful Lays.'
Note: A reprint of no. 1351.

1361. Mar. 18, 1757 *NHG* №24.
'The pleasing Task be mine, sweet Maid.'
Note: A reprint of no. 1352.

1362. Mar. 21, 1757 *NYG* №741, 1/1.
'Oh! why is British Virtue at a Stand?'
Note: A reprint of no. 1353.

1363. Mar. 25, 1757 *NHG* №23.
'Peace with your Fiddling there—It shall be spoke.'
Note: A reprint of no. 1347.

1364. Mar. 26, 1757 *CG* #103.
'The Man of upright Heart and Soul.'
T: 'The Bold Soldier. Inscrib'd to Major-General [Phinias] Lyman.'
¶ No: 56 lines.

1365. Apr. 15, 1757 *NHG* #28, 4/2.
'Oh! why is British Virtue at a Stand?'
Note: A reprint of no. 1353.

1366. Apr. 27, 1757 *PJ* #803.
'Ye power divine, assist my hand and heart.'
T: 'On the Evil of Pride.' ¶ No: 52 lines. ¶ A: 'By a Female Hand.'

1367. Apr. 29, 1757 *NHG* #30.
'Virginians! rouse! and from your Borders drive.'
T: [From Va. Centinel, No. XVIII.] ¶ No: 26 lines. ¶ A: [Rev.
James Maury?]
Note: Cf. no. 1324.

1368. Apr. 1757 *Gent Mag* XXVII, 178.
'Peace with your fiddling there—It shall be spoke.'
A: 'By the Rev. Mr. Smith, Provost of the College of Philadelphia.'
Note: A reprint of no. 1347.

1369. Apr. 1757 *Gent Mag* XXVII, 178–9.
'To rouse the slumb'ring *virtue* of the free.'
A: 'By the same' [i.e., Provost William Smith].
Note: A reprint of no. 1349.

1370. Apr. 1757 *Gent Mag* XXVII, 179.
'To Thee, sweet harmonist! in grateful lays.'
Note: A reprint of no. 1351.

1371. Apr. 1757 *Gent Mag* XXVII, 179.
'The pleasing task, sweet maid! be mine.'
Note: A reprint of no. 1352.

1372. May 2, 1757 *BG* #109, 1/1.
'Oh! why is British Virtue at a Stand?'
Note: A reprint of no. 1353.

1373. May 2, 1757 *BG* #109, 3/2–3.
'O Quem futurum pectore finxeram.'
T: 'In obitum Magnae spei Juvenis, Nathanaelis Smiberti, &c.' ¶
No: 64 lines. ¶ A: 'Jo. Beveridge.'
Note: Dated 'Hartford, Connecticutensium, 1757.' Cf. no. 1375.
Reprinted 1) *In obitum Magnae Spei Juvenis ...* (Boston, 1757);
2) in Beveridge, *Epistolae Familiares* (Phila., 1765), pp. 44–46;
3) in H. W. Foote, *John Smibert, Painter* (Cambridge, Mass.,
1950), pp. 259–260.

1374. May 30, 1757 *BEP* ⚹1135, 1/2.
'God prosper long our noble King.'
T: 'Courge and Conduct display'd. To the Tune of *Chevy-Chace.*' ¶
No: 76 lines.
Note: 'From the Halifax Gazette, April 30, 1757.' 'A True Relation
of a bloody Engagement which is to happen on the Seventh Day
of June next, between a Privateer of this Place, and a large
French Merchant Ship: Wherein is shewn the Effects of Courage,
when duly tempers with Discretion. Now made publick for the
Benefit of all young Privateer Captains.' Cf. no. 819.

1375. May 1757 *Lon Mag* XXVI, 255.
'Vincere si rigidam posset eruditio mortem.'
T: 'In Obitam Juvenis ornatissimi (ac Amici mei charissimi) Joannis
Smiberti, Evangelij Praeconis. Mortaletatem autem expletus est
undecimo Mensis Martij, 1757.' ¶ A: 'A Millar, Taodumensis.'
Note: Cf. no. 1373.

1376. June 17, 1757 *NHG* ⚹37.
'For The[e], the Soldiers, with Heroik Grace.'
T: [On money.] ¶ No: 12 lines.
Note: Probably from *The Pleasant Art of Money Catching.*

1377. July 4, 1757 *NYM* ⚹256, 1/3.
'What's the spring or the sweet smiling rose.'
T: 'Verses ... on the Liberties of the Nation.' ¶ No: 20 lines. ¶ A:
'by a young Lady.'
Note: Reprinted in McCarty, I, 324–325.

1378. July 22, 1757 *NHG* ⚹42.
'In Gold and Silver what unseen Deceit.'
T: 'The Mischief of Gold and Silver.' ¶ No: 12 lines.

1379. July 29, 1757 *NHG* ⚹43.
'O the Immense, the Amazing Height.'
T: 'The God of Thunder.' ¶ No: 20 lines.

1380. Aug. 25, 1757 *SCG* ⚹1200, 4/2.
'The Means and Arts that to Perfection bring.'
T: 'Extract of a Peom, entitled Indico, Being the First in the Col-
lection.' ¶ No: 5 lines. ¶ A: [Charles Woodmason.]
Note: 'Just Published. Proposals for Printing, by Subscription, A
Collection of Poems, On various Subjects: By a Resident of South
Carolina ... Subscriptions will be taken in, by Mr. William Hen-
derson, Master of the Free School in Charles Town, by Mr.
Robert Wells, Bookseller and Stationer in Elliott Street, and Mr.
William Bampfield, Merchant in Broad Street. By Mr. Joseph
Brown, Merchant, and Dr. Charles Fyfe, in George Town. By

Mr. Daniel Dunbibin in North-Carolina. And by Messrs. Francis Stuart and John Gordon, Merchants in Port Royal.' The 'Extract of a Poem,' like the *Proposals*, attempted to drum up interest in a collection of Woodmason's poems—which was never published. Reprinted in Hennig Cohen, 'A Colonial Poem on Indigo Culture,' *Agricultural History*, XXX (1956), 42–43.

1381. Oct. 13, 1757 *MG*.
'To see my Friends some Distance out of Town.'
T: 'The Stage-Coach from Bourn, imitated: and addressed to Mr. Hogarth.' ¶ No: 34 lines. ¶ A: 'By the author of *The Little Book*.' 'X' [John Mercer].
Note: Dated 'Belmont on Occoquon, in Virginia, August 31st, 1757.' Good, competent, amusing verse. This poem 'The production of a Friend of mine' was sent to Jonas Green by 'J. D.' 'The Little Book' was a euphemism for the 'Dinwiddeanae,' a series of satiric poems aimed principally at Virginia's Governor Robert Dinwiddie. For an edition of 'The Little Book,' see Richard Beale Davis, 'The Colonial Virginia Satirist,' *Transactions* of the Am. Philos. Soc., N. S., LVII, pt. 1 (1967); and for confirmation of the suggestion that it was written by John Mercer (1704–1768), lawyer, of 'Marlborough,' Stafford Co., Va., see J. A. Leo Lemay's review of Davis, in the *Va. Mag. of Hist. and Biog.*, LXXV (1967), 491–3. For another poem in the style of Prior, see no. 1202.

1382. Oct. 14, 1757 *NHG* ℳ54.
'What shocking sound has rouz'd me thus from sleep ?'
Note: A reprint of no. 1318.

1383. Oct. 1757 *Scots Mag* XIX, 528–9.
'From these lone walls, and this ungrateful shore.'
T: 'Epistle to a Friend.' ¶ No: 91 lines.
Note: Dated 'Fort George.'

1384. Oct. 1757 *Am Mag* I, 44.
'Thus to a young despairing swain.'
T: 'The Progress of Love. A Cantata.' ¶ No: 32 lines.

1385. Oct. 1757 *Am Mag* I, 44–5.
'Hark! hark! the [s]weet vibrating lyre.'
T: 'Ode on Music. Written at Philadelphia by a young Gentleman of 17, on his beginning to learn the Harpsicord.' ¶ No: 36 lines. ¶ A: [Francis Hopkinson.]
Note: Cf. no. 1387. Reprinted in Hopkinson's *Miscellaneous Essays* III, pt. II, pp. 5–6. See Hastings (no. 1352), p. 62.

1386. Oct. 1757 *Am Mag* I, 45.
'Tuneful sisters! sacred nine.'
T: 'Ode on a late Marriage.' ¶ No: 74 lines.
Note: Dated 'Philadelphia, September 12th, 1757.'

1387. Nov. 1757 *Am Mag* I, 84–6.
'Hence Melancholy, Care and Sorrow!'
T: 'L'Allegro. Humble inscribed to B. C[*he*]w, Esq.' ¶ No: 216
lines. ¶ A: 'By the Author of the Ode on Music, published in
our last.' [Francis Hopkinson.]
Note: Line 140: 'The lawyer—here forgive me *Chew.' *'The
Author studies Law under him.' Reprinted in Hopkinson's *Mis-
cellaneous Essays*, III, pt. 2 (Philadelphia, 1792), 21–27.

1388. Nov. 1757 *Am Mag* I. 86–8.
'Vanish mirth and vanish joy.'
Il Penseroso. By the same. Humbly inscribed to the Rev. Mr. S[mi]th.'
¶ No: 210 lines. ¶ A: [Francis Hopkinson.]
Note: Line 18: Reveals that Provost William Smith 'was the Au-
thor's preceptor in Philosophy,' and line 73, mentions 'A Night-
bird vulgarly called the Wipperwill.' Reprinted in Hopkinson's
Miscellaneous Essays, III, pt. 2 (Philadelphia, 1792), 28–35.

1389. Nov. 1757 *Am Mag* I, 88.
'Imagine not those lines are writ.'
T: 'To a young Lady at a Boarding School' ¶ No: 56 lines.

1390. Dec. 1, 1757 *MG* #656.
'Fleet! Spread thy Canvass Wing.'
T: 'Admiral Hawke's Health; Or, Success to his Expedition. A New
Toast, Tune, God save our Noble King.' ¶ No: 14 lines.
Note: Reprinted from 'New York, Nov. 21.' Reprinted, no. 1392.

1391. Dec. 1, 1757 *MG* #656.
'Man should weigh well the Nature of Himself.'
T: [On Man.] ¶ No: 15 lines. ¶ A: Alexander Lord Colville?
Note: Reprinted from Boston (Green & Russell's paper, Nov. 14).
'The following Lines are beautifully wrote with a Diamond on a
Pane of Glass in a Casement of the House in this Town, some
Time since inhabited by the Right Honourable Alexander Lord
Colville.'

1392. Dec. 2, 1757 *NHG* #61.
'Fleet! spread thy Canvas Wing.'
Note: A reprint of no. 1390.

1393. Dec. 15, 1757 *PG* #1512.
'Hail learned Bard! who dost thy Power dispense.'
T: 'On the Author of that excellent Book, entitled, The Way to
Health, long Life and Happiness.' ¶ No: 66 lines. ¶ A: 'By a
Female Hand.'
Note: On Thomas Tyron's *Way to Health.*

1395. Dec. 1757 *Am Mag* I, 128–9.
'An amorous youth inclining to wed.'
T: 'Socrates on Matrimony.' ¶ No: 12 lines.
Note: Dated 'Philadelphia, Dec. 19, 1757.' Title from 'Contents.'

1396. Dec. 1757 *Am Mag* I, 129.
'First form'd and bred within some musing brain.'
T: 'Enigma.' ¶ No: 17 lines.
Note: Dated 'Lewes, Dec. 2, 1757.' See the 'Answer by 'Annandius'
(no. 1416); and the reply to 'Annandius' (no. 1437).

1397. Dec. 1757 *Am Mag* I, 129.
'To a fifth of the wind, that pierces us most.'
T: 'A Rebus.' ¶ No: 6 lines. ¶ A: 'Amelia.'
Note: See the 'Answer,' no. 1415.

1398. Dec. 1757 *Am Mag* I, 130.
'O King of heav'n and hell, of earth and sea.'
T: 'A Fragment from Orpheus.' ¶ No: 18 lines. ¶ A: 'By —.'
Note: Dated 'Maryland, Dec. 1, 1757.' See no. 1399.

1399. Dec. 1757 *Am Mag* I, 130.
'The body sick, we for the doctor send.'
T: 'A Fragment from Menander.' ¶ No: 4 lines. ¶ A: 'By the Same.'
Note: See no. 1398.

1400. Dec. 1757 *Am Mag* I, 131–2.
'Awake, my heart! awake, my lyre!'
T: 'Ode On the Nativity of Christ.' ¶ No: 108 lines. ¶ A: 'By —.'
Note: Dated 'Philadelphia, Dec. 25, 1757.'

1758

1401. Jan. 9, 1758 *NYG* #781, 2/1.
'Long had a mungrel *French* and *Indian* brood.'
Note: A reprint of no. 1354.

1402. Jan. 9, 1758 *BEP* #1167, 2/1.
'With the New-Year, O could my rural Muse.'
T: [New Year's Verses.] ¶ No: 70 lines. ¶ A: 'Roger More.'
Note: 'From the American Country Almanack, for the Year 1758.'

1403. Jan. 9, 1758 *BG* ✻145, 3/2.
'As Cloe with affected Air.'
T: 'The Lady and the Wasp.' ¶ No: 10 lines.
Note: Reprinted, no. 1405.

1404. Jan. 9, 1758 *NYM* ✻282, 1/1.
'Dear to each Muse, to thy Country dear.'
T: 'To the Honorable Col. Peter Schuyler.' ¶ No: 12 lines. ¶ A:
[Annis (Boudinot) Stockton.]
Note: 'The following Lines were wrote by a young Lady of the
Province of New Jersey, during the few Minutes Col. Schuyler
staid at Prince-Town, the last Week, in his way to Trenton, and
presented him in the most agreeable Manner. As they discover so
fruitful and uncommon a Genius in their fair Author.' A holo-
graph copy is in Annis B. Stockton, [Colonial and Revolutionary
Verse. A Commonplace Book], pp. 9–10, Princeton Univ. Li-
brary. Reprinted *New Jersey Archives*, XX, 169. Reprinted, no.
1412. A recent article is Lyman H. Butterfield, 'Morven: A Colo-
nial Outpost of Sensibility With Some Hitherto Unpublished
Poems by Annis Boudinot Stockton,' *Princeton U. Lib. Chron.*, VI
(1944), 1–15.

1405. Jan. 13, 1758 *NHG* ✻67.
'As Cloe with affected Air.'
Note: A reprint of no. 1403.

1406. Jan. 23, 1758 *BG* ✻147, 2/2–3.
'Long had a mungrel *French* and *Indian* brood.'
Note: A reprint of no. 1354.

1407. Jan. 30, 1758 *BWA* ✻24.
'Scarce had the Sun resign'd the Winter Sky.'
T: 'The following Piece was written during the late Total Eclipse of
the Moon.' ¶ No: 46 lines.

1408. Jan. 1758 *Am Mag* I, 183–4.
'Haste, Sylvia! haste, my charming maid!'
T: 'The Invitation*' ¶ No: 48 lines. ¶ A: 'Junius' [Thomas God-
frey.]
Note: Dated 'Philadelphia, Jan. 20, 1758.' '*This little poem was
sent to us by an unknown hand, and seems dated as an original. If
it be so we think it does honour to our city.' Godfrey's authorhsip
is revealed by nos. 1474 and 1483. Reprinted in Godfrey's *Juven-
ile Poems on Various Subjects* (Philadelphia, 1765), pp. 11–13.

1409. Jan. 1758 *Am Mag* I, 186–7.
'Carmina me poscis? dare vellem, sed neque sacri.'
T: 'Ad Mr. Gardner.' ¶ No: 54 lines. ¶ A: 'I. B.' [John Beveridge.]

Note: Dated 'Falmouth, Id. Jan. 1753.' In *Am Mag*, June, 1758, I, 437, Provost William Smith identified the author. Reprinted in Beveridge, *Epistolae Familiares* (Philadelphia, 1765), pp. 23–24. Cf. no. 1493, Gardner is Nathaniel Gardner, Jr. (1719–1760), a poet who graduated from Harvard in 1739. See Shipton, X, 366–368, and see Leo M. Kaiser, 'Latin Teacher 1754' *Classical Journal*, LXIII (1968), 300–303.

1410. Jan. 1758 *Am Mag* I, 187–8.
'Arise! and see The morning sun.'
T: 'Ode on the Morning.' ¶ No: 48 lines. ¶ A: 'By the Author of L'Allegro and Il Penseroso.' [Francis Hopkinson.]
Note: Cf. nos. 1387, 1388. Reprinted in Hopkinson's *Miscellaneous Essays* III, pt. 2 (Philadelphia, 1792), 36–38.

1411. Jan. 1758 *New Am Mag* I, 15.
'Divinely warn'd to meet the mortal hour.'
T: 'Part of a funeral elegy, composed upon another occasion; but now justly inscribed to his excellency, Jonathan Belcher, Esqr; deceas'd, late governor of New-Jersey.' ¶ No: 18 lines. ¶ A: 'By a particular friend.'

1412. Jan. 1758 *New Am Mag* I, 16.
'Dear to each muse, and to thy country dear.'
Note: A reprint of no. 1404.

1413. Jan. 1758 *New Am Mag* I, 16.
'Ye swains, who your wit to display.'
T: 'A Pastoral Ballad. Occasioned by a late occurrence in —.' ¶ No: 64 lines.
Note: Sent by 'A Subscriber,' dated 'B[run]s[wic]k, Jan. 9, 1758.' Richardson, p. 133, n. 155, writes 'The same author (see line 23) later contributed "A Pastoral" [no. 1442] ... and "A Pastoral Ballad" [no. 1453].'

1414. Feb. 1758 *Am Mag* I, 238.
'Since Guido's skilful hand, with mimic art.'
T: 'Upon seeing the Portrait of Miss **—** by Mr. West.' ¶ No: 24 lines. ¶ A: 'Lovelace' [Joseph Shippen].
Note: Dated 'Philadelphia, February 15, 1758.' Smyth, p. 33, follows Griswold, p. 24, and Tyler, p. 469, in attributing the poem to Shippen. The poem had also been attributed to Francis Hopkinson and to 'Mr. [William?] Hicks; see Richardson, p. 115. On Joseph Shippen (1732–1810), the best sketch is Thomas Balch, ed., *Letters and Papers Relating Chiefly to the Provincial History of Pennsylvania with some Notices of the Writers* (Philadelphia, 1855,)

pp. lxvii-lxxi. For two other poems by Shippen, see the *Penna. Mag. of Hist. and Biog.*, II (1878), 157, and XVI (1892), 247. Reprinted in Griswold, p. 24.

1415. Feb. 1758 *Am Mag* I, 238.
'The northwind, 'Tis granted, still pierces us most.'
T: 'Answer to the Rebus in Dec. Mag, 1757.' ¶ No: 8 lines.
Note: A reply to no. 1397.

1416. Feb. 1758 *Am Mag* I, 238.
'To you learn'd curious enigmatic friend.'
T: 'Answer to the Enigma in December 1757.' ¶ No: 4 lines. ¶ A: 'Annandius.' [Joseph Shippen ?]
Note: Dated from 'Lewes.' A reply to no. 1396. Smyth, p. 33, attributes no. 1425, signed 'Annandius,' to Shippen. The Library of Congress copy of the *Am. Mag.* attributes the poem to Shippen—see Richardson, p. 119, n. 88.

1417. Feb. 1758 *Am Mag* I, 238.
'The world's a *Comedy*, in which we act.'
T: 'Wrote upon the Back of the Title-Page of a Comedy.' ¶ No: 14 lines. ¶ A: ['Annandius' ?] [Joseph Shippen ?]
Note: For Shippen's authorship, see no. 1416.

1418. Feb. 1758 *Am Mag* I, 238–240.
'Fair autumn! now her pride is fled.'
T: 'Winter a Poem.' ¶ No: 147 lines. ¶ A: 'By the same' ['Annandius'] [Joseph Shippen].
Note: For Shippen's authorship, see no. 1416. The Library of Congress copy attributes the poem to Shippen—see Richardson, p. 119, n. 88.

1419. Feb. 1758 *Am Mag* I, 240.
'Hail matchless monarch! prince renown'd.'
T: 'Ode on the late Victory obtained by the King of Prussia.' ¶ No: 54 lines. ¶ A: 'By the same' ['Annandius'] [Joseph Shippen].
Note: Dated 'Philadelphia, Feb. 10, 1758.' For Shippen's authorship, see no. 1416. The Library of Congress copy attributes the poem to Shippen—see Richardson, p. 119, n. 88.

1420. Feb. 1758 *Am Mag* I, 240.
''Tis he! 'Tis he! I hear from afar.'
T: 'On the compleat Victory gain'd by his *Prussian Majesty* over the French and Imperial Army, the 5th of November, 1757. A Pindaric Ode.' ¶ No: 91 lines. ¶ A: 'Philandreia.'
Note: Dated 'Philadelphia, Feb. 25,' On Frederick II of Priussa. Cf. nos. 1423, 1425, 1447, 1472, 1519.

1421. Feb. 1758 *New Am Mag* I, 38.
'Turn Thee, *Strephon*, and behold.'
T: 'The Prospect: A Moral Ode.' ¶ No: 46 lines. ¶ A: 'A. Z.'

1422. Feb. 1758 *New Am Mag* I, 40.
'Now hours of mirth, salute the coming year.'
T: 'Verses on the beginning of the New-Year, 1758. To a Sett of Ladies.'

1423. Mar. 17, 1758 *NHG* #76, 2/20.
'O! Thou undaunted Prince! whom millions own.'
T: To the King of Prussia, on his late Success.' ¶ No: 52 lines.

1424. Mar. 17, 1758 *NHG* #76, 3/2.
'In dawn of Life she wisely sought her God.'
T: 'On a Young Lady deceas'd.' ¶ No: 14 lines.

1425. Mar. 1758 *Am Mag* I, 280.
'My muse! again attempt the lyre.'
T: 'On the glorious Victory obtained by the HEROICK KING of Prussia over the Imperial Army near Newmark in Silesea, the 5th of December 1757.' ¶ No: 90 lines. ¶ A: 'Annandius' [Joseph Shippen].
Note: Dated 'March 11, 1758.' Cf. no. 1420. Smyth, p. 33, attributed this poem to Shippen, and so does a note in the Library of Congress copy of the poem; see Richardson, p. 119, n. 88.

1426. Mar. 1758 *Am Mag* I, 281–290.
'These lays, ye *Great*! to Richardson belong.'
T: 'A Poem. On the Invention of Letters and the Art of Printing. Addrest to Mr. Richardson in London, the Author and Printer of Sir Charles Grandison, and other works, for the Promotion of Religion, Virtue and polite Manners, in a corrupted Age.' ¶ No: 270 lines. ¶ A: [James Sterling.]
Note: Dated 'Kent County in Maryland, December 15th, 1757.' On the strength of a contemporary ms notation in the British Museum copy of the *Am Mag.*, Smyth, p. 37, attributed the poem to Sterling. Richardson, pp. 119–120, and Wroth (see no. 96) p. 36, concur. Wroth pointed out that the poem is ascribed to Sterling in a ms note in the Library of Congress copy of the *Am Mag.* Smyth thought it 'the most remarkable poem' in the *Am Mag.* It is actually a much enlarged and revised version of no. 96.

1427. Mar. 1758 *New Am Mag* I, 63–4.
'From wild retreats, allur'd by France.'
T: 'Verses occasioned by the late depredations committed upon our frontiers.' ¶ No: 30 lines.

1428. Mar. 1758 *New Am Mag* I, 64.
     'From all the noisy cares of Town.'
     T: 'A Song.' ¶ No: 12 lines. ¶ A: 'C.'

1429. Mar. 1758 *New Am Mag* I, 64.
     'What a constant round of pain.'
     T: 'Life a Bubble.' ¶ No: 12 lines.

1430. Mar. 1758 *New Am Mag* I, 64.
     'Happy when I see Thy eyes.'
     T: 'From Ausonius.' ¶ No: 8 lines.

1431. Mar. 1758 *New Am Mag* I, 64.
     'A Poor man once a judge besought.'
     T: 'The Poor Man and the Judge. A Fable. In Imitation of Stern-
     hold and Hopkins.' ¶ No: 20 lines.

1432. Apr. 10, 1758 *NYM* #295, 1/2.
     'Great Edwards dead! how doleful is the Sound?'
     T: [Epitaph on Jonathan Edwards.] ¶ No: 16 lines.
     Note: At the end of Edwards' obituary. Reprinted *New Jersey Ar-
     chives*, XX, 191.

1433. Apr. 21, 1758 *NHG* #81, 2/2–3.
     'To injur'd Troops Thus gallant Brunswick spoke.'
     T: 'Speech of the Prince of Brunswick to the Hanoverian and Hes-
     sian Troops.' ¶ No: 18 lines.
     Note: Dated 'Portsmouth Apr. 20, 1758.' Crum T2994.

1434. Apr. 1758 *Am Mag* I, 332–335.
     'When vile corruption, like a general pest.'
     T: 'The Patriot. A Poem.' ¶ No: 124 lines. ¶ A: [James Sterling.]
     Note: Attributed to Sterling by Richardson, p. 121, and Wroth (see
     no. 96), p. 36, because of stylistic reasons; and I agree.

1435. Apr. 1758 *Am Mag* I, 335.
     'When cruel Peter over *Cyprus* reign'd.'
     T: 'The Dame of Cyprus.' ¶ No: 29 lines. ¶ A: [James Sterling?]
     Note: This poem, in style and content typical of Sterling, appears in
     the *Am Mag* between two other poems (nos. 1434 and 1436) by
     him.

1436. Apr. 1758 *Am Mag* I, 335–336.
     'Leda's Twin-sons, when they together shin'd.'
     T: 'epigram.' ¶ No: 4 lines of English + 4 lines of Latin. ¶ A:
     [James Sterling.]

Note: Dated 'Kent in Maryland.' Wroth (see no. 96), p. 36, attributed this charming *vers de société* to Sterling because of the date line.

1437. Apr. 1758 *Am Mag* I, 336.
'Your answer kind sir, with the marginal note.'
T: 'Epigram on the Second Answer [by 'Annandius'—see no. 1416] to a riddle in the February Magazine.' ¶ No: 8 lines.
Note: This is probably by the author of no. 1396.

1438. May 1, 1758 *NYM* #298, 2/3.
'Lo! Farmer now, no more does act below.'
T: 'On the Death of Captain Jasper Farmer.' ¶ No: 12 lines.
Note: Follows the obituary notice: Farmer was a merchant of N.Y., & Capt. of the 2nd Independent Artillery Co., age 51.

1439. May 12, 1758 *NHG* #84.
'Rouse Sons of Earth, to War, to War.'
T: 'On the present Expedition.' ¶ No: 48 lines.
Note: 'From the Boston News Letter, May 5.' Dated 'Deerfield, Apr. 22, 1758.' Reprinted, no. 1449 (where a different date is given.)

1440. May 12, 1758 *NHG* #84.
'We're of one common stock.'
T: 'April 30th 1758. To the Publisher...Please to insert in your publick Paper, for the Entertainment of both Parents and children, what follows (as in Representation) of the Sentiments &c. of a large Family of Children; on Occasion of their several Names, and some other distinguishing circumstances.' ¶ No: 68 lines.

1441. May 1758 *Am Mag* I, 390–397.
'Pierian nymphs that haunt Sicilian plains.'
T: 'A Pastoral. To his Excellency George Thomas, Esq., formerly Governor of Pennsylvania, and now General of the Leeward Islands.' ¶ No: 218 lines. ¶ A: [James Sterling.]
Note: There is a correction in the 'Contents' page for this poem. Contemporary ms. annotations in the British Museum and Library of Congress copies of the *Am Mag*, attribute this poem to Sterling: Smyth (p. 37), Richardson (p. 120), and L. C. Wroth (see no. 196), p. 36. Sterling wrote the poem in 1744, on the death of Pope. The poem uses the *translatio studii* theme. The copy in the BM has manuscript revisions and an added couplet. See Theodore Hornberger, 'Mr. Hicks of Philadelphia,' *Penna. Mag. of Hist. and Biog.*, LIII (1929), 347. The first part of the poem is reprinted in Silverman, pp. 328–331.

1442. May 1758 *New Am Mag* I, 117–119.
'To Tune the slender reed on *Indian* plains.'
T: A PASTORAL. Inscrib'd to DIGNUS. ¶ No: 120 lines.
Note: See no. 1413.

1443. May 1758 *New Am Mag* I, 120.
'Hear heav'n! on this propitious day!'
T: 'To Miss M. K. on her birth-day.' ¶ No: 24 lines. ¶ A: 'W. S.'
Note: Crum H529 gives the title 'Presented to the Widow Carbonnel' and suggests an attribution to the artist Gabriel Lepipre (d. 1698), for whom, see the *DNB*.

1444. May 1758 *New Am Mag* I, 120.
'Tell me no more of whig and Tory.'
T: 'A Song. On occasion of the present war.' ¶ No: 28 lines.

1445. June 2, 1758 *NHG* ♯87.
'Where shall an infant Muse such Numbers find.'
T: 'On the News of the Arrival of our Fleet.' ¶ No: 39 lines.
Note: Dated 'Portsmouth May 18.'

1446. June 9, 1758 *NHG* ♯88.
'Hope! 'Tis in vain to rest it where.'
T: 'A Timely Caution on the present Expedition.' ¶ No: 44 lines.

1447. June 16, 1758 *NHG* ♯89.
'Here taught by Thee, we view with raptur'd eyes.'
T: 'On seeing an armed bust of the King of Prussia, curiously imprinted on a Porcelain Cup of the Worcester Manufacture with the Emblim of his Victories, Inscribed to the Maker.' ¶ No: 38 lines.
Note: Cf. no. 1420.

1448. June 16, 1758 *NHG* ♯89.
'See! how the fair creation round.'
T: 'A Hymn in a Spring Morning.' ¶ No: 48 lines.

1449. June 19, 1758 *BEP* ♯1190.
'Rouse Sons of Earth, to War, to War.'
Note: Dated 'Boston, April 13th, 1758.' A reprint of no. 1439, but with a different date.

1450. June, 1758 *Am Mag* I, 437.
'Taedium longi maris et viarum.'
T: 'Ad Rev. Jacob: Innesium V.D.M. in Parochia de Merton ad ripam Tuedae in Britannia Septentrionali.' ¶ No: 40 lines. ¶ A: 'I. B.' ('John Beveridge')

Note: Smith, in an editorial note, refers to Beveridge's 'elegant latin poem in the *Mag* for December.' Smith says that Beveridge was appointed 'at a full meeting on the 13th of this month, unanimously ... professor of languages and master of the latin school; in the room of Mr. Paul Jackson, whose public spirit has induced him to accept of the command of a company in the provincial service, during the expedition to the westward.' See no. 1451. Reprinted in Beveridge, *Epistolae Familiares* (Philadelphia, 1765), pp. 21–22.

1451. June, 1758 *Am Mag* I, 437–8.
'I've now o'ercome the long fatigue.'
T: 'The following is a Translation of the above Letter by the reverend Dr. Jonathan Mayhew at Boston.' 'To *Reverend* Mr. J. Innes, &c.' ¶ No: 51 lines. ¶ A: Jonathan Mayhew.
Note: See no. 1450. Reprinted in John Beveridge, (see no. 1450), pp. 75–76.

1452. June, 1758 *New Am Mag* I, 141.
'See how that once-lov'd flower neglected lyes.'
T: 'The Withered Rose.' ¶ No: 24 lines. ¶ A: 'Sophia Meanwell.'

1453. June, 1758 *New Am Mag* I, 142–3.
'Once more, O ye muses, my song.'
T: 'A Pastoral Ballad. Written in the Month of *May*, of the Year 1758.' ¶ No: 64 lines. ¶ A: 'By the Author of the Pastoral inscrib'd to Dignus, [no. 1442].'
Note: Good verse. With prefatory letter saying 'That the intellectual soil here, like the natural is extremely rich and fertile, capable of the finest productions, under due culture and encouragement.' See no. 1413. Reprinted, no. 1612.

1454. June, 1758 *New Am Mag* I, 143–4.
'Just as the morn had spread the skies.'
T: 'Schuylkill Side.' ¶ No: 56 lines.
Note: Good local description.

1455. June 1758 *New Am Mag* I, 144.
'When Wintry blasts and riffling storms expire.'
T: 'The Spring.' ¶ No: 60 lines. ¶ A: 'C.'

1456. June, 1758 *Scots Mag* XX, 306.
'To wed, or not to wed—that is the question.'
T: 'The Bachelor's Soliloquy.' ¶ A: 'P—d.'
Note: Dated 'Aberdeen, June 30, 1758.'

1457. July 17, *NYG* ⌗811, 2/top.
'Upon the object and foundation.'
T: 'A Medical Essay on Hunger. In the Manner of a Dissertation on the Hooping-Cough.'

1458. July 21, 1758 *NHG* ⌗94.
'Hah! is Meserve dead? too true, he's gone.'
T: 'Spoken on the News of Colonel Meserve's Death.' ¶ No: 12 lines.
Note: On Nathaniel Meserve of Portsmouth, N.H.

1459. July 24, 1758 *BG* ⌗173.
'Rise! Britons, Rise! defend your righteous Cause.'
T: 'On the present Expedition.' ¶ No: 26 lines. ¶ A: 'By a young Genius.'
Note: Reprinted, no. 1460.

1460. July 28, 1758 *NHG* ⌗95, 2/2.
'Rise! Britons, Rise! defend your righteous Cause.'
Note: A reprint of no. 1459.

1461. July 31, 1758 *BEP* ⌗1196, 4/2.
'Raise thee my Muse, thy aid once more.'
T: [On war.] ¶ No: 44 lines. ¶ A: 'Philalethes.'
Note: Dated 'Boston, July 20, 1758.' Reprinted, no. 1470.

1462. July, 1758 *Am Mag* I, 499–500.
'Thou little wond'rous miniature of man.'
T: 'A Father's Reflections on the Birth of a Son.' ¶ No: 40 lines. ¶ A: 'Virgineanus Hanoverensis' [Rev. Samuel Davies.]
Note: Dated 'August 20, 1752.' See no. 1463, Smyth, p. 45, attributes this pseudonym to Davies. Reprinted in Davies *Sermons* (1792), III, 431–432, with the title 'On the Birth of John Rogers Davies, The Author's Third Son.' Reprinted in Davis (see no. 1035), pp. 198–200.

1463. July, 1758 *Am Mag* I, 500.
'Hark! saith the Lord, what moving sound.'
T: 'A Paraphrase on Jer. XXXI. 18, 19, 20.' ¶ No: 44 lines. ¶ A: 'By the same' [Rev. Samuel Davies.]
Note: See no. 1462. Reprinted in Davis (see no. 1035), pp. 201–202.

1464. July, 1758 *Am Mag* I, 501.
'To-day the living streams of grace.'

T: 'The Invitations of the Gospel. Annext to a Sermon on Rev. XXII. 17. April 9, 1753.' ¶ No: 24 lines. ¶ A: [Rev. Samuel Davies.]

Note: Reprinted in Davis (see no. 1035), pp. 203–204.

1465. July, 1758 *Am Mag* I, 502.
'Sitting by the streams, that glide.'
T: ['Version' of the 139th psalm.] ¶ No: 40 lines. ¶ A: [Samuel Davies.]
Note: Reprinted in Davis (see no. 1035), pp. 205–206. Cf. no. 1623. Davies' poem is modeled upon Thomas Carew's imitation of the 137th psalm. Davies' entire first stanza (5 lines) is the same, and phrases throughout the poem echo Carew. For Carew's poem, see Rhodes Dunlap, *The Poems of Thomas Carew* (Oxford, 1949), p. 149. Carew's imitation was originally printed in Henry Lawes, *Select Psalmes* (London, 1655). Crum S776 lists Carew's poem.

1466. July, 1758 *Am Mag* I, 502.
'With eager eyes and heart refin'd.'
T: [Translation of 'Euseb. Praep. Evang. L. 13.'] ¶ No: 10 lines. ¶ A: [Samuel Davies.]
Note: Reprinted in Davis (see no. 1035), p. 207.

1467. July 1758 *Am Mag* I, 502–3.
'While in a thousand open'd veins.'
T: 'A Hymn adapted to the Present State of public affairs: In Allusion to Isai. 32. 13–18.' ¶ No: 28 lines. ¶ A: [Samuel Davies.]
Note: Reprinted in Davis (see no. 1035), pp. 194–195.

1468. July, 1758 *Am Mag* I, 503.
'Eternal spirit! source of light.'
T: 'A Criticism on 1 Thess. V. 19. Quench not the spirit.' ¶ No: 24 lines. ¶ A: [Samuel Davies.]
Note: Reprinted in Davis (see no. 1035), pp. 189–190.

1469. July, 1758 *New Am Mag* I, 169.
'Sing heav'n-born muse, and may thy strain.'
T: 'A Hymn to the Creator.' ¶ No: 84 lines. ¶ A: 'By a Youth under Seventeen.'

1470. Aug. 11, 1758 *NHG* ₦97.
'Raise thee my Muse, thy aid once more.'
Note: A reprint of no. 1461.

1471. Aug. 14, 1758 *BEP* ₦1198, 2/2.
'Harsh to the Heart, and grating to the Ear.'

T: In ad for 'The Polite Philosopher: Or, An Essay on that Art, which makes a Man *happy* in Himself and agreeable to Others.' ¶ No: 12 lines.

1472. Aug. 1758 *Am Mag* I, 550–2.
'Mistaken astronomers, gaze not so high:'
T: 'The Royal Comet.' ¶ No: 98 lines. ¶ A: [James Sterling.]
Note: Dated 'Kent in Maryland, July 14th, 1758.' On Frederick II of Prussia. Cf. no. 1420. Richardson, p. 121, attributed the poem to Sterling on the basis of an annotation in the Library of Congress copy of the *Am. Mag.* Wroth (see no. 96), p. 37, attributed it to Sterling because of the dateline.

1473. Aug., 1758 *Am Mag* I, 552–3.
'At length Tis done! The glorious conflict's done!'
T: 'On the taking of Cape-Breton.' ¶ No: 65 lines. ¶ A: 'F. H.' [Francis Hopkinson].
Note: Dated 'Philadelphia, August 23d, 1758.' Reprinted in Hopkinson's *Miscellaneous Essays*, III, pt. 2 (Philadelphia, 1792), 47–49.

1474. Aug., 1758 *Am Mag* I, 554–6.
'Friendship, all hail! Thou dearest tye.'
T: 'A Pindaric Ode on Friendship, by the Author of the Invitation.' ¶ No: 119 lines. ¶ A: [Thomas Godfrey.]
Note: 'Contents' for Sept., 1758: 'Pindaric Ode on Wine by Mr. Godfrey, author of The Invitation.' Reprinted in Godfrey's *Poems* (see no. 1408), pp. 15–19.

1475. Aug., 1758 *New Am Mag* I, 201.
'NEglected long has lain my useless lyre.'
T: 'On the late defeat at TEONDEROGA' [sic.] ¶ No: 50 lines. ¶ A: ['By a Lady in America.']
Note: Reprinted (with several changes), no. 1560.

1476. Aug., 1758 *New Am Mag* I, 201.
'When mighty roast beef was the Englishmen's food.'
T: 'The following Old England Ballad may correspond very well with the present times in America, and be properly adopted to the behaviour of some of our G–r–ls in the late Expeditions.' ¶ No: 33 lines + 2 line refrain 'O the roast beef of Old England.'
Note: Two stanzas on Lord Howe are inserted in the poem. For *Viscount* (George Augustus) Howe, see nos. 1484, 1495, 1496, 1497. This is one of the numerous expansions of Henry Fielding's 'Roast Beef of Old England.'

1477. Aug., 1758 *NE Mag* I, [i–ii].
'You are the Man who Counsel can bestow.'
T: 'A Poetical Dedication to a good Old Gentleman.' ¶ No: 54 lines.
¶ A: 'Urbanus Filter' [B. Mecom?]
Note: The editor of the *NE Mag* was Benjamin Mecom, who prob-
ably addressed this poem to his uncle Benjamin Franklin.

1478. Sept. 1, 1758 *SCG*, 1/1.
'Fair Flower, cropt by Death's remorseless Hand.'
T: 'On the Death of a young Child.' ¶ No: 109 lines.

1479. Sept. 4, 1758 *BEP* ⚹1201, 3/2.
'Old-fashioned Writings and select Essays.'
T: [ad for *New England Magazine*] ¶ No: 10 lines. ¶ A: [Benjamin
Mecom.]
Note: Dated 'Thurs. Aug. 31, 1758'; repeated Sept. 11, 1758 *BEP*.

1480. Sept. 4, 1758 *BG* ⚹179, 4/1.
'Alluring *Profit* with *Delight* we blend.'
T: [Ad for 'The New-England Magazine.'] ¶ No: 14 lines. ¶ A:
[Benjamin Mecom.]
Note: Repeated *BG*, Sept. 18.

1481. Sept. 14, 1758 *MG*.
'Britons rejoice at Heav'n's indulgent Smile.'
T: 'On Admiral Boscawen's Success, 1758.' ¶ No: 18 lines. ¶ A:
'A young gentleman of 15.'
Note: Poor verse. 'The following is a Performance of a young
Gentleman of fifteen; who has our Thanks for this his first
Favour.' Reprinted, nos. 1498, 1502.

1482. Sept. 29, 1758 *NLS* ⚹8, 4/2.
'Envy, detraction, seek your dark retreat.'
T: 'On Col. Bradstreet's Success.' ¶ No: 16 lines. ¶ A: 'Americanus.'
Note: Reprinted, nos. 1501, 1504, 1512.

1483. Sept., 1758 *Am Mag* I, 604.
'Come! let Mirth our hours employ.'
T: 'A Pindaric Ode on Wine. By the Author of The Invitation.' ¶
No: 77 lines. ¶ A: [Thomas Godfrey.]
Note: William Smith writes a long note on Godfrey as a 'Preface' to
the 'Poetical Essays,' *Am Mag*, I (Sept., 1758), 602–3. Cf. no.
1408. Reprinted in Godfrey's *Poems* (see no. 1408), pp. 34–37.
Reprinted in Duyckinck, I, 206–7; in Stedman and Hutchinson,
II, 493–94.

1484. Sept., 1758 *Am Mag* I, 604–5.
    'Patriots and chiefs! Britannia's mighty Dead.'
    T: 'Epitaph on the late Lord Howe.' ¶ No: 22 lines. ¶ A: [James
        Sterling.]
    Note: Dated 'Kent in Maryland, August 14th, 1758.' Attributed to
        Sterling by Smyth, p. 39; Richardson, p. 119; and Wroth (see no.
        96), p. 37. Reprinted, nos. 1517, 1565, 1570.

1485. Sept., 1758 *Am Mag* I, 605–7.
    'While *Vice* Triumphant lords it o'er the plain.'
    T: 'To Thyrsis.' ¶ No: 83 lines. ¶ A: [Rev. Thomas Cradock?]
    Note: Dated 'Maryland, Baltimore County, written in the Year
        1744.' Both the Rev. Thomas Chase and the Rev. Thomas
        Cradock, Anglican ministers of Baltimore Co., wrote poetry, and
        this religious poem is probably by one of them. Cradock was the
        more prolific.

1486. Sept., 1758 *Am Mag* I, 607–8.
    'Let others mix in faction's giddy throng.'
    T: 'Verses inscribed to Mr. Wollaston.' ¶ No: 60 lines. ¶ A: 'F. H.'
        [Francis Hopkinson.]
    Note: Praise for John Wollaston & Benjamin West; ut pictura poesis
        genre. Dated 'Philadelphia, September 18th, 1758.' Griswold, p.
        25, attributes the poem to Hopkinson, and so does Richardson, p.
        115.

1487. Sept., 1758 *Am Mag* I, 609.
    'Ad Jovis arbitrium referunt duo numina causam.'
    T: 'Elogium.' ¶ No: 34 lines. ¶ A: [James Sterling.]
    Note: Dated 'E. Comitatu Cantii, in Mariae Provincio.' On the
        French and Indian War. Richardson, p. 118, n. 83, mistakenly
        attributes this poem to Beveridge. Wroth (see no. 96), p. 37,
        attributes it to Sterling.

1488. Sept., 1758 *Am Mag* I, 609–10.
    'Pergis extremas, bone dux, in oras.'
    T: 'Ad Illustrissimum, ac sublimi Virtute, Optimâ Eruditione or-
        natum virum, Gulielmum Shirley, &c.' ¶ A: 'Johann: Beveridge.'
    Note: A reprint of no. 1189.

1489. Sept., 1758 *New Am Mag* I, 233.
    'A Neat quaker girl in her Sabbeth-day gown.'
    T: 'Bourne's Fæmina Manditiis simplex, &c. *imitated*.' ¶ No: 16
        lines.
    Note: Cf. no. 1490, and no. 1525.

1490. Sept., 1758 *New Am Mag* I, 233.
'From sacred seat, above the rest advanc'd.'
T: 'Bourne's Fanaticas imitated.' ¶ No: 24 lines.
Note: Sent in by 'M.' Pref. letter—'Observing in your Poetical
Essays for May, a piece entitled The Enthusiastick Preacher,
taken from the Gentleman's Magazine, which appears to have
been intended for something *like* a Translation of Mr. Bourne's
Fanaticus, in latin ... your readers perhaps will not be displeased
with having a fair opportunity of comparing an American with an
English manufacture.' Cf. no. 1489.

1491. Sept., 1758 *New Am Mag* I, 233.
'Little but too powerful tie.'
T: 'The Wedding-Ring.' ¶ No: 10 lines. ¶ A: 'C.'

1492. Sept., 1758 *New Am Mag* I, 233–4.
'While all my soul's with anxious care opprest.'
T: 'To Mrs. E. S.' ¶ No: 16 lines. ¶ A: 'X.'

1493. Sept. 1758 *New Am Mag* I, 234.
'Michare Gardner, dic aganippidas.'
T: 'An Ode. By a gentleman in New-England, to his friend in
Boston.' ¶ No: 28 lines. ¶ A: [John Beveridge.]
Note: Sent in by 'P,' dated 'New-Brunswick, Sept. 12, 1758.' who
sneers at the 'romantic' turn of 'Lucinda,' 'Pedagogue' & 'Petti-
fogger.' This is another of Beveridge's poems to Nathaniel
Gardner, Jr. For the earlier, see no. 1409. Reprinted in Beveridge
(see no. 1409), pp. 24–25.

1494. Sept., 1758 *New Am Mag* I, 234.
'Opress'd with grief, in heavy strains I mourn.'
Note: A reprint of no. 280.

1495. Sept., 1758 *New Am Mag* I, 235.
'Illustrious man! why so intrepid brave.'
T: 'In memory of the honourable and brave lord Howe, who was
unfortunately slain at the head of a small party, near Ticonderoga.'
¶ No: 10 lines.
Note: Cf. no. 1476. Reprinted, no. 1499.

1496. Sept., 1758 *New Am Mag* I, 235.
'Oh! valiant Howe!'
T: ['Verses' on Howe.] ¶ No: 36 lines. ¶ A: 'Philo-Patria.'
Note: Cf. no. 1476.

1497. Sept., 1758 *Scots Mag* XX, 480.
'Britannia Triumphs; yet her eyes o'erflow!'
T: 'On the Death of Lord Howe.' ¶ No: 30 lines.
Note: Cf. no. 1476.

1498. Oct. 5, 1758 *BNL* ⚥2934, 1/2.
'Britons rejoice at Heaven's indulgent smile.'
Note: A reprint of no. 1481.

1499. Oct. 9, 1758 *BEP* ⚥1206, 3/2.
'Illustrious Man! why so intreprid brave.'
Note: A reprint of no. 1495.

1500. Oct. 9, 1758 *BWA* ⚥60, 4/1.
'My Muse, I ask Assistance for my Lays.'
T: 'On the Success of the British Arms.' ¶ No: 20 lines. ¶ A: 'Philander.'
Note: Reprinted, no. 1503.

1501. Oct. 12, 1758 *BNL* ⚥2935, 3/1.
'Envy, detraction, seek your dark retreat.'
Note: A reprint of no. 1482.

1502. Oct. 13, 1758 *NHG* ⚥106.
'Britons rejoice at Heaven's indulgent Smile.'
Note: A reprint of no. 1481.

1503. Oct. 13, 1758 *NH Gaz* ⚥106.
'My Muse, I ask Assistance for my Lays.'
Note: A reprint of no. 1500.

1504. Oct. 20, 1758 *NHG* ⚥107.
'Envy, detraction, seek your dark retreat.'
Note: A reprint of no. 1482.

1505. Oct., 1758 *Am Mag* I, 641.
'Rerum parentem te, genitor, canam.'
T: 'Psal. CIV.' ¶ No: 100 lines. ¶ A: 'Joh. Beveridge.'
Note: With an account of Beveridge on p. 640. Reprinted in Beveridge, *Epistolae Familiares* (Philadelphia, 1765), pp. 40–42.

1506. Oct., 1758 *Am Mag* I, 642.
'Clamavit Phoebus, sibi quae nunc arrogat Harpax.'
T: 'Apollinis Querela, Sive Epigramma.' ¶ No: 30 lines. ¶ A: [James Sterling.]
Note: This poem, complimenting John Beveridge, is reprinted in Beveridge's *Epistolae Familiares* (Philadelphia, 1765), pp. 46–47, where it is attributed to 'Author Rev. Ja. Sterlino.' See Beveridge's reply, no. 1530A.

1507. Oct., 1758 *Am Mag* I, 642–3.
'The Christian hero, pure from sin.'
T: 'The 22d Ode of the first Book of Horace imitated; and inscribed to the Lady of his late Excellency Samuel Ogle, Esquire.' ¶ No: 48 lines. ¶ A: [James Sterling.]
Note: Dated 'Kent in Maryland, October 25th, 1758.' On the basis of a contemporary ms. notation in the Library of Congress copy of the *Am Mag*, Richardson (p. 121) attributed the poem to Sterling; Wroth (see no. 96), p. 37, ascribed it to him because of the date line. It is actually a revised version of a poem that Sterling wrote in Ireland: see *The Poetical Works of the Reverend James Sterling* (Dublin, 1734), pp. 17–21. Reprinted in Silverman, pp. 331–333.

1508. Oct., 1758 *Am Mag* I, 644–5.
'How awful is the night, beneath whose shade.'
T: 'A Night Piece.' ¶ No: 60 lines. ¶ A: 'By Mr. Godfrey.'
Note: Reprinted in Godfrey's *Poems* (see no. 1408), pp. 39–41. The poem pays a passing compliment to Godfrey's childhood friend, the artist John Green (c. 1738–1802).

1509. Oct., 1758 *Am Mag* I, 645–8.
'As when the winds from ev'ry corner blow.'
T: 'Roxana to Alexander at the Siege of Tyre.' ¶ No: 166 lines. ¶ A: By 'a young lady in a neighbouring government.'
Note: Provost William Smith complimented the 'real feeling and beautiful perplexity of thought' in this poem.

1510. Oct., 1758 *Gent Mag* XX, 530.
'Britannia mourns her youthful hero slain.'
T: 'On the death of Lord Howe.'
Note: Dated 'Nottingham, Oct. 23.'

1511. Oct., 1758 *New Am Mag* I, 258–60.
'There flourish'd in a market Town.'
T: 'The Basket. A Tale.'
Note: Reprinted, no. 1522.

1512. Oct., 1758 *New Am Mag* I, 260.
'Envy, detraction, seek your dark retreat.'
Note: A reprint of no. 1482.

1513. Oct., 1758 *New Am Mag* I, 277–8.
'Where have I been Till now? what have I done?'
T: 'The Convert's Soliloquy.' ¶ No: 106 lines. ¶ A: 'R— in Berk's Co., in Penna.'
Note: Fair blank verse. Sent in by 'Sylvances Agrecolus,' 'September 3, 1756.'

1514. Oct. 1758 *NE Mag* no. 2, p. 56–7.
'The Golden Age, a specious cheat.'
T: 'Golden Age *fabulous.*' ¶ No: 36 lines. ¶ A: ['Said to be wrote by a Lady of New-York'.]

1515. Oct., 1758 *NE Mag* #2, pp. 59–60.
'Ye Charmers who shine.'
T: 'Mira. A Song. Tune, Bumper Squire Jones.' ¶ No: 54 lines. ¶ A: [Rev. William Shervington.]
Note: '[By the Author of a Poem entitled The *Antigonian Beauties,* some Time ago applied to an Assembly of Bostonian Beauties.]' Reprinted from Shervington's *Occasional Poems* (Antiqua, 1749), pp. 80–82.

1516. Nov. 13, 1758 *BWA* #65, 4/1.
'No longer now does favour'd Strephon roam.'
T: 'Upon a young Lady's Marriage.' ¶ No: 34 lines. ¶ A: ['By a young Gentleman.']
Note: Reprinted, no. 1563.

1517. Nov. 16, 1758 *MG.*
'Patriots and Chiefs! Britannia's mighty Dead.'
Note: A reprint of no. 1484.

1518. Nov. 17, 1758 *NHG* #111.
'Men need not fear, to preach or hear.'
T: 'A Word of Advice to New England Protestants, to shun Antichristian Slavery.' ¶ No: 16 lines.
Note: Dated 'Stratham, N. H., Nov. 8, 1758.' See reply, no. 1520.

1519. Nov. 23, 1758 *MG.*
'He is the Assertor of Liberty.'
T: 'A True Character of the King of Prussia.' ¶ No: 15 lines.
Note: Cf. no. 1420.

1520. Nov. 24, 1758 *NHG* #112.
'Men need both fear, to *Preach* and *Hear.*'
T: 'A Word of Instruction to the Author of the Verses dated at This Place the 8th Instant, inserted in the New Hampshire Gazette the last Week.' ¶ No: 16 lines.
Note: A reply to no. 1518.

1521. Nov. 24, 1758 *NHG* #112.
'Ye Nymphs! that boast your Charms, see here.'
T: [Elegy on Miss Elizabeth Gilman, dau. of Col. Peter Gilman.] ¶ No: 32 lines.
Note: A shortened form of no. 717.

1522. Nov. 27, 1758 *NYG* #830, 2/2–3.
'There flourish'd in a market Town.'
Note: A reprint of no. 1511.

1523. Nov., 1758 *New Am Mag* I, 282–3.
'Fair *Maria* tell me why.'
T: 'To Miss M. A.' ¶ No: 23 lines. ¶ A: 'A.'
Note: Cf. nos. 1588, 1653.

1524. Nov., 1758 *New Am Mag* I, 283.
'Beauty like heaven's various bow.'
T: ['Ode on beauty.'] ¶ No: 32 lines. ¶ A: 'Z.'

1525. Nov. 1758 *New Am Mag* I, 283.
'How sweetly looks and smiles the lovely lass.'
T: 'On Miss —. The verses in your magazine ... for September, on
the Quaker-girl, gave rise to the following rhimes.' ¶ No: 22
lines. ¶ A: 'J— G—g.'
Note: The verses to the quaker girl are evidently no. 1489.

1526. Dec. 1, 1758 *SCG*, 1/1.
'Yet Summer Follows best your Crops ensure.'
T: 'An Extract of the Poem of Indico.' ¶ No: 25 lines. ¶ A: [Charles
Woodmason.]
Note: Sent in by 'Agricola.' Reprinted in Cohen (see no. 1380), pp.
43–44.

1527. Dec. 8, 1758 *NHG* #114.
'All Things, beneath the Circle of the Sun.'
T: 'On The Mutability of *Words* and *Things*.' ¶ No: 12 lines.

1528. Dec. 14, 1758 *BNL* #2989, 3/1.
'Methinks I see Britannia's Genius here.'
T: 'Lines ... upon General Amherst's leading his Troops from Bos-
ton, after the Conquest of Louisbourg, to join our Army that had
been repulsed at Ti[c]onderoga.' ¶ No: 26 lines. ¶ A: 'Written
by a Lady.'
Note: Reprinted, nos. 1530, 1538, 1551, 1554. Crum M340, with
the same first line, is entitled 'A Prologue ... 9 Dec. 1745 ...
Theater Royal ... Drury Lane, when the whole Receipt of the
House was apply'd to ... Giving ... Soldiers ... Flannel Waistcoats.'

1529. Dec. 18, 1758 *NYM* #331, 1/3.
'Amherst, while Crouds attend you on your Way.'
T: 'The following Lines were designed to have been presented to
General Amherst, as he passed thro' Long-Island, had not the
Young Gentlemen who composed them been unfortunately dis-

appointed of the Pleasure of seeing him.' ¶ No: 41 lines. ¶ A: 'Nassovicus' [Benjamin Young Prime].
Note: Reprinted, nos. 1536, 1537, 1540, 1552. For a satirical reply, see no. 1545. Reprinted in Prime's *Patriot Muse* (London, 1764), pp. 39–41. For Prime, see no. 1274.

1530. Dec. 22, 1758 *NHG* #116.
'Methinks I see Britannia's Genius here.'
Note: A reprint of no. 1528.

1530A. Dec. 28, 1758 *PJ* #838, 2/1.
'Carmina num redolent vigilem, Sterline, Lucernam?'
T: 'An Answer to the Epigram in your last Magazine, entitled Apollinis Querila ... Rev. D. Jac: Ster: Harpax, alias J: B: S: P: D:' ¶ No: 42 lines. ¶ A: 'J. B.' [John Beveridge].
Note: Dated 'Phila. Nov. 20th, 1758.' Beveridge's answer to Rev. James Sterling's compliment (no. 1506). Reprinted in Beveridge, *Epistolae Familiares* (Philadelphia, 1765), pp. 48–49.

1531. Dec., 1758 *New Am Mag* I, 309.
'O May the joyful voice of praise.'
T: 'Hymn of thanksgiving for the success of our arms and those of our ally, and the reduction of Louisbourg and Fort Dequesne, and the demolishing of Fort Frontenac in the present year, 1758.' ¶ No: 32 lines. ¶ A: 'Z.'

1532. Dec., 1758 *New Am Mag* I, 390–10.
'Remote from liberty and truth.'
T: 'Stanzas found on a Gentleman's window shutters in the country.' ¶ No: 24 lines. ¶ A: [Robert Nugent.]
Note: Praise of Moore and James Harrington. Sent in by 'P,' dated from New-Brunswick, Oct. 7, 1738. Cf. no. 1533. This popular eighteenth-century poem usually has the title 'Ode to William Pulteney.' On Nugent (1702–1788), see the *CBEL*, II, 323. The *DNB* article contains a good account of this poem. Printed in Dodsley, II, 210. Crum R143.

1533. Dec. 1758 *New Am Mag* I, 310.
'Our grandsires were all papists.'
T: 'An Epigram. Wrote on a pain of glass in the same room, in imitation of Horace's Davinosa quid non immenint dies, &c.' ¶ No: 4 lines.
Note: Cf. no. 1532.

1534. Dec., 1758 *New Am Mag* I, 310.
'With parrots, and such Trifles Tir'd.'

T: 'Sir, a friend of mine in this town who sometimes amuses himself with sending little pieces of poetry to the ladies of his acquaintance, being ask'd why Delia alone escaped his muse, gave his reason in the following lines.' ¶ No: 58 lines.
Note: Not bad verse. Sent in by 'P.'

1535. Dec., 1758 *New Am Mag* I, 310.
'Curs'd be the wretch, that's bought.'
T: 'On Liberty.' ¶ No: 22 lines.

1759

1536. Jan. 1, 1759 *BEP* ⋕1218, 3/2.
'Amherst, while Crouds attend you on your Way.'
Note: A reprint of no. 1529.

1537. Jan. 1, 1759 *BG* ⋕196, 1/2–3.
'Amherst, while Crouds attend you on your Way.'
Note: A reprint of no. 1529.

1538. Jan. 1, 1759 *NYG* ⋕835, 3/1.
'Methinks I see *Britania's* Genius here.'
Note: A reprint of no. 1528.

1539. Jan. 4, 1759 *MG*.
'Ye *Maids*, whom Nature meant for *Mothers*.'
T: 'A Batchelor's address, or Proposal to the Maidens.' ¶ No: 58 lines. ¶ A: 'Cynthio.'
Note: Good verse.

1540. Jan. 5, 1759 *NHG* ⋕118.
'Amherst, while Crouds attend you on your Way.'
Note: A reprint of no. 1529.

1541. Jan. 5, 1759 *NLS* ⋕22.
'Mark with what different Zeal each Nation arms.'
T: 'On the Clemency shewn the French at Louisburg, and the Cruelty shewn by the French at Fort Duquesne, now Pittsborough.' ¶ No: 8 lines.
Note: Reprinted, no. 1562.

1542. Jan. 8, 1759 *NYM* ⋕334, 2/2.
'To this new World, from fam'd Britannia's Shore.'
T: 'Prologue Spoken by Mr. Hallam ... at the opening of the new Theatre, in this City.'

Note: Prefatory note by David Douglas: 'They [prologue & epilogue] were both written in North America, and generously sent us by the ingenious Author.' See no. 1543. This is a reprint of no. 1184.

1543. Jan. 8, 1759 *NYM* ⚹334, 2/2–3.
'Much has been said at this unlucky Time.'
T: 'Epilogue spoken by Mrs. Douglas.' ¶ No: 55 lines. ¶ A: [Dr. Adam Thomson.]
Note: See no. 1542. This is a revised and enlarged version of no. 1185.

1544. Jan. 8, 1759 *NYG* ⚹836, 3/1.
'Hail Western World, begin Thy better Fate.'
T: 'On the taking of Cape Breton.' ¶ No: 46 lines.
Note: Good imaginative, romantic verse. Reprinted, no. 1550.

1545. Jan. 15, 1759 *BG* ⚹198, 3/1.
'Res augus ta Domi Musam confundit amicam--'
T: 'Dogma Poeticam.' 'The following Lines by Way of Condolance with the young Gentleman, who unhappily miss'd the Opportunity of presenting his Poem to General Amherst, as he pass'd through Long-Island.' ¶ No: 14 lines. ¶ A: 'Philo—Metros.'
Note: A reply to no. 1529.

1546. Jan. 27, 1759 *CG* ⚹199, 1/1–2/1.
'My muse, assume a grateful strain.'
T: 'Grateful Reflections upon the divine Goodness in the remarkable Success vouchsafed his Majesty's Arms, especially in North-America, in the current Year, in a poetical Essay, occasioned by the happy News of the late Acquisition of Fort Du Quesne, on the Ohio, by General Forbes.' ¶ No: 136 lines.
Note: Dated 'Conn., Dec. 29, 1758.'

1547. Jan., 1759 *New Am Mag* I, 331–2.
'The hoary winter now conceals from sight.'
T: 'Winter.' ¶ No: 34 lines.
Note: Reprinted, no. 1909.

1548. Jan., 1759 *New Am Mag* I, 332.
'Silence! soft daughter of nocturnal shades!'
T: 'A Night Piece.' ¶ No: 52 lines. ¶ A: 'Al—s' [Princeton author; B. Y. Prime?]
Note: Dated 'E. Jersey,' signed 'Nass—al Fil— Al—.' Nos. 1575, 1596, 1597, and 1627, are all by a Princeton alumnus and probably by the same person. Cf. no. 1627.

1549. Jan., 1759 *New Am Mag* I, 332–3.
'Thrice happy *Damon!* to thy longing arms.'
T: 'To a successful Rival.' ¶ No: 48 lines. ¶ A: 'Thyrsis.'

1550. Jan., 1759 *New Am Mag* I, 333.
'Hail western world! begin thy better fate.'
Note: A reprint of no. 1544.

1551. Jan., 1759 *New Am Mag* I, 333–4.
'Methinks I see Britannia's genius here.'
Note: A reprint of no. 1529.

1552. Jan., 1759 *New Am Mag* I, 334.
'Amherst, while crowds attend you on your way.'
Note: A reprint of no. 1529.

1553. Jan., 1759 *New Am Mag* I, 334.
'To part, or not to part:—that is the question.'
T: 'Shakespeare parody'd.' ¶ No: 33 lines. ¶ A: 'By an Officer of the army.'
Note: Reprinted in the *Columbian Magazine* II (Feb., 1788), 112, as 'A Parody written during the Late War.'

1554. Feb. 8, 1759 *MG* #718.
'Methinks I see Britannia's Genius here.'
Note: A reprint of no. 1528.

1555. Feb. 15, 1759 *PJ* #845, 2/2–3.
'Forbes! to thee the muse her tribute brings.'
T: 'To the Honourable Brigadier-General [John] Forbes.' ¶ No: 58 lines.

1556. Feb. 16, 1759 *NHG* #124.
'Hear, Peggy, since the single State.'
T: 'Advice to a Young Lady, lately Married.' ¶ No: 96 lines. ¶ A: 'By an unmarried Lady.'

1557. Feb. 22, 1759 *BNL* #2999, 2/1.
'Hail, noble Forbes! embark'd in *Briton's* Cause.'
T: 'Verses ... wrote soon after the Reduction of Fort Du Quesne.' ¶ No: 52 lines. ¶ A: ['By a New-England Friend.']
Note: Reprinted (with fuller title and author information), no. 1567.

1558. Feb. 26, 1759 *NYM* #341, 1/1.
'Tell me, says Cato, where you found.'
T: 'To S. B. Esq; On the Death of his Son, Colonel Bever, who was killed in the Engagement at Ticonderoga.' ¶ No: 28 lines.

Note: On Lt. Col. Samuel Bever. 'J. G.' submits the Lines 'without Leave of the Author; for though the Style and Manner will easily point him out to many of your Readers, you may be assured he will excuse the Publication; being indifferent to either Praise or Censure for such petty Compositions.'

1559. Feb., 1759 *Gent Mag* XXIX, 81.
'Attend! and favour! as our fires ordain.'
T: 'A description of an ancient Festival honoured with a Solemn Sacrifice for procuring a Blessing on the Fields. From a late elegant Translation of Tibullus. Book the Second. Elegy the First.' ¶ No: 104 lines. ¶ A: 'By Dr. [James] Grainger.'
Note: On Grainger (1721 ?–1766), see the *CBEL*, II, 363. Cf. no. 1991.

1560. Feb., 1759 *London Mag* XXVIII, 102.
'Neglected long had lain my useless lyre,'
T: 'On the Defeat at Ticonderoga, or Carelong.' ¶ A: 'By a Lady in America.'
Note: A reprint of no. 1475.

1561. Feb., 1759 *Universal Mag* XXIV, 104.
'Thou bed! in which I first began.'
T: 'M. Brockes a son Lit (Vol. XXIV. p. 40.) Imitated.' ¶ No: 28 lines. ¶ A: 'R. B.' [Robert Bolling ?]
Note: Robert Bolling (1738–1775) of Chellow, Buckingham Co., Va., a planter, county justice, county sheriff, member of the House of Burgesses 1761-1765, and delegate for Buckingham Co. to the Va. Convention of July, 1775, was the most prolific poet of pre-revolutionary Virginia. The initials 'R. B.,' coupled with the fact that Brock's French poem and Bolling's translation of his *jeu d'esprit* are in two of Bolling's manuscript volumes of verse ('Hl: arodiana,' p. 49, microfilm at the Univ. of Va. Library, MS 8708; and 'La Gazetta di Parnasso,' p. 37, Huntington Library, Brock collection), suggest that the imitation may be his. Reprinted, no. 1692. Reprinted in the *Columbian Magazine*, I (July, 1787), 560.

1562. March 2, 1759 *NHG* #126.
'Mark with what different Zeal each Nation arms,'
Note: A reprint of no. 1541.

1563. March 2, 1759 *NHG* #126.
'No longer now does favour'd Strephon roam.'
A: 'By a Young Gentleman.'
Note: A reprint of no. 1516.

1564. March 2, 1759 *NHG* #126.
  'Once on a Time it by chance came to pass.'
  T: 'An old fashioned rhyming Tale.' ¶ No: 26 lines.
  Note: Cf. no. 848 for a variant. This poem also appeared in *Poor
    Richard* for 1743 (reprinted in the *Franklin Papers*, II, 373–374).

1565. March 2, 1759 *NHG* #126.
  'Patriots and Chiefs! Britannia's mighty *Dead.*'
  Note: A reprint of no. 1484.

1566. March 5, 1759 *MG* 2/2.
  'Good Cust'mers are (without all Jeering).'
  T: 'A Friendly Caveat.' ¶ No: 12 lines. ¶ A: 'R. P.'

1567. March 9, 1759 *NHG* #127.
  'Hail, noble Forbes! embark'd in Briton's cause.'
  T: 'To General Forbes, soon after the Reduction of Fort Du Quesne.'
    ¶ A: 'By a New-England Friend.'
  Note: A reprint of no. 1557.

1568. March 19, 1759 *BG* #207, 1/3.
  'My Tho'ts do coincide in Part.'
  T: 'Some Remarks On the Dialogue between Tom and Dick, in the
    last Week's Paper.' ¶ No: 30 lines. ¶ A: 'Phil. Anthropos.'

1569. March 19, 1759 *BPB* #83.
  'From War's rude Scenes, to sport with milder Fires.'
  T: 'Acrostick.' ¶ No: 24 lines.
  Note: Spells out 'For the club of Anti danglers.'

1570. March 19, 1759 *NYG* #846, 4/1.
  'Patriots and Chiefs! Britania's mighty *Dead.*'
  Note: A reprint of no. 1484.

1571. March 23, 1759 *NHG* #129.
  'Time is a short Parenthesis.'
  T: 'On Time.' ¶ No: 42 lines.

1572. March 26, 1759 *WNYG* #6, 1/1–2.
  'Great-Britain with a deal of Pelf.'
  T: 'The Crisis, or Demonstration; being a Translation of a late
    memorable Speech from the original Arabic.' ¶ No: 104 lines. ¶
    A: 'By P. W., Professor of the oriental Languages, in Harvard
    College, Cambridge.'
  Note: Hudibrastic verse satirizing a [governor's?] speech asking for
    funds to prosecute the war.

1573. March 29, 1759 *BNL* #3004, 2/1.
  'As thro' the Waves the faithless Shepherd bore.'
  T: 'Horace, Lib I, Od. 15.' ¶ No: 42 lines.

1574. March 29, 1759 *BNL* #3004, 2/1.
'Is this a Time to fiddle, sing and dance.'
T: 'On the present Expedition.' ¶ No: 39 lines. ¶ A: 'By a Quaker.'
Note: Dated 'The 26th day of the 3d Mo. 1759.' Reprinted, no.
1582.

1575. March, 1759 *New Am Mag* I, 406–7.
'Oft before *Phoebus* gilds the highest hills.'
T: 'The Solemn Pensive.' ¶ No: 91 lines. ¶ A: 'Fil. Nass. Ale—s'
[Princeton author; B. Y. Prime?]
Note: Dated 'East Jersey.' Richardson, p. 132, refers to the author
as a woman, but I suspect that the author was B. Y. Prime. See
no. 1548.

1576. March, 1759 *NE Mag* #3, pp. 49–50.
'A Gentleman of a spotless character.'
Note: A reprint of no. 1051.

1577. Apr. 16, 1759 *BG* #211, 2/1.
'Galliâ ruente, surgat Omnis Heros.'
T: 'Canticum Novum.' ¶ No: 16 lines.

1578. Apr. 16, 1759 *NYG* #850, 1/3.
'A God there is, the whole Creation tells.'
Note: A reprint of no. 854.

1579. Apr. 16, 1759 *NYM* #348, 3/2.
'Hah! there it flames, the long expected star.'
T: [On the comet.] ¶ No: 30 lines.
Note: The comet was seen on April 3 'about 3 o'clock in the morn-
ing.' The author 'being without any advantage of making nice
astronomical observations, could do no more than compose the
following lines.' Reprinted, nos. 1588, 1591, 1592, 1595, 1600.

1580. Apr. 23, 1759 *BG* # 212, 2/3.
'A Dexter'ous Trader of the Town.'
T: 'The Auctioneer enrag'd.' ¶ No: 18 Lines.
Note: Evidently by the auctioneer. See the reply, no. 1583.

1581. Apr. 23, 1759 *NYM* # 349, 3/3.
'Pale night succeeds the Sun's Career.'
T: 'Two and Forty Lines in Meter.' ¶ No: 42 lines.
Note: The mutability of men and empires.

1582. Apr. 27, 1759 *NHG* # 134.
'Is this a Time to fiddle, sing and dance.'
Note: A reprint of no. 1574.

1583. Apr. 30, 1759 *BG* ✳ 213, 2/3.
    'Johnny, Why art so Touchy grown.'
    T: 'To the Auctioneer, on his Advertisement in last Thursday's
    Paper.' ¶ No: 20 lines. ¶ A: 'Philo Metros.'
    Note: A reply to no. 1580.

1584. Apr., 1759 *New Am Mag* I, 434–5.
    'Behold how gay the flow'ng mead.'
    T: 'On the approaching Spring.' ¶ No: 28 lines. ¶ A: 'Philo-Musae-
    us' [Dr. Adam Thomson].
    Note: Nationalistic note in prefatory letter. Richardson, p. 133, n.
    155, praises the poem.

1585. Apr., 1759 *New Am Mag* I, 435–6.
    'In what fond accents shall my thoughts have vent.'
    T: 'To Col. R—s in Spain.' ¶ No: 67 lines. ¶ A: 'Z.'
    Note: A 'paraphrase of ... Spectator. Vol. 3, No. 204.'

1586. Apr., 1759 *New Am Mag* I, 436.
    'May I presume in humble lays.'
    T: 'To a lady fond of Dancing.' ¶ No: 25 lines. ¶ A: 'Z.'
    Note: Crum M242.

1587. Apr., 1759 *New Am Mag* I, 436–7 and May, 1759, 468–9.
    'Oh! happy swains, did they know how to prize.'
    T: 'O Fortunatos Nimium, &c. paraphras'd.' ¶ No: 141 lines. ¶ A:
    'C.'
    Note: Signed 'O' at end of April selection, but 'C' at end of piece (p.
    469).

1588. Apr., 1759 *New Am Mag* I, 437.
    'This morning to pen, ink, and paper I flew.'
    T: 'To Miss M. A.' ¶ No: 8 lines. ¶ A: 'A.'
    Note: Cf. nos. 1523, 1653.

1589. Apr., 1759 *New Am Mag* I, 438.
    'Hah! there it flames, the long expected star!'
    Note: A reprint of no. 1579.

1590. Apr., 1759 *New Am Mag* I, 438.
    'I'll haste me to some shady grove.'
    T: 'The Constant Swain: In imitation of The Constant Fair, set to
    musick in the Gentleman's Magazine for October 1756.' ¶ No: 24
    lines.
    Note: See no. 1613 for another poem by this author.

1591. May 3, 1759 *BNL* ❡3009, 1/3.
      'Hah! there it flames, the long expected star.'
      Note: A reprint of no. 1579.

1592. May 11, 1759 *NHG* ❡136, 4/1.
      'Hah! there it flames, the long expected Star.'
      Note: A reprint of no. 1579.

1593. May 21, 1759 *NYG* ❡855, 4/3.
      'With Beat of Drum, and Trumpet's Heroic Poem.'
      T: 'Extract from the Freeholder of Kent's Heroic Poem.' ❡ No: 28
      lines.
      Note: 'N.B. The Public are desired to take Notice, that the author ...
      in the year 1753 gave the World a plain Hint of those remarkable
      Slaughters that have since been made among the Austrians,
      French, and Russians.'

1594. May, 1759 *Gent Mag* XXIX, 228–9.
      'While Damon whistles o'er the plain.'
      T: 'Myrtilla to Damon.' ❡ No: 24 lines. ❡ A: 'Myrtilla' [i.e., Ben-
      jamin Waller].
      Note: Dated 'May 17, 1759' The manuscript is in the Waller Papers
      at Colonial Williamsburg, Inc. On Waller (1710–1786), lawyer,
      of Williamsburg, Va., see James A. Servies and Carl P. Dol-
      metsch, eds., *The Poems of Charles Hansford* (Chapel Hill, N.C.,
      1961), pp. xvii–xix, and p. 78.

1595. May, 1759 *Gent Mag* XXIX, 229.
      'Hah! there it flames, the long expected star.'
      Note: A reprint of no. 1579.

1596. May, 1759 *New Am Mag* I, 467–8.
      'Far in a wild retired gloom.'
      T: 'True Politness.' ❡ No: 66 lines. ❡ A: 'F— N—ae. d—.'
      [Princeton author; B. Y. Prime?].
      Note: Cf. no. 1548.

1597. May, 1759 *New Am Mag* I, 468.
      'O Peaceful mansion! how thy rural face.'
      T: 'On coming to a house in the country. April 4th, 1759.' ❡ No: 25
      lines. ❡ A: 'A—' [Princeton author? B. Y. Prime?].
      Note: Retirement theme. Cf. no. 1548.

1598. May, 1759 *New Am Mag* I, 469–70.
      'There once liv'd in repute a substantial freeholder.'
      T: 'The Electioneer.' ❡ No: 62 lines.

1599. May 1759 *New Am Mag* I, 470–1.
'To print, or not to print,--that is the question.'
T: 'Hamlet's Soliloquy, imitated.' ¶ No: 32 lines. ¶ A: [Richard Jago.]
Note: Printed in Dodsley, V, 82.

1600. May, 1759 *Scots Mag* XXI, 254.
'Hah! there it flames, the long-expected star.'
Note: A reprint of no. 1579.

1601. June 22, 1759 *NHG* #142, *Postscript.*
'Look see the mighty Hero stand.'
T: 'On the King of Prussia's Speech to the States of Holland.' ¶ No: 25 lines.

1602. June 29, 1759 *NHG* #143.
'Forbear to ask what France or Spain.'
T: 'Imitation of Horace, Lib ii. Ode XI.' ¶ No: 30 lines.

1603. June, 1759 *Gent Mag* XXIX, 283.
'Beneath yon Turf lies *Gamble's* dust.'
T: 'An Epitaph on the late Dr. Gamble, one of the Denomination of Quakers, in Barbadoes.' ¶ No: 10 lines.
Note: Reprinted, no. 1937A.

1604. June, 1759 *Lon Mag* XXVIII, 334.
'The swains in a bantering way.'
T: 'Two Pastoral Ballads, wrote in North America. In the Manner of Mr. Shenston. Ballad I. The Quarrel. Written in the Month of January, 1758.' ¶ No: 64 lines.
Note: Cf. no. 1612.

1605. June, 1759 *New Am Mag* I, 508–10.
'Some husbands on a winters day.'
T: 'The Pig: A Tale.' ¶ No: 208 lines.
Note: Cf. no. 1615. This is a reprint (revised?) of no. 485.

1606. June, 1759 *New Am Mag* I, 510.
'In beauty, or wit.'
T: 'A panegyric on a learned and worthy Lady.' ¶ No: 30 lines.
Note: Crum I1247 entitles the poem 'Upon the Learned Mary Wortly Montagu' and attributes it to Swift, but the poem is not mentioned in Harold Williams' standard edition of Swift's *Poems*, nor in Arthur H. Scouten's revision of Teerink's *Bibliography of ... Swift* (Philadelphia, 1963).

1607. June, 1759 *New Am Mag* I, 510.
    'Near where Euphrates silent stream.'
    T: 'Aenigma.' ¶ No: 29 lines.
    Note: Reprinted in the *Columbian Mag*, I (Aug., 1787), 610.

1608. June, 1759 *New Am Mag* I, 510.
    'Yet oft our fond affections want controul.'
    T: 'Fragment.' ¶ No: 26 lines. ¶ A: 'Z.'

1609. June, 1759 *Universal Mag* XXIV, 319–20.
    'An austere Sage, in ancient days.'
    T: 'Friar Philip's Geese: A Tale. From La Fontain.' ¶ No: 138
    lines. ¶ A: 'Row. Rugeley.'
    Note: Dated 'St. Ives.' Rowland Rugeley (1735?–1776) emigrated
    to South Carolina, c. 1765.

1610. July 2, 1759 *BPB* #98.
    'How chang'd the Scene, since from their native Reign.'
    ¶ No: 26 lines. ¶ A: 'By a young Gentleman.'

1611. July 13, 1759 *NHG* #145.
    'Vile Wretch! who sacrifices all to wealth.'
    T: 'The Miser.' ¶ No: 30 lines. ¶ A: 'Liberalitas.'

1612. July, 1759 *London Mag* XXVIII, 390.
    'Once more, O ye Muses, my song.'
    T: 'Ballad II, after Reconciliation. Written in the Month of May,
    1758.'
    Note: Cf. no. 1604. A reprint of no. 1453.

1613. July, 1759 *New Am Mag* I, 547.
    'Ye sacred guardians of the good and fair!'
    T: 'A Hymn.' ¶ No: 8 lines. ¶ A: 'By the author of the Constant
    Swain.'
    Note: See no. 1590 for 'the Constant Swain.'

1614. July, 1759 *New Am Mag* I, 547–8.
    'Hail! sov'reign leaf, whose virtue can dispense.'
    T: 'Upon a Dish of Tea. Addressed to a young Lady.' ¶ No: 52
    lines.

1615. July, 1759 *New Am Mag* I, 548–60.
    'Two sparks were earnest in debate.'
    T: 'The Sequal to the Pig. Or, The Wager. A Tale.' ¶ No: 240
    lines.
    Note: 'The Pig' is no. 1605 (i.e., no. 485). A shortened reprint of
    no. 929.

1616. Aug. 3, 1759 *NHG* #148.
'Sing melancholly Muse the awful Stroke.'
T: 'Some Verses on the Death of a young Lady.' ¶ No: 54 lines. ¶
A: 'By a young Gentleman.'

1617. Aug. 3, 1759 *NHG* #148.
'Boscaw'n, that great auspicious Name.'
T: 'A Verse upon the Taking of Louisbourg.' ¶ No: 66 lines. ¶ A:
'By a Female Hand in the Country.'

1618. Aug. 6, 1759 *WNYG* #25, 1/1–2.
'What! can an infant Muse attempt to sing.'
T: 'On the Heroism of the Royal Frederick. The Patriotism of the
Honourable Pitt--and Fall of the brave General Howe.' ¶ No:
131 lines. ¶ A: 'Done by a young Gentleman.'

1619. Aug. 11, 1759 *CG* #227.
'Tho' Life is but a narrow Span.'
T: [*Tempus fugit.*] ¶ No: 16 lines.

1620. Aug. 24, 1759 *NHG* #151.
'He is the Emblem of Fear.'
T: 'The following Character of C–m–e J—n M—e, was found, the
Night after his arrival at Barbados, on all the Tavern doors there.'
¶ No: 10 lines. ¶ A: 'Philo Veritatis.' Pluto Justicia.
Note: Dated 'Boston, Aug. 20, Extract of a Letter from Barbados.
July 16, 1759.' Reprinted, no. 1621. On Commodore John Moore.

1621. Aug. 31, 1759 *NLS* #56.
'He is the Emblem of Fear.'
Note: A reprint of no. 1620.

1622. Aug., 1759 *Gent Mag* XXIX, 383.
'Yea, sweeter far than sweetest flow'r that grows.'
T: 'Upon a Rose given me by Damon.' ¶ No: 28 lines. ¶ A:
'Myrtilla.'
Note: Dated 'July 18, 1759.' Cf. no. 1594.

1623. Aug., 1759 *New Am Mag* I, 588.
'Great God! thou guardian of each hour.'
T: 'Psalm 139.' ¶ No: 60 lines.
Note: Cf. no. 1465.

1624. Aug., 1759 *New Am Mag* I, 588–9.
'You ask, if the thing to my choice were submitted.'
T: 'The Choice of a Husband. In a Letter to a Friend.' ¶ No: 40
lines.
Note: Reprinted (in 44 lines), no. 1724. Reprinted in the *Am. Museum*, VI (Oct., 1789), 332.

1625. Aug., 1759 *New Am Mag* I, 590.
'What Shepherd or nymph of the grove.'
T: 'A Pastoral Song. To the Tune of Colin's Complaint.' ¶ No: 40 lines.

1626. Sept. 29, 1759 *SCG* #1308, 4/1.
'What fine antitheses, what flow'ry phrase.'
T: 'To Cliophil. Answers. To the Verses written under the Portraits, &c.' ¶ No: 22 lines. ¶ A: By a 'young gentleman' at school ('Misandogmaticus'?).
Note: Cf. nos. 1631, 1633, 1641.

1627. Sept., 1759 *New Am Mag* I, 621.
'Has Neptune and Apollo join'd.'
T: 'Louisburg Taken: An Ode.' ¶ No: 90 lines. ¶ A: 'Al—s.' [Princeton author; B. Y. Prime?].
Note: Dated 'E. Jersey, Aug. 1, 1759' and additionally signed 'Nassovean—' Cf. no. 1548. Possibly imitated by no. 1650. Oscar G. T. Sonneck, *Francis Hopkinson and James Lyon* (Washington, 1905), p. 124, attributes this poem to James Lyon, following the suggestion of William Nelson in *New Jersey Archives*, XX, 383; see also Nelson in *Collections of the New Jersey Hist. Soc.*, IX, 161. But Nelson's suggestion seems unlikely to me, for Lyon is not known to have written any poetry.

1628. Sept., 1759 *New Am Mag* I, 622.
'Parent of all, Omnipotent.'
T: 'The Patriot's Prayer.' ¶ No: 24 lines.

1629. Oct. 1, 1759 *NYG* #874, 3/2.
'Friend *Weyman*, doubtless having oft observ'd.'
T: [J. Parker's attack on Weyman.] ¶ No: 42 lines. ¶ A: 'J. Parker.'
Note: James Parker and William Weyman were both New York printers. For an account of this quarrel, see Beverley McAnear, 'James Parker versus William Weyman,' N.J. Hist Soc., *Proc.*, LIX (1941), 1–24.

1630. Oct. 1, 1759 *NYM* #372.
'Chearful, fearless and at ease.'
T: Under date 'Nassau Hall, Sept. 27, 1759: Yesterday the annual Commencement, ... The whole Ceremony concluded with the following Ode, set to Music by Mr. James Lyon, one of the Students.' ¶ No: 42 lines. ¶ A: [Samuel Davies.]
Note: Reprinted in *New Jersey Archives*, XX, 383. Reprinted, no. 1640. The attribution is given in Jonathan Bayard Smith, 'Commonplace Book of Verse, 1759' (Princeton MS, AM 1361). Reprinted in Davis (see no. 1035), pp. 208–219 (from no. 1640).

1631. Oct. 6, 1759 *SCG*, 4/2.
    'Tho' Billingsgate most copious Stile.'
    T: 'To S. Q.' ¶ No: 8 lines. ¶ A: 'Misandogmaticus.'
    Note: Cf. no. 1626.

1632. Oct. 6, 1759 *SCG*, 4/2.
    'What has been prov'd, to prove again.'
    T: 'To S. Q. and Aletheia, on their Verses in the South Carolina
    weekly Gazette.' ¶ No: 4 lines. ¶ A: 'Scriblerus.'
    Note: Cf. no. 1626.

1633. Oct. 13, 1759 *SCG*, 3/1.
    'Enough chastis'd has *Hurlo* felt thy dart.'
    T: 'To Mis-andogmaticus.' ¶ No: 8 lines. ¶ A: 'A By Stander.'
    Note: Cf. no. 1626.

1634. Oct. 15, 1759 *BG* #237, 1/2.
    'What Honours Wolfe should thy brave Brows adorn ?'
    T: ['On the Death of General Wolfe.'] ¶ No: 14 lines. ¶ A: 'Massa-
    chutensis.'
    Note: This poem also appeared in two other newspapers on this
    date, nos. 1635 and 1636. It was reprinted, nos. 1638, 1645, 1647,
    1654. Reprinted in McCarty, III, 7–8 (from no. 1645). Cf. no.
    1669A.

1635. Oct. 15, 1759 *BEP* #1259, 3/1.
    'What Honours, Wolfe, should they brave Brows adorn ?'
    Note: See no. 1634.

1636. Oct. 15, 1759 *BPB* #113, 3/2.
    'What Honours, Wolfe, should thy brave Brows adorn ?'
    Note: See no. 1634.

1637. Oct. 15, 1759 *NYG* #876, 1/1.
    'Wake! awake the plaintive Strain.'
    T: 'Elegy. On the Death of his Excellency George Haldane, Esq.' ¶
    No: 36 lines. ¶ A: 'Square-Cap.'
    Note: Dated 'Kingston, (in Jamaica) July 27, 1759.' Reprinted, no.
    1656, with additional information.

1638. Oct. 18, 1759 *BNL* #2042, 1/3.
    'What Honours, Wolfe, should Thy brave Brows adorn ?'
    Note: A reprint of no. 1634.

1639. Oct. 18, 1759 *BNL* #2042, 3/3.
    'Whilst War now rages with impetuous Roar.'
    T: [Elegy on Wolfe.] ¶ No: 60 lines. ¶ A: 'Americanus.'
    Note: Reprinted, nos. 1642, 1643, 1646, 1648, 1661.

1640. Oct. 19, 1759 *NHG* ⚹159.
'Chearful, fearless, and at ease.'
Note: A reprint of no. 1630.

1641. Oct. 20, 1759 *SCG*, 4/3.
'Away great Johnson, and each worn-out Theme.'
T: [On Cliophil and Misandogmaticus.] ¶ No: 14 lines.
Note: In mock advertisement of a Proposal for printing by poem on the literary war between 'Cliophil and Misandogmaticus' 'By Shenkin ap Evan, ap Lewis, ap Morgan, The Welsh Geneaologist.' Notes that an Epitaph 'in Hudibrastic Stile' will conclude the piece.

1642. Oct. 22, 1759 *BG* ⚹238, 1/2.
'Whilst War now rages with impetuous Roar.'
Note: A reprint of no. 1639.

1643. Oct. 22, 1759 *BEP* ⚹1260, 4/2.
'Whilst War now rages with impetuous Roar.'
Note: A reprint of no. 1639.

1644. Oct. 22, 1759 *BPB* ⚹114, 3/1.
'Could lays harmonious speak thy high desert.'
T: 'On the Death of General Wolfe, who was kill'd in defeating the French Army near Quebec, on the 13th of September, 1759.' ¶ No: 26 lines. ¶ A: 'Bostoniensis.'
Note: Cf. 1669A. Reprinted, no. 1662.

1645. Oct. 25, 1759 *PG* ⚹1609.
'What Honours, WOLFE, should thy brave Brows adorn?'
Note: A reprint of no. 1634.

1646. Oct. 29, 1759 *NYM* ⚹376, 3/1–2.
'Whilst War now rages with impetuous Roar.'
Note: A reprint of no. 1639.

1647. Oct. 29, 1759 *NYG* ⚹878, 3/2.
'What Honours, Wolfe, should thy brave Brows adorn?'
Note: A reprint of no. 1634.

1648. Oct. 29, 1759 *NYG* ⚹ 878, 3/2.
'Whilst War now rages with impetuous Roar.'
Note: A reprint of no. 1639.

1649. Oct., 1759 *New Am Mag* I, 665.
'The plains recede, the sylvan hillock's rise.'
T: 'A Poem, humbly inscribed to his Excellency Francis Bernard,

Esq; Governor in Chief, in and over the Province of New-Jersey, &c. Occasioned by some differing Sentiments, observed among the Indian Savages in one of the late treaties at Easton.' ¶ No: 118 lines. ¶ A: 'Martinus Scriblerus.'

Note: Richardson, p. 132, says Martinus Scriblerus is 'of Hunterdon, New Jersey.' Good verse. Cf. no. 1650.

1650. Oct., 1759 *New Am Mag* I, 667–8.
'Britons! attend the song.'
T: 'A Loyal Prayer; or, an Ode. In imitation of one compos'd [on] the late war.' ¶ No: 90 lines. ¶ A: 'Martinus Scriblerus.'
Note: Cf. no. 1649. This may refer to no. 1627. Set to the tune of 'God save The King.'

1651. Oct., 1759 *New Am Mag* I, 668.
'G—ey, waste not thy precious Time.'
T: 'Advice to Miss G—e C—xe.' ¶ No: 16 lines.

1652. Oct., 1759 *New Am Mag* I, 668.
'In Times of old, the poets lays.'
T: 'An Epigram.' ¶ No: 14 lines.

1653. Oct., 1759 *New Am Mag* I, 668.
'Think, bright Maria, when you see.'
T: 'To Miss M. A.' ¶ No: 8 lines. ¶ A: 'F.'
Note: Cf. nos. 1523, 1588.

1654. Oct., 1759 *New Am Mag* I, 668.
'What honours Wolfe, should thy brave brows adorn?'
Note: A reprint of no. 1634.

1655. Oct., 1759 *Scots Mag* XXI, 526.
'On younder plain what awful form appears.'
T: 'Elegy on the death of Gen. Wolfe.' ¶ No: 36 lines.
Note: Reprinted, no. 1751.

1656. Oct., 1759 *Scots Mag* XXI, 526.
'Wake! awake! the plaintive strain.'
A: 'G. S.'
Note: 'From the Kingston gazette.' A reprint of no. 1637.

1657. Oct., 1759 *Scots Mag* XXI, 526–7.
'Amidst these Triumphs, This excess of joy.'
T: 'Lines occasioned by the death of Gen. Wolfe.' ¶ No: 44 lines.

1658. Oct., 1759 *Scots Mag* XXI, 527.
'Ah me! what sorrows are we born to bear!'
T: 'To the memory of an officer killed before Quebec.' ¶ No: 74 lines. ¶ A: 'J. M'P.'
Note: Dated Oct. 30, 1759. Reprinted, no. 1862.

1659. Oct., 1759 *Scots Mag* XXI, 527.

'The great Epaminondas conq'ring, dy'd.'

T: 'Extempore. Upon the news of the Gen. Wolfe and Montcalm being both killed in the same action.' ¶ No: 4 lines.

1660. Nov. 1, 1759 *PJ* ⚹882, 3/1–2.

'Brittan I mourn! Great Wolfe in Arms no more.'

T: 'On the Death of General Wolfe.' ¶ No: 19 lines. ¶ A: 'Pennsylvanicus.'

Note: 'Pennsylvanicus' wrote a number of political essays in the *PJ*, 1758–9. Reprinted, no. 1683.

1661. Nov. 2, 1759 *NHG* ⚹161, 4/1–2.

'Whilst war now rages with impetuous roar.'

Note: A reprint of no. 1639.

1662. Nov. 2, 1759 *NHG* ⚹161, 4/2.

'Could lays harmonious speak Thy high desert.'

Note: A reprint of no. 1644.

1663. Nov. 3, 1759 *SCG* ⚹1315, 1/3.

'To all those Youths, whose noble Hearts.'

T: 'The following Song, written extempore, upon reading one published in the Paper called. Supplement to the South Carolina weekly Gazette, No. 49 (by a Volunteer in the Army) is just come to Hand.' ¶ No: 32 lines + 4 line refrain.

Note: The poem referred to is not extant in the source cited, but see no. 1670.

1664. Nov. 5, 1759 *BG* ⚹240, 1/1–2.

'Hail, auspicious, happy Day.'

T: 'On the Reduction of Quebec by General Wolfe.' ¶ No: 97 lines. ¶ A: 'G. B.'

Note: 'a young Author.'

1665. Nov. 8, 1759 *PG* ⚹1611.

'Thy Merits, Wolfe, transcend all Human Praise.'

T: 'On the Death of the much lamented General Wolfe.' ¶ No: 36 lines.

Note: Reprinted in McCarty, I, 300–301; in part in Dyckinck, I, 449; in Stedman and Hutchinson, II, 477–78; and in Stevenson, p. 123. Ll. 5–6: 'Had I Duché's or Godfrey's magic skill,/Each line to raise, and animate at will.' These lines suggest local, younger author--perhaps Evans or Hopkinson. Reprinted, no. 1671.

1666. Nov. 12, 1759 *BG* ⚹241, 1/1.

'By Base retreat how were those honours stain'd.'

T: 'The Contrast.' ¶ No: 12 lines. ¶ A: ['T.']

Note: Acrostic: Byng, Boscawen. Reprinted, no. 1748 (where the initial 'T' is given for the author).

1667. Nov. 17, 1759 *SCG* ⌗1317, 2/3–3/1; cont. Nov. 24, 2/1; Dec.22, 1–2.
'Aloft in air, the bright Astraea sat.'
T: 'A Poem. On the glorious success of his majesty's arms at Quebec.' ¶ No: 194 lines. ¶ A: [Thomas Godfrey?]
Note: Good poetry. Godfrey was currently in Charleston and advertised his merchandise in the *SCG* Dec. 22, 1759, 1/1. Reprinted, nos. 1750, 1770.

1668. Nov. 17, 1759 *SCG* ⌗1317, 3/3.
'Peace to thy silent shade, dear worthy friend!'
T: 'To the memory of the late Mr. John Hunt.' ¶ No: 12 lines.

1669. Nov. 19, 1759 *BPB* ⌗118.
'Here rests from Toil, in narrow Bounds confin'd.'
T: 'An Essay to an Epitaph on the mighty, great, and justly lamented Major-General Wolfe, who fell Victorious before Quebec, September 13, 1759.' ¶ No: 22 lines. ¶ A: ['By Valentine Nevil ... Purser of his Majesty's ship Oxford.']
Note: Reprinted, nos. 1684, 1691, 1694, 1696 (where the author is given). Reprinted, McCarty, I, 306–307 (where the source is cited as the *New York Gazette* Dec. 13, 1759). In his poem *The Reduction of Louisbourg* (Portsmouth, Eng., 1758), Wegelin 281, Nevill is described as 'of Greenwich in Kent, Secretary to the Honourable Admiral Townsend.'

1669A. Nov. 20, 1759 *NM* ⌗75, 3/2.
'My Boston Babes, who are so dear.'
T: Verses 'in Imitation of, *Milk for Boston Babes*.' ¶ No: 16 lines. ¶ A: [John Maylem?]
Note: Satire on 'Boston 'ensis' (see no. 1644) and 'Massachusetensis' (see no. 1634). The best-known Newport poet of the day was John Maylem, and this verse seems very like his, but in late 1759 he was living in New York. See Lawrence C. Wroth, 'John Maylem: Poet and Warrior,' Col. Soc. of Mass., *Pubs.*, XXXII (1932–37), 87–120, esp. p. 105. Cf. no. 1764, and no. 1827A.

1670. Nov. 26, 1759 *NYG* ⌗882, 2/2.
'To all those Youths, whose noble Hearts.'
T: 'A New Song, for all True Hearts and Sound Bottoms, designed against the Cherokees.' ¶ No: 44 lines. ¶ A: '(By a Volunteer)'.
Note: Cf. no. 1663.

1671. Nov. 30, 1759 *VG*.
'Thy Merits, Wolfe, transcend all Human Praise.'
Note: A reprint of no. 1655.

1672. Nov., 1759 *New Am Mag* I, 689.
'Night forc'd a truce: The batt'ries ceas'd to roar.'
T: 'The Worm and the Monarch: A Fable.'

1673. Nov., 1759 *New Am Mag* I, 690–2.
'Along the main.'
T: 'An Ode. [On Britain's glory]. ¶ A: 'Martius Scriblerus.'

1674. Nov., 1759 *New Am Mag* I, 692.
'A Holy Friar, as Tis said.'
T: 'Epigram.' ¶ No: 8 lines. ¶ A: 'Martius Scriblerus.'

1675. Nov., 1759 *New Am Mag* I, 692.
'As Bob was a reeling one night, full of drink.'
T: 'Epigram.' ¶ No: 8 lines. ¶ A: 'Martius Scriblerus.'

1676. Nov., 1759 *New Am Mag* I, 692.
'Of late we have heard how that Hungary's dame.'
T: 'An Epigram on the Pope's conferring the title of Apostolic
Majesty on the Queen of Hungary.' ¶ No: 11 lines. ¶ A: 'Martius
Scriblerus.'

1677. Nov., 1759 *New Am Mag* I, 692–3.
'Hail! Empress of the star-bespangled sky!'
T: 'The Moonlight Night.' ¶ No: 61 lines. ¶ A: 'Martius Scribler-
us.'

1678. Dec. 1, 1759 *CG* ✳243, 1/1.
'Here Strangers and the Age to come.'
T: 'An Epitaph upon Roger Wolcott, Esq; Who was One of The
Honourable Council of the Colony of Connecticut, and a Judge of
Their Superior Court; who died October the 19th, 1759; in the
56th Year of his Age.' ¶ No: 38 lines.

1679. Dec. 3, 1759 *NYG* ✳883, 2/3.
'Blest Youth! whose Soul, with genuine Virtue warm.'
T: 'On General Wolfe.' ¶ No: 56 lines.

1680. Dec. 17, 1759 *BPB* ✳122; cont. Jan. 14, 1760, 3/2.
'Now view the maid, the love-inspiring maid.'
T: 'A few lines from *A Paraphrase on the Oeconomy of Human Life.*'
¶ No: 46 lines. ¶ A: James Bowdoin's paraphrase of Robert Dods-
ley.
Note: The best sketch of Bowdoin is Shipton, XI, 514–550.

1681. Dec. 20, 1759 *PJ* ℥889, 1/2.
'Nos tibi devoti Juvenes, Dynasta verende.'
T: 'Ad virum dignissimum Jacobum Hamilton, Pennsylvaniae Prae-
fectum, Juventutis Academicae Laurea donatae & donandae, Car-
men Salutatorium.' ¶ No: 42 lines. ¶ A: John Beveridge.
Note: 'A rev. Jac: Duche, A. B. pub: Oratore habitum; Authore
Joan: Beveridge, A. M. Ling. Profess:' These verses compli-
menting Gov. James Hamilton were declaimed by Rev. Jacob
Duché at a ceremony at the College of Philadelphia. Cf. no. 1682.
An account of the ceremony is given in Thomas H. Montgomery,
A History of the Univ. of Pa. (Philadelphia, 1900), pp. 345–6. A re-
vision is printed in Beveridge, *Epistolae Familiares* (Philadelphia,
1765), pp. 51–52.

1682. Dec. 20, 1759 *PJ* ℥889, 1/2.
'Once more we strike the long-neglected Lyre.'
T: 'Delivered by Mr. William Hamilton, attended by a Deputation
from the lower Schools.' ¶ No: 39 lines. ¶ A: [Provost William
Smith?]
Note: Cf. no. 1681.

1683. Dec. 29, 1759 *NHG* ℥169, 4/2.
'Brittain I mourn! Great Wolfe in Arms no more.'
Note: A reprint of no. 1660.

1684. Dec. 29 *NHG* ℥169, 4/2.
'Here rests from Toil, in narrow Bounds confin'd.'
Note: A reprint of no. 1669.

1685. Dec. 31, 1759 *NYG* ℥887, 3/Top.
'Whilst tuneful Bards prepare to sing.'
T: 'Occasioned by the late glorious Success of his Majesty's Arms
against the French.' ¶ No: 72 lines. ¶ A: 'P. S.'

1686. Dec., 1759 *New Am Mag* I, 751.
'When cold translation clings to copied thought.'
T: 'Prologue to a late Play, call'd Alyria; or, Spanish insult re-
pented.' ¶ No: 64 lines.
Note: Sent in by 'Z.'

1687. Dec., 1759 *New Am Mag* I, 752–3.
'That God! The sov'reign of the earth and sky.'
T: 'An Idea of God, and his Power: From Racine's Tragedy of
Esther. Imitated in English.' ¶ No: 20 lines. ¶ A: 'M. Scriblerus.'

1688. Dec., 1759 *New Am Mag* I, 753.
'Hail Britain! queen of arms and arts confest.'

T: 'From an English Oration, that was intended to have been pro-
nounc'd at the late Commencement of New-Jersey College: The
author, after an historical account of the British Worthies, those
especially famous in the polite arts, introduces the following
Panegyric.' ¶ No: 34 lines.

1689. Dec., 1759 *New Am Mag* I, 753.
'O Happiness where's thy resort?'
T: 'On Happiness.' ¶ No: 14 lines.

1690. 1759 *Annual Register* II, 451–2.
'Britons, the work of war is done.'
T: 'An Ode to Miss L—. On the death of General Wolfe.' ¶ No: 30
lines.
Note: Reprinted, nos. 1729A, 1730, 1743.

1691. 1759 *Annual Register* II, 452.
'Here rests from toil, in narrow bounds confin'd.'
Note: A reprint of no. 1684.

1692. 1759 *Annual Register* I, 456–7.
'Thou bed! in which I first began.'
Note: A reprint of no. 1561.

1693. Supp., 1759 *Universal Mag* XXV, 375–6.
'It happen'd once a cit mouse.'
T: 'The City Mouse and Country Mouse: A Fable.' ¶ No: 100 lines.
¶ A: 'Row. Rugeley.'
Note: Dated 'St. Ives.' An altered version appeared in Rugeley's
Misc. Poems (Cambridge, 1763), pp. 1–9.

1760

1694. Jan. 3, 1760 *MG*.
'Here rests from Toil, in narrow Bounds confin'd.'
Note: A reprint of no. 1669.

1695. Jan. 3, 1760 *MG*, 1/1.
'Shall echoing Joys thro' all the Land rebound.'
T: 'Verses. Occasioned by the Success of the British Arms in the
Year 1759.' ¶ No: 210 lines. ¶ A: [James Sterling?]
Note: Uses the translatio studii theme. Praises Addison and Pope.
Style, content, and place of publication suggest Sterling's author-
ship. Reprinted, Silverman, pp. 339–344.

1696. Jan. 7, 1760 *BEP* ℣1271, 4/1.
'Here rests from Toil, in narrow Bounds confin'd.'
A: '[By Valentine Nevil, Esq; Purser of his Majesty's Ship *Oxford*.]'
Note: A reprint of no. 1669.

1697. Jan. 7, 1760 *BPB* ⚹125, 2/1.
'To wake the Soul by Tender Strokes of Art.'
T: 'Prologue to Cato, intended to be spoke in the Character of an
   Officer of the Army.' ¶ No: 42 lines.
Note: Reprinted, nos. 1705 (where the background is given), 1735.

1698. Jan. 10, 1760 *BNL* ⚹2054, *Postscript.*
'L[oui]s ce grand Faiseur d'Impots.'
T: [Epigram.] ¶ No: 9 lines.
Note: The editor asks for a translation. See nos. 1701, 1702, and
   1704.

1699. Jan. 10, 1760 *BNL* ⚹2054, *Postscript.*
'Repond moi, cher Echo, c'est Louis qui te parle ?'
T: 'Dialogue entre Louis Quinze et l'Echo.' ¶ No: 18 lines. ¶ A:
'Par un des 243 officiers, prisoniers à la Battaille de Tonhausen le
   1me d'Aout.'
Note: For translations, see nos. 1700, 1703.

1700. Jan. 17, 1760 *BNL* ⚹2055, 1/1.
'Dear Echo, answer me, 'Tis Louis who speaks.'
T: 'Translation of the dialogue between Louis XV. and Echo' ...
Note: See no. 1699.

1701. Jan. 17, 1760 *BNL* ⚹2055, 1/1.
'L[oui]s, who grinds both great and small.'
T: [A translation of the Epigram.] ¶ No: 12 lines.
Note: See no. 1698.

1702. Jan. 17, 1760 *BNL* ⚹2055, 1/1.
'Opprest with Taxes L[oui]s' vassals groan.'
T: 'Translation of the French epigram printed in the Postscript to
   the Boston News-Letter, Jan. 10.' ¶ No: 14 lines.
Note: See no. 1698.

1703. Jan. 17, 1760 *BNL* ⚹2055, 1/2.
'Dear Echo reply, 'Tis I Louis that speak.'
T: [Translation of the 'Dialogue'] ¶ No: 18 lines.
Note: See no. 1699. Reprinted, no. 1729.

1704. Jan. 17, 1760 *BNL* ⚹2055, 1/2.
'Lewis, whose heart is case'd with stone.'
T: [A translation of the epigram.] ¶ No: 12 lines.
Note: See no. 1698.

1705. Jan. 18, 1760 *NHG* ⚹172.
'To wake the Soul by Tender Strokes of Art.'
Note: 'From the Boston Post Boy, Jan. 7. The Gentlemen who had

proposed to amuse themselves, and Friends, by the Representa-
tion of a Play, wish the wise Men of Boston to understand that
the Piece they had made Choice of for that Purpose was Mr.
Addison's Cato, and that they are very sorry they should have
been suspected to be Promoters of Vice, Impiety, Immorality, &c.
And as it was intended to have been introduced by the Original
Prologue, a little alter'd, to adapt it to the Times, I send you a
copy thereof to insert in your next Paper.' A reprint of no. 1697.

1706. Jan. 21, 1760 *BG* #251, 2/2.
   'In the Name of God, I Thomas Oakam.'
   T: 'The Last Will and Testament of a British Tar.' ¶ A: 'Thomas
    Oakam.'

1707. Jan. 21, 1760 *BG* #251, 2/3.
   'When James, assuming Right from God.'
   T: 'Revolution Ode ... occasioned by the Abdication of K. James II^d
    and the Acceptation of the Prince of Orange (K. Wm. III^d) to the
    British Throne.' ¶ No: 48 lines + 4 line refrain.

1708. Jan. 21, 1760 *BPB* #127.
   'Whilst raptur'd Bards from ev'ry Corner spring.'
   T: 'Written on the Death of General Wolfe.' ¶ No: 64 lines. ¶ A:
    'Juvenilis Cantabrigiensis.'

1709. Jan. 24, 1760 *BNL* #2056, 3/2.
   'All Hail, O Hind! Heav'n safe Thy Charge convey.'
   T: 'The following Lines were sent to the Purser of the Hind Man of
    War, upon his carrying Home a fine young Lady of this Town,
    whom he had just married.' ¶ No: 14 lines.
   Note: Reprinted, no. 1710.

1710. Jan. 28, 1760 *BEP* #1274, 3/2.
   'All Hail, O Hind! Heav'n safe Thy Charge convey.'
   Note: A reprint of no. 1709.

1711. Jan. 28, 1760 *BG* #252, 3/3.
   'In Poetry S—h takes delight.'
   T: [Attack on poet 'S—h'.] ¶ No: 8 lines.

1712. Jan., 1760 *New Am Mag* II, 29.
   'The ladies claim right.'
   T: [An answer to some ladies who want to be free-masons.] ¶ No:
    18 lines. ¶ A: 'Esop Coon.'
   Note: Dated 'New York, Jan. 15, 1760.' Cf. no. 1727.

1713. Jan., 1760 *Scots Mag* XXII, 32.
'Sprung from an ancient, honour'd race.'
T: 'Ode addressed to the late Gen. Wolfe. Written after the reduction of Louisburg.' ¶ No: 30 lines.

1714. Jan., 1760 *Scots Mag* XXII, 33.
'While to brave Wolfe such clouds of incense rise.'
T: 'A Call to the Poets. On the taking of Quebec.' ¶ No: 28 lines. ¶ A: 'T. D.'

1715. Feb. 1, 1760 *NHG* #174.
'Underneath, a Hero lies.'
T: 'Epitaph on General Wolfe.' ¶ No: 6 lines.

1716. Feb. 4, 1760 *NYG* #892, 3/top.
'A Princely huntsman once did live.'
T: 'The Chase. A Ballad.' ¶ No: 56 lines. ¶ A: 'P. L. C.'
Note: 'To the Tune of Chevy Chase.'

1717. Feb. 11, 1760 *NYG* #893, 3/1.
'Well, now Friend Z, you see what Caution.'
T: 'Wrote on reading a Paragraph, or Section, in Mr. Weyman's New-York Gazette, of the 21st of January last,--to the following Purpose, Mr. Z, if he pleases, may call for the Piece he sent us last Week, &c we will return half the Money he sent; his Subject being unfit, &c.' ¶ No: 40 lines. ¶ A: 'Risarius.'

1718. Feb. 15, 1760 *NHG* #176.
'Must Babel's Lofty Towers submit to Fate?'
T: 'On Fate.' ¶ No: 12 lines.

1719. Feb. 16, 1760 *SCG* #1331, 3/1.
'Disease malignant fills the Air.'
T: 'Virginibus pueresque canto.' ¶ No: 17 lines.
Note: On smallpox innoculation.

1720. Feb. 18, 1760 *BPB* #131.
'To God our Saviour and our King.'
T: 'Maschil, or, A Song of Praise for the Sons of New-England.' ¶ No: 28 lines.

1721. Feb. 21, 1760 *BNL* #2060.
''Tis now the midnight Hour, when all lies hush'd.'
T: 'on the Anniversary Night of the Death of a Friend.' ¶ No: 49 lines.
Note: Dated 'Boston, Feb. 16, 1760.'

1722. Feb. 22, 1760 *NHG* #177.
'From Pole to Pole, while ecchoing Fame resounds.'
T: 'On General Wolfe.' ¶ No: 43 lines. ¶ A: 'By a young Lady.'

1723. Feb. 25, 1760 *NYG* #895, 4/1.
'Whilst other Muses tune the sounding lyre.'
T: 'An Elegy, Inscribed to the Memory of Brigadier General Prideaux; Killed before Niagara, July 20, 1759.' ¶ No: 58 lines.
Note: Reprinted, no. 1742.

1724. Feb. 29, 1760 *NHG* #178.
'You ask, if the Thing to my Choice were submitted.'
T: 'The Choice of a Husband. In a Letter to a Friend.' ¶ No: 44 lines. ¶ A: 'Caroline.'
Note: Note on Mar. 7: 'The Piece sent Yesterday, sign'd Caroline, to be inserted in this Paper, must be deferr'd for further Consideration.' A reprint, enlarged, of no. 1624.

1725. Feb., 1760 *London Mag* XXIX, 101.
'Bright source of bliss! whose cheering rays inspire.'
T: 'To Contentment.' ¶ No: 52 lines. ¶ A: 'R. R.' [i.e., Rowland Rugeley].
Note: Dated 'St. Ives.' Reprinted in Rugeley's *Misc. Poems* (Cambridge, 1763), pp. 10–12.

1725A. Feb., 1760 *Imperial Mag* I, 102–3.
'First, in these fields, I sport in rural strains.'
T: 'Sacharissa. A Pastoral.' ¶ No: 127 lines. ¶ A: [Evidently a 'Carolina' poet.]

Note: An interesting and pretty good poem. Ll. 2–4: 'And sound the Doric reed on Indian plains;/May Carolina now with Greece compare,/ as fam'd in Song, as fertile, and as fair.' The poet sings 'fair Sacharissa's praise,' but makes love to 'Africk's swarthy dames.'

1726. Feb., 1760 *New Am Mag* II, 68–9.
'The solitary bird of night.'
T: 'Ode to Wisdom.' ¶ No: 90 lines. ¶ A: 'By a Female genius.' [Elizabeth Carter.]
Note: For Carter (1717–1806), see *CBEL*, II, 842. Printed in Dodsley, III, 209.

1727. Feb., 1760 *New Am Mag* II, 69.
'Since you well know.'
T: 'Lines in answer to those of Esop Coon.' ¶ No: 18 lines. ¶ A: 'Clorinda Cora.'
Note: Dated 'New York, Feb. 12, 1760.' Cf. no. 1712.

1728. Feb., 1760 *New Am Mag* II, 69–70.
'The remedy, *Dick*.'
T: 'The Little Boy's Companion through Life.' ¶ No: 80 lines.

1729. Mar. 1, 1760 *SCG* #1333, 1/2.
'Dear Echo reply, 'Tis I Louis that speak ?'
Note: A reprint of no. 1703.

1729A. Mar. 1, 1760 *NM* #91, 2/2.
'Britons, the work of war is done!'
Note: A reprint of 1690.

1730. Mar. 3, 1760 *BG* #257, 1/2.
'Britons, the work of war is done!'
Note: A reprint of no. 1690.

1731. Mar. 3, 1760 *WNYG* #56, 3/3.
'Ye Maids of Honour, mind your ways.'
T: 'The Fall.' ¶ No: 36 lines.

1732. Mar. 6, 1760 *MG*.
'Lo! To new Worlds th' advent'rous Muse conveys.'
T: 'Prologue, spoken by Mr. Douglass.' ¶ No: 38 lines. ¶ A:
'Written by a Gentleman in This Province, whose poetical Works
have render'd him justly Admir'd by all Encouragers of the Liber-
al Arts.' [James Sterling ?]

Note: Good verse. Nationalistic. See also no. 1733. Jonas Green
prefaced these two poems (nos. 1732 and 1733) with an account
of the opening night's performance. Reprinted in George O. Seil-
hamer, *History of the American Theatre Before the Revolution*
(Philadelphia, 1888), 116. Reprinted in Silverman, pp. 345–346.

1733. Mar. 6, 1760 *MG*.
'Well!--since the dreadful bus'ness is all over--'
T: 'Epilogue, spoken by Mrs. Douglass.' ¶ No: 46 lines. ¶ A:
[James Sterling ?]
Note: See also no. 1732. Reprinted in Seilhamer (see no. 1732), pp.
116–117.

1734. Mar. 13, 1760 *PG* #1629.
'When gen'rous Amherst heard the Tube of Fame.'
T: 'Panegyrical Verses on The Death of General Wolfe.' ¶ No: 96
lines. ¶ A: [James Sterling].
Note: Dated 'Kent, in Maryland, November 18, 1759.' the prefatory
note indirectly identifies the author: 'Being a Production of this
Country, and containing a sufficient Share of that Energy of Ex-

pression, Dignity of Sentiment, and Glow of Spirit which charac-
terize all the Performances of the reverend and worthy author of
the Epitaph on Lord Howe [no. 1484] ... from whose Hand they
come.' Reprinted, nos. 1746, 1763.

1735. Mar. 27, 1760 *MG.*
'To wake the Soul by tender Strokes of Art.'
Note: A reprint of no. 1697.

1736. Mar., 1760 *Lon Mag* XXIX, 157–8.
'Farewell, thou earth.'
T: 'Written in imitation of **Dr.** Young's Ode, entitled, Ocean.' ¶
No: 114 lines.
Note: Dated 'Boston, New England, June 24, 1758.'

1737. Mar., 1760 *Lon Mag* XXIX, 158.
'I Boast existence long ere man.'
T: 'An Enigma.' ¶ No: 22 lines. ¶ A: 'R. R.' [Rowland Rugeley?]
Note: Cf. no. 1725, which is undoubtedly by Rugeley.

1738. Mar., 1760 *Lon Mag* XXIX, 158.
'Sing to the Lord, exalt his name.'
T: 'A Thanksgiving Hymn. To St. George's Tune, common Metre.'
¶ No: 32 lines.
Note: Refers to death of Wolfe and has American subject matter.
Reprinted, no. 1784.

1739. Mar., 1760 *New Am Mag* II, 105–6.
'Strike, O muse, the sounding lyre.'
T: 'A Panegyric Ode. On the late General Wolfe, on the taking of
Quebec.' ¶ No: 89 lines. ¶ A: [Nathaniel Evans.]
Note: Dated 'Philadelphia Jan. 10, 1760.' Reprinted (revised) in
Evans, *Poems on Several Occasions* (Phila., 1772), pp. 12–16.

1740. Mar., 1760 *New Am Mag* II, 106.
'From climes deform'd with frost severe.'
T: 'The Glooms of Ligonier, A Song.' ¶ No: 24 lines. ¶ A: 'By an
officer of The Pennsylvania Regiment, stationed at Ligonier,
(formerly Loyalhanning) in the winter 1759' [Joseph Shippen].
Note: Reprinted in *Penna. Mag. of Hist. and Biog.*, XXIV (1900),
120. Tyler, p. 469, also attributes the poem to Shippen, following
Griswold, p. 24.

1741. Mar., 1760 *New Am Mag* II, 107.
'Enough of raptur'd fancy's Trivial Lays.'
T: 'A Translation of Mr. Masters' Greek Ode on the Crucifixion.'
¶ No: 38 lines. ¶ A: Sent in by 'Z.'

1742. Mar., 1760 *New Am Mag* II, 108.
  'Whilst other muses Tune the sounding lyre.'
  Note: A reprint of no. 1723.

1743. Apr. 5, 1760 *CG* #261, 1/1.
  'Britons, the work of war is done!'
  Note: 'From the Gentleman's Magazine, for November 1759.' A
    reprint of no. 1690.

1744. Apr. 12, 1760 *SCG* #1339, 2/2.
  'Be still, nor anxious thoughts employ.'
  T: 'To a friend in great distress, for the loss of his — by the small-
    pox, and under daily apprehensions of losing his —' ¶ No: 20
    lines. ¶ A: 'Z. Z.'

1745. Apr. 14, 1760 *NYG* #901, 4/1.
  'Long had sad Albion mourn'd her coward Race.'
  T: 'On our many Glorious and Rapid Victories.' ¶ No: 48 lines. ¶
    A: 'Cynthio.'

1746. Apr. 14, 1760 *NYG* #901, 4/1–2.
  'When gen'rous Amherst heard the Tube of Fame.'
  Note: A reprint of no. 1734.

1747. Apr. 19, 1760 *SCG* #1340, 2/2.
  'Spoiler of Beauty! for this once forbear.'
  T: 'Address to the Small-Pox. Inscrib'd to Miss —' ¶ No: 16 lines.

1748. Apr. 21, 1760 *NYG* #902, 2/3.
  'By base Retreat how were Those Honours stain'd.'
  A: 'T.'
  Note: A reprint of no. 1666.

1749. Apr. 26, 1760 *SCG* #1341, 3/3.
  'Mount, mount, aspiring Soul.'
  T: 'The Transport. An irregular Ode.' ¶ No: 31 lines. ¶ A: 'Z. Z.'

1750. Apr. 28, 1760 *NYG* #903, 2/1–2.
  'Aloft in air, the bright Astrea sat.'
  Note: A reprint of no. 1667.

1751. Apr. 28, 1760 *NYG* #903, 2/2.
  'On Yonder plain what awful form appears.'
  Note: A reprint of no. 1655.

1752. Apr., 1760 *Gent Mag* XXX, 195.
  'Amidst these loud acclaims which rend the sky.'
  T: 'On the Death of General Wolfe.' ¶ No: 40 lines.
  Note: Ugh.

1753. Apr., 1760 *Lon Mag* XXIX, 211.
'Cloe, her naked breast display'd.'
T: 'The Fall of Cupid. Occasioned by a gentleman's beating a China image of Cupid from a chimney piece, in bowing to a young lady.' ¶ No: 18 lines. ¶ A: 'R. R.' [Rowland Rugeley?]

1754. Apr., 1760 *Scots Mag* XXII, 203.
'Bless'd Liberty! how absolute thy pow'r.'
T: 'Occasioned by the death of Gen. Wolfe.' ¶ A: 'F. D.'
Note: Dated 'Aberdeen, Feb. 13, 1760.'

1755. May 2, 1760 *NHG* ※187, 3/3.
'When Cato view'd the generous Marcus dead.'
T: 'On the Death of General Wolfe.' ¶ No: 20 lines. ¶ A: 'Nov. Anglicus.'
Note: 'From The Conn. Gazette' (not extant). Cf. 1861.

1756. May 3, 1760 *SCG* ※1342, 1/1–2.
'Long had Despair approach'd Britannia's Shore.'
T: 'On the Reduction of Guadaloupe.' ¶ No: 169 lines. ¶ A: 'By the Rev. Mr. [Michael] Smith of Cape-Fear.'
Note: On Smith (1698-post 1760), see Weis, *Va.*, p. 90; and Lawrence Lee, *The Lower Cape Fear in Colonial Days* (Chapel Hill, 1965), p. 211.

1757. May 9, 1760 *NHG*.
'The Spring returns, Nature in Bloom appears.'
T: 'On the Death of Mr. Daniel Treadwell, of this Town, who was Professor of the Mathematicks at New York; a young Gentleman, whose many useful Accomplishments, render'd his Loss universally lamented.' ¶ No: 46 lines.
Note: Refers to Epps. Treadwell who graduated from Harvard in 1754; d. April 18, 1760--obituary in *NHG*, May 30th. A biographical sketch is in Shipton, XIII, 495–7.

1758. May 12, 1760 *NYG* ※905, 1/1.
'Once a Solicitor of high Renown.'
T: 'Reynard out-witted, or —, caught in his own Trap.' ¶ No: 30 lines.
Note: Dated 'N.Y., 25th Ap., 1760.'

1759. May 12, 1760 *NYG* ※905, 1/1.
'Pretty Insect, Summer's child.'
T: 'The Butterfly.' ¶ No: 16 lines.

1760. May 15, 1760 *MG*.
'Ye gen'rous Fair, ere finally we part.'

T: 'The following Epilogue, addressed to the Ladies, was spoken by Mrs. Douglass.' ¶ No: 40 lines.

Note: At closing of theater for season, on Mon., May 12th after the performance of the *Gamester* and *Toy-Shop*.

1761. May 17, 1760 *SCG* #1344, 2/3.
'Hail! happy days! whose glad returning rays.'
T: 'On Miss Al—n's recovery from the Small-Pox.' ¶ No: 38 lines.

1762. May 17, 1760 *SCG* #1344, 2/3.
'Thais condemns the gen'rous Soul.'
T: 'Epigram.' ¶ No: 8 lines. ¶ A: 'Z. Z.'

1763. May 26, 1760 *BG* #269, 1/1–2.
'When gen'rous Amherst heard the Tube of Fame.'
Note: A reprint of no. 1734.

1764. June 2, 1760 *WNYG* #69, 3/2.
'When noble Deeds, and friendly Actions done.'
T: 'W. Hawxhurst's Character of Mr. James Mills.' ¶ No: 42 lines. ¶ A: 'Done into Verse by Mr. John Maylem.'
Note: Cf. 1669A. This poem, not found by Wroth, supplements the information given in his study of Maylem (see no. 1669A), esp. pp. 105–7.

1765. June 6, 1760 *NYG* #908, 3/1.
'Again the blossom'd hedge is seen.'
T: 'Spring.' ¶ A: 'J. Copywell.'

1766. June 14, 1760 *SCG* #1349, 4/3.
'Accept, my Dear.'
T: 'Verses to a Lady.' ¶ No: 36 lines. ¶ A: 'W. B.'
Note: '[omitted in our last]'

1767. June, 1760 *Lon Mag* XXIX, 318.
'The snows are gone, and nature spreads.'
T: 'Translation of the 7th Ode of the 4th Book of Horace. Inscribed to Mr. William Draper.' ¶ No: 34 lines. ¶ A: 'Row. Rugeley.'
Note: Dated 'St. Ives.' An altered version is in Rugeley's *Misc. Poems* (Cambridge, 1763), pp. 91–92.

1768. July 4, 1760 *NHG* #196.
'May all the Pow'rs of Harmony combine.'
T: 'The following Lines would have been inserted before, had Room permitted; however, if the Portrature be genuine, (as no doubt it is) the inserting them now will be as agreeable as if the Honey Moon was not expired.' ¶ No: 42 lines.
Note: An epithalamium on a local doctor's marriage.

1769. July 12, 1760 *CG* #275, 3/2.
'Lorenzo, warm in Youth; Thy Cares remove.'
T: 'The following Lines from a Gentleman, who has favour'd us
with several compositions that do honour to his Taste and Judg-
ment, and to our Paper.' ¶ No: 11 lines.

1770. July 12, 1760 *SCG* #1353, 1/1–3.
'Aloft in air, the bright Astraea sat.'
Note: 'We are glad of an Opportunity, in the present Scarcity of
News, of obliging several of our Friends, who desired that the
following ingenious Poem (written immediately upon the first
Receipt of the News here of the Reduction of Quebec) which was
begun in this Gazette Numb. 1317, continued in 1318, and con-
cluded in 1322, might be reprinted undivided.' A reprint of no.
1667.

1771. July 12, 1760 *SCG* #1353, 1/3.
'Blest thought! from whence proceeds this joy.'
T: 'Happiness. A Thought.' ¶ No: 45 lines.

1772. July 14, 1760 *NYM* #413, 2/2.
'Thine Eyes, dear Girl, are clos'd in Night.'
T: 'On the much lamented Death of Miss Rickets.' ¶ No: 28 lines.
Note: Follows her obituary notice: Polly Rickets, daughter of Col.
William Rickets of Elizabeth-Town. For a simultaneous printing,
see no. 1773. Reprinted in *New Jersey Archives*, XX, 456.

1773. July 14, 1760 *WNYG* #75, 3/2.
'Thine Eyes, dear Girl, are clos'd in Night.'
Note: See no. 1772.

1774. Aug. 7, 1760 *PG* #1650, 1/1.
'Why will soft Sorrow thus o'erwhelm my Soul?'
T: 'An Elegy, to the Memory of Mr. Theophilus Grew, late Pro-
fessor of Mathematicks in the Philadelphia College.' ¶ No: 84
lines. ¶ A: [Nathaniel Evans.]
Note: Reprinted in Nathaniel Evans, *Poems* (Philadelphia, 1772)
pp. 16–19.

1775. Aug. 9, 1760 *SCG* #1357.
'Goddess of numbers, and of thought supreme!'
T: 'On the Death of Capt. Manly Williams, who commanded a
Company of Light-infantry of His Majesty's First or Royal Regi-
ment of Foot, and was killed by the Cherokee Indians, near Et-
chowee, on the 27th of June, 1760. A Pindaric Ode.' ¶ No: 35
lines. ¶ A: 'Anglicanus.'

1776. Aug. 14, 1760 *NYG* #919, 3/1.
'The Soldier longs for Arms (the Ensigns of his Trade).'
T: '... English of the four Latin Hepameters, lately inserted in Wey-
man's Paper ...' ¶ No: 6 lines.

1777. Sept. 4, 1760 *NYG* #922, 4/1.
'Dear Tom, this Brown Jug, that now foams with wild ale.'
T: 'Toby reduc'd; or The Brown Jug.' ¶ No: 18 lines. ¶ A: [Joseph
Green?]
Note: Opposite the poem is written 'Mr. Carmalt' in photostatic
edition at New York Hist. Soc. Cf. broadside at the Pa. Hist.
Soc., which begins 'Dear Sir this Brown Jug that now foams with
raild Ale/Was once Toby Filpot a thirsty Old Soul.' This broad-
side was 'Sold by Jas. Lumsden Engraver Glasgow.' Mather
Byles also wrote a similar poem, entitled 'Bug Barret transformed
into a Brandy Bottle,' with the first line 'Assist, Ye Gods, since
ye alone can tell,' which is copied in Benjamin Church's 'Common-
place Book' (Harvard MS Am 1369). It is possible, though un-
likely, that the above poem may be a reply by Green to Byles.

1778. Sept. 5, 1760 *NHG* #205.
'Had not New England been his Place of Birth.'
T: 'A sudden Thought concerning the late Capt. John Rous upon
Sight of some Verses on Land and Sea Officers.' ¶ No: 4 lines.
Note: From the *Royal Mag.* for March, 1760.

1779. Sept. 19, 1760 *NHG* #207, 3/3.
'Her Temper charming, affable and kind.'
T: 'The following short, but true character of the late Mrs. M[ar]-
g[are]t W[a]rn[e]r, was design'd in Season for the Press, but by
Accident was mislaid.' ¶ No: 10 lines.
Note: 'Last Tuesday died here, greatly lamented, Mrs. Margaret
Warner of this Town'--*NHG*, Sept. 5, 1760 #205.

1780. Sept. 22, 1760 *BG* #286, 2/1.
'When martial Heroes greatly buy Applause.'
T: 'On the Death of Judge Sewall.' ¶ No: 44 lines.
Note: For Stephen Sewall (1702–1760), a nephew of Samuel Sewall
and a Harvard graduate of 1721; see the long obituary in *BG*,
Sept. 22, 1760, 1/1–2; and Shipton, VI, 561–7. Reprinted, see no.
1782.

1781. Sept., 1760 *Lon Mag* XXIX, 487.
'A Vehicle by love employ'd.'
T: 'A Rebus.' ¶ No: 14 lines. ¶ A: 'Row. Rugeley.'
Note: Dated 'St. Ives.'

1782. Oct. 3, 1760 *NHG* #209.
'When martial Heroes greatly buy Applause.'
Note: A reprint of no. 1780.

1783. Oct. 4, 1760 *SCG* #1366, 2/2.
'This lofty theme! This pure etherial flame!'
T: 'Ode on Friendship.' ¶ No: 40 lines. ¶ A: 'Britanicas.'
Note: Dated 'Sept. 3, 1760.'

1784. Oct. 9, 1760 *NYG* #927, 3/2.
'Sing to the Lord, exalt his Name.'
Note: A reprint of no. 1738.

1785. Oct. 23, 1760 *MG*.
'Of polish'd Manners, and of gen'rous Mind.'
T: 'On The Death of The Hon. Benjamin Tasker, junr. Esq.' ¶ No:
10 lines. ¶ A: 'T. J.' [Thomas Jennings?]
Note: Mediocre verse, 'On Friday Evening last [Oct. 17], died here,
in the 40th Year of his Age, The Honourable Benjamin Tasker,
junior, Esq; Secretary of this Province.' Thomas Jennings, law-
yer, was later the Poet Laureate of the Annapolis Hominy Club.

1786. Oct., 1760 *Gent Mag* XXX, 480–1.
'An humble muse, unus'd to rude alarms.'
T: 'On the Taking of Montreal by Gen. Amherst.' ¶ No: 80 lines. ¶
A: ['J. W.']
Note: Reprinted, nos. 1790, 1813 (where author and source are
given).

1787. Nov. 1, 1760 *CG* #291, 4/1.
'New-England, raise thy grateful Voice.'
T: 'A Thanksgiving Hymn, for New-England.' ¶ No: 44 lines.
Note: Cf. no. 1738. Reprinted, no. 1789.

1788. Nov. 17, 1760 *BPB* #170, 1/1–2.
'Muse, resume the sounding Lyre.'
T: 'Ode. On the Total Reduction of Canada.' ¶ No: 149 lines.

1789. Nov. 21, 1760 *NHG* #216.
'New England, raise Thy grateful Voice.'
Note: A reprint of no. 1787.

1790. Nov., 1760 *Scots Mag* XXII, 580.
'An humble muse, unus'd to rude alarms.'
Note: A reprint of no. 1786.

1791. Dec. 4, 1760 *NYG* ✳935, 1/2.
    'More sad than when the much-lov'd Ovid's Tongue.'
    T: 'To the Memory of Capt. John Seabury, (late of New-London, in
        Connecticut), Commander of a Troop of Rangers ... who died ...
        on the 24th of October, 1760.' ¶ No: 31 lines. ¶ A: 'N. A.'
    Note: Dated 'Charles-Town, (in South Carolina) Nov. 1.'

1792. Dec. 10, 1760 *MG*.
    'Britannia, from her rock listening to the Bards (who recite the
        praises of the Heroes) on a signal from Neptune of the Queen's
        Approach, descends to receive and gratulate her Arrival.'
    No: 24 lines.
    Note: Ode welcoming Queen Charlotte.

1793. Dec. 16, 1760 *SCG* ✳1376, 2/2.
    'To fields of light where angels sing.'
    T: 'The Happy Youth.' ¶ No: 52 lines. ¶ A: 'N. E.'

1794. Dec. 24, 1760 *NYG* ✳938.
    'From younder beauteous Realms of Light.'
    T: 'The Nativity Song.' ¶ No: 48 lines.

1795. Dec. 25, 1760 *BNL* ✳2947, *Postscript*, 2/2.
    ''We tho't father *Abraham* had a large Dose.'
    T: 'To Mr. Ames, on his rivalling the foreign *Vintages* by the
        Gardens of America.' ¶ No: 48 lines. ¶ A: ['H—k.']
    Note: Dated 'From Vintner's-Hall Dec. 22, 1760.' Cf. no. 1840 for
        Ames' reply, and no. 1850 for this author's further attack. In no.
        1854, Ames seems to give his opponent's initials as 'H—k.'

1761

1796. Jan. 1, 1761 *BNL* ✳2918, 3/2.
    'What time the Julian arms assail'd the coast.'
    T: 'On the Death of His late Majesty, and The Accession of King
        George III.' ¶ No: 67 lines. ¶ A: 'A* C**' 'By a Gentleman here
        [Boston].'
    Note: Six prefatory lines from Tasso.

1797. Jan. 1, 1761 *BNL* ✳2918, 4/3.
    'And is This all, one poor unfinish'd Lay.'
    T: 'An Elegy On the Death of His late Majesty, of blessed Memory.
        ¶ No: 50 lines.
    Note: Dated 'Boston.' Reprinted, no. 1804.

1798. Jan. 1, 1761 *BNL* ☼2918, 4/3.
'Hear, all ye People! hear.'
T: 'On the Death of his late Majesty King George the Second, who
  died October 25th, 1760.' ¶ No: 14 lines. ¶ A: Lad '11 years old.'
Note: For author's age, see *BNL*, Jan. 8, 1/1.

1799. Jan. 1, 1761 *PG, Sup.*
'To write of Scenes of Blood, or War's alarms.'
T: 'The New-Year Verses, Of the Printers Lads, who carry about
  the Pennsylvania Gazette to the Customers.'
Note: Broadside in Harvard file of *PG*.

1800. Jan. 5, 1761 *BG* ☼301, 1/3.
'Transfix'd by Death, with solemn Rites interr'd.'
T: 'On the much lamented Thomas Ward, Esquire [d. Dec. 23,
  1760] late Secretary of This [i.e., R. I.] Colony. An Accrostic.' ¶
  No: 10 lines.

1801. Jan. 5, 1761 *BPB* ☼177.
'My mournful Muse recluse from Human View.'
T: 'An Elegy on the Death of our late Sovereign George the Second,
  of blessed Memory.' ¶ No: 28 lines, + 4 line preface, + 2 Latin
  lines. ¶ A: 'H. R.' [Hebar?]
Note: In the preface, the poet says of himself 'Old *Hebar* will exert
  his Rustic Art.' Reprinted, no. 1805.

1802. Jan. 6, 1761 *SCG* ☼1379, 3/1.
'The setting Year in shades of Night.'
T: 'Ode Written on New-Year's Day.' ¶ No: 24 lines.
Note: Reprinted, no. 1848A.

1803. Jan. 6, 1761 *SCG* ☼1379, 3/1.
'With opening wings the infant year.'
T: 'On the New Year.' ¶ No: 32 lines.

1804. Jan. 9, 1761 *NHG* ☼223.
'And is this all, one poor unfinish'd Lay.'
Note: A reprint of no. 1797.

1805. Jan. 23, 1761 *NHG* ☼225.
'My mournful Muse recluse from Human View.'
Note: A reprint of no. 1801.

1806. Jan. 26, 1761 *BPB* ☼180, 3/2.
'As Wolfe all glorious lately stood.'
T: 'An Ode Compos'd and Sung by an Officer of the Montreal-Club,
  At Boston.' ¶ No: 40 lines.

1807. Jan. 26, 1761 *NYM* #442, 1/1–2.
'Why heaves the bosom with continual Sighs ?'
T: 'The following Piece, on the Death of his late Majesty King George the Second.' ¶ No: 172 lines. ¶ A: 'An ingenious young Gentleman in this Province' [Benjamin Young Prime.]
Note: Reprinted in Prime's *Patriot Muse* (London, 1764), pp. 72–77. For Prime, see no. 1274.

1808. Jan. 26, 1761 *WNYG* #105, 1/1.
'A Grand Court conven'd on important occasion.'
T: 'On the Addresses of Addresses lately presented to his Ex—y Bernardus Francisco, and, published in the B–ston Gazette of December 29, 1760; in one of which addresses, speaking of the Blessings derived to Great-Britain, from the Loyalty of the Colonies in general, there are these Words, "and from the Efforts of the Province in particular; which, for more than a Century past, has been waiding [!] in Blood, and laden with the Expence of repelling the common Enemy; without which efforts, Great-Britain before this Day might have had no Colonies to defend."' ¶ No: 57 lines.
Note: A satirical attack on the egotism of Boston & Mass, with a parody of Gov. Francis Bernard's speech.

1809. Jan. 29, 1761 *PG* #1675.
'See! pale *Britannia* clad in sable Woe.'
T: 'On the Death of His late Majesty *King* GEORGE the Second.' ¶ No: 20 lines. ¶ A: 'Fidelia.'
Note: Editorial Note: 'Fidelia is desired to send for the *Money* which accompanied the above Lines, as we take no Gratuity for obliging the Public with such Performances.'

1810. Feb. 7, 1761 *CG* #305, 3/2.
'It was no vulgar Mind.'
T: [Epitaph on John Humphry of Simsbury, Conn. (d. Nov. 2, 1760).] ¶ No: 12 lines.

1811. Feb. 7, 1761 *SCG* #1384, 1/2.
'Sweetest of blessings, heavenly light!'
T: 'Ode on the Morning.' ¶ No: 32 lines. ¶ A: 'J.'

1812. Feb. 9, 1761 *BEP* #1328, 3/1.
'The Verse above Mysterious is.'
T: [Attack on lines that had appeared in 'Edes & Gill' [*BG*]: 'Ah Thea Bohea!/Quid placet insigni ut decem Codices Pacintono ?'] ¶ No: 24 lines.

1813. Feb. 12, 1761 *NYG* #945, 1/1–2.
'An humble Muse, unus'd to rude alarms.'
A: 'J. W.'
Note: 'From the London General Evening Post.' A reprint of no.
1786.

1814. Feb. 13, 1761 *NHG* #228.
'Your charming Thoughts in softest Words express'd.'
T: 'A Gentle Whisper, in Answer to the Ladies Objections to some
useful Arguments in your Paper, No. 226 [Jan. 30th].' ¶ No: 16
lines. ¶ A: 'Yeoman Youch.'
Note: With accompanying article.

1815. Feb. 14, 1761 *CG* #306, 4/1.
'Go, Thrice lamented! quit this mortal Stage.'
T: 'To the Memory of Mr. David Phelps, late of Simsbury.' ¶ No:
26 lines.

1816. Feb. 16, 1761 *BEP* #1329, 3/2.
'Here lies our Captain and Major.'
Note: A reprint of no. 401 A.

1817. Feb. 20, 1761 *NHG* #229.
'From Pole to Pole.'
T: 'Portsmouth. The Following Poem was wrote before the News of
King's Death.' ¶ No: 56 lines.
Note: Poem in praise of George II.

1818. Feb. 21, 1761 *CG* #307, 1/1–2.
'Another gone! how thick the arrows fly!'
T: 'Elegaic Thoughts, occasioned by the sudden Death of Joseph
Buckingham, Esq; Soon after the Death of John Humphry, Esq;
who, both were Justices of the Peace for the County of Hartford;
and Judges of The County Court; and often Members of the
General Assembly, of the Colony of Connecticut; and died in the
Month of November 1760.' ¶ No: 97 lines. ¶ A: 'W. W.'

1819. Feb. 23, 1761 *WNYG* #109, 1/2–3.
'An Ass once left his master's home.'
T: 'The Countryman and his Ass.' ¶ No: 32 lines.

1820. Apr. 2, 1761 *NYG* #952, 1/2–3.
'Struck with religious awe, and solemn dread.'
T: 'A Soliloquy written in a Church-yard.'
Note: Crum S1259 attributes this to 'the Revd—Moore of Corn-
wall.'

1821. Apr. 2, 1761 *NYG* #952, 1/2–3.
 ''Twas He, who once descending from the Height.'
 T: 'The following Translation of a Latin Poem of Doctor Watts, in
   his Horae Lyricae, On the divine Love and Sufferings of our
   Saviour Jesus Christ for Mankind, By the Rev. Mr. Davies, late
   President of the College in New-Jersey, was intended for our
   Paper in Easter Week, but omitted by Accident.' ¶ No: 64 lines.
   ¶ A: Samuel Davies.
 Note: Reprinted in Davis (see no. 1035), pp. 212–214.

1822. Apr. 4, 1761 *CG* #313, 4/2.
 'The dry, dull, drowsy Batchelor, surveys.'
 T: [On Batchelors.] ¶ No: 18 lines. ¶ A: 'A. Z.'
 Note: 'From the *Boston Gazette*.' Reprinted, nos. 1990, 2022.

1823. Apr. 13, 1761 *BEP* #1337, 1/3.
 'Mark my gay Friend, that solemn Toll.'
 T: 'occasioned by hearing the Sound of a Passing-Bell.' ¶ No: 57
   lines.

1824. Apr. 24, 1761 *NHG* #238.
 'While Nations die.'
 T: 'An Ode on Peace. Set to Music by *James Lyon*, A.B. and Sung
   at the *public Commencement* in Nassau Hall, September the 24th,
   1760.' ¶ No: 36 lines. ¶ A: Samuel Davies.
 Note: There is also a broadside of the poem in the Princeton Univ.
   Library. Reprinted in Davis (see no. 1035), pp. 210–211.

1825. Apr. 30, 1761 *NYG* #956, 1/2.
 'Painter, all thy pow'r exert.'
 T: 'Directions to a Painter.' ¶ No: 53 lines. ¶ A: 'a young Lady.'

1826. May 1, 1761 *NHG* #239.
 'Science! bright Beam of Light Divine!'
 T: 'Science. An Ode. For the Commencement September 24, 1760 ...
   Set to Music by James Lyon, A.B.' ¶ No: 20 lines. ¶ A: Samuel
   Davies.
 Note: Reprinted in Davis (see no. 1035), p. 215.

1827. May 4, 1761 *BPB* #194, 2/1.
 'A Ship of War, a Second Rate.'
 T: 'The Ship and the Wind. A Fable.' ¶ No: 46 lines.

1827A. May 19, 1761 *NM* #144, 3/2–3.
 'In ancient days, 'Twas God's most sacred will.'
 T: 'The Boston Sabbath.' ¶ No: 29 lines. ¶ A: [John Maylem.]

Note: Printed in *New England Quarterly*, VII, 325–326, by Carl Bridenbaugh. Printed by Wroth 'Maylem,' (see no. 1669A), p. 108, from a ms. copy. Reprinted in the *American Museum*, I (Feb. 1787), 186, where it is entitled 'The Connecticut Sabbath.'

1828. June 12, 1761 *NHG* #245.
    'Assist me, Muse divine.'
    T: 'An Ode on George III.'
    Note: Dated 'Portsmouth.'

1829. June 19, 1761 *NHG* #246.
    'If gen'rous Friendship and harmonious Love.'
    T: 'The Merits of Free-Masonry Display'd.' ¶ No: 17 lines.
    Note: Dated 'Portsmouth.' There is an ad for Feast of St. John the Baptist in paper of same date. Officers are: William Pearson, Master; Wiseman Clagett, Sec.; Hugh Hall Wentworth and Theodore Atkinson, Wardens; Samuel Levermore, Treasurer. Reprinted, no. 1830.

1830. June 29, 1761 *BEP* #1348, 3/1.
    'If gen'rous Friendship and harmonious Love.'
    Note: A reprint of no. 1829.

1830A. June, 1761 *Imperial Mag.* II, 325.
    'O wou'dst thou know what secret Charm.'
    T: 'Song.' ¶ No: 16 lines. ¶ A: 'Prometheus' [Robert Bolling].
    Note: A copy is in Bolling's ms. volume 'La Gazzetta di Parnasso' (see no. 1561) p. vii, where he notes 'This Song was Twice printed in The imperial Magazine & it was afterwards admitted into a Collection of Songs printed at Philadelphia.'

1830B. June, 1761 *Imperial Mag* II, 326.
    'And sure this is the age of gold.'
    T: 'The Satyr's Imprecation, in Tasso's Aminta, *imitated*.' ¶ No: 13 lines. ¶ A: [Robert Bolling?]
    Note: This follows a poem by Bolling (no. 1830A) who wrote numerous imitations of Tasso.

1831. July 10, 1761 *NHG* #249.
    'From Adam downward to this Evening Knell.'
    T: 'On the Death of King George II.' ¶ No: 16 lines.

1832. July 10, 1761 *NHG* #229.
    'Hail George the Third, of Predecessors, Great, Sublime.'
    T: 'On the Accession of King George III to the Throne of Great-Britain.' ¶ No: 20 lines.

1833. July 10, 1761 *NHG* #299.
'No more the woful Scenes of Death and Slaughter.'
T: 'A Prospect of the Millenium.' ¶ No: 34 lines.

1834. July, 1761 *Imperial Mag* II, 380.
'A Doctor sent to me his darling son.'
T: [Translation of Greek.] ¶ No: 10 lines. ¶ A: 'S. Henley.'
Note: This may be the Rev. Samuel Henley, who was currently teaching at William and Mary College.

1835. July, 1761 *Universal Mag* XXIX, 43.
'Pan sighs for Echo o'er the lawn.'
T: 'Adyllium VI. of Moschus: Capricious Love.' ¶ No: 14 lines.

1836. Aug., 1761 *Gent Mag* XXXI, 375.
'Learning and piety, with ev'ry grace.'
T: 'Written in the West Indies, on reading some Memoirs of the Life of Mr. Abernethy (Author of Discourses on the Being and Attributes of God) affixed to his Posthumous Sermons.' ¶ No: 18 lines.

1837. Sept. 4, 1761 *NHG* #257.
'Come, heav'nly pensive Contemplation, come.'
T: 'The following Verses were composed by a pious Clergyman in Virginia, who preaches to seven Congregations, the nearest of which meets at the Distance of five Miles from his House, as he was returning home in a very gloomy and rainy Night.' ¶ No: 73 lines. ¶ A: [A Virginia Clergyman; Samuel Davies?]
Note: Davies' poetry was frequently printed in the *NHG*.

1838. Sept. 11, 1761 *NHG* #258.
'Of my dear Flock one more is gone.'
T: 'A Clergyman's Reflections on the Death of one of his pious Parishioners.' ¶ No: 30 lines. ¶ A: [Samuel Davies?]
Note: See no. 1837.

1839. Sept. 14, 1761 *BPB* #213, 2/3.
'Quis Labor infandus! Quis tam Crudelis, et asper.'
T: 'Ad Deminum S. P.' ¶ No: 18 lines.

1839A. Sept., 1761 *Imperial Mag* II, 495–6.
'When time hangs heavy on my hands.'
T: 'A Satire.' ¶ No: 189 lines. ¶ A: ['Prometheus'; Robert Bolling.]
Note: Bolling has corrected two words in his copy of the *Imperial Mag.* at the Huntington Library and has scratched out the attribution ('Prometheus') at the end. The satire is about a girl in Providence, R. I., who abandoned her American fiancé for an Englishman.

1839B. Oct., 1761 *Imperial Mag* II, 552–3.
  'O Melancholy, pensive maid.'
  T: 'The Complaint.' ¶ No: 60 lines. ¶ A: [Robert Bolling.]
  Note: Bolling attributed this poem to himself in his own copy of the
    magazine, which is at the Huntington Library. There is also a
    version of the poem in his 'La Gazetto di Parnasso' (see no.
    1561), pp. 26–28. Reprinted (in a shorter version), no. 1960.

1840. Nov. 30, 1761 *BEP* #1370, 3/2.
  'Like Priests of *Baal* they crav'd the Muses Aid.'
  T: 'Urania descending from the forky Summet of Parnassus de-
    livered me a Rod, sent by the whole Choir of Muses, to Chastise
    the Insolence of the Vintners, whom they never lov'd, and with
    whom they are highly offended for a Piece of Rhyme directed to
    Me in the *Postscript* of the Boston Weekly News-Letter, Thurs-
    day 25th December 1760, on the Receipt I published in my last
    Year's Almanack, to make Currant Wine.' ¶ No: 27 lines. ¶ A:
    Nathaniel Ames.
  Note: 'From Ames's Almanack for 1762.' A reply to no. 1795. See
    also no. 1850. Reprinted in Briggs (see no. 1344), p. 324.

1841. Nov., 1761 *Lon Mag* XXX, 607.
  'When Venus erst in Cytherean bow'rs.'
  T: 'The First Bascum of Johannes Secundus Imitated.' ¶ A: J.
    Glasse.
  Note: Dated 'Kingston near Taunton.'

1842. Dec. 24, 1761 *NYG* #990, 3/1.
  'Begin the high celestial strain.'
  Note: Accompanies a local essay. A reprint of no. 536.

1843. Dec. 25, 1761 *NHG* #273.
  'What Sounds harmonious strike the Ears.'
  Note: A reprint of no. 385.

1844. Dec. 31, 1761 *NYG* #991, 2/3.
  'Old Time, alas! with stealing pace.'
  T: 'Winter.' ¶ No: 40 lines.

1845. Dec. 31, 1761 *NYG* #991, 2/3.
  'Revolving Years their steady course pursue.'
  T: 'Upon the first Day of the Year.' ¶ No: 20 lines.

1846. Dec. 31, 1761 *NYG* #991, 2/3–3/1.
  'Thy grateful sons, O queen of isles.'
  T: 'Ode for the New Year. To the Tune of *When Britain's first*, at
    heaven's command &c.' ¶ No: 40 lines.

1762

1847. Jan. 11, 1762 *NYM* ✷495, 1/2–3.
'To This new World; from fam'd Britannia's Shore.'
T: 'Prologue Spoken by Mr. Hallam.' ¶ No: 36 lines. ¶ A: [Dr. Adam Thomson.]
Note: 'The following Prologue and Epilogue were written by a Gentleman in this City, for the Opening of the Play-House on Cruger's Wharf, in the Year 1758; at the Desire of several Gentlemen they were Spoken last Monday, with some Additions and Alterations by the Author, in which dress they are now presented to the Public, 'Tis thought they have a considerable Share of Merit, and convey in an elegant Poetical Manner, a just Representation of the Nature and Tendency of Dramatic Entertainments.' Cf. no. 1848. A revision of no. 1184.

1848. Jan. 11, 1762 *NYM* ✷495, 1/3–2/1.
'Much has been said at this censorious Time.'
T: 'Epilogue Spoken by Mrs. Douglass.' ¶ No: 68 lines.
Note: Accompanies 1847. This is a revised and enlarged version of no. 1185.

1848A. Jan. 22, 1762 *NHG* ✷277, 2/3.
'The setting Year in Shades of Night.'
Note: A reprint of no. 1802.

1849. Jan., 1762 *Universal Mag* XXX, 43.
'In search of her son to the list'ning croud.'
T: 'Idyllium I. of Moschus.' ¶ No: 50 lines.

1850. Feb. 1, 1762 *BEP* ✷1379, 4/1–2.
'To tell a Tale I'm sure no Man can blame us.'
T: [Reply to Nathaniel Ames (see no. 1840).] ¶ No: 100 lines.
Note: Cf. *BNL Postscript*, Dec. 25, 1760; *BEP*, Nov. 30, 1761; Feb. 22, 1762. See no. 1795 for the start of this war on Ames.

1851. Feb. 4, 1762 *MG*.
'While loftier Bards in sweeter Numbers, raise.'
T: 'Verses, Occasion'd by the Marriage and Coronation of George III.' ¶ No: 72 lines. ¶ A: 'a young Bard.'
Note: *Translatio studii* theme, interesting poem.

1852. Feb. 11, 1762 *PG* ✷1729.
'Ye *Dryads* fair, whose Temples round.'
T: 'The following RURAL ODE, wrote by an ingenious young Gentleman of this place, at a very early Time of Life, we flatter ourselves will be agreeable to our Readers.' ¶ No: 84 lines. ¶ A: [Nathaniel Evans.]
Note: Reprinted in Evans, *Poems* (Philadelphia, 1772), 30–35.

1853. Feb. 12, 1762 *VG*.
'Three Pints of Wine, the Grave and Wise.'
T: 'The Rule of Drinking—from the Greek of Eubulus.' ¶ No: 12 lines. ¶ A: [Robert Bolling ?]
Note: This accompanies an essay entitled 'Hints for making Wine in America.' Bolling published a series of essays on viniculture in the *VG*.

1854. Feb. 22, 1762 *BEP* #1382, 3/3.
'H—k my Muse disdains.'
T: [Nathaniel Ames replies to H—k.] ¶ No: 89 lines. ¶ A: 'Nathaniel Ames.'
Note: Dated 'Dedham, Feb. 11, 1762. Cf. *BNL Postscript*, Dec. 25, 1760; *BEP*, Nov. 30, 1761, Feb. 1, 1762. See no. 1795.

1855. Feb., 1762 *Gent Mag* XXXII, 87.
'Eliza! harmonist divine!'
T: 'Verses occasioned by reading Miss Carter's Poems.' ¶ No: 16 lines. ¶ A: 'Z.'
Note: Elizabeth Carter's *Poems on several occasions* are advertised in the *Gent Mag* for Mar., 1762, p. 147. See *CBEL*, II, 842.

1856. Mar. 13, 1762 *SCG* #1442, 2/1.
'Hail! fair charmer wafted from Britannia's shore.'
T: 'To Miss J. W.' ¶ No: 20 lines. ¶ A: 'C.' 'Britannicus.'

1856A. Mar. 20, 1762 *Am. Chron.*, 3/3.
'Grant me, Gods, a little Seat.'
Note: A reprint of no. 711.

1857. Mar. 25, 1762 *PG* #1735.
'Thrice blest is he whose placid Birth.'
T: 'Ode to a Friend.' ¶ No: 36 lines. ¶ A: 'By the Author of the RURAL ODE ...' [Nathaniel Evans.]
Note: See no. 1852. Reprinted in Evans, *Poems* (Phila., 1772), pp. 35–37.

1858. Apr. 16, 1762 *NHG* #289.
'O Leuconoe! cease from anxious care.'
T: 'The 11th Ode of the 1st Book of Horace translated.' ¶ No: 14 lines. ¶ A: 'E. E.'
Note: Dated 'Portsmouth, April 1st, 1762.'

1859. Apr. 19, 1762 *BEP* #1389, 2/3.
'A Lottery, like a magic spell.'
T: 'A few Thoughts on Lotteries.' ¶ No: 32 lines.
Note: Reprinted, no. 1860.

1859A. Apr. 19, 1762 *Am. Chron.*, 2/3–3/1.
    'Within these peaceful Walls retir'd.'
    T: 'Britannia: An Ode. Occasioned by the Reduction of Martinico.'
    ¶ No: 42 lines. ¶ A: 'Composed by a young Gentleman of the Col-
    lege of New Jersey. [Benjamin Young Prime?] Set to Music by
    another Gentleman [James Lyon] of the same College, and pub-
    lickly performed in Nassau-Hall.'
    Note: S. Farley has an ed. note in *Am. Chron.* of April 12 saying that
    'The Ode entitled *Britannia;* will be inserted in our next.' Re-
    printed, no. 1864. Since Prime, a Princeton graduate, was con-
    tributing poetry to the *Am. Chron.* at this time (see no. 1865A),
    he is the probable author.

1860. Apr. 23, 1762 *NHG* ⚹290.
    'A Lottery, like a magic spell.'
    Note: A reprint of no. 1859.

1861. Apr. 26, 1762 *BPB* ⚹245, 2/3.
    'Musa canit tristis Mortem, Tum Vulnera Mortis.'
    T: 'Carmen Elegiacum. Thema Pax Bello potior--.' ¶ No: 38 lines.
    ¶ A: 'Nov-Anglus.'
    Note: Cf. no. 1756.

1862. Apr., 1762 *Gent Mag* XXXII, 186–7.
    'Ah me! what sorrows are we born to bear!'
    Note: A reprint of no. 1658.

1863. May 6, 1762 *PG* ⚹1741.
    'Welcome my *Corydon*, to these glad arms.'
    T: 'A Dialogue, occasioned by the Reduction of Martinico.' ¶ No:
    63 lines. ¶ A: 'X. Z.'
    Note: The 'first production' of a 'Youth.'

1864. May 7, 1762 *NHG* ⚹292.
    'Within these peaceful Walls retir'd.'
    Note: A reprint of no. 1859A.

1865. May 10, 1762 *BPB* ⚹247, 2/2.
    'Great are thy Works which thy worthy Name.'
    T: [On General Monckton.] ¶ No: 34 lines. ¶ A: 'Academicus.'
    Note: 'From a young Gentleman.'

1865A. May 10, 1762 *Am. Chron.*, 1/2–3.
    'Where Tyrants Rule with Arbitrary sway.'
    T: ['On the Liberty of the Press. To Mr. F— Printer, at New York;
    1762.] ¶ No: 69 lines. ¶ A: 'Phileleutherius' [Benjamin Young
    Prime].

Note: Dated 'Long-Island.' Reprinted in Prime's *Patriot Muse* (London, 1764), pp. 82–84, from where the title is taken. The dating and place of publication suggest that no. 1865B is also by Prime. See also no. 1866A.

1865B. May 17, 1762 *Am. Chron.*, 3/3.
    'Lewis worsted on the Ocean.'
    T: An Epigrammatic Song on the Spanish War.' ¶ No: 24 lines. ¶
    A: [Benjamin Young Prime?]
    Note: Dated 'Long-Island.' Cf. no. 1865A.

1866. May 31, 1762 *BEP* ❊1395, 4/2.
    'Dull *Grave!* thou spoil'st the Dance of youthful Blood.'
    T: [Epitaph on William Jackson (d. May 28), son of Col. Joseph
    Jackson.] ¶ No: 11 lines.

1866A. May 31, 1762 *Am. Chron.*
    'Montibus in summis occisa est gloria gentis.'
    T: 'Eligia Davidica.' ¶ A: 'Phileleutherius' [Benjamin Young
    Prime.]
    Note: 'a Latin Translation of the celebrated Elegy of David, over
    Saul and Jonathan.' The pseudonym and place of publication (cf.
    no. 1856A) suggest Prime was the author.

1867. May, 1762 *Gent Mag* XXXII, 233–4.
    'Of old, when *Thessaly's* selected band.'
    T: 'Verses on the Return of a young Lady from Jamaica in very bad
    Weather.' ¶ No: 24 lines. ¶ A: 'A. B.'

1868. May, 1762 *Lon Mag* XXXI, 270.
    'Here dormant, with a vulgar tribe.'
    T: 'Epitaph' [on 'Pug']. ¶ No: 20 lines. ¶ A: 'S. D.'
    Note: Dated 'Cambridge, New England, 10th Feb., 1762.'

1869. June 3, 1762 *PG* ❊1745.
    'Now had the Beam of Titan gay.'
    T: 'Hymn to May.' ¶ No: 89 lines. ¶ A: [Nathaniel Evans.]
    Note: Reprinted in Evans, *Poems* (Phila., 1772), pp. 38–41; in
    Kettell, I, 113–14, and in Stedman and Hutchinson, II, 501–2.

1869A. June 7, 1762 *Am. Chron.*
    'All human Bliss we liken to a Span.'
    T: 'Hamlet's Reflections in the Scene of the Grave Digger, imitated.'
    'Sacred to the Memory of a Friend.' ¶ No: 28 lines.

1870. June 24, 1762 *PG* ❊1748.
    'When Vice Triumphant rul'd the Roman Court.'

T: 'To the unknown Author of the late Satire, called, The Manners of the Times.' ¶ No: 14 lines. ¶ A: 'Philo-Philadelphienses.'

Note: Praises the author 'Philadelphienses,' who wrote *The Manners of the Times; A Satire* (Philadelphia, 1762), Evans 9240.

1871. July 22, 1762 *NYG* #1020, 1/1.
'In farmer's yard, one summer's day.'
T: 'The Cock and the Doves. A Fable. Inscribed to a Friend.' ¶ No: 74 lines.

1872. July, 1762 *Gent Mag* XXXII, 332.
'When *William* by *Britannia* fought.'
T: 'Song at the Revolution-Club in Newport, Nov. 16, 1761. To the Tune of Rule Britannia, rule the Waves.' ¶ No: 32 lines plus 2-line refrain.

1873. July, 1762 *Gent Mag* XXXII, 382.
'Not like the rooted plants that grow.'
T: 'Ode by Capt. Petrie (who died at Barbadoes 1753) to the Rev. Mr. H. S.' ¶ No: 36 lines. ¶ A: 'Capt. Petrie.'
Note: References in poem to Barbadoes. For a simultaneous publication, see no. 1874.

1873A. July, 1762 *Imperial Mag* III, 374.
'Aenigma knotters, rebus cooks.'
T: 'To the Modern Witlings.' ¶ No: 34 lines. ¶ A: 'Periturus' [Robert Bolling].
Note: Bolling's copy of the *Imperial Magazine* at the Huntington Library has the attribution 'By R. Bolling junr.' In addition, his manuscript volume 'A Collection of Diverting anecdotes,' Huntington Library, BR 164, contains the poem, pp. 161-163. There is a reply to this poem in the *Imperial Magazine* for Sept. 1762 (III, 480), by John Clarke, dated 'Lincoln, Aug. 7th, 1762.' Cf. no. 1873B.

1873B. July, 1762 *Imperial Mag* III, 374.
'In *Lincolnshire* a grazier dwelt.'
T: 'An Epigram.' ¶ No: 8 lines. ¶ A: 'Prometheus' [Robert Bolling].
Note: Bolling's own copy of the *Imperial Mag* at the Huntington Library attributes the poem to him. Like the immediately preceding poem, it refers to John Clarke.

1873C. July, 1762 *Imperial Mag* III, 374.
'Sweet dove, Thy solitary sounds.'
T: 'To a Turtle-Dove.' ¶ No: 35 lines. ¶ A: 'Prometheus' [Robert Bolling].

Note: In his copy of the *Imperial Mag* at the Huntington Library,
Bolling has identified 'Delia' in l. 6 as 'Nancy Miller.' There is a
version of the poem in Bolling's ms. 'La Gazzetta di Parnasso' (see
no. 1561), pp. 29–30.

1873D. July, 1762 *Imperial Mag* III, 375.
'Here lie, beneath this heap of stones.'
T: 'Epitaph on a Lady.' ¶ No: 20 lines. ¶ A: 'Prometheus' [Robert
Bolling].
Note: Bolling's copy of the *Imperial Mag* at the Huntington Library
attributes the poem to him.

1873E. July, 1762 *Imperial Mag* III, 375.
'Let prudence each petition guide.'
T: 'Take-Care.' ¶ No: 78 lines. ¶ A: 'Prometheus' [Robert Bolling].
Note: Bolling's copy of the *Imperial Mag* at the Huntington Library
notes, 'I'm sorry to say, by me—Robt. Bolling junr.'

1874. July, 1762 *Scots Mag* XXIV, 376.
'Not like the rooted plants that grow.'
Note: For a simultaneous publication, see no. 1873.

1875. Aug. 19, 1762 *BNL* #3034, 2/3.
'Today we've made the French and Spaniards fly.'
T: 'A comparative, satyrical, and moral View of To-Day & To-
morrow.' ¶ No: 12 lines.
Note: Reprinted, nos. 1877, 1880.

1876. Aug. 19, 1762 *MG*.
'To wed, or not to wed—That's the Question.'
T: 'The Batchelor's Soliloquy. In Imitation of the celebrated Solilo-
quy of Hamlet.' ¶ No: 35 lines.
Note: Cf. no. 733.

1877. Aug. 23, 1762 *BG* #386, 3/2.
'Today we've made the French and Spaniards fly.'
Note: A reprinting of no. 1875.

1878. Aug. 26, 1762 *BNL* #3035, 4/1–2.
'Arise, Britannia, from the Dust arise.'
T: 'A Poem on the Accession of King George III.' ¶ No: 118 lines.
¶ A: 'by a young Gentleman in this Town.'

1879. Aug. 26, 1762 *NYG* #1025, 3/2.
''Twas Evening mild--the Sun's refulgent Ray.'
T: 'An Elegy Sacred to the Memory of Josiah Martin, Esq., jun.
who died in the island of Antigua, the—day of June, MDCCLXII.'
¶ No: 48 lines. ¶ A: F. H. [Francis Hopkinson].

Note: Dated 'Philadelphia, August 16th, 1762.' The authorship is given in the reprints, nos. 1935, 1939. Reprinted in Hopkinson's *Miscellaneous Essays*, III, pt. 2 (Philadelphia, 1792), 70–72.

1880. Aug. 30, 1762 *NYM* #526, 3/2.
'*Today* we've made the French and Spaniards fly.'
Note: A reprinting of no. 1875.

1880A. Aug., 1762 *Imperial Mag* III, 429.
'With all my heart,--his lordship may.'
T: 'O, if I cou'd! imitated from the Italian, and very humbly inscribed to Miss Randolph, of Chatsworth.' ¶ No: 26 lines. ¶ A: 'Prometheus' [Robert Bolling].
Note: Bolling's copy of the *Imperial Mag* at the Huntington Library attributes the poem to himself.

1880B. Aug., 1762 *Imperial Mag* III, 429.
'You're fair, dear maid, so very fair.'
T: 'To Miss Patty Daugerfield. Imitated from Ariosto.' ¶ No: 12 lines. ¶ A: 'Prometheus' [Robert Bolling].
Note: In his copy of the magazine at the Huntington Library, Bolling has corrected the epigram from Ariosto.

1880C. Aug., 1762 *Imperial Mag* III, 429–430.
'With thee, fair maid, thy merit dies.'
T: 'To an amiable young Lady, on her determination to live single.' ¶ No: 14 lines. ¶ A: 'Prometheus' [Robert Bolling].
Note: Bolling's copy of the *Imperial Mag* at the Huntington Library identifies 'Miss Betty Randolph' as the 'amiable young Lady.' For a revised, enlarged reprint, see no. 2049A.

1881. Sept. 16, 1762 *PG* #1760, 4/1.
'In Advertisement now I tell.'
T: [Advertisement verse.] ¶ No: 26 lines. ¶ A: 'Moses Peters.'

1881A. Sept., 1762 *Imperial Mag* III, 481–2.
'Forgive, if while you pass each day.'
T: 'To Stella.' ¶ No: 48 lines. ¶ A: 'Prometheus' [Robert Bolling.]
Note: Bolling identified 'Stella' in his own copy of the *Imperial Magazine*, but then crossed it out. He also revised a couplet at the end of the poem and identified 'Cynthio' (who is passionately burning for 'Stella') as 'Will Fleming.'

1881B. Sept., 1762 *Imperial Mag* III, 482.
'Old Mag, some forty years ago.'

T: 'Happy Pair.' ¶ No: 33 lines. ¶ A: 'Prometheus' [Robert Bolling].

Note: In his copy of the *Imperial Mag* at the Huntington Library, Bolling has noted 'An ideal Picture by R. Bolling if that can be called so which was suggested by the Happiness and Circumstances of his Parents.'

1882. Oct. 11, 1762 *BG* #393, 1/1–2.
'In fame's bright annals shall *New-Hampshire* stand.'
¶ No: 82 lines.
Note: dated 'Portsmouth, Oct. 1, 1762.'

1883. Oct. 15, 1762 *NHG* #315.
'In the Boston Gazette of last Monday past.'
T: [Scurrilous reply to *BG*.] ¶ No: 18 lines.
Note: Reprinted, no. 1885. Reply, no. 1886.

1884. Oct. 15, 1762 *NHG* #315.
'Should George the Third, the best of Kings.'
T: [On Massachusetts politics.] ¶ No: 12 lines.
Note: Reprinted from *BG*, not extant.

1885. Oct. 18, 1762 *BEP* #1415, 3/1.
'In the Boston Gazette of last Monday past.'
Note: A reprint of no. 1883.

1886. Oct. 18, 1762 *BG* #394.
'In the *Hampshire* Gazette of last Friday past.'
T: 'In Answer to the *Hampshire Gazette.*' ¶ No: 26 lines.
Note: A reply to no. 1883.

1886A. Oct., 1762 *Imperial Mag* III, 538.
'Whene'er I press my lips to thine.'
T: 'The Kiss. To M.A.R.O.C.I.R.V.I.A.' ¶ No: 8 lines. ¶ A: 'Prometheus' [Robert Bolling].
Note: In his copy of the *Imperial Mag* at the Huntington Library, Bolling expanded the abbreviations: 'Mary Anne Randolph of Curles James River Virginia in America.' Cf. no. 1886B.

1886B. Oct., 1762 *Imperial Mag* III, 538.
'See, from my lovely Stella's eyes.'
T: 'On M. A. Randolph.' ¶ No: 10 lines. ¶ A: 'Prometheus' [Robert Bolling].
Note: In his copy of the *Imperial Mag* at the Huntington Library, Bolling attributed the poem to himself. 'M. A. Randolph' is evidently Mary Anne Randolph, see no. 1886A.

1886C. Oct., 1762 *Imperial Mag* III, 538.
'Whoever wants a great estate.'
T: 'Tenant by the Curtesy. From the 35th Section of Littleton's Institutes.' ¶ No: 22 lines. ¶ A: 'Prometheus' [Robert Bolling].
Note: In his copy of the *Imperial Mag* at the Huntington Library, Bolling attributed the poem to himself.

1886D. Oct., 1762 *Imperial Mag* III, 538.
'Now, wretched Joque, thou art a guest.'
T: 'On a Parasite.' ¶ No: 8 lines. ¶ A: 'Prometheus' [Robert Bolling].
Note: Bolling has substituted *Cock* for *Joque* in his copy of the magazine at the Huntington Library.

1887. Dec. 10, 1762 *NLS* #227.
'Plenty three years our crowded Graneries fill'd.'
T: [Almanack verse for 1763.] ¶ No: 8 lines. ¶ A: 'Nathaniel Ames.'
Note: Repeated Dec. 17. Reprinted in Briggs (see no. 1344), p. 333.

1888. Dec. 11, 1762 *CG* #401.
'Let daring bands attune the sounding lyre.'
T: 'Sacred to the Memory of the late ingenious Doct. Nathaniel Hubbard.' ¶ No: 40 lines.
Note: On Hubbard, age 23, son of Col. Hubbard of New Haven; see obit, *CG*, Nov. 27, 1762, 2/1.

1889. Dec. 30, 1762 *PG* #1775, 2/2.
'Suppress, dear Delia, thy too constant Sighs.'
T: 'On the Death of John Moland, Esq; Counsellor at Law. To a Lady.' ¶ No: 56 lines. ¶ A: 'D.'

1890. Dec. 30, 1762 *PG* #1775, 2/2–3.
'Hail Heav'n-born Science! whose enliv'ning Touch.'
T: 'On hearing the Organ, at St. Paul's Church, on Christmas Day, 1762.' ¶ No: 41 lines. ¶ A: 'C. W. P.'
Note: Praises Philip Fyring, maker of the organ. Reprinted, no. 1899.

1891. Dec. 30, 1762 *PJ* #1047, 2/1.
'Now to my arms, submits the pride of Spain.'
T: 'Verses wrote immediately on reading the Extraordinary Gazette, on the taking of the Havanna.' ¶ No: 30 lines. ¶ A: 'Eugenio.'
Note: Reprinted, no. 1901.

1892. 1762 *Annual Register*, pp. 206–7.
'The youth, whose birth the sisters twin.'
T: 'Lib. IV. Ode 3. Horace. Imitated.' ¶ No: 48 lines. ¶ A: 'R. B.' [Robert Bolling?].

1763

1893. Jan. 6, 1763 *BNL* ✳3081, 1/2.
'England, for martial Deeds renown'd.'
T: 'Verses on taking the Great Guns at the Havannah, called the Twelve Apostles.' ¶ No: 12 lines. ¶ A: 'By a Lady.'
Note: Cf. no. 1898. Reprinted, nos. 1897, 2079.

1894. Jan. 6, 1763 *PG* ✳1776, 1/1–2.
'On a soft Bank, wrapt in the gloomy Groves.'
T: 'Victory. A Poem.' ¶ No: 132 lines. ¶ A: 'By Mr. [Thomas] Godfrey.'
Note: Reprinted in Godfrey's *Poems* (see no. 1408), pp. 65–71.

1895. Jan. 8, 1763 *CG* ✳405, 1/3.
'From France and Spain we're called to the Field.'
T: '[The following lines were delivered by the Rev. Mr. Booge, of Farmington, in his Thanksgiving Sermon, The 8th of Nov. last.]'
¶ No: 50 lines. ¶ A: Rev. Mr. [Ebenezer] Booge.
Note: On the Rev. Ebenezer Booge (1716–1767), who graduated from Yale in 1748, see Weis, *New England*, p. 36.

1896. Jan. 8, 1763 *Prov. G.* ✳12, 4/1.
'A Term full as long as the Siege of Old Troy.'
T: 'A New Song.' ¶ No: 24 lines plus 2-line refrain: ''Tis Time enough yet.'

1897. Jan. 10, 1763 *BG* ✳406, 3/1.
'England, for martial Deeds renoun'd.'
Note: A reprint of no. 1893.

1898. Jan. 10, 1763 *BG* ✳406, 3/1.
'As Grain with latent Fire well fraught.'
T: 'To the Author of the above Lines.' ¶ No: 28 lines. ¶ A: 'G[eorge] Cockings.'
Note: Cockings writes a 4-line compliment to the poetess who wrote no. 1897, and a 24-line poem on the same theme. There is a brief, supercilious sketch of Cockings in the *DNB*.

1899. Jan. 10, 1763 *NYM* ✳545, 1/2.
'Hail Heav'n born Science! whose enliv'ning Touch.'
Note: A reprint of no. 1890.

1900. Jan. 11, 1763 *BNL* ✳3082, 3/2.
'When Albion 'woke, and rouz'd, midst War's Alarms.'
T: 'An Acrostic.' ¶ No: 18 lines. ¶ A: George Cockings.
Note: On 'William Pitt Esquire.' Reprinted, no. 1902.

1901. Jan. 21, 1763 *NHG* ⚹329.
'Now to my arms; submits the pride of Spain.'
Note: A reprint of no. 1891.

1902. Jan. 21, 1763 *NHG* ⚹329.
'When Albion woke, and rouz'd, 'midst War's Alarms.'
Note: A reprint of no. 1900.

1903. Jan. 24, 1763 *BEP* ⚹1429, 1/2.
'Behold the Lillies and the gorgeous Flowers.'
T: 'A Poem. On Occasion of the Death of Dr. Thomas Mather,
Surgeon to the Troops of the Massachusetts-Province, at Halifax;
address'd to his Father in Boston.' ¶ No: 79 lines. ¶ A: 'By a
young Gentleman intimately acquainted with the late Doctor.'
Note: News of his death is in *BEP*, Dec. 20, 1762, 3/1: 'lately died--
Son of the Rev. Samuel Mather.'

1904. Jan. 27, 1763 *BNL* ⚹3084, 4/2.
'With ardent love for ancient wisdom fir'd.'
T: 'Lines dedicated to Benjamin Prat.' ¶ No: 14 lines. ¶ A: 'Y. Z.'
['T. Z—y'].
Note: An elegy on Benjamin Prat. Reprinted, nos. 1911 and 1919
(where a fuller title is given). Copied in Jeremy Belknap's green
notebook (see no. 71) where Belknap writes that the author is
'T. Z—y.'

1905. Feb. 18, 1763 *NLS* ⚹237.
'A Monarch in my rustick bower.'
T: 'The Hermit's Empire.' ¶ No: 24 lines.
Note: A reprint of no. 919.

1906. Feb. 21, 1763 *BEP* ⚹1433, 4/1.
'Friendship, the heav'nly Theme, I sing.'
T: 'On Friendship.' ¶ No: 39 lines. ¶ A: 'Philanthropos.'

1907. Feb. 21, 1763 *BEP* ⚹1433, 4/1.
'How we tremble 'midst the Snow!'
T: 'Winter. An Ode.' ¶ No: 26 lines.

1908. Feb. 21, 1763 *BG* ⚹412, 1/1.
'The lab'ring Mountains were in Pieces torn.'
T: [Satire on two writers.] ¶ No: 71 lines. ¶ A: 'Hudibras Paro-
diy'd.'
Note: Enjoyable satire. Cf. no. 1916.

1909. Feb. 26, 1763 *Prov. G.* ⚹19, 4/1.
'The hoary winter now conceals from sight.'
Note: A reprint of no. 1547.

1910. Feb. 28, 1763 *BEP* #1434, 3/1.
    'Bless'd are the dead, when dying in the Lord.'
    T: [Elegy on Samuel Hill.] ¶ No: 24 lines. ¶ A: 'George Cockings.'
    Note: Hill was a 'noted Shopkeeper,' a. 68. His obituary is in *BEP*,
        Feb. 21, 1763, 3/2. He died Feb. 18, 1763.

1911. Feb. 28, 1763 *WNYG* #220, 1/2.
    'With ardent Love for ancient Wisdom fir'd.'
    Note: A reprint of no. 1904.

1912. Mar. 2, 1763 *NLG* #16, 4/2.
    'Hark, my gay friend, that solemn bell.'
    T: 'The Unknown World. Verses occasioned by hearing a Pass-
        Bell.' ¶ A: 'By the Rev. Mr. St—p.'
    Note: Crum H249 notes that it is by 'the Rev. Mr. St----n.'

1913. Mar. 4, 1763 *NHG* #335.
    'How hard my Lot! and ah! how cruel Fate!'
    T: 'On the Death of a favourite beautiful Taby colour'd CAT.' ¶
        No: 28 lines.
    Note: Cf. no. 766. Reprinted, no. 1917.

1914. Mar. 7, 1763 *NYG* #553, 2/3–3/1.
    'Scarce had the dark'ned Sky, which Night had borne.'
    T: 'Description of the Morning.' ¶ No: 24 lines.

1915. Mar. 11, 1763 *NHG* #336.
    'Believe my Sighs and Tears my Dear.'
    T: 'A young Gentleman to Miss P[oll]y J—n.' ¶ No: 16 lines. ¶ A:
        'J— F—.'
    Note: Dated 'Portsmouth.'

1916. Mar. 14, 1763 *BG* #415, 1/1.
    'A Grub street bard is hen coop'd twice sev'n days.'
    T: 'Most noble Festus, I am not Mad, but speak the Words of
        Truth; and when I have clear'd the Stage of a little dirty Rubbish
        of Thine own making, it shall be found that I can also speak those
        of Soberness.' ¶ A: 'Parodisticon Hudibrasticon.'
    Note: Probably a reply to no. 1908.

1916A. Mar. 14, 1763 *NM* #236, 1/3.
    'Like all the num'rous Sins, which lawless Rage.'
    T: 'Advice to profane Swearers.' ¶ No: 12 lines.

1917. Mar. 19, 1763 *CG* #415, 2/1.
    'How hard my Lot! and ah! how cruel Fate!'
    No: 28 lines.
    Note: A reprint of no. 1913.

1918. Mar. 24, 1763 *PG* ⚡1787, 2/1.
'While you, dear Hal, are forc'd to roam.'
T: 'Ode: attempted in the Horatian Style. To the Ingenious Mr.
Th[oma]s G[o]df[re]y. By Mr. *— *—. Mat to Hal.' ¶ No: 42
lines. ¶ A: [Nathaniel Evans.]
Note: Nathaniel Evans' poem to Thomas Godfrey is reprinted in
Evans, *Poems*, pp. 50–52; and in Kettell, I, 112–13.

1919. Mar. 25, 1763 *NHG* ⚡338.
'With ardent Love for ancient Wisdom fir'd.'
T: 'The following Lines dedicated to the Memory of the Honour-
able Benjamin Pratt, Esq; late Chief Justice of New-York, and a
Member of his Majesty's Council; ... was wrote and published in
Boston, Jan. 26, 1763.'
Note: A reprint of no. 1904.

1921. Apr. 2, 1763 *Prov. G.* ⚡24, 3/3.
'Old Tenor breathing out her last.'
T: 'On the Conviction of Old Tenor before her Death; wrote by a
Spectator, after hearing the Debates on the Petition, February
Session, at Providence, 1763.' ¶ No: 20 lines. ¶ A: 'A. Z.'
Note: Joseph Green wrote two similar poems: *A Mournful Lamen-
tation for the Sad and Deplorable Death of Mr. Old Tenor* (Boston,
1750), Evans 6512, Ford 915, and Wegelin 187; and *The Dying
Speech of Old Tenor* (Boston, 1750), Ford 912.

1922. Apr. 4, 1763 *BEP* ⚡1439, 1/1–2.
'Fathers, Friends, Fellow-Citizens and Countrymen!'
T: [Satirical verification of James Otis's speech as moderator at
Town meeting which was printed in *BEP*, Mar. 21, 1763, 2/1–2.]
¶ No: 87 lines. ¶ A: 'J. Philanthrop' [Samuel Waterhouse or
Joseph Green?]
Note: These verses are similar to a number of burlesques written by
Joseph Green in the 1730's, but the author is more probably
Samuel Waterhouse. See no. 2035.

1922A. April 28, 1763 *GG* ⚡4.
'Whence, Britons, these desponding cares.'
T: Ode [to the people 'apprehensive of future broils if peace is given
... upon such terms' as the preliminary articles of peace signed at
Fontainbleau]. ¶ No: 44 lines.

1923. Apr. 23, 1763 *Prov. G.* ⚡27, 3/2.
'The choice came on, Fame told the Success round.'
T: 'On the late Town meeting.' ¶ No: 6 lines. ¶ A: 'By a Youth.'

1923A. May 2, 1763 *NM* #243, 1/1.
'It must be so--Milton, thou reason'st well.'
T: 'The Maid's Soliloquy.' ¶ No: 30 lines.
Note: An imitation of Addison's *Cato*, I, i. Cf. no. 872.

1923B. May 12, 1763 *GG* #6, 3/1.
'When Physick saw her younger hope expire.'
T: 'On the Death of a Physician's Child.' ¶ No: 4 lines.

1924. May 14, 1763 *Prov. Gaz.* #30, 3/3.
'As Fame of late in merry Mood.'
T: [Political verse.] ¶ No: 28 lines.

1925. May 14, 1763 *Prov. Gaz.* #30, 3/3.
'Sincerity! thou sweetest thing in Life.'
T: 'Lines, on Sincerity.' ¶ No: 18 lines. ¶ A: 'By a young Lady.'

1926. May 26, 1763 *PG* #1796, 1/1.
'Not with more Pleasure o'er the fragrant Lawn.'
T: 'Extract from the Dialogue on Peace, pronounced at the late
public Commencement [May 17] in the College of this City.' ¶
No: 60 lines. ¶ A: [Nathaniel Evans.]
Note: Reprinted in Evans, *Poems*, pp. 74–76. Reprinted, no. 1928,
1929A.

1927. May 28, 1763 *Prov. G.* #32, 1/1.
'Whilst *Britain* led by Royal George.'
T: 'Verses on Dr. Mayhew's *Book of Observations on the Charter
and Conduct of the Society for the Propagation of the Gospel in
Foreign Parts, with notes critical and explanatory.' ¶ No: 36
lines. ¶ A: 'By a Gentleman of Rhode-Island Colony' [John
Aplin].
Note: Reprinted, no. 1929B. On June 4, 1/1, the fifth stanza was re-
printed, and on June 11, 1/1, the last four stanzas were reprinted.
The poem, with the long notes, was reprinted as a pamphlet. For
an excellent reprint, see Bernard Bailyn, *Pamphlets of the American
Revolution* (Cambridge, Mass., 1965), pp. 273–291.

1928. May 30, 1763 *WNYG* #233, 2/3.
'Not with more Pleasure, o'r the fragrant Lawn.'
Note: A reprint of no. 1926.

1929. May, 1763 *Gent Mag* XXXIII, 251.
'Hail sacred muse! thou harbinger of fame.'
T: 'Extract from an Ode on the late glorious Successes of his
Majesty's Arms, and present Greatness of the English Nation;
from a Pamphlet lately published in Philadelphia.' ¶ No: 108
lines. ¶ A: [Nathaniel Evans.]

Note: Reprinted in Evans, *Poems* (Philadelphia, 1772), pp. 64–71, where the title is 'Heroic Stanzas, On the Success of his Majesty's Arms, and the Greatness of the English Nation, 1762.'

1929A. June 6, 1763 *NM* #248, 2/2.
'Not with more Pleasure o'er the fragrant Lawn.'
Note: A reprint of no. 1926.

1929B. June 6, 1763 *NM* #248, 4/1–3.
'While *Britain* led by Royal *George*.'
Note: A reprint of no. 1927.

1930. June, 1763 *Scots Mag* XXV, 347.
'Come, chear up, my lads, to our country be firm.'
T:' 'Liberty: A Song.' ['Hearts of Oak.'] ¶ A: [David Garrick.]
Note: Chorus: 'Hearts of oak are we still, for we're sons of those men Who always were ready; steady boys, steady, To fight for our freedom again and again.' This popular English song was imitated by many Revolutionary American songs.

1931. July 9, 1763 *Prov G* #38, 3/3.
'Heav'n's sacred Will, *Leaconoé*, wait.'
T:' The 11th Ode of the 1st Book of Horace, translated.' ¶ No: 22 lines. ¶ A: 'By a young Gentleman of this town.'

1932. July 15, 1763 *NHG* #354.
'What smiling Seraph courts my ravish'd eyes.'
T: [To Silvia.] ¶ No: 50 lines.
Note: Good verse.

1933. July 21, 1763 *BNL* #3109, 3/3.
'A Shrouded Corpse! ah me, who yonder lies?'
T: 'An Elegy to the Memory of a Lady. Occasioned by a View of the Corpse.' ¶ No: 72 lines.

1934. July, 1763 *Scots Mag* XXV, 403.
'Why should I tempt the raging main.'
T: 'An Irregular Ode. To a friend, on being desired to go to Jamaica.'
Note: Dated 'Tweedside, July 20, 1763.'

1935. Aug., 1763 *Gent Mag* XXXIII, 407.
''Twas ev'ning mild, the sun's refulgent ray.'
A: 'F. Hopkinson.'
Note: A reprint of no. 1879.

1936. Sept. 1, 1763 *BNL* #3115, 2/1.
'Quid frustra erepte fatis quaeramus amici.'

T: 'In Obitum Roberti Kennedi juvenum sui saeculi facile principis, qui ab Nov Eboraco ad insulan Statten transgrediens mari demerus praematuris et violentibus fatis concessit, XVI Kalend: Septemb: Anna Aerae Christianae vulgaris MDCCLXIII Aetat: sua vix XXVIII. ¶ No: 56 lines. ¶ A: 'William Hooper.'

Note: The attribution is added in manuscript in a contemporary hand. The poem is dated 'Boston, Aug. 31.' The best sketch of Hooper, a Signer, is in Shipton, XIV, 624–637.

1937. Sept. 1, 1763 *BNL* #3115, 3/1.
'Fair Chloe's Dress (which Venus self might wear).'
T: 'On a Young Lady's Dress.' ¶ No: 22 lines.

1937A. Sept. 19, 1763 *NM* #263.
'Beneath yon turf lies Gamble's dust.'
Note: A reprint of no. 1603.

1938. Sept. 26, 1763 *BPB* #319, 1/1.
'Hail glorious Peace, 'tis thy refreshing smiles.'
T: [On the 'Proclamation for Peace.'] ¶ No: 54 lines. ¶ A: 'Z. A.'

1939. Sept., 1763 *Lon Mag* XXXII, 495–6.
''Twas evening mild--the sun's refulgent ray.'
Note: A reprint of no. 1879.

1940. Oct. 6, 1763 *BNL* #3120, 2/3.
'Behold the Prophet in the awful Shade.'
T: 'Verses Sacred to the Memory of the Rev. Mr. Cumming.'¶ No: 22 lines.
Note: Rev. Alexander Cumming's obituary in *BNL*, Aug. 25, 1763.

1941. Oct. 13, 1763 *PG* #1816, 1/1.
'O Death! thou Victor of the human Frame!'
T: 'Elegy To the Memory of Mr. Godfrey, 1763.' ¶ No: 68 lines. ¶ A: 'E.' [Nathaniel Evans].
Note: Cf. no. 1918. Reprinted, no. 1966 (with fuller title, and with author given). Reprinted in Godfrey, *Poems* (see no. 1408), pp. 5–7; in Evans, *Poems* (Phila., 1772), pp. 104–107; and in Kettell, I, 117–18.

1942. Nov. 3, 1763 *PG* #1819, 3/1.
'Heaven oft before the fatal Bolt is hurl'd.'
T: 'On Sunday last, about a Quarter after Four in the Afternoon, we had a smart Shock of an Earthquake here, which so alarmed the Congregations of most of the Places of Worship in Town, that the Service was immediately broke up; but happily no Damage ensued.--The following Lines were sent us on the Occasion.' ¶ No: 10 lines. ¶ A: 'I. F.'

Note: Reprinted, nos. 1943, 1944 (where the author's initials are given as 'J. F.'), 1945.

1943. Nov. 12, 1763 *Prov Gaz* #56, 3/2.
'Heav'n oft before the Bolt is hurl'd.'
Note: A reprint of no. 1942.

1944. Nov. 14, 1763 *BEP* #1471, 2/3.
'Heav'n oft before the bolt is hurl'd.'
¶ A: 'J. F.'
Note: A reprint of no. 1942.

1945. Nov. 14, 1763 *BPB* #326, 2/2.
'Heav'n oft before the fatal Bolt is hurl'd.'
Note: A reprint of no. 1942.

1946. Nov. 17, 1763 *MG.*
'Stranger, whoe'er Thou art, one Moment stay.'
T: 'Epitaph, On the late Rev. Mr. James Sterling.' ¶ No: 21 lines.
¶ A: 'Euphranor.'
Note: The epitaph accompanies a long obituary on Sterling by 'Euphranor.'

1947. Nov. 17, 1763 *PG* #1821, 1/1.
'Death's Iron Jav'lins thro' the Globe are hurl'd.'
T: 'To the Memory of Mr. John Bingham, late Student in the College of Philadelphia.' ¶ No: 38 lines.

1947A. Dec. 26, 1763 *NM* #277.
'In man too oft a well dissembled part.'
T: 'True Pourtrait of the Essence of Virtue.' ¶ No: 125 lines.

1948. Dec. 31, 1763 *Prov G* #63, 1/3.
'God of my Life, Thy constant Care.'
T: 'For New Year's Day.' ¶ No: 16 lines.

1949. 1763 *Annual Register*, pp. 239–41.
'Begin, begin the sorrow-soothing theme.'
T: 'An Elegy. On the death of General Wolfe.' ¶ No: 108 lines.

1764

1950. Jan. 5, 1764 *BNL* #3124, 3/3.
'Like as a Damask Rose you see.'
T: 'On the Shortness of Human Life.' ¶ No: 36 lines.
Note: Good verse. Reprinted in the *Armenian Mag*, II (April, 1790), 205–6, and in *The Telescope*, II (May 20, 1826), 204. The first line is similar to Crum L383 and L409–11.

1951. Jan. 23, 1764 *BPB* ☿336, 3/2.
'Give me a Girl if e'er I take a Wife.'
T: 'The Choice.' ¶ No: 10 lines.
Note: Dated 'New Boston, 21st Jan. 1764.'

1952. Jan., 1764 *Lon Mag*, XXXIII, 45.
'Ye Fair, with youth and beauty vain.'
T: 'Time's Address to the Ladies. This Imitation of Tasso, is most
humbly inscribed to Miss E. Randolph, of James River, in Vir-
ginia.' ¶ No: 67 lines. ¶ A: 'Rob. Bolling, jun.'
Note: Reprinted in the *American Museum*, VII (Appendix, 1790), 30.

1953. Jan., 1764 *Lon Mag*, XXXIII, 45.
'Circle has a daughter fair.'
T: 'The Choice.' ¶ No: 15 lines. ¶ A: 'Prometheus' [Robert Bolling].
Note: This is Bolling's pseudonym--and the poem is printed be-
tween two others by him.

1954. Jan., 1764 *Lon Mag*, XXXIII, 45–6.
'Dear Polly, yes: My days with thee.'
T: 'To my wife.' ¶ No: 45 lines. ¶ A: 'R. B.' [Robert Bolling].
Note: Dated 'Virginia, June 6, 1763.'

1955. Feb. 2, 1764 *BNL* ☿3128, 1/1.
'Quis lacrymas retinere potest dum fatur Amicus.'
T: 'Threnodia. In Conflagrationem Aulae Harvardinae, Canta-
brigiae Nov-Anglorum die 24⁰ Janj 1764.' ¶ No: 20 lines. ¶ A:
'Philomusus.'

1956. Feb. 3, 1764 *NHG* ☿383.
'If Women Chins are made both smooth and Fair.'
T: 'Mr. [William] Scott has his Picture drawn by Mr. [Joseph]
Badger, under which is the following Lines, composed by him-
self.' ¶ No: 3 lines--but with a 15-line answer.
Note: Cf. no. 1957.

1957. Feb. 3, 1764 *NHG* ☿383.
'Man love Women with Lips quite bare.'
T: 'Mr. Fowle, Please to print the following Lines, as they shew the
Poetical Genius of Mr. William Scott, a Shoemaker in Boston,
wrote with his own Hand.' ¶ No: 34 lines. ¶ A: 'William Scott.'
Note: Cf. no. 1956.

1958. Feb. 6, 1764 *BPB* ☿338.
'Omnis Agyrta audax Regiones perque vagatur.'
T: 'Monitum Bostoniensibus oblatum Descriptio Agyrtae Emi-
grantis Emphatica.' ¶ No: 10 lines. ¶ A: 'Galenicus.'

1959. Feb. 6, 1764 *WNYG* #269, 1/2.
'No more are Mars's blust'ring Sons.'
T: 'A New and mild Method totally to extirpate the Indians out of No. America. It was wrote at Philadelphia on a particular Occasion.' ¶ No: 46 lines. ¶ A: [Benjamin Franklin?]
Note: 'Aid us, than more than all the Nine,/*Poetic Hartshorn*, good old Wine!' Franklin humorously suggested in his *Autobiography* (New Haven, 1764), p. 199, that rum might be 'the appointed Means' for annihilating the Indians. There was an H. Hartshorn, of Burlington, who, judging from his taking in subscriptions for Provost William Smith's *American Magazine* (see *PG*, Jan. 18, 1759, 1/3), evidently had some literary interests.

1960. Feb., 1764 *Lon Mag*, XXXIII, 101.
'O Melancholy, pensive maid.'
T: 'Hymn to Melancholy. Inscribed to Miss A. Miller, of V.' ¶ No: 48 lines. ¶ A: 'Prometheus' [Robert Bolling].
Note: A shortened version of no. 1839B.

1961. Feb., 1764 *Lon Mag*, XXXIII, 101.
'See, from Stella's sloe-black eyes.'
T: 'The Flamers.' ¶ No: 10 lines. ¶ A: 'Prometheus' [Robert Bolling].

1962. Feb., 1764 *Lon Mag*, XXXIII, 101–2.
'While exil'd in this solitude.'
T: 'To my Flute.' ¶ No: 20 lines. ¶ A: 'Robert Bolling, jun.'

1963. Feb., 1764 *Universal Mag*, XXXIV, 92.
'Say, why like a little fawn.'
T: 'To Miss Nancy Blair of Williamsburg in Virginia, this Imitation of Horace is most humbly inscribed.' ¶ No: 14 lines. ¶ A: 'Prometheus' [Robert Bolling].

1964. Feb., 1764 *Universal Mag*, XXXIV, 94.
'Stella's waving hair flows down.'
T: 'A Canzonet of Chiabura imitated.' ¶ No: 46 lines. ¶ A: 'Robert Bolling, jun.'
Note: Dated 'Virginia.'

1965. Mar. 5, 1764 *BEP* #1787, 3/2.
'The People of *Taunton* they lately have seen.'
¶ No: 10 lines.
Note: Dated 'Taunton, Mar. 1, 1764.'

1965A. Mar. 12, 1764 *NM* #288, 2/1.
'In Hymen's bonds united prove.'
T:' To ----, coming into Marriage with the amiable Miss ----.' ¶ No: 24 lines.

1966. Mar., 1764 *Lon Mag*, XXXIII, 152–3.
'O Death! thou victor of the human frame!'
T: 'Elegy. To the Memory of Mr. Thomas Godfrey, who died near
   Wilmington, North-Carolina, August 3ᵈ, 1763.' ¶ A: 'By N.
   Evans, of Philadelphia.'
Note: A reprint of no. 1941.

1967. Apr. 26, 1764 *BNL* ⸸3140, 3/3.
'Alas! how am I chang'd! Revolving Suns.'
T: 'The Lamentation of Harvard.' ¶ No: 64 lines. ¶ A: 'SPQR.'
Note: On the fire. Mentions the Harvard poets of the day: 'Where is
   my Ch—ch, my L–w–ll, H–p–r, D—n,/The *Popes* and *Priors* of
   our western world?' See *BNL*, May 3, 1764, for an account of
   the fire. See the reply, no. 1969. The poets referred to may be Dr.
   Benjamin Church, Jr., John Lovell, the Rev. Samuel Cooper, and
   the Rev. Samuel Deane, respectively. The poem has been re-
   printed in *Pubs. of the Col. Soc. of Mass.*, XIV (1911–13), 8–11,
   and I follow the suggestion of F. Apthorp Foster that H–p–r is a
   misprint for C–p–r, a contributor to Harvard's volume *Pietas et
   Gratulatio* (Boston, 1761).

1968. Apr., 1764 *Gent Mag* XXXIV, 188.
'Frail man, thro' life's uncomfortable gloom.'
T: 'Elegy To the Memory of the Rev. Isaac Teale, A.M. Late of the
   Island of Jamaica.' ¶ No: 44 lines. ¶ A: 'Bryan Edwards.'
Note: Lines 25–28 reveal that Teale was a poet. Dated 'Jamaica,
   Jan. 11, 1764.'

1969. May 3, 1764 *BNL* ⸸3141, 3/3.
'Thou foundling Bard, I've trac'd thy Labor thro'.'
T: 'To the Author of that florid Piece in the Massachusetts Gazette
   of April 26, 1764 entitled "The Lamentation of Harvard."' ¶ No:
   21 lines. ¶ A: 'Farewell.'
Note: An editorial note, *BNL*, May 10, 1764: 'S.P.Q.R. is desired
   to excuse our not inserting his Reply to that in our last, as what
   has hitherto been published, has not been agreeable to our
   Readers.' A reply to no. 1967.

1970. May 14, 1764 *BG* ⸸476, 2/3.
'Snatch'd in the Morn of Life alas! too soon.'
T: 'On the Death of two blooming young Ladies.' ¶ No: 30 lines.
Note: Dated 'Boston, May 11, 1764.'

1971. May 17, 1764 *PG* ⸸1847, 1/1.
'If in this Wild pleasing Spot we meet.'
T: 'extracted from an *Epistle to a Friend*, from Fort Henry, dated
   August, 1758.' ¶ No: 12 lines. ¶ A: Thomas Godfrey.

Note: This extract is found in an advertisement for Godfrey's *Poetical Works*. Reprinted, no. 1972. Cf. no. 1973.

1972. May 17, 1764 *PJ* ⚹1119, 1/1.
'If in this Wild pleasing Spot we meet.'
Note: A reprint of no. 1971.

1973. May 24, 1764 *PG* ⚹1848, 1/1.
'Curiosity's another name for Man.'
T: 'Extracts from the Tragedy of the *Prince of Parthia*' [in ad for Godfrey's *Poetical Works*]. ¶ No: 45 lines. ¶ A: Thomas Godfrey.
Note: This extract is found in an advertisement for Godfrey's *Poetical Works*. Reprinted, no. 1974. Also reprinted in *PJ*, 14 and 28 June, and 19 and 26 July.

1974. May 31, 1764 *PJ* ⚹1121, 4/1.
'Curiosity's another name for Man.'
Note: A reprint of no. 1973.

1975. June 7, 1764 *BNL* ⚹3146, 3/1.
'And must thou go? Farewell thou sacred Guide!'
T: 'Addressed to the Rev. Mr. Whitefield, on his Departure.' ¶ No: 20 lines.
Note: Reprinted, nos. 1976A, 1980. Cf. nos. 1976, 1977.

1976. June 11, 1764 *BEP* ⚹1501, 3/1.
'And art thou gone? Fly swift thou baneful Star!'
T: 'A Contrast' [Attack on Whitefield]. ¶ No: 20 lines.
Note: Although the poem seems to be an attack on Whitefield, the author wrote a note in *BEP* of June 18, saying that he meant the poem as a 'Jeu d'Esprit, a Matter of Humour on the Poet of Thursday preceding [no. 1975], and not pointed at the respectful Subject of the Elegy published by Mr. Draper.' For replies see nos. 1977, 1978, 1979. Cf. no. 1985.

1976A. June 11, 1764 *NM* ⚹301, 3/1.
'And must thou go? Farewell thou sacred Guide!'
Note: A reprint of 1975.

1977. June 14, 1764 *BNL* ⚹3147, 3/2.
'Rail on, vile Atheist; let your Tongue blaspheme.'
T: 'Lines addressed to the Author "A Contrast," published in Yesterday's Evening-Post.' ¶ No: 28 lines. ¶ A: 'H. P.'
Note: Dated 'Boston, June 12, 1764.' A reply to no. 1976. Reprinted, no. 1986.

1978. June 14, 1764 *BNL* ⚹3147, 3/2.
'Ungen'rous Bard! Th' hast shot thy Bolt in haste.'

T: 'To the Author of The Contrast, in the Evening Post.' ¶ No: 10
lines. ¶ A: 'Farewell.'
Note: Another reply to no. 1976. Reprinted, no. 1987.

1979. June 14, 1764 *BNL* #3147, 3/2.
'What wretched Rhymes with polluted Stains.'
T: 'To the Author of The Contrast.' ¶ No: 22 lines.
Note: Another reply to no. 1976.

1980. June 15, 1764 *NHG* #402.
'And must thou go? Farewell thou sacred Guide!'
Note: A reprint of no. 1975.

1981. July 2, 1764 *BG* #483, 2/2.
'To satyrize the Dead.'
T: 'Encomiastes.' ¶ No: 18 lines.
Note: This answers the mock obituary dated 'Wickingham.'

1982. July 5, 1764 *BNL* #3150, 3/2.
'Hail Marriage! sacred Rite, whose mystic Tie.'
T: [On marriage.] ¶ No: 57 lines. ¶ A: 'Philander.'

1983. July 5, 1764 *NYG* #1122, 3/1.
'Near some cool Grot and purling Rill.'
T: 'His Choice.' ¶ No: 12 lines. ¶ A: By a 'young Gentleman' (who
has only had 'a little common Schooling').
Note: The same author wrote no. 1984.

1984. July 5, 1764 *NYG* #1122, 3/1.
'Thus pensive as I tread the Strand.'
T: 'Reflections occasion'd by a Walk on the Sea Shore, on the East
End of Long Island.' ¶ No: 72 lines. ¶ A: 'By a young Gentle-
man.'
Note: The same author wrote no. 1983.

1985. July 13, 1764 *NHG* #402, 4/3.
'Quite mad with Zeal, the Biggots raves.'
T: [Anti-enthusiast; attack on Whitefield.] ¶ No: 18 lines.
Note: A defense of no. 1976. For a reply, see no. 1994.

1986. July 13, 1764 *NHG* #406.
'Rail on, vile Atheist; let your Tongue blaspheme.'
Note: A reprint of no. 1977.

1987. July 13, 1764 *NHG* #406.
'Ungen'rous Bard! Th' has shot thy Bolt in haste.'
Note: A reprint of no. 1978.

1988. July 16, 1764 *BEP* ₩1506.
  'Haec Tibi, sancte senex, funebria maesta dicamus.'
  T: 'In Obitum dolendum Josiae Crockeri, A.M. qui fatis concessit immaturis Easthami Nov. Ang. XII Kalend. Jun. Anno Aeta Christianae vulgaris MDCCLXIV, Aetatis suae XXIV: Ad Patrem ejus superstitem.' ¶ No: 53 lines. ¶ A: 'H.'
  Note: Dated, 'Apud Bostonum: XVII Kalend. Aug. A.D. MDCC-LXIV.'

1989. July 26, 1764 *NYG* ₩1125, 3/2.
  'What is that Vice that still prevails.'
  T: [On Slander.] ¶ No: 20 lines.

1990. July 27, 1764 *NHG* ₩408.
  'The dry, dull, drowsy *Batchelor* surveys.'
  Note: A reprint of no. 1822.

1990A. July 30, 1764 *NM* ₩308, 1/1.
  'Proteus, as ancient poets tell you.'
  T: 'Patriotism! A Farce. As is acted by his Majesty's Servants. Prologue.' ¶ No: 46 lines.

1991. July, 1764 *Gent Mag* XXXIV, 342.
  'Soon as young Reason dawn'd in Junio's breast.'
  T: 'The Story of Junio and Theana, an Episode, from the second Book of the Sugar-Cane, a Poem, by James Grainger, M.D. just published.' ¶ No: 126 lines. ¶ A: 'James Grainger' M.D.
  Note: Cf. no. 1559. For another printing, see no. 1992.

1992. July, 1764 *Scots Mag*, XXVI, 395–6.
  'Soon as young Reason dawn'd in Junio's breast.'
  Note: See no. 1991.

1993. Aug. 9, 1764 *PJ* ₩1131, 3/1.
  'A Speech there is, which no Man spoke.'
  T: 'Advertisement, and not a Joke.' ¶ No: 14 lines.

1994. Aug. 10, 1764 *NHG* ₩410.
  'And must God's Truth, the Glory of our Land.'
  T: [On Whitefield.] ¶ No: 40 lines.
  Note: A reply to no. 1985.

1995. Aug. 24, 1764 *NHG* ₩412.
  'Indulgent God, whose bounteous care.'
  T: 'An Evening Hymn.' ¶ No: 24 lines.
  Note: Crum I 1673.

1996. Sept. 13, 1764 *BNL* ₩3160, 3/2.
  'Foelix ille fuit, qui Rebus (tempore quôdam).'
  T: 'Frugalitas.' ¶ No: 10 lines. ¶ A: 'Valete, Nov-Angli.'

1997. Sept. 24, 1764 *BPB* #371.
    'Sat mihi, quod satyrâ videaris gnavus et asper.'
    T: 'Ad Criticum (in Acrostichiden) nuper jactatem.' ¶ No: 10 lines.

1998. Sept., 1764 *Lon Mag*, XXXIII, 478.
    'Born I was to raging grief.'
    T: 'Another from the same.' [I.e. from Metasasio.] ¶ No: 8 lines. ¶
    A: 'Varignano' [Robert Bolling].

1999. Sept., 1764 *Lon Mag*, XXXIII, 478.
    'Hail mystick art! which men like angels taught.'
    T: 'The Art of Printing, a Poem.' ¶ No: 18 lines. ¶ A: [Robert
    Bolling?]
    Note: Between other poems by Bolling.

2000. Sept., 1764 *Lon Mag*, XXXIII, 478.
    'I shall Lavinia see no more.'
    T: 'Madrigal, attributed to Abbe Chaulieu, imitated, in Memory of
    Mrs. M. Bolling.' ¶ No: 6 lines. ¶ A: [Robert Bolling.]
    Note: Mary (Burton) Bolling was Robert Bolling's wife.

2001. Sept., 1764 *Lon Mag*, XXXIII, 478.
    'Time, in pity to my woes.'
    T: 'Air to be set to Music. From Metasasio.' ¶ No: 8 lines. ¶ A:
    'Varignano' [R. Bolling].
    Note: Reprinted, with music, no. 2012.

2002. Nov. 5, 1764 *NYM* #680, 3/2.
    'Two Bars of a Gate.'
    T: 'A Rebus.' ¶ No: 18 lines.

2003. Nov. 12, 1764 *NYM* #681, 2/3.
    'With Bars and with Grates.'
    T: 'Solution of the Rebus inserted in our last' 'That your charmer's
    Miss B— L—l.' ¶ No: 12 lines.

2004. Nov. 12, 1764 *SCG* #1557, *Supp.*, 4/1–2.
    'Thou enemy to wit!--Thy fatal darts.'
    T: [Dialogue between Apollo and Death, on the death of Robert
    Skiddy, A.B., of Dublin, age 40, who died in Dublin in February.]
    ¶ No: 74 lines. ¶ A: 'W. G.'
    Note: Sent in by 'A gentleman in Charles-Town.'

2005. Nov. 19, 1764 *BEP* #1524, 2/3.
    'I do not expect in a female to find.'
    T: 'The Choice.' ¶ No: 20 lines.
    Note: Copied in B. Wadsworth's Commonplace Book (see no. 988),
    p. 4.

2006. Dec. 10, 1764 *BPB* ₰382, 3/2.
'An easy mein, engaging in Address.'
T: 'The Character.' ¶ No: 16 lines.
Note: Reprinted, no. 2011A.

2007. Dec. 20, 1764 *MG* ₰1024.
'Beneath this stone lies Katharine Gray.'
T: [Epitaph on Katharine Gray.]
Note: The poem is mutilated, but see no. 2013. Crum B319 gives
the title 'Katherine Gray, an old woman, seller of Pots in
Chester.'

2008. Dec. 21, 1764 *No Car Mag* I, ₰29, p. 227.
'O Lord our God arise.'
T: 'The Anthem sung at Chester.' ¶ No: 21 lines.
Note: On Franklin's sailing for England from Chester. The editors
of the *Franklin Papers*, XI, 447, note that this is an adaptation of
'God Save the King.'

2009. Dec. 29, 1764 *Prov G* ₰115, 2/3.
'Long had the World in gloomy Shades.'
T: 'On Christ's Appearance.' ¶ No: 20 lines.
Note: With a prefatory note; accompanies no. 2010.

2010. Dec. 29, 1764 *Prov G* ₰115, 2/3.
'Remark, my Soul, the narrow Bounds.'
T: 'For New Year's Day.' ¶ No: 20 lines.
Note: Accompanies no. 2009.

2011. Dec. 31, 1764 *CC* ₰6, 3/2.
'To us, This Day, a Child is born.'
T: 'The following Hymn was sung in St. Andrew's Church, Syms-
bury, upon Christmas-Day last; being composed [for] that Time
and Place. From Isiah IX, 6 and 7.' ¶ No: 32 lines.
Note: Either the Rev. William Gibbs or the Rev. Roger Viets is the
probable author.

2011A. Dec. 31, 1764 *NM* ₰330, 3/2.
'An easy mien, engaging in address.'
Note: A reprint of 2006.

2012. Dec., 1764 *Lon Mag*, XXXIII, 651.
'Time, in pity to my woes.'
T: 'The Air from Metastasio, Set to Music by W. Atkinson, of
Lincoln.'
Note: A reprint of no. 2001.

1765

2013. Jan. 3, 1765 *MG* ✸1026.
'Beneath this Stone, lies Katharine Gray.'
T: 'Explanation of the Epitaph inserted in one of our last Year's
    Gazettes, No. 1024.' ¶ No: 10 lines.
Note: An anagram. See no. 2007.

2014. Jan. 12, 1765 *Prov G* ✸117, 2/1.
'Nor House, nor Hut, nor Fruitful Field.'
T: [On the hardships of the first settlers.] ¶ No: 12 lines. ¶ A:
    [Gov. Stephen Hopkins?]
Note: On the condition of the first settlers in Providence--in an
    article, 'An Historical Account of the Planting and Growth of
    Providence.' The poem echoes William Bradford's *Of Plymouth
    Plantation*. Reprinted in William Eaton Foster, *Early Attempts at
    Rhode Island History*, R.I. Hist. Soc., *Coll.*, VII (1885), 20–21.
    For Hopkins (1707–1785), author of the article and thus perhaps
    of the poem, see the *DAB*.

2015. Jan. 17, 1765 *PG* ✸1882, 1/2.
'Just now is published some Rhimes.'
T: ['Rhimes Relating to the present times.'] ¶ No: 12 lines.
Note: This is an advertisement for a poetic pamphlet, entitled by
    Hildeburn *Rhymes Relating to the Present Times* (Philadelphia,
    1765); Hildeburn 2164. But no copy is extant. Hildeburn (fol-
    lowed by Evans 10159 and Sabin 70772) probably made up the
    title from this advertisement--but I doubt that the advertisement
    paraphrased the actual title. The advertisement was repeated
    Jan. 24, 1765, 4/1.

2016. Jan. 19, 1765 *Prov G* ✸118, 4/1.
'How can we adore.'
T: 'As CXLIth Psalm.' ¶ No: 24 lines.

2017. Jan. 19, 1765 *Prov Gaz* ✸118, 4/1.
'Ye Wise, instruct me to endure.'
Note: A reprint of no. 924.

2018. Jan. 21, 1765 *BEP* ✸1533, 3/2.
'Pensive I lay, e'en from the dead of Night.'
T: 'Elegy on a Tallow-Candle.' ¶ No: 24 lines. ¶ A: 'W. P.'

2019. Jan. 24, 1765 *BNL* ✸3179, 2/1–2.
'The Prophet's Soul has bid adieu to Earth.'
T: 'Sacred to the Memory of Dr. [Edward] Wigglesworth.' ¶ No:
    118 lines. ¶ A: 'Sympathes' [Joseph Willard].

Note: 'Joseph Willard' has been added in a contemporary manu-
script note to the photostat edition. The reprint reveals that the
author was currently 'a student in the college' (no. 2020). Cf. no.
2026. On Joseph Willard, later President of Harvard, see the
DAB.

2020. Feb. 1, 1765 *NHG* #434.
'The Prophet's Soul has bid adieu to Earth.'
Note: The Author is 'a student in the College.' A reprint of no.
2019.

2021. Feb. 4, 1765 *BG* #514, 1/1.
'When Phebus had withdrawn his genial Rays.'
T: 'Prognosticon, or The Vision.' ¶ No: 52 lines.
Note: Harbottle Door (1730–1794) noted that the poem was 'Sup-
posed to allude to Nat Wheelwright's Failing.' Door, a Boston
businessman, Son of Liberty, and Selectman, kept an annotated
file of Massachusetts newspapers, 1765–1776, which have been
published on microfilm by the Massachusetts Historical Society.

2022. Feb. 4, 1765 *WNYG* #322, 1/4.
'The dry, dull, drowsy *Batchelor* surveys.'
Note: A reprint of no. 1822.

2023. Feb. 11, 1765 *NYM* #694, 2/3.
'Heavenly Friendship, Balm of Woe.'
T: 'To Friendship. An Ode.' ¶ No: 42 lines. ¶ A: 'In the King's
College, in this City, the Students generally have *Liberty*, instead
of a weekly *Latin Theme*, to write a Copy of Latin or English
Verses. On such an Occasion, one of the young Gentlemen, of
only fifteen years of age, wrote the following.'

2024. Feb. 14, 1765 *MG*.
'The very silliest Things in Life.'
T: 'The Spirit of Contradiction. A Tale.' ¶ No: 92 lines. ¶ A: 'R.
Lloyd, M.A.'
Note: On Robert Lloyd (1733–1764), see the *CBEL*, II, 370.

2025. Feb. 18, 1765 *BEP* #1537, 3/1.
'In Youth's fair days, when first our infant love.'
T: 'Epistle from a Gentleman in Town to his Wife in the Country,
retired on account of the Small-Pox (last Winter).' ¶ No: 44
lines.

2026. Mar. 4, 1765 *BEP* #1539, 1/2.
'Wherefore this change ?--'
T: 'On the Death of the Rev. Doctor Wigglesworth; written Tues-
day February 19th 1765, the day on which the Doctor used to

read his public lectures.' ¶ No: 47 lines. ¶ A: 'Philophron.' ['by a
student of the College, in his second year there, and the 16th of
his age.']

Note: Cf. no. 2019.

2027. Mar. 4, 1765 *BPB* ⚹394.
    'Thus Adam look'd, from the Garden driven.'
    T: 'The following Lines were spoken Extempore by a Gentleman
    lately desired to quit the Presence of a young Lady with whom he
    was greatly in Love.' ¶ No: 6 lines. ¶ A: 'John Damon.'
    Note: Dated 'Newport, R.I., Feb. 25, 1765.' Reprinted no. 2029.
    Crum T2524 attributed this to Sir William Young (1749–1815),
    evidently in error.

2028. Mar. 7, 1765 *MG*.
    'Calm, tho' not mean, courageous without Rage.'
    T: 'Inscription on a Dog.' ¶ No: 14 lines.

2029. Mar. 8, 1765 *NHG* ⚹439.
    'Thus Adam look'd, from the Garden driven.'
    Note: A reprint of no. 2027.

2030. Mar. 18, 1765 *BPB* ⚹396.
    ''Twas on the Day, our great Convention met.'
    T: 'The *Contrast*, or rather *Battle*, between Ariell and Umbriell,
    and their Auxiliaries.' ¶ No: 38 lines.
    Note: The poet uses Pope's *Rape of the Lock* to satirize Massachu-
    setts politics. Reprinted, no. 2034.

2030A. Mar. 21, 1765 *GG* ⚹103, 2/2.
    'Too often name and thing are distant far.'
    T: 'The Mourning.' ¶ No: 33 lines. ¶ A: 'n. m. y.'
    Note: Dated 'Savannah, March 21.'

2031. Mar. 23, 1765 *SCG* ⚹1576, 2/3.
    'Happy *Pompey!* which can be.'
    T: 'Ode to Pompey, A Puppy, playing with *Constantia* in Bed. In
    Imitation of Metastasio.' ¶ No: 36 lines. ¶ A: 'Veramor' [Robert
    Bolling?].
    Note: Bolling wrote numerous imitations of Metastasio.

2032. Mar. 25, 1765 *CC* ⚹18, 1/1.
    'Since Life's a dear precarious Thing.'
    T: 'To the Public.' ¶ No: 61 lines. ¶ A: 'Philopacis.'
    Note: Dated 'Hartford.'

2033. Apr. 1, 1765 *CC* ⚹19, 3/2.
    'Three Fourths of a Weed, universally known.'
    T: 'A Rebus.' ¶ No: 10 lines.
    Note: Dated 'Hartford, March 29, 1765.'

2034. May 3, 1765 *NHG* #447.
'"Twas on the day, our great *Convention* met.'
Note: A reprint of no. 2030.

2035. May 13, 1765 *BEP* #1549, 2/1.
'And Jemmy is a silly dog, and Jemmy is a fool.'
T: 'Jemmibullero: A Fragment of an Ode of Orpheus; Freely Trans-
lated from the original Tongue, and adopted to British Music.' ¶
No: 48 lines plus 2-line refrain. ¶ A: 'Peter Minim' [Samuel
Waterhouse].
Note: Shipton, XI, 263–4, in his account of James Otis, attributes
the poem to Waterhouse. Shipton also notes that the poem was
reprinted as a ballad in New York: Evans 10426. The poem at-
tacks 'Jemmy' Otis. Cf. no. 2036. For an earlier parody of Otis,
see no. 1922.

2036. May 20, 1765 *BEP* #1550, 3/2.
'As quick as Lightning's winged Beam.'
T: 'Stanzas meditated in the Thunder Storm succeeding the last
Election of Deputies.' ¶ No: 16 lines.
Note: On James Otis, cf. no. 2035.

2037. May 27, 1765 *BG* #530, *Sup.* 2/2.
'Ecce Leo lucis habitans impastus opacis.'
T: 'Fabula Neotreicu vel Dialogus Inter Leonem et Murem.' ¶ No:
24 lines.

2038. May, 1765 *Lon Mag*, XXXIV, 259.
'The north-east wind did briskly blow.'
T: 'Bryan and Pereene. A West-Indian Ballad. Founded on a real
Fact, that happened in The Island of St. Christopher's about two
years ago.' ¶ No: 56 lines.
Note: Reprinted, no. 2091 (with added phrase 'from Reliques of
ancient English Poetry'). Crum T1093.

2039. June 13, 1765 *PJ* #1175, 1/2.
'"Tis done--Your patient ear we greet no more.'
T: 'Dialogue, Air, and Chorus at the Commencement in the College
of Philadelphia, May 30th, 1765.' ¶ No: 73 lines. ¶ A: [Richard
Peters.]
Note: Hildeburn 2159 [Richard Peters], *Dialogue, &c For the Com-
mencement* ... [Phila., 1765], notes: 'The original manuscript in the
author's handwriting is in the possession of D. McN. Stauffer.'
Reprinted, nos. 2040, 2052, 2053.

2040. June 13, 1765 *PG* #1903, 2/3–3/1.
'"Tis done--Your patient Ear we greet no more.'
Note: See no. 2039.

2041. June 17, 1765 *BEP* #1554, 3/2.
'When here, Lucinda, first we came.'
T: 'Arno's Vale.' ¶ No: 16 lines.

2042. July 4, 1765 *NYG* #1174, 3/3.
'Since Terms are confounded, & Words on the Rack.'
T: 'An Essay on the Virtues of the Word Virtue or Virtual.' ¶ No:
56 lines.
Note: A satire on the 'Virtual' representation of Americans in Parliament. Reprinted, nos. 2044, 2086.

2043. July 15, 1765 *BEP* #1558.
'Once warm with Zeal in honest Virtue's Cause.'
T: 'Written Extempore, on hearing of the Death of Oxenbridge
Thacher, Esq; on a Supposed View of the Corps.' ¶ No: 14 lines.
¶ A: 'S. Y.'
Note: The elegy follows Thacher's obituary notice. Reprinted, nos.
2046, 2047, 2051. Reprinted in Shipton's sketch of Thacher, X,
327.

2044. July 15, 1765 *BPB* #413, 2/3.
'Since Terms are confounded, & Words on the Rack.'
Note: A reprint of no. 2042.

2045. July 18, 1765 *BNL* #3204, 3/1.
'Thy worth, blest spirit, claims my humble lays.'
T: 'To the memory of that late Friend to Liberty and valuable Member of Society, Joseph Green, Esq; who departed this Life, July
the 1st, 1765, Aet. 62 by an intimate Friend.' ¶ No: 46 lines.
Note: This is Joseph Green (1701–1765), son of the Rev. Joseph
Green (Harvard, 1695), and not to be confused with the Boston
poet, Joseph Green.

2046. July 18, 1765 *BNL* #3204, 3/2.
'Once warm with Zeal in honest Virtue's Cause.'
Note: A reprint of no. 2043.

2047. July 19, 1765 *NHG* #458.
'Once warm with Zeal in honest Virtue's Cause.'
Note: A reprint of no. 2043.

2048. July 22, 1765 *CC* #35, 3/1.
'Sol, in the East, from Neptune's watry Bed.'
T: 'Copy of a Letter.' ¶ No: 70 lines. ¶ A: 'Somniator.'

2049. July 25, 1765 *PG* #1909.
'In sorrowing Verse to mourn the pious Dead.'
T: 'Elegy Sacred to the Memory of Dr. Edward Young.' ¶ No: 84
lines. ¶ A: 'T. H.'

2049A. Aug. 2, 1765 *VG*.
'With thee fair maid thy merit dies.'
T: 'Old Maiden-age. To a single Lady.' ¶ No: 42 lines. ¶ A: [Robert Bolling.]
Note: Although this issue of the *VG* is not extant, the poem, with the note 'Printed in the Virginia Gazette Aug. 2, 1765,' is in Robert *Bolling's* 'La Gazzetta di Parnaso' (see no. 1561), pp. 15–16. There are four prefatory lines from Tasso. A revised, enlarged reprint of no. 1880C.

2050. Aug. 19, 1765 *BPB* #418, 3/3.
'Snow, Hail, and Rains descend from wintry clouds.'
T: 'Elegy XV.' ¶ No: 27 lines.
Note: 'the following Translation of an Elegy in the *Pietas et Grat. Col. Cantab. Nov. Aug.* ... being the only Greek Performance in that Collection.'

2051. Aug. 1, 1765 *CG*.
'Once warm with Zeal in honest Virtue's Cause.'
Note: A reprint of no. 2043.

2052. Aug., 1765 *Lon Mag*, XXXIV, 429–30.
'Tis done--your patient ear we greet no more.'
Note: A reprint of no. 2039.

2053. Aug., 1765 *Scots Mag*, XXVII, 434.
''Tis done--your patient ear we greet no more.'
Note: A reprint of no. 2039.

2054. Aug., 1765 *Universal Mag*, XXXVII, 97–8.
'Adieu, my fair! this hapless day.'
T: 'The Parting. La Parterza. From Metastasio.' ¶ No: 42 lines. ¶ A: [Robert Bolling ?]

2055. Sept. 6, 1765 *CG* #480, 3/2.
'He who for a Post, or base sordid Pelf.'
T: [On Dr. Thomas Moffat & Martin Howard, Jr., sailing for England]. ¶ No: 16 lines plus refrain.
Note: Refrain: 'Sing Tentara, burn all, burn all.' Revolutionary American poetry, resulting from the Stamp Act. Reprinted, no. 2056, 2057 (with a testimony to its popularity). Reprinted in the Mass. Hist. Soc. *Proceedings*, LV (1921–22), 234–237; it was included in a letter from William Almy to Elisha Story, dated Newport, August 29, 1765, which told of the hanging in effigy of Martin Howard and Dr. Thomas Moffat. It is listed by Arthur M. Schlesinger, 'A Note on Songs as Patriot Propaganda,' *William and Mary Quarterly*, XI (1954), 82.

2056. Sept. 6, 1765 *NHG* ⋕465.
    'He who for a Post, or base sordid Pelf.'
    Note: A reprint of no. 2055.

2057. Sept. 9, 1765 *NYM* ⋕724, 3/2.
    'He who for a Post, or base sordid Pelf.'
    Note: 'The following Song has been sung thro' the Streets of New-
        port and Boston.' A reprint of no. 2055.

2058. Sept. 13, 1765 *CG* ⋕481, 2/3.
    'Behold a Giant vile and base.'
    T: [Anti-Stamp Act.] ¶ No: 16 lines. ¶ A: 'Antonius.'
    Note: Reprinted, no. 2059.

2059. Sept. 23, 1765 *BEP* ⋕1567, 3/1.
    'Behold a Giant vile and base.'
    Note: A reprint of no. 2058.

2060. Sept. 27, 1765 *CG* ⋕483.
    'I am inform'd that it is said.'
    T: 'A Parody.' ¶ No: 75 lines.
    Note: Harbottle Door (see no. 2021) explains that this is a parody
        on Gov. Bernard's speech, published in *BEP*, Sept. 9, 1765. Re-
        printed, nos. 2061, 2061A, 2064.

2061. Sept. 30, 1765 *BG* ⋕548, 3/1.
    'I am inform'd that it is said.'
    Note: A reprint of no. 2060.

2061A. Sept. 30, 1765 *NM* ⋕369, 2/1.
    'I am inform'd that it is said.'
    Note: A reprint of 2060.

2062. Sept., 1765 *Lon Mag*, XXXIV, 478–9.
    'Colour apart--beneath yon Turf doth lie.'
    T: 'An Elegy on Miss B's Juliet, a Negro Girl, who died in Barba-
        does, Dec. 24, 1764, at less than eight years of Age.' ¶ No: 55
        lines.

2063. Oct. 3, 1765 *HG* ⋕223, 2/2.
    'Would you take the morning Air.'
    T: 'The Morning Air.' ¶ No: 16 lines. ¶ A: 'Compos'd by Mr.
        Granom.'

2064. Oct. 4, 1765 *NLG* ⋕99, 2/3.
    'I am inform'd that it is said.'
    Note: A reprint of no. 2060.

2064A. Oct. 7, 1765 *PM* #38, 1/2–3.
'In Days of yore and pious Times.'
T: 'The Silver Age, A Lilliputian Tale.' ¶ No: 85 lines. ¶ A: 'Quinbas Flestrin.' [William Parker, Jun.]
Note: Sent in by 'T. Q.' ['William Parker jun'—contemporary manuscript note, Mass. Hist. Soc. copy.] Judge William Parker (1731–1813) graduated from Harvard in 1751; see Shipton, XIII, 121–124. Jeremy Belknap copied this into his Commonplace Book B (unnumbered pages in the back), Mass. Hist. Soc. The poem satirizes Gov. Benning Wentworth's appointment of unqualified magistrates.

2065. Oct. 14, 1765 *BEP* #1570, 2/1–2.
'One Night as I lay slumb'ring in my Bed.'
T: [A 'Dream' on the Stamp Act.] ¶ No: 154 lines. ¶ A: 'B. C.' [Benjamin Church].
Note: Reprinted, nos. 2065A, 2067. Harbottle Door (see no. 2021) noted that 'B. C.' was Benjamin Church.

2065A. Oct. 21, 1765 *PM* #40, 1/1–2.
'One Night as I lay slumb'ring in my Bed.'
Note: A reprint of 2065.

2066. Oct. 24, 1765 *HG* #226, 2/1.
'Genteel is my Damon, engaging his air.'
T: '... The following copy of verses is handed about, said to be the production of the greatest lady in this nation, and will serve (if so) not only to convince us of her extraordinary proficiency in the English language, but also the greatness of her natural genius.' ¶ No: 16 lines. ¶ A: 'The greatest lady in this nation.'

2067. Oct. 25, 1765 *NHG* #473, 1/2–2/1.
'One Night as I lay slumb'ring in my Bed.'
Note: A reprint of no. 2065.

2068. Oct. 31, 1765 *BNL* #3239, Extra, 1/3.
'Amid this loud Clamour.'
T: 'Advice from the Country.' ¶ No: 78 lines.
Note: This 'Song sung at Boston' advocates thrift as a patriotic act. It is noted by Schlesinger (see no. 2055), p. 82. Reprinted, no. 2090.

2069. Nov. 4, 1765 *BG* #553.
'What, Brother H[anco]ck this is bad ?'
T: [Libel on 'J[oh]n H[anco]ck.] ¶ No: 14 lines.
Note: Reprinted, no. 2071.

2070. Nov. 4, 1765 *BG* #553.
'Your Servant Sirs, do you like my Figure?'
T: [Libel on 'G[*eor*]ge G[*re*]nv[*il*]le.'] ¶ No: 10 lines.
Note: Reprinted, no. 2072.

2071. Nov. 4, 1765 *BPB* #429, *Extra.*
'What Brother H—k? why is this bad?'
Note: A reprint of no. 2069.

2072. Nov. 4, 1765 *BPB* #429, *Extra.*
'Your servant Sirs! do you like my Figure?'
Note: A reprint of no. 2070.

2073. Nov. 7, 1765 *HG* #228, 2/3.
'With joy, sweet Rosalind, we hear.'
T: 'Poetry. To a Young Lady, on her fine Ear for Music.' ¶ No: 20
lines.

2074. Nov. 7, 1765 *NYG* #1192, 1/2–3.
'Some Twelve months ago.'
T: 'Old Ballad on the Fifth of November.' ¶ No: 78 lines. ¶ A:
'Communicative.' [Philip Hawkins].
Note: Crum S1010 attributes the poem to Hawkins (c. 1725–1798).

2075. Nov. 14, 1765 *HG* #225.
'An open heart, a generous mind.'
T: 'The Rake.' ¶ No: 27 lines. ¶ A: 'By a Lady in New England.'
Note: A reprint from Robert Dodsley's *Collection of Poems by
Several Hands* (London, 1758), IV, 318. Crum A1226.

2076. Nov. 21, 1765 *HG* #230, 2/3.
'If I am doom'd the marriage chain to wear.'
T: 'On the Choice of a Husband.' ¶ No: 18 lines. ¶ A: 'By a young
Lady.'
Note: Crum I809.

2077. Nov. 21, 1765 *HG* #230.
'Jehovah is my sole support.'
T: 'The 23d Psalm paraphras'd.' ¶ No: 24 lines.

2078. Nov. 25, 1765 *BG* #556, 2/1–2.
'Gentlemen of the C—l and of the H—se.'
T: 'A Speech.' ¶ No: 143 lines. ¶ A: 'B. F.'
Note: This parodies Gov. Francis Bernard's speech of Nov. 8, 1765,
printed in the *BG*, Nov. 11, 1765, 2/1–2. Reprinted, no. 2087.

2078A. Nov. 25, 1765, 4/1.
'Eaton so fam'd, so wise, so meek, so just.'

T: 'Inscription on a tomb Stone at New Haven in This Colony.' ¶
No: 6 lines.
Note: On Gov. Theophilus Eaton (d. Jan. 7, 1657/8).

2079. Nov. 28, 1765 *HG* #231, 2/2.
'England, for martial Deeds renown'd.'
Note: A reprint of no. 1893.

2080. Nov. 28, 1765 *HG* #231.
'Enrag'd with *Delia's* coy disdain.'
T: 'The Lover's Resolution.' ¶ No: 40 lines.

2081. Nov. 28, 1765 *HG* #231.
'Stay passenger, and spend a Tear.'
T: 'An Accrostic Epitaph.' ¶ No: 17 lines.
Note: On Sussannah Tellcock.

2082. Nov. 28, 1765 *HG* #231.
'When *Delia* shews her beauteous face.'
T: 'A Song.' ¶ No: 16 lines.

2083. Nov., 1765 *Gent Mag*, XXXV, 526.
'While in a soft Savannah's cool retreat.'
T: 'An Indian's Speech to his Countrymen.' ¶ No: 101 lines. ¶ A:
'An Idler.'
Note: 'Imitated from the Second Vol. of the *Idler*.' Samuel Johnson's
Idler No. 81 appeared Nov. 3, 1759.

2084. Dec. 2, 1765 *BG* #657, 2/3.
'Spurn the Relation--She's no more a Mother.'
T: [3 epigrams, revolutionary sentiment, dated 'America, Nov'r
1765.'] ¶ No: 10 lines. ¶ A: 'Bostoniensis.'

2085. Dec. 2, 1765 *NYM* #736, 2/3.
'Great Pitt, hast thou in Pity to our Nation.'
T: [On Pitt.] ¶ No: 29 lines.
Note: '[The Printer was paid for inserting the following Piece.]'

2086. Dec. 5, 1765 *HG* #232.
'Since terms are confounded, & Words on the Rock.'
Note: A reprint of no. 2042.

2087. Dec. 9, 1765 *WNYG* #395, 4/2-3.
'Gentlemen of the Council and of the House.'
T: '[His Excellency Bernardus Francisco's Speech versify'd--Note,
Where some Lines are short in their proper Measure, there are
others long enough to make amends.]'
Note: A reprint of no. 2078.

2088. Dec. 23, 1765 *BEP* ⋕1580, 2/1.
'Until th' important day, the day when truth.'
T: [Attack on 'Stultus Minds.'] ¶ No: 10 lines. ¶ A: 'Y. Z.'

2089. Dec. 30, 1765 *BG* ⋕561.
'It must be so--my Sons ye reason well!'
T: 'Cato's Soliloquy imitated. Scene the Senate House in B—n.

America Sola, sitting a thoughtful Posture: In her Hand the R—s—lves of the H—se. The S—p A–t on the Table by her.' ¶ No: 31 lines. ¶ A: 'T. T.'
Note: Another attack on the Stamp Act.

2090. Dec., 1765 *Gent Mag* XXXV, 591 [i.e., 575].
'Amid this load clamour.'
Note: A reprint of no. 2068.

2091. 1765 *Annual Register*, pp. 292–4.
'The north-east wind did briskly blow.'
Note: A reprint of no. 2068.

Indexes

First Line Index

A

A Bag-wig of a jauntee air, 1247.
A British Admiral, of late, assign'd, 1098.
A common Theme a flatt'ring Muse may fire, 189, 216.
A Country Spark, addressing charming She, 1132.
A Dexter'ous Trader of the Town, 1580.
A Dog impleads a Sheep, pretends a Debt, 931.
A Doctor sent to me his darling son, 1834.
A famous Prophet in this year appears, 332.
A famous Title now you boast on, 19.
A Gentleman of a spotless Character, 1051, 1052, 1576.
A Gentleman whilst walking in his Ground, 632.
A God there is, the whole Creation Tells, 854, 1578.
A Good repute, a virtuous name, 398.
A Grand Court conven'd on important occasion, 1808.
A Grub street bard is hen coop'd twice sev'n days, 1916.
A Holy Friar, as Tis said, 1674.
A Kid, an heifer, and a lambkin mild, 1220, 1231.
A Lottery, like a magic spell, 1859, 1860.
A Man of Wisdom may disguise, 640, 801.
A Monarch in my rustic bower, 919, 1905.
A Monkey, to reform the Times, 642.
A Muskito just starv'd, in a sorry condition, 672.
A Neat quaker girl in her Sabbeth-day gown, 1489.
A New Creation charms the ravish'd light, 434, 436.
A Pipe of strong and sparkling Wine, 1003.
A Port there was where Wormwood knew, 791.
A Poor man once a judge besought, 1431.
A Princely huntsman once did live, 1716.
A Pritty Bird did lately please my sight, 263.
A Ship of War, a Second Rate, 1827.
A Shrouded Corpse! ah me, who yonder lies, 1933.
A Slice of pudding, once, a man divine, 688.
A Speech there is, which no Man spoke, 1993.
A, stands for *Andrew*, the Saint so renown'd, 299, 301.
A Swain who musing on the various cares, 244, 321.
A Table, Chairs, and pair of Bellows, 337.
A Term full as long as the Siege of Old Troy, 1896.
A Town fear'd a Siege, and held Consultation, 673.
A Tract of Land of vast Extent, 29.
A Trout, the plumpest in the Tide, 988, 1117.
A Vehicle by love employ'd, 1781.
A wak'ning Thought! Must Time expire indeed, 1264.
A Worthy merchant in wealth did so abound, 1154.
A Wretch who Triumphs o'er her Neighbours Woe, 1074.
A Year of Wonders now behold, 671.
Accept, dear Jens, this humble Chair, 1161.
Accept, Dear Ma'am, the fabled lay, 977.
Accept, great shade, the Tribute of a lay, 759.
Accept, my Dear, 1766.
Accept, O Lloyd, the Tribute of a Muse, 1143A.

Accomplish'd *Gurney* charms my ravish'd ear, 435.
Active spark of heav'nly Fire, 1001.
Ad Jovis arbitrium referunt duo numina causam, 1487.
Adieu, my fair! this hapless day, 2054.
Adieu native plains, where blithsome I've rov'd, 731.
Adieu! Thou Saint of God, Adieu, 616, 637.
Admitting that you have been arch, 1079.
Adventus vester cunctes gratissimus hic est, 893.
Aequore germanos glacies infida relinquens, 79.
Aenigma knotters, rebus cooks, 1873A.
Again fair Nymph, you Charm our wond'ring Eyes, 89.
Again the blossom'd hedge is seen, 1769.
Again the pictur'd page displays, 1164.
Against my Negro man nam'd Parris, 291.
Ages our Land a barb'rous Desert stood, 131, 133.
Agrippa next, a Bard unknown to Fame, 242.
Ah! *Braddock* why did you persuade, 1284.
Ah me! What horrid Noise is this! Tis sure, 1317.
Ah me! what sorrows are we born to bear, 1658, 1862.
Ah, modest M[oorh----]d, vain are all, 667.
Aid me Phoebus, aid me ye sacred nine, 344, 346.
Alas! how am I chang'd! Revolving Suns, 1967.
Alas, how frail is Man! ah hapless Race, 1169.
Alas poor Shad, 124.
Alas, poor Soul! Those youthful Days are fled, 50.
Alas! whilst aching pains declare, 741.
All attendants, apart, 336.
All bounteous Nature! in the varied Year, 809.
All gracious Heaven, how intricate Thy Ways, 1205, 1206, 1207, 1212.
All Hail, My Sons, who can so justly trace, 176.
All Hail, O Hind! Heav'n safe Thy Charge convey, 1709, 1710.
All hail, ye Fields, where constant Peace attends, 428.
All hail, ye great *Preservers* of our Land, 1311.
All human Bliss we liken to a Span, 1869A.
All Men have Follies, which they blindly trace, 211.
All Night invoking sleep's balsamic Dew, 1340.
All on that Main, the verdant Trees abound, 1138.
All Things, beneath the Circle of the Sun, 1527.
All which, by full Experience plain doth show, 101.
Alluring *Profit* with *Delight* we blend, 1480.
Almighty Archer of the Skies, 1177.
Almighty Monarch! How Thy glorious Name, 370.
Aloft in air, the bright Astraea sat, 1667, 1750, 1770.
Along the main, 1673.
Along the Road, as, in an open Chair, 1062, 1065.
Amherst, while Crowds attend you on your Way, 1529, 1536, 1537, 1540, 1552.
Amid this loud Clamour, 2068, 2090.
Amidst the vast Profusious of Delight, 266.
Amidst these Io'Peans of the crowd, 724.
Amidst these loud acclaims which rend the sky, 1752.
Amidst these Triumphs, This excess of joy, 1657.
Among some Roses, with dull Sleep opprest, 466
Among the Divines there has been much Debate, 660.
An amorous youth inclining to wed, 1395.

An Ass once left his master's home, 1819.
An austere Sage, in ancient days, 1609.
An easy mein, engaging in address, 2006, 2011A.
An humble Muse resumes the plantive Strain, 1345.
An humble muse, unus'd to rude alarms, 1786, 1790, 1813.
An Irish Mungrel, lately Run away, 320.
An open heart, a generous mind, 2075.
And art thou gone? Fly swift thou baneful Star, 1976.
And did the Omnipotent, Eternal Mind, 1139.
And has Charissa her whole Heav'n of Charms, 478.
And is old *Merrymak* come to an End, 371.
And is Pope gone?--Then mourn ye Britons! mourn, 779.
And is the Infant snacht away, 727.
And is This all, one poor unfinish'd Lay, 1797, 1804.
And Jemmy is a silly dog, and Jemmy is a fool, 2035.
And live we yet by Power Divine, 1312.
And must God's Truth, the Glory of our Land, 1994.
And must thou go? Farewell thou sacred Guide, 1975, 1976A, 1980.
And sure this is the age of gold, 1830B.
And why, my friend, these melting tears, 894.
Another gone! how thick the arrows fly, 1818.
Another Sun!--'Tis true;--but not the Same, 765.
Anxious and Trembling for the future Hour, 590.
Apollo's Sons, where'er the Wealthy die, 1026, 1029.
Arah, dear joy, suave all your faushes, 349.
Argo, that ship renown'd of ancient Greece, 968.
Arise! and see the morning sun, 1410.
Arise, and soar, my tow'ring soul, 747.
Arise, Britannia, from the Dust arise, 1878.
Arise! my Muse, extend thy trembling wing, 644.
Arise my Muse, salute the dawning Day, 1225.
Arra Joy! My monthly Macasheen shall contain Sheets four, 610.
Artful Painter, by this Plan, 1304, 1310.
Artist, that underneath my Table, 275.
As blustering Winds disturb the calmest Sea, 462.
As Bob was a reeling one night, full of drink, 1675.
As Cloe with affected Air, 1403, 1405.
As *Damon* one Day with his fair One was sate, 1163.
As Fame of late in merry Mood, 1924.
As Grain with latent Fire well fraught, 1898.
As it is the Fashion in quiet Times, 940.
As late I mus'd on fortune's ebb and flow, 917.
As late I stray'd on H--m--d's lonsome Plain, 1091, 1092, 1111.
As many People now-a-days, 969, 970.
As mornful *Philomel* the Groves supply, 855.
As, near *Porto Bello* lying, 593.
As nigh a river's silver stream, 891.
As once in Solyma, the sacred Town, 756.
As once the Shame of *Gath* with impious Boast, 87.
As quick as Lightning's winged Beam, 2036.
As Sir Toby reel'd home, with skin full of wine, 394.
As soon as the bless'd Sabbeth dawns, and all, 601.
As soon as to the Temple you retire, 650.
As sounding Brass and Tinkling Cymbals ring, 441.

As stormy Winds disturb the calmest Sea, 471.
As th' Eagle soaring in the lofty Skies, 786A, 789.
As thro' the Waves the faithless Shepherd bore, 1573.
As we appear unto Beholders, 910.
As when the winds from ev'ry corner blow, 1509.
As whilom roving o'er the lonely Plain, 1127.
As Wolfe all glorious lately stood, 1806.
Aspiring men (swell'd with ambition) rose, 43.
Asseris in Satyrâ atroci ta velle Magistrum, 1280.
Assist me, Muse divine, 1828.
Assist, my muse, while I with fear relate, 710.
Assist, ye greater Bards assist, 1303.
At Delaware's broad Stream, the View begin, 117.
At length our fine winter for spring has made way, 1135.
At length the wintry horrors disappear, 184, 187, 198, 215, 252A, 254, 258.
At length Tis done! The glorious conflict's done, 1473.
At length we see the Day auspicious shine, 308.
At Midnight when the Fever rag'd, 262.
At Milton, near the Paper-Mill, 271.
At Ten this Morn, Dear Friend, *Your most*, 100.
At Tu iterum Trucidas P. M. sarcasticé cantat, 1267.
At Will, while *Fortune* turns the wheel, 964.
Attend! and favour! as our fires ordain, 1559.
Attend ye Fair, Calliope the Song, 798.
Attwood, while those, whose yearly Thousands bring, 324.
Auspicious *Chiefs*, your great Designs pursue, 586, 606.
Awake, Britannia's Guardian Pow'r, 592.
Awake, my heart! awake, my lyre, 1400.
Awake, my Soul, your Haleluyahs sing, 1109.
Awake O Arnold from Thy drousie Den, 554.
Away great Johnson, and each worn-out Theme, 1641.
Awful Hero, Cato, rise, 431.

B

Be all thy Labours, all thy Cares pursu'd, 1322, 1325.
Be still, nor anxious Thoughts employ, 1744.
Beat on proud Billows! Boreas blow, 537.
Beauteous Venus Queen of Love, 645.
Beauty like heaven's various bow, 1524.
Begin, begin the sorrow-soothing theme, 1949.
Begin, just *Satyr*, lash those who pretend, 217.
Begin, my Muse, but softly sing, 735.
Begin the high celestial Strain, 536, 1842.
Begin, ye Muses, that delight to rove, 564.
Behold a Giant vile and base, 2058, 2059.
Behold how gay the flow'ry mead, 1584.
Behold how Papal Wright with Lordly Pride, 391.
Behold the Lillies and the gorgeous Flowers, 1903.
Behold the Prophet in the awful Shade, 1940.
Behold the Sons of Antichristian Saul, 33.
Behold the wond'rous Power of Art, 1125.
Belcher, once more permit the muse you lov'd, 457.
Believe my Sighs and Tears my Dear, 1915.
Beneath an aged *holm?*, whose arms had made, 1047.

Beneath some *Indian* shrub, if chance you spy, 1268, 1270.
Beneath the baleful Yews unfruitful Shade, 294.
[Beneath this stone lies Katherine Gray], 2007, 2013.
Beneath yon Turf lies *Gamble's* dust, 1603, 1937A.
Berkley, farewell,--on Earth an honour'd Name, 1133.
Beware, fond Youths, of Nymphs deceitful Charms, 9.
Bless'd are the dead, when dying in the Lord, 1910.
Bless'd in himself, no dangers move, 780.
Bless'd Liberty! how absolute Thy pow'r, 1754.
Blest husbandman! where horny hands have Till'd, 326.
Blest Leaf, whose aromatick Gales dispense, 414.
Blest martyr, for whose fate, 397, 400.
Blest thought! from whence proceeds this joy, 1771.
Blest Youth! whose Soul, with genuine Virtue warm, 1679.
Bold Heroes, who undaunted dare engage, 639.
Born I was to raging grief, 1998.
Boscaw'n, that great auspicious Name, 1617.
Both man and chylde is glad to here tell, 885.
Brethren, this comes to let you know, 704.
Bridges! whene'er thy *Little World* we view, 1298, 1305, 1321.
Bright *Hymen* now the pleasing Knot has Ty'd, 764.
Bright source of bliss! whose chearing rays inspire, 1725.
Britain, lament! How great thy Cause of Woe, 1031.
Britannia, from her rocky seat, 1792.
Britannia mourns her youthful hero slain, 1510.
Britannia strove a Carthage to gain, 780B, 782, 784, 785.
Britannia Triumphs; yet her eyes o'erflow, 1497.
Britons! attend the song, 1650.
Britons rejoice at Heav'n's indulgent Smile, 1481, 1498, 1502.
Britons, the work of war is done, 1690, 1729A, 1730, 1743.
Brittan I mourn! Great Wolfe in Arms no more, 1660, 1683.
Bullies, like Dunghill cocks, will strut and Crow, 22.
Burnet, To Thee the daring Muse would sing, 92.
But lest you think me deaf or rude, 565.
By Base retreat how were those honours stain'd, 1666, 1748.
By various arts we thus attempt to please, 356.
By what I know and ye perceive, 518.
Byfield beneath in peaceful slumber lies, 264, 268.

C

Cain, the first Murd'rer, when from Eden driven, 813.
Calm, tho' not mean, courageous without Rage, 2028.
Calmly repos'd upon a pleasant Green, 892, 1021.
Can you suppose ill Language will prevail, 722.
Candide doctarum praeses, Cytharaede, sororum, 638.
Candidus, ah! Sociis grato officiusus Amico, 655.
Captain *Whole-Bones* is come in, 643, 646.
Carmina me poscis? dare vellem, sed neque sacri, 1409.
Carmina num redolent vigilem, Sterline, Lucernam, 1394.
Celestial Maid, whom endless Smiles adorn, 1143.
Charmer of a lonesome hour, 899.
Chearful, fearless and at ease, 1630, 1640.
Ciel, grand Gouverneur, ne vous avoct fuit naitre, 419.
Circe has a daughter fair, 1953.

Clamavit Phoebus, sibi quae nunc arrogat Harpax, 1506.
Cloe, her naked breast display'd, 1753.
Clos'd are those Eyes, that beam'd Seraphic Fire, 138, 150.
Cold as the Arctick Pole in Winter Time, 243.
Colour apart—beneath you Turf doth lie, 2062.
Come, chear up, my lads, to our country be firm, 1930.
Come deck, you drooping Nine, your Fav'rite's Herse, 739, 745.
Come from the House of Grief, let us my Friend, 1057.
Come, heav'nly pensive Contemplation, come, 1837.
Come hither, *Friend*, who like with me to rove, 1196.
Come! let Mirth our hours employ, 1483.
Come, let us join our God to bless, 658.
Come on ye Critics, find one Fault who dare, 1061.
Come, see this Edifice in Ruin lye, 965.
Come, ye great spirits, Cavendish, Raleigh, Blake, 1235.
Come ye whose Souls harmonious sounds inspire, 763.
Compassion proper to our Sex appears, 306.
Conceal the flame, dear Charmer, from the Swain, 333.
Contented thus I lead a rural Life, 531.
Continual Wars I wage without Expence, 715.
Cosby the Mild, the happy, good and great, 284.
Could I but emulate thy glorious Strain, 28.
Cou'd I the grateful Tribute pay, 213.
Could lays harmonious speak thy high desert, 1644, 1662.
Criticks avaunt! Tobacco is my Theme, 415.
Critics in Verse, as Squibs on Triumphs waif, 1077.
Curiosity's another name for Man, 1973, 1974.
Curs'd be the wretch, that's bought, 1535.
Custom, alas! doth partial prove, 425, 690.

D

Dame *Law*, to maintain a more flourishing State, 426.
Damon, no more implore the fair, 659.
Damon Thy look presages me no good, 511.
Dear Charmers! with meleodious Strains, 1075.
Dear Collen prevent my warm Flushes, 443, 452.
Dear Echo, answer me, 'Tis Louis who speaks, 1700.
Dear Echo reply, 'Tis I Louis that speak, 1703, 1729.
Dear Kitty! now my Counsel take, 677.
Dear Miss, of Custom you complain, 692.
Dear nymph! in vain has *Ramsay* shown his art, 1224.
Dear Nymph, the Single say of thee, 11.
Dear Polly, yes: My days with thee, 1954.
Dear Sir, 'tis with pleasure the following I write, 1333.
Dear to each Muse, and to thy Country dear, 1404, 1412.
Dear Tom, this brown Jug, that now foams with wild ale, 1777.
Death's Iron Jav'lins thro' the Globe are hurl'd, 1947.
Descend, Contentment! from thy seat above, 1158.
Descend my Muse to sing the noble Fray, 696, 699, 700.
Descend, Urania, and inspire my verse, 721, 725, 727A, 728.
Dick join'd in nuptial Conjugation, 863.
Die mihi, musa, virum saccli qui gloria nostri, 569.
Disease malignant fills the Air, 1719.
Distracted with Care, 222.

Father of All! in every Age, 510.
Fathers, Friends, Fellow-Citizens and Countrymen, 1922.
Fear God, Honour the King, 342.
Fear not, you've conquer'd your undaunted Foes, 767.
Feeble and tuneless are my native Lays, 1282.
First form'd and bred within some musing brain, 1396.
First, in these fields, I sport in rural strains, 1725A.
First lay some Onions to keep the Pork from burning, 1046, 1048.
Five times ten Miles from Town, a clyme there lies, 111.
Flavia complains of dull Restraint, 629.
Fleet! Spread thy Canvass Wing, 1390, 1392.
Fly hence ambition far from hence be gone, 563.
Foelix ille fuit, qui Rebus (tempore quôdam), 1996.
For Barclay's learn'd Apology is due, 865.
For heaps of Gold let plodding misers Toil, 649.
For once let me ask you a Question, good Sir, 269.
For the[e], the Soldiers, with Heroick Grace, 1376.
For these nocturnal thieves, huntsman prepare, 389.
For you, dear Sir, the Muse unus'd to sing, 1043.
Forbear to ask what France or Spain, 1602.
Forbes! to thee the muse her tribute brings, 1555.
Forgive, if while you pass each day, 1881A.
Forgive the Scribler when he writes in Rhime, 5.
Foul winds, foul weather vex'd us fore, 748.
Frail man, thro' life's uncomfortable gloom, 1968.
France, Spain, and Sardinia, together conspire, 376.
Free is my Heart, and just my Cause, 1320, 1323.
Freed from the tyrant Rage of Winter's sway, 1130.
Friend *Weyman*, doubtless having oft observ'd, 1629.
Friend, when a rival Poem you peruse, 1008.
Friends! Countrymen! or, if a nobler Name, 1324, 1330.
Friendship, all hail! Thou dearest tye, 1474.
Friendship, the heav'nly Theme, I sing, 1906.
Friendship, thou sacred name, my muse inspire, 744.
From a small Acorn see the Oak arise, 607.
From Adam downward to this Evening knell, 1831.
From all the noisy cares of town, 1428.
From climes deform'd with frost severe, 1740.
From climes where hot Phoebus is scorching my skin, 1300.
From Courts remote, and Europe's pompus Scenes, 206.
From dear Chloe, I stole two kisses in Play, 1011.
From Delawarian banks, the Muses seat, 427.
From distant Climes, and desart Woods, where no, 313.
From earth remov'd, in ev'ry virtue warm, 938.
From envious Tales, and idle Life refrain, 851.
From fair Cypria's Fane I'm forced away, 311.
From favr'd *Barbados* on the western Main, 719B.
From France and Spain we're called to the Field, 1895.
From *Georgia* t' *Augustine* the General goes, 674.
From Hearts devout the Tear sincerely falls, 686.
From luxury and care, from dear quadril, 369.
From native *Britain's* verdant plains, 689.
From peaceful Solitude, and calm Retreat, 691.
From Pole to Pole, 1817.

H

Had I a field, it soon should be, 488.
Had I, O had I all the tuneful Arts, 68.
Had not New England been his Place of Birth, 1778.
Haec tibi, sancte senex, funebria maesta dicamus, 1988.
Hah! is Meserve dead? too true, he's gone, 1458.
Hah! there it flames, the long expected star, 1579, 1589, 1591, 1592, 1595, 1600.
Hail, auspicious, happy Day, 1664.
Hail Bard Seraphick! tell what Generous Fire, 46.
Hail Britain! queen of arms and arts confest, 1688.
Hail Britains, who, in western Regions dwell, 1329.
Hail Brother Trade! What brought you here, 958.
Hail *Carolina*, hail! Fill up the Bowl, 514.
Hail! charming Poet whose distinguish'd lays, 70.
Hail Critick! from whose furious scorching Tongue, 192.
Hail! D[aven]p[or]t of wondrous fame, 661.
Hail! Empress of the star-bespangled sky, 1677.
Hail! fair charmer wafted from Britannia's shore, 1856.
Hail George the Third, of Predecessors, Great, Sublime, 1832.
Hail, gracious God! thou goodness' source, 681.
Hail glorious Peace, 'tis thy refreshing smiles, 1938.
Hail! great Instructor of Mankind, 229.
Hail! Great good Man, hail! Patron of the Poor, 1096, 1108.
Hail! happy day! whose glad returning rays, 1761.
Hail happy Man! New-England's genuine Son, 170.
Hail, happy Pair, for you these Vows ascend, 596.
Hail happy virgin of celestial race, 401.
Hail Heav'n-born Science! whose enliv'ning Touch, 1890, 1899.
Hail! House of Salem, let it, pray, be shown, 696.
Hail! Joyful Bride, your Eyes are brought to see, 522.
Hail king supreme! all wise and good, 1269.
Hail learned Bard! who dost thy Power dispense, 1393.
Hail Marriage! sacred Rite, whose mystic Tie, 1982.
Hail matchless monarch! prince renown'd, 1419.
Hail mighty Sires! whose bright Refulgence shines, 683.
Hail, much-lov'd man! forgive the aspiring Muse, 737.
Hail, mystick art! which men like angels taught, 1999.
Hail, noble Forbes! embark'd in *Briton's* Cause, 1557, 1567.
Hail! pious, learn'd and eloquent Divine, 309.
Hail Raleigh! Venerable Shade, 250.
Hail sacred Art! thou Gift of Heaven, design'd, 95, 97, 1118, 1122, 1128.
Hail sacred muse! thou harbinger of fame, 1929.
Hail! Sol supream the glory of the skies, 319.
Hail! sov'reign leaf, whose virtue can dispense, 1614.
Hail the dear Angels of the Lord, 668.
Hail wedded Love! mysterious Law! true Source of human Offspring, 1172.
Hail Western World, begin thy better Fate, 1544, 1550.
Hail wondrous Wit! Immortal 'Nezer, 41.
Happy Pompey! which can be, 2031.
Happy that Man, that has per Ann, 762.
Happy the Maid, whose Body pure and chaste, 1149, 1175.
Happy the Man! Thrice happy he, 214.
Happy's the Man, who with just Thoughts, and clear, 272.
Happy when I see thy eyes, 1430.

Hark! hark! the [s]weet vibrating lyre, 1385.
Hark--how the Groves and Woods resound, 1072.
Hark! methought I heard the death-betok'ning knell, 857.
Hark, my gay friend, that solemn bell, 1912.
Hark! saith the Lord, what moving sound, 1463.
Harmonious maids, assist my artless flame, 1005.
Harsh to the Heart, and grating to the Ear, 1471.
Has Neptune and Apollo join'd, 1627.
Haste, Sylvia! haste, my charming maid, 1408.
Have you e'er seen the raging stormy Main, 51.
Have you not seen at Country Wake, 888.
He comes! great Watts, he comes! (thy Vows prevail,) 159.
He is not form'd for Arms, the Soldier's Pride, 1291.
He is the Assertor of Liberty, 1519.
He is the Emblem of Fear, 1620, 1621.
He that to *Wit* has no pretence, 239A.
He who for a Post, or base sordid Pelf, 2055, 2056, 2057.
Hear, all ye People! hear, 1798.
Hear heav'n! on this propitious day, 1443.
Hear me with patience while a motion is made, 843.
Hear, Peggy, since the single State, 1556.
Heaven oft before the fatal Bolt is hurl'd, 1942, 1943, 1944, 1945.
Heavenly Friendship, Balm of Woe, 2023.
Heav'n's sacred Will, *Leaconoé*, wait, 1931.
Hence Melancholy, Care and Sorrow, 1387.
Hence ye Prophane, ye puny Slaves retire, 509.
Hendrick, bold Sachem of the Mohawk race, 1295, 1332.
Her Temper charming, affable and kind, 1779.
Here are such rare Conceits and Merriment, 325.
Here dormant, with a vulgar tribe, 1868.
Here lie, beneath this heap of stones, 1873D.
Here lie I fix'd in Earth full low, 1078.
Here lies, and here's likely to lie, after all the Trouble, 1040.
Here lies old Cole; but how or why, 54.
Here lies our Captain and Major, 1816.
Here rests from Toil, in narrow Bounds confin'd, 1669, 1684, 1691, 1694, 1696.
Here Strangers and the Age to come, 1678.
Here taught by thee, we view with raptur'd eyes, 1447.
Here, wife, let's see my slippers, cap and gown, 413.
He's not the happy man, to whom is giv'n, 920.
Heu! Generosus abest Faneuil. Et temperet ulluo, 680.
Hibernian Jack, the saddest D--g, 669.
High on the bright Expanse of azure Skies, 776.
His Host (as Crowds are superstitious still), 375.
Historic Muse, awake!--and from the shade, 769.
H--k my Muse disdains, 1854.
Hoc juxta Marmor S. E., 525.
Hold, Censure hold! a timrous Virgin spare, 1281.
Hope! 'Tis in vain to rest it where, 1446.
Hosier! with indignant Sorrow, 613.
Houses, Churches, mix'd together, 1157.
How awful is the night, beneath whose shade, 1508.
How bless'd her State! in innocence array'd, 1167.
How can we adore, 2016.

How chang'd the Scene, since from their native Reign, 1610.
How cruel Fortune, and how fickle too, 406.
How do'st thou do, my Dear; you look as pale, 815.
How every [da]y unworthy of thy love, 1140A.
How gaily is at first begun, 193, 314.
How great, how just Thy zeal, advent'rous youth, 481.
How happy is a Woman's Fate, 707.
How hard is my Fate!--to be thus over match'd, 451.
How hard my Lot! and ah! how cruel Fate, 766, 1913, 1917.
How is my honest Soul oppress'd, 121.
How kind has Heav'n adorn'd this happy Land, 1337, 1338, 1341, 1343.
How lovely sacred Pourtraiture appears, 147.
How mighty silly your Resolves, 355.
How now! proud Queen, what dost thou strutting here, 31.
How pleasant is it, to behold on shore, 317.
How shall I tune my Lyre! How Shall I show, 729.
How shall my feeble Muse attempt, 824.
How shall the Muse find Language to express, 1036.
How shall the muse in elegiac lay, 860.
How sweet a Face, what magic Charms, 456.
How sweetly looks and smiles the lovely lass, 1525.
How sweetly opening with the blushing morn, 323.
How vain is Man! how fickle his estate, 152.
How vain is Man! How fluttering are his Joys!, 1308.
How we Tremble 'midst the Snow, 1907.
How welcome this, when fill'd with Fear, 1306.
How wretched is a Woman's Fate, 706.
Hypocrisy, the thriving'st calling, 507.

I

I am a thing of ugly form, 651.
I am inform'd that it is said, 2060, 2061, 2061A, 2064.
I Boast existence long ere man, 1737.
I do not expect in a female to find, 2005.
I knew that the Song, which I lately did send, 447.
[I] know thee Janus, both what thou art, and who, 274.
I know you Lawyers can, with Ease, 185, 303.
I Lov'd no King in forty one, 684.
I praise their Ardor, that with generous Pride, 234.
I shall Lavinia see no more, 2000.
I sicken at the Nonsense of the Crowd, 1030.
I Sing thy Praise, most famous Thomas, 777.
I stroll'd one day into a room, 718.
I, Who long since did draw my Pen, 440.
If a lawful Excuse, I can plead for my Muse, 959, 962.
If Aught, fair Maid: could add new Grace, 1069.
If Bees a Government maintain, 161.
If ever Dram to thee was dear, 576.
If ever I should change my State of Life, 1010.
If gen'rous Friendship and harmonious Love, 1829, 1830.
If great Mens Frown divert your Enterprize, 23.
If human Life, in prosp'rous Station plac'd, 1102, 1104, 1112, 1115, 1121.
If I am doom'd the marriage chain to wear, 2076.
If in this Wild pleasing Spot we meet, 1971, 1972.

In some calm midnight, when no whisp'ring breeze, 112.
In sorrowing Verse to mourn the pious Dead, 2049.
In the Almighty's Pow'r how great is Man, 1296, 1301.
In the Boston Gazette of last Monday past, 1883, 1885.
In the desk or the pulpit, when Rufus appears, 951.
In the first place, reverse what all schoolmasters use, 1271.
In the *Hampshire* Gazette of last Friday past, 1886.
In the immense Expanse above, 429.
In the Name of God, I Thomas Oakam, 1706.
In the name of Good Liquor, Amen, I J--n C---s--y, 472.
In the sprightly Month of May, 248.
In this judicious Piece, the Work of Years, 972.
In this our Town I've heard some Youngsters say, 307.
In times of old, the poets lays, 1652.
In Transport rise, ye Sons of Britain, rise, 1331.
In truth, dear ladies! 'tis a curious matter, 408.
In vain alas! (do lazy mortals cry), 1198.
In vain, *Almeria*, do you this way strive, 627.
In vain, fond Youth, dost thou attempt to move, 834.
In vain is all you speak, and all you Write, 58.
In vain th' Indulgence of the warmer Sun, 340.
In various Shapes have I been shewn, 148.
In Virtue's Cause to draw a daring Pen, 712.
In what a maze of Errour do I stray, 670, 675.
In what fond accents shall my thoughts have vent, 1585.
In Youth's fair days, when first our infant love, 2025.
Indulgent Death, prepare thy gentle Dart, 409.
Indulgent God, whose bounteous care, 1995.
Insatiate fiend! thy purple slaughter cease, 1007.
Inspiring Phoebus! warm my friendly Mind, 952.
Interdum Euphrates tribuit terrore dolores, 36.
Is Lee snatch'd from us ? Is his soul then fled, 1059.
Is this a Time to fiddle, sing and dance, 1574, 1582.
It can't be Treason in our own Defence, 411.
It grieves me much to hear my Friend complain, 720.
It happen'd once a city mouse, 1693.
It must be so--*Machiavel* reasons well, 1060.
It must be so--Milton thou reason'st well, 872, 1009, 1923A.
It must be so--my Sons ye reason well, 2089.
It was, as learn'd Traditions say, 1020.
It was no vulgar Mind, 1810.
I've now o'ercome the long fatigue, 1451.
I've wrote a Book and fix'd my Name, 736B.

J

Jehovah is my sole support, 2077.
Johnny, Why art so touchy grown, 1583.
Just as the morn had spread the skies, 1454.
Just in his youthful Prime and Bloom of Age, 841.
Just now is published some Rhimes, 2015.

K

Katherine is sometimes called *Kate*, 907.

L

Ladies! there's something happen'd now so queer, 1223, 1228, 1230, 1240.
Last Wednesday Night L----'e you know, 602.
Law, Physic, and Divinity, 1170.
Learning and piety, with ev'ry grace, 1836.
Learning that Cobweb of the Brain, 218.
Leda's twin-sons, when they together shin'd, 1436.
Let all the Works of Heaven's Eternal KING, 366.
Let daring bands attune the sounding lyre, 1888.
Let gloomy Groves, let awful Rocks and Hills, 143.
Let grovelling Misers count Their sordid store, 351.
Let grov'ling rhymers court an awkward Muse, 88.
Let loftier Bards the Hero's Acts relate, 453.
Let *others* mix in faction's giddy throng, 1486.
Let others muse on sublunary things, 1178, 1194, 1195, 1197.
Let other Pens th' ungrateful News declare, 119.
Let Philadelphia's generous Sons excuse, 122.
Let prudence each petition guide, 1873E.
Let *Rome* no more her antient triumphs boast, 407.
Let Romes Anathemas, be Dead, 3.
Let thankless Slaves for Favours humbly *ask*, 1201.
Let this give Notice to my Friends, 128.
Let's away to *New Scotland*, where Plenty sits queen, 963, 973.
Lewis, whose heart is case'd with stone, 1704.
Lewis worsted on the Ocean, 1865B.
Libertas nomen; bonitas confuncta colori, 37.
Life's but a Feast; and when we die, 438.
Like all the num'rous Sins, which lawless Rage, 1916A.
Like as a Damask Rose you see, 1950.
Like Priests of *Baal* they crav'd the Muses Aid, 1840.
Little but too powerful tie, 1491.
Lo! Farmer now, no more does act below, 1438.
Lo! from yon solitary, sad recess, 971.
Lo, the swift Courier hov'ring on the Eye, 1279.
Lo! to new Worlds th' advent'rous Muse conveys, 1732.
Londini domus est in Nigris Fratribus, Hansdon, 49.
Lonely Chloe, pretty creature, 424.
Long did *Euphrates* make us glad, 372.
Long e'er the Sun usurp'd with flaming Light, 923.
Long for an Answer have I staid, 862.
Long had a mungrel *French* and *Indian* brood, 1354, 1355, 1401, 1406.
Long had Despair approach'd Britannia's Shore, 1756.
Long had mankind with darkness been oppress'd, 194, 237, 241, 246.
Long had sad Albion mourn'd her coward Race, 1745.
Long had the Rulers prudent Care, 7.
Long had the World in gloomy Shades, 2009.
Long has *New England* groan'd beneath the Load, 93.
Long have the learned Pastors of the age, 582, 584, 600, 605.
Long have the weaker Sons of Harvard Strove, 24.
Long since I bade the pleasant Muse adieu, 129, 130.
Long Time, alas! by our great Grandsire's Fall, 34.
Long us'd this World's vain Greatness to despise, 494.
Look, see the mighty Hero stand, 1601.
L--d have Mercy on us!--the Capitol! the Capitol! is burnt down, 839, 840, 842.

Lorenzo, warm in Youth! thy Cares remove, 1769.
Love, the most fav'rite Gift design'd, 1002.
Love! thou divinest good below, 904.
Lovely Queen of soft Desires, 736.
Low, in the gloomy vale of thought, confin'd, 486, 493.
L---s ce grand Faiseur d'Impots, 1698.
L---s, who grinds both great and small, 1701.
Lucinda, qui novit numeris constringere justis, 153.
Lucinda, what d'you call this frosty Jaunt, 1064, 1067.
Luke, on his dying Bed, embrac'd his Wife, 870.
Lull'd in pleasing Sleep old Cornell lies, 873.

M

Make way for Hymen with his Lights, 118.
Man should weigh well the Nature of Himself, 1391.
Man was a happy Favourite above, 367.
Marino!--welcome from the Western Shore, 53, 396.
Mark my gay Friend, that solemn Toll, 1823.
Mark with what different Zeal each Nation arms, 1541, 1562.
Mars, O God of War, why hast thou, 878.
Masters should have sound Wit, and Documents that's plain, 134.
Mauginio says, I am a Fool, and I, 624.
May all the Pow'rs of Harmony combine, 1768.
May I presume in humble lays, 1586.
May none but fair and pleasant Gales, 381.
Mayst Thou, Great Man, withstand a misled Throng, 587, 595.
Melpomene, assist my mournful Theme, 163.
Men love Women with Lips quite bare, 1957.
Men need both fear, to *Preach* and *Hear*, 1520.
Men need not fear, to preach or hear, 1518.
Menedemus the stoic, once heartily jaded, 749.
Methinks I see Britannia's Genius here, 1528, 1530, 1538, 1551, 1554.
Michare Gardner, dic aganippidas, 1493.
Might I, like others, make Request, 1090, 1095, 1105, 1114, 1119.
Mine, and the F---ies Sons, why are your Lyres, 177.
Minorca's gone! Oswego too is lost! 1344.
Miss Bett, --pray, what think you's the reason, 657.
Miss Molly, a fam'd toast, was fair and young, 947.
Mistaken astronomers, gaze not so high, 1472.
Mistress A----y, 202, 212, 220, 231, 235.
Moments, wing'd with smiling pleasure, 758.
Montibus in summis occisa est gloria gentis, 1866A.
More sad than when the much-lov'd Ovid's tongue, 1791.
Most Gracious Sovereign Lord, May't please, 72.
Mount, mount, aspiring Soul, 1749.
Much has been said at this censorious Time, 1848.
Much has been said at this unlucky Time, 1543.
Much has been said in this reforming Age, 1185, 1200.
Much honoured Muse! accept this grateful Verse, 734A.
Musa canit tristis Mortem, tum Vulnera Mortis, 1861.
Muse, extend thy sable Wing, 630.
Muse, resume the sounding Lyre, 1788.
Music has Power to melt the Soul, 283.
Must Babel's Lofty Towers submit to Fate, 1718.

Nor wings, nor feet, unto my share have fell, 916.
Nos tibi devoti Juvenes, Dynasta verende, 1681.
Not all that parent earth can give, 918.
Not ev'ry temper rural scenes delight, 265, 285.
Not like the rooted plants that grow, 1873, 1874.
Not with more Pleasure o'er the fragrant Lawn, 1926, 1928, 1929A.
Now blessed be this present Age, 292.
Now gloomy Winter shews his hoary head, 900.
Now had the Beam of Titan gay, 1869.
Now had the Son of *Jove* mature, attain'd, 1056.
Now his last level Rays the Sun hath cast, 66.
Now hostile Fury every Breast inspires, 1327.
Now hours of mirth, salute the coming year, 1422.
Now lay your Politics aside, 282.
Now mantled with an hoary Garb, the Earth, 388.
Now Mars with double Fury has arose, 560.
Now Nature with her various Verdure glows, 316.
Now, O ye Nine! if all your Pow'rs can paint, 83.
Now on the Town an Angel flaming stands, 17.
Now the full Harvest of the golden Year, 1082, 1083.
Now the *Summer's* sultry Beams, 1088.
Now to my arms, submits the pride of Spain, 1891, 1901.
Now view the maid, the love-inspiring maid, 1680.
Now when the War of Elements is o'er, 1035.
Now while the Sun revolving feasts each sense, 881.
Now will I Guard against my Morning Fall, 114.
Now, wretched Joque, thou art a guest, 1886D.

O

O Bless the Lord, *my Soul*, with Rapture sing, 74.
O Blessed Man, great Tennent! what shall we, 619.
O Cruel Fate, could'st thou not miss, 334.
O Death! thou Victor of the human Frame, 1941, 1966.
O! For the tuneful Voice of Eloquence, 1087.
O Happiness where's thy resort, 1689.
O Happy Virgin Land! still Self-producing, 599.
O Hartopp! born of a Superior Race, 774.
O Heavenly Muse my daring Breast inspire, 557.
O King of heav'n and hell, of earth and sea, 1398.
O Leuconoe! cease from anxious care, 1858.
O Lord our God arise, 2008.
O May the joyful voice of praise, 1531.
O Melancholy, pensive maid, 1839B, 1960.
O Mournful One of Nine, ne'er known to smile, 664.
O Peaceful mansion! how thy rural face, 1597.
O Quem futurum pectore finxeram, 1373.
O *Stella* fair, whose Cheeks bestows, 820A.
O the Immense, the Amazing Height, 1379.
O Thou matur'd by glad hesperian Suns, 416.
O! thou undaunted Prince! whom millions own, 1423.
O Walter! Thou for great Atchievments born, 1085.
O when shall (long-lost) Honour guide the war, 869.
O wou'dst thou know what secret Charm, 1830A.
Objicis egregiis mihi quae convicia nugis, 838.

One Evening I courted my Muse, 240.
One lovely maid alone my thoughts employs, 1081, 1093.
One Night as I lay slumb'ring in my Bed, 2065, 2065A, 2067.
One Thing I of *Paturia* must confess, 179.
Oppress'd with grief, in heavy strains I mourn, 280, 1494.
Opprest with taxes L—s' vassals groan, 1702.
Orpheus to seek his Wife decreed, 482.
Orpheus to seek his Wife 'tis said, 483.
Others their Beauty heighten and improve, 136.
Oui, je l'ai dit cent fois, ce n'est que fiction 418.
Our Fathers crost the wide Atlantick Sea, 164, 166.
Our Fathers left *Britannia's* fruitful Shore, 769B, 771.
Our Fathers pass'd the great Atlantic Sea, 172.
Our grandsires were all papists, 1533.
Our humble *Prologue* means not to engage, 1190, 1192, 1219.
Over the Hills with Heart we go, 1211, 1251.

P

Painter, all thy pow'r exert, 1825.
Painter, display, in honour of the state, 836.
Painters shall use their fading arts no more, 359.
Pale night succeeds the Sun's Career, 1581.
Pan sighs for Echo o'er the lawn, 1835.
Panting for Air beneath the scorching Sun, 939.
Parent of all, Omnipotent, 1628.
Parthanissa's Beauty blooming, 63.
Pass o'er this grave without concern, 837.
Passing those Fields where Negroe slaves are found, 115.
Patriots and chiefs! Britannia's nightly Dead, 1484, 1517, 1565, 1570.
Peace to thy silent shade, dear worthy friend, 1668.
Peace with your Fiddling there--It shall be spoke, 1347, 1348, 1357, 1363, 1368.
Peggy, Pride of heav'nly Muses, 561.
Pensive I lay, e'en from the dead of Night, 2018.
Pensive my thoughts descend to shades below, 382.
Pensively pay the Tribute of a Tear, 534.
Pergis extremas, bone Dux, in oras, 1189, 1488.
Permit, lamented shade, an humble Muse, 404, 612.
Peter his Lord and Master, did deny, 648.
Pharaoh's proud Heart was not with Wonders mov'd, 574.
Phoebus, Wit-inspiring Lord, 169, 175.
Pierian nymphs that haunt Sicilian plains, 1441.
[P]lain, Gen'rous, Honest, Merciful, and Brave, 420.
Plainman and Truman cease your hate, 566.
Plenty three Years our crowded Graneries fill'd, 1887.
Poor *Pompy's* dead! and likewise skin'd, 374, 377.
Poor Swain! the Doubled say of thee, 10.
Port Royal plains, let ever balmy dew, 1049.
Poverty's bitter, but a wholesome Good, 634.
Pray Master CLIO now take care, 990.
Presumptuous Traytor, we can make't appear, 168.
Pretty Insect, Summer's Child, 1759.
Pretty Tube of mighty power, 417.
Propitious pale! we had thy healing power, 732.
Proteus, as ancient poets tell you, 1990A.

Proud France, why such excessive Joy, 789A, 790.
Prussia's proud Prince, the Story goes, 882.
Pure was this Lady, and the fairest Dane, 1243.
Pursuant to your late command, 755.

Q

Qui te cunque movit carmen dispandere tuum, 835.
Quickquid in buccam venerit, effutit, 1273.
Quid frustra erepti fatis quaeramus amici, 1936.
Quis Labor infandus! Quis tam Crudelis, et asper, 1839.
Quis lacrymas retinere potest dum fatur Amicus, 1955.
Quite mad with Zeal, the Biggots raves, 1985.
Quoth modest S[mi]th in me combine, 547.
Quoth Simon to Thomas (and shew'd him his Wife), 856.

R

Rachel appears with bleating Flocks afar, 56.
Rail on, vile Atheist; let your Tongue blaspheme, 1977, 1986.
Rais'd on a Throne of Block-work see him sit, 42, 874, 877.
Raise thee my Muse, thy aid once more, 1461, 1470.
Rejoyce not in Beauty, ye Masons, beware, 491.
Rejoyce, O ye *Ladies*, and cast away Care, 501.
Rejoyce, O ye Masons,! and cast away Care, 500.
Relentless Death! Still shall thy rugged hand, 1328.
Remark, my Soul, the narrow Bounds, 2010.
Remote from liberty and truth, 1532.
Repond moi, cher Echo, c'est Louis qui te parle, 1699.
Rerum parentem te, genitor, canam, 1505.
Res augusta Domi Musam confundit amicam, 1545.
Revolving Years their steady course pursue, 1845.
Reynard for Cunning is Renown'd, 123.
Right trusty and expert Commanders, 517.
Rise! Britons, Rise! defend your righteous Cause, 1459, 1460.
Rise, *Britons!* rise, with all your father's might, 1259.
Rise Heavenly Muse, but rise with *heavy* Wings, 75, 77, 78, 80.
Rome shall lament her ancient Fame declin'd, 1151.
Rouse Sons of Earth, to War, to War, 1439, 1449.
Rouze up my Soul, awake thy active Pow'rs, 81, 82.
Rowe, like the Queen of Love, would studious save, 641.
Rowse Haddock, rowse thee from inglorious Sleep, 618.
Rufus by nature form'd unfit, 950.

S

Salkeld, from silent Sitting, slow would rise, 544, 551.
Sat mihi, quod satyrâ videaris gnavus et asper, 1997.
Say, Cadmus, by what Ray divine inspir'd, 96, 98.
Say, I conjure thee, Damon, say, 227.
Say, mighty Love, and teach my Song, 178, 186, 224.
Say, mournful Muse, declare thy rising Woe, 69.
Say muse, what Numbers shall relate, 135, 142.
Say, smiling Muse, what heav'nly strain, 621.
Say, why like a little fawn, 1963.
Scarse Egypt's Land more dire Disasters knew, 433.

Scarce had the dark'ned Sky, which Night had borne, 1914.
Scarce had the Sun resign'd the Winter Sky, 1407.
Scarce in an Age one Twigg of Laurel grows, 979.
Science! bright Beam of Light Divine, 1826.
See dusky clouds, the welkin overspread, 716.
See, from my lovely Stella's eyes, 1886B.
See, from Stella's sloe-black eyes, 1961.
See Heaven born Tennent from Mount Sinai flies, 617, 631.
See how that once-lov'd flower neglected Lyes, 1452.
See! how the fair creation round, 1448.
See! lonly Wastes and barren Wilds proclaim, 788.
See! pale *Britannia* clad in sable Woe, 1809.
Seek you to know what keeps the mind, 890, 913.
Serene as Light is *Whitefield's* soul, 570.
Shall Blazing Stars drop from their Spheres, 636.
Shall boastful Pomp, the high imperial Name, 983.
Shall brave New-England's Glory fly, 802, 808.
Shall *Celia's* fav'rite Bird lie dead, 775.
Shall echoing Joys thro' all the Land rebound, 1695.
Shall Freedom, now, her care for Britain o'er, 812.
Shall virtuous *Molly* unlamented die, 535.
Shall Wesley's Sons, o'er rule all human Kind, 757, 768.
She comes! she comes! ye Nine, strike every String, 1222, 1227, 1229, 1239.
She Nature's Master-piece, is form'd to please, 773.
She's gone, ah! gone, for evermore secure, 804.
Shine thou bright Sun, with a distinguish'd Ray, 1019.
Shirley, whilst War it's Desolation spreads, 1215.
Shou'd it e'er be my Lot, with a Husband to live, 1245.
Should George the Third, the best of Kings, 1884.
Should the whole Earth of growing Numbers stand, 1309.
Silence! soft daughter of nocturnal shades, 1548.
Since all men must, 345.
Since, as the serious preach, and prudent say, 395.
Since B—lay's Praise, the Poet has proclaim'd, 954.
Since *Guido's* skilful hand, with mimic art, 1414.
Since injur'd Wit is thus reliev'd, 442.
Since Life's a dear precarious Thing, 2032.
Since no Adven'trous Muse her voice will raise, 666.
Since Polly, you ev'ry Charm possess, 901.
Since Scandal and ill Nature take their Rounds, 302.
Since Terms are confounded, & Words on the Rack, 2042, 2044, 2086.
Since, th'am'rous Bard has thus essay'd, 207.
Since we see the long *Surplice*, and else the short *Cloak*, 221.
Since Worms your Study wholly now engage, 1018.
Since you well know, 1727.
Since you've provok'd my humble Rage, 105.
Sincerity! thou sweetest Thing in Life, 1925.
Sing heav'n-born muse, and may thy strain, 1469.
Sing melancholly Muse the awful Stroke, 1616.
Sing, O my Muse (as well you may), 1012.
Sing the Hero in strains so sublime, O my Muse, 542.
Sing to the Lord, exalt his name, 1738, 1784.
Sit licet in Satyrâ P.M. nimis acer & ordens, 1279.
Sitting by the streams, that glide, 1465.

Six bottles of Wine, right old, good and clear, 1202.
Sixteen, d'ye say ? Nay then tis time, 912.
Snatch'd in the Morn of Life alas! too soon, 1970.
Snow, Hail, and Rains descend from wintry clouds, 2050.
So Fam'd for Rhymes, for Mockery and Myrth, 528.
So farewell to the little Good you bear me, 1162.
Soar now, my Muse, exert thy utmost Lays, 239.
Soft as the downy plumage of the dove, 742.
Soft Babe! sweet Image of a harmless Mind, 1023, 1124.
Sol, in the East, from Neptune's watry Bed, 2048.
Some Birds (it is no News to tell), 1068, 1070, 1071.
Some Husbands on a Winter's Day, 485, 487A, 1120, 1605.
Some purchase Land, some stately Buildings raise, 278.
Some Twelvemonths ago, 2074.
Soon as young Reason dawn'd in Junio's breast, 1991, 1992.
Spoiler of Beauty! for this once forbear, 1747.
Sprung from an ancient, honour'd race, 1713.
Spurn the Relation--She's no more a Mother, 2084.
Stay gentle Nymph, nay, pray thee stay, 581.
Stay passenger, and spend a Tear, 2081.
Stella's waving hair flows down, 1964.
Still shall the Tyrant Scourge of Gaul, 1335, 1336, 1339, 1342.
Stop Passenger, until my Life you read, 387.
Strange Aspects in New Haven late were seen, 30.
Stranger, whoe'er thou art, one Moment stay, 1946.
Stream on my Eyes, with generous Grief o'erflow, 57.
Strephon, a Youth extremely modest, 32.
Strike, O muse, the sounding lyre, 1739.
Struck with religious awe, and solemn dread, 1820.
Such, gracious sir, your province now appears, 259.
Suppress, dear Delia, thy too constant Sighs, 1889.
Surprizing Being! Which we Nature call, 719.
Sweet bird! whose fate and mine agree, 1183.
Sweet dove, thy solitary sounds, 1873C.
Sweet Nature smiles! and to the raptur'd Eyes, 833.
Sweet Philomel renew thy sacred strains, 508.
Sweetest of blessings, heavenly light, 1811.
Sweetness and Strength in Silvia's Voice unite, 460, 477.
S—y Pride of Grubstreet Muses, 562.
Sylvia! with the Wheel I send, 1166.
Sylvius! let *Reason* rule thy breast, 911.

T

Taedium longi maris et viarum, 1450.
Take Courage, Friends, for in this G[*loom*]y shade, 178A.
Tell me no more of whig and tory, 1444.
Tell me, Old Man, with stooping Head, 140.
Tell me, poor peevish Bard! what Muse in spight, 48.
Tell me, says Cato, where you found, 1558.
Thais condemns the gen'rous Soul, 1762.
That God! the sov'reign of the earth and sky, 1687.
That *Sawney* might kill two Birds with one Stone, 1038.
That with all dazzling Splendor strike the Eye, 445.
That you Salute me on one Cheek alone, 662.

That your Petitioner was born, and bred at Home, 1072A.
That your Work does abound, 1039.
The Age of the fortunate Man in your last, 1134.
The Beau, with his delicate Womanish Face, 1055.
The bleak Norwest begins his dreaded Reign, 238.
The bleak North-west with nipping rigour reigns, 1099, 1113, 1116.
The body sick, we for the doctor send, 1399.
The *British* lion from his slumber wakes, 1252.
The Choice came on, Fame told the Success round, 1923.
The Christian hero, pure from sin, 1507.
The coolest Time in a Summer's Day, 461.
The Counsel of a Friend Belinda hear, 328.
The Dean would Visit Market-Hill, 155.
The Doctors in *Charles-Town* have lately agreed, 1262.
The dry, dull, drowsy Batchelor, surveys, 1822, 1990, 2022.
The Fate of *Dommett* is not singly hard, 530.
The fiercest Animals that range the Wood, 937.
The Fool by his Wit, 13.
The French will grant that Shirley's Schemes, 800.
The Friend, who proves sincere and true, 476.
The gloomy Horrors all around, 884.
The Golden Age, a specious cheat, 1514.
The great *Epaminondas* conqu'ring, dy'd, 1659.
The Great Jehovah from Above, 35.
The great Jehova is my Friend, 633.
The greatest Authors of our modern Age, 736A.
The greatful Tribute of these rural Lays, 174.
The hoary winter now conceals from sight, 1547, 1909.
The hostile Fleet, Brave Warren! strait ingage, 936.
The Humble Springs of stately Plimouth *Beach*, 38A.
The January Riddle I swear by Jove, 555.
The kingly ruler of the plain, 338.
The lab'ring Mountains were in Pieces torn, 1908.
The ladies claim right, 1712.
The Lawyer, Orator, Divine, 550.
The lazy morn as yet undrest, 1181.
The Loom, the Comb, the Spinning Wheel, 967, 1147.
The Man in vertue's sacred paths sincere, 734B.
The Man of upright Heart and Soul, 1364.
The Man that Happiness enjoys, is he, 702.
The Man that wou'd in Health his Life prolong, 1255.
The Man, who seeks to win the Fair, 1024.
The Man, whose Heart from Vice is clear, 1254.
The Means and Arts that to Perfection bring, 1380.
The Members of the *ancient* Tuesday Club, 995.
The Mind oppress'd, with heavy Cares of state, 519.
The Moon grows red, pale, big, and walks by Night, 1013.
The Muse an Ode select prepares, 927.
The Muse that us'd in Silvan Strains to sing, 1233, 1234, 1236, 1241, 1242.
The north-east wind did briskly blow, 2038, 2091.
The northwind, 'tis granted, still pierces us most, 1415.
The number of our years (Sir) I nearly —, 1131.
The nymphs of Plaistow fields begin my Song, 273.
The Parson says, my Verse I stole, 879.

The People of *Taunton* they lately have seen, 1965.
The Persian King, when he his Troops survey'd, 787.
The plains recede, the sylvan hillock's rise, 1649.
The pleasing Task be mine, sweet Maid, 1352, 1361, 1371.
The Poet is mad, 976.
The Pow'r of *LETTERS* can't be weak, 230.
The pow'rful Prince, by Lust of Empire driv'n, 827, 830.
The Prelates and their Impositions, 40.
The price of rice, or talk on *'Change*, 1137.
The Prophet's Soul has bid adieu to Earth, 2019, 2020.
The Raven Phoebus' fav'rite Bird was long, 622.
The remedy, *Dick*, 1728.
The Rose's Age is but a Day, 1168.
The round-headed Tribe, 14.
The *Russ* loves Brandy, *Dutchman* beer, 380.
The setting Year in shades of Night, 1802, 1848A.
The snows are gone, and nature spreads, 1767.
The Soldier longs for Arms (the Ensigns of his Trade), 1776.
The solid Joys of human Kind, 473.
The solitary bird of night, 1726.
The Spring returns, Nature in Bloom appears, 1757.
The swains in a bantering way, 1604.
The tuneful Muse, in lofty strains, 358.
The Twenty-third of April is ever the Day, 253.
The Verse above Mysterious is, 1812.
The very silliest Things in Life, 2024.
The wish'd Supports of Wealth are vain, 985.
The wond'rous Draught, the Pencil's daring Stroke, 635.
The world's a *Comedy*, in which we act, 1417.
The World's great Lord commands the *Dove* to fly, 1246, 1248.
The youth, whose birth the sisters twain, 1892.
The Zeal that in Thy Godlike Bosom glows, 339, 362.
Their Fathers crost the wide Atlantick Sea, 165, 167.
Then 'tis decreed--the vain exulting *Gaul*, 1288, 1289, 1290, 1292.
There are a number of us creep, 430, 439.
There curst Canadia's motley-savage Herd, 1283, 1285, 1286, 1293.
There flourish'd in a market town, 1511, 1522.
There is a man that most does know, 1155.
There is a Thing which oft the Vulgar see, 832.
There is no Ill on Earth which Mortals Fly, 190.
There once liv'd in repute a substantial freeholder, 1598.
There was an old Dame aged Ninety and Eight, 52.
There's not an Ear that is not deaf, 343.
These lays, ye *Great!* to Richardson belong, 1426.
They have a Right to write who understand, 861, 867.
Thine Eyes, dear Girl, are clos'd in Night, 1772, 1773.
Things that are bitter, bitterer than Gall, 390.
Think, bright Maria, when you see, 1653.
Think what you list, yet he that trains, 55.
This City's lost their Pedagogue of Art, 335.
This day young Mars in wedlock Bands was ty'd, 191.
This Earth, the Sun, and yonder Stars of Light, 1110.
This is to let you know, that I have seen, 611.
This lofty theme! this pure etherial flame, 1783.

This morning to pen, ink, and paper I flew, 1588.
This Town would quickly be reclaim'd 295, 297.
Tho' Angles could infuse their holy Fire, 106.
Tho' Billingsgate most copious Still, 1631.
Tho' for a while the Wretch escapes, 1086.
Tho' heav'nly Musick dwelt upon my Tongue, 210.
Tho' Life is but a narrow Span, 1619.
Tho' now we may with Transport gaze, 267.
Tho' plagu'd with algebraic lectures, 726.
Tho' Rhyme serves the thoughts of great Poets to fetter, 437.
Tho *Rome* blaspheme the Marriage-Bed, 2, 4.
Tho' sage Philosophers have said, 746.
Tho' unconfin'd Spinosa rov'd abroad, 287.
Thomas loves *Mary* passing well, 902.
Those who, quite careless, leave unshut my Gate, 626.
Thou bed! in which I first began, 1561, 1692.
Thou enemy to wit!--thy fatal darts, 2004.
Thou fondest Partner, of my Joy, my Grief, 803.
Thou foundling Bard, I've trac'd thy Labor thro, 1969.
Thou hast, great Bard, in thy Mysterious Ode, 25.
Thou little wond'rous miniature of man, 1462.
Thou perverse, adverse, Caleb D'Anvers, 149.
Thou source of all that's great and good, 1221.
Though long extinguish'd the poetic Fire, 993.
Thou'rt gone, dear Prop of my declining Years, 935.
Three Fourths of a Weed, universally known, 2033.
Three learned Gothicks, in their furious Zeal, 889.
Three Pints of Wine, the Grave and Wise, 1853.
Thrice blest is he whose placid Birth, 1857.
Thrice happy *Damon!* to thy longing arms, 1549.
Thrice happy he, whom providence has plac'd, 1054.
Thrice happy were the golden Days, 1037.
Thro' all Mankind impatient ardours reign, 61.
Thro' what romantick scenes does *Fancy* stray, 908, 915, 925.
Thus Adam look'd, from the Garden driven, 2027, 2029.
Thus pensive as I tread the Strand, 1984.
Thus to a young despairing swain, 1384.
Thy charming lines, all pleasing, reach my hands, 723.
Thy dreadful Pow'r, Almighty God, 73.
Thy formost Sons of War, 685.
Thy Frowns, O Fortune, I contemn, 628.
Thy Funeral Honours weeping Friends have paid, 934.
Thy grateful sons, O queen of isles, 1846.
Thy heavenly Notes, like Angel's musick cheer, 353.
Thy Merits, Wolfe, transcend all Human Praise, 1665, 1671.
Thy Pow'r, O Lord, in the great Deep is shown, 553.
Thy worth, blest spirit, claims my humble lays, 2045.
Time, in pity to my woes, 2001, 2012.
Time is A short Parenthesis, 1571.
Time's Measurer, the radiant Sun, 714.
'Tis come! attend thou blest seraphick Throng, 1253.
'Tis done--Your patient ear we greet no more, 2039, 2040, 2052, 2053.
'Tis he! 'tis he! I hear him from afar, 1420.
'Tis not yet Day, and sure it must be nigh, 1073.

Too long Britania! gentle to her Foes, 1260, 1261, 1265.
Too long have Party-Broils usurpt the Song, 103.
Too often name and thing are distant far, 2030A.
Transfix'd by Death, with solemn Rites interr'd, 1800.
Trees once could speak, some Authors say, 1076.
Tu commissa diu fuerat cui mascula Pubea, 676.
Tuneful sisters! sacred nine, 1386.
Turbida nox Tenebras duplices dedit una Nov-Anglis, 39A.
Turn thee, *Strephon*, and behold, 1421.
'Twas Evening mild-- the Sun's refulgent Ray, 1879, 1935, 1939.
'Twas He, who once descending from the Height, 1821.
'Twas on the Day, our great Convention met, 2030, 2034.
'Twas when a gloom my pensive Soul o're spread, 183.
Twenty-third, did I say! no--that will be *Sunday*, 208.
Two annual Courses Time has run, 765A.
Two Bars of a Gate, 2002.
Two handsome chairs, 866.
Two Hotspurs unnoted for martial adventures, 379.
Two Limbs of the Law (so capricious is Fate), 465.
Two sparks were earnest in Debate, 929, 1615.

U

Unde nova haec rerum focies miserabilis? eheu, 653.
Underneath, a Hero lies, 1715.
Unerring *Nature* learn to follow close, 348.
Ungen'rous Bard! Th' hast shot thy Bolt in haste, 1978, 1987.
Unhappy Bard! Sprung in such Gothic Times, 144.
Unhappy Day! distressing Sight, 479.
Unhappy Youth, that could not longer stay, 695.
Until th' important day, the day when truth, 2088.
Unus'd to Love's Imperial Chain, 496.
Unwise and thoughtless! impotent and blind, 609.
Upon the object and foundation, 1457.

V

Vain fears, and idle doubts, begone, 817.
Vainest of Mortals crub thy mad Carreer, 59.
Vanish mirth and vanish joy, 1388.
Vast Happiness enjoy thy gay Allies, 905.
Vice admiral Vernon!--Ipswich!--Suffolk!--how, 1145.
Victorious Wisdom whose supreme Command, 276.
Vile Wretch! who sacrifices all to wealth, 1611.
Vincere si rigidam posset eruditio mortem, 1375.
Virginians! rouse! and from your Borders drive, 1367.
Virtue and Vice, two mighty Powers, 864.
Virtue here lyes, a Pattern for any, 459.
Virtue, thou ornament of human life, 286.
Vital Spark of heavenly Flame, 1313.

W

Wake! awake the plaintive Strain, 1637, 1656.
War, mournful War, I sing my Country's Woe, 1299.
We dare not own your Piece for Publick Use, 8.
We justly triumph in your righteous Fate, 27.

What will you then, requires a youthful Friend, 761.
What Words, what sense sufficient can express, 887.
What wretched Rhymer with polluted Stains, 1979.
Whate're Men speak by this New Light, 821.
What's the spring or the sweet smiling rose, 1377.
When a Comet presumes, 489.
When Albion 'woke, and rouz'd, midst War's Alarms, 1900, 1902.
When Cato view'd the generous Marcus dead, 1755.
When cold translation clings to copied thought, 1686.
When cruel Peter over *Cyprus* reign'd, 1435.
When Daphne o'er the Meadows fled, 1015.
When *Delia* shows her beauteous face, 2082.
When e'er the Eagle and the Lilly join, 769A.
When fair Intention has been slighted, 1129.
When faithless *Gallia*, proud of guilty pow'r, 810.
When fam'd Apelles drew the beauteous Face, 1146.
When filial Words describe a Daughter's Grief, 853.
When first Columbus touch'd this distant Shore, 354.
When first from Nothing at th' Almighty's Call, 1041.
When first I tun'd the Lyric Strings, 432.
When first the seals the good lord *King* resign'd, 474.
When foolish Calves in Forests walk astray, 580.
When General Mathew pass'd this mortal Bound, 1148, 1150, 1176.
When gen'rous Amherst heard the Tube of Fame, 1734, 1746, 1763.
When George our King shall learn his Foes to fear, 807.
When glorious Actions we would fain rehearse, 792.
When glorious Anne *Britannia's* Scepter sway'd, 780A, 781, 783, 786.
When God was pleas'd with Truth divinely bright, 137, 181.
When here, Lucinda, first we came, 2041.
When his immortal part by heaven, 949.
When I am to chuse a Woman, 868.
When I consider my Disgrace, 513.
When Israel's Daughters mourn'd their past Offences, 247.
When James, assuming Right from God, 1707.
When Life hath fail'd one; (and Life's but a Bubble), 981, 986.
When, *Lydia*, you, the manly charms, 1179.
When martial Heroes greatly buy Applause, 1780, 1782.
When Masons write in Masons Praise, 997.
When mighty roast beef was the Englishmen's food, 1476.
When noble Deeds, and friendly Actions done, 1764.
When now no more the summer's scorching sun, 1180.
When on the banks of Babel's rolling Flood, 378.
When on thy ever blooming charms, 322.
When pale Disease th' affected blood assails, 527.
When *Pharoah's* Pride brought down on Egypt's Land, 1028.
When Pharoh's sins provok'd th' Almighty's hand, 393.
When Phebus had lain off his Golden Vest, 512.
When Phebus had withdrawn his genial Rays, 2021.
When Physick saw her younger hope expire, 1923B.
When plastick nature moulds the wondrous clay, 752.
When sad Distempers rage, then Doctors strive, 1263.
When *Talbot* ravag'd all the Plains of France, 463.
When the old World was sunk in Vice, 647.
When the proud Philistines for war declar'd, 90.

Whilst anxious mortals strive in vain, 1006.
Whilst *Britain* led by Royal George, 1927.
Whilst Celia sings, let no intruding breath, 197A.
Whilst God inspir'd the pious fervent Youth, 575.
Whilst I lov'd thee, and thou wer't kind, 469.
Whilst other Muses tune the sounding lyre, 1723, 1742.
Whilst savage Brutes, stirr'd up by *Gallic* Arts, 820B.
Whilst th' *Arian* Preacher *Christ* his God denies, 571, 598.
Whilst thirst of fame and dreadful War's alarms, 549.
Whilst to relieve a generous Queen's Distress, 734.
Whilst tuneful Bards prepare to sing, 1685.
Whilst War now rages with impetuous Roar, 1639, 1642, 1643, 1646, 1648, 1661.
Whilst with glad Voice united Nature sings, 709.
Whitefield! that great, that pleasing Name, 538, 539, 540, 541, 548.
Whitefield to what End do you preach, 583.
Who can describe the horrors of that night, 1050, 1064A.
Who dare affirm, my Pow'r is weak, 201, 228.
Who don't remember the last Hurricane, 1287.
Who on the Earth, or in the Skies, 625.
Who says we have not gained a mighty Thing, 844.
Who wou'd have thought that Bella's Frown, 533.
Whoe'er you be that on this Ground may tread, 845.
Whoever picks your Bone will swear, 1272.
Whoever wants a great estate, 1886C.
Why, Celia, is your spreading waist, 895.
Why do the Heathen Rage, or Why, 1278.
Why heaves the bosom with continual Sighs, 1807.
Why how now, old Grandsir, what is it you mean, 196.
Why should I tempt the raging main, 1934.
Why should our Joys transform to Pain, 559.
Why should the Nations angry be, 687.
Why will soft Sorrow thus o'erwhelm my Soul, 1774.
Wipe clean your Pen, my Friend and lay it by, 847.
With a White Stone, Macrinus, mark this Day, 703.
With all my heart,--his lordship may, 1880A.
With ardent love for ancient wisdom fir'd, 1904, 1911, 1919.
With Bars and with Grates, 2003.
With Beat of Drum, and Trumpet's Heroic Poem, 1593.
With close Attack, I lately woo'd a Maid, 589.
With eager eyes and heart refin'd, 1466.
With ev'ry Patriot Virtue crown'd, 1294.
With Heart untouch'd, and Look serene, 1025.
With joy, sweet Rosalind, we hear, 2073.
With Majesty and Glory clad, 126.
With opening wings the infant year, 1803.
With parrots, and such trifles tir'd, 1534.
With quick vibrations of aetherial flame, 1136.
With spotless Innocence, that chears the Mind, 480.
With vast amazement we survey, 281.
With the New-Year, O could my rural Muse, 1402.
With thee, fair maid, thy merit dies, 1880C, 2049A.
With youth and perfect Beauty blest, 719A.
Within these peaceful Walls retir'd, 1859A, 1864.
Within this doleful tomb, at length there lies interr'd, 941.

Within this tomb of water, not of stone, 558.
Would you, as sure you would, with utmost care, 373.
Would you Attempt to lash a guilty Age, 62.
Would you be concern'd to know, 363.
Wou'd you pass thro' Life with Pleasure, 914.
Would *Heaven* propitious with my *Wish* comply, 464.
Would you lead a peaceable, undisturb'd life, 468.
Would you, my Fair, triumphant lead along, 778.
Would you take the morning Air, 2063.

Y

Ye Britons be merry, because you've grown wise, 1014.
Ye Charmers who shine, 1515.
Ye cruel Winds that blow from North to East, 1187, 1188.
Ye deities who rule the deep, 1203, 1204.
Ye *Dryads* fair, whose Temples round, 1852.
Ye fair, whose worth I so esteem, 730.
Ye Fair, with youth and beauty vain, 1952.
Ye gen'rous Fair, ere finally we part, 1760.
Ye good people all, who of cordage have need, 1097.
Ye hostile Nations! let your Fury cease, 826.
Ye Ladies who to *Boston-Town* are come, 197.
Ye lovely maids! whose yet unpractis'd hearts, 987.
Ye Maids of Honour, mind your ways, 1731.
Ye *Maids,* whom Nature meant for *Mothers,* 1539.
Ye Muses, Hail the Roial Dame, 423.
Ye nymphs of *Salem,* who, with hallow'd lays, 797.
Ye Nymphs! that boast your Charms, see here, 717, 1521.
Ye paultry scriblers of a foggy clime, 980.
Ye power divine, assist my hand and heart, 1366.
Ye Quacks be gone, with all your Ills, 524.
Ye sacred guardians of the good and fair, 1613.
Ye swains, who your wit to display, 1413.
Ye tuneful Nine, who all my Soul inspire, 160.
Ye Virgin Pow'rs defend my Heart, 315.
Ye Wise! instruct me to endure, 924, 2017.
Yes, sweeter far than sweetest flow'r that grows, 1622.
Yet oft our fond affections want controul, 1608.
Yet Summer Fallows best your Crops ensure, 1526.
You are the Man who Counsel can bestow, 1477.
You ask, Dear Friend, that I ressume the Lyre, 156.
You ask, if the thing to my choice were submitted, 1624, 1724.
You ask me how this sultry clime, 492.
You know where you did despise, 249.
You who in London youthful Passions fir'd, 120.
You wish in vain, it cannot be, 754.
Your answer kind sir, with the marginal note, 1437.
Your charming Thoughts in softest Words express'd, 1814.
Your Petitioners being reduc'd to a wretched Condition, 330, 365.
Your Riddle I, observed to be, 604.
Your sage and moralist can show, 289, 368, 546.
Your Servant Sirs, do you like my Figure, 2070, 2072.
You're fair, dear maid, so very fair, 1880B.
You're so choice of your wine, 975.
Your's I received, but the Date, 39.

Name, Pseudonym, and Title Index

Titles refer only to works mentioned. For drama, see titles under *plays*. For Greek and Roman authors, see under *classical authors* in the subject and genre index. For the names of colleges, see under *colleges* in the subject and genre index.

A

'A,' 1523.

'A----' (see *Princeton author*), 1597.

'A., A.,' 355.

'A., *Miss* M.,' 1523, 1588, 1653.

'A., N.,' 1791.

'A., Z.,' 1938.

'A-s-q,' *Dr.*, 980.

'A---ty,' 954.

'AE' [Matthew Adams], 66.

Abbey, Matthew, 199 (203, 204, 219, 225, 226).

Abbey, *Mrs.* Matthew, 202 (212, 220, 231, 235).

Abernethy, *Mr.*, 1836.

'Academicus,' 1865.

Adams, *Rev.* John, 61, 70, 74, 106, 366, 806, 1043; mentioned 17.

Adams, Matthew (see also Philo-Musus [of Boston]), author 17, 66, 83, 87; mentioned, 60, 61, 69, 806.

Addison, *Rev.* Henry, 876.

'Agricola,' 1526.

'Aishmella,' 1089.

Al---n, Miss, 1761.

'Al--s,' (see *Princeton author*), 1548, 1627.

'Aletheia,' 1632.

Algeo, David, 1069.

Allen, John, 722.

Allen, William (Chief Justice of Pa.), 182, 557.

Amator, Ruris, 363.

'Amelia,' 10, 11, 1397.

'American Fables,' 1068, 1076, 1129.

'Americanus,' 393, 394, 395, 1269, 1331, 1482.

Ames, Nathaniel, 1344, 1795, 1840, 1850, 1854, 1887.

Amherst, Jeffrey, *Baron*, 1528 (1530, 1538, 1551, 1554), 1529 (1536, 1537, 1540, 1552), 1545, 1786 (1790, 1813).

'Amintor,' 456, 589.

'Amoroso,' 32.

'Anglicanus,' 1775.

'Annandius' [Joseph Shippen?] author: 1416, 1417, 1418, 1419, 1425; mentioned: 1396, 1437.

Antigonian Beauties, 1515.

'Antonius' 2058 (2059).

Aplin, John, 1927, 1929B.

Applewhaite, Thomas (of Barbadoes, d. 1749), 941, 949.

Archer, Henry (of Eton), 726.

'Ariosto' 1880B.

Armstrong, *Col.* John, 1335.

Associators of Pennsylvania, 886.

Atherton, Humphry (d. 1681), 401A, 1816.

Atkinson, Theodore, 1829 (1830).

Atkinson, W., 2012.

Attwood, *Capt.* [William?], 324.

'Ausonius,' 1430.

B

'B., A.,' 629, 884, 1027, 1036, 1867.

'B., C.,' 1266, 1267, 1273.

B., E., 588.

'B., G.,' 1664.

B., J., 1137.

'B., M.,' 229, 355.

B., R., 1892.

'B., T.,' 1072, 1082 (1083).

'B., W.,' 1766.

'B--lay,' 952, 954.

Bacon, *Lt.* John, 1211 (1251).

Bacon, *Rev.* Thomas, 1072, 1082, 1211 (1251).

Badger, Joseph (1708–1765), 1956.

Baker, —, 391.

Baker, Henry, 200 (277, 520).

Barbadoes, 859.

Barbary, 823.

Barber, *Mrs.* Mary, 437.

Barret, Bug, 1777.

Barthlo, *Capt.*, 983.

Bayard, John R., 1328.

Belcher, *Gov.* Jonathan 156, 157, 158, 159, 161, 164, 165, 166, 167, 168, 170, 172, 176, 177, 178A, 457, 1411.

Belcher, *Mrs.* Jonathan (d. 1736), 526.

'Belinda,' 32, 207.

Belknap, Jeremy, 71, 81, 90, 94, 160, 267, 326, 336, 401A, 1904 (1911, 1919).

Fitch, James, 38, 47.

Fleming, Will, 1881A.

'Florella,' 227.

'Florinda,' 89.

Forbes, *General* John, 1546, 1555, 1557 (1567).

'Forecast, Timothy,' 468.

Foster, *Mr.*, 847.

Foxcraft, Elizabeth, 956.

Foxcraft, *Hon.* Francis, 956.

Foxcraft, *Rev.* Thomas, 777.

Frankland, *Captain* Thomas, 643 (646), 663 (665), 691, 767, 770.

Franklin, Benjamin (see also *Kitelic Poetry*) author: 25, 161, 195, 272, 390, 610, 839 (840, 842), 865, 1959; subject: 24, 274, 765, 886, 1164, 1178 (1194, 1195, 1197), 1477, 2008; *Poor Richard*: 185, 200 (277, 520), 390, 660, 671, 672, 673, 674, 848, 861 (867), 869, 870, 871, 1564; his file of *NEC* cited: 5, 6, 7, 8, 9, 10, 11, 13, 14, 16, 17, 18, 19, 20, 21; mentioned: 17, 28, 59, 111, 122, 167, 174, 282, 288, 349, 427, 850, 1165, 1198; 'Silence Dogood': 24; 'Busy-Body': 105, 109, 111; *The Papers of Benjamin Franklin* cited: 25, 111, 185, 195, 200, 274, 282.

Franklin, James, 5, 7, 8, 9, 11, 18, 19, 21, 27, 32, 51, 332.

Frederick II of Prussia, 1420, 1423, 1425, 1447, 1472, 1519, 1601, 1618.

Freneau, Philip, 188, 1168.

Fyring, Philip, 1890 (1899).

G

G., J., 1558.

'G---, P---,' 883.

'G., W.,' 2004.

'G---g, J---,' 1525.

Gamble, *Dr.*, 1603 (1937A).

Garden, *Rev.* Alexander, 571 (598).

Gardner, Nathaniel, 20; mentioned: 17.

Gardner, Nathaniel, Jr., 1409, 1493.

Gay, John, 185 (303), 398, 642, 819 (1374).

'Gentleman of Virginia,' 1042.

George I, King of England, 45, 69, 83.

George II, King of England, 69, 72, 157, 239, 957, 1225, 1233, 1817; death: 1796, 1797 (1804), 1798, 1801 (1805), 1807, 1809, 1831.

George III, King of England. Accession: 1796, 1828, 1832, 1851, 1878, 1884.

Georgia, 330.

Geraldino, Don Thomas, 577.

Gibbs, Rev. William (1715–1777) (Harvard, 1734), 2011.

Gibson, Benjamin, 39a.

Gilman, Elizabeth, 1521.

Gilman, *Col.* Peter, 1521.

Glover, Richard, 593.

Godfrey, Thomas, author: 1408, 1474, 1483, 1508, 1667 (1750, 1770), 1894; extracts printed in advertisement: 1971 (1972), 1973 (1974); mentioned: 1665; subject: 1918, 1941 (1966).

Godin, Benjamin (d. 1748), 880.

Gooch, *Sir* William, 432, 545 (597), 839 (840, 842), 948.

Gooch, William, Jr., 596.

Goodhue, *Rev.* Francis (d. 1707), 37.

Gordon, Rev. John, 876.

Gordon, *Gov.* Patrick, 182, 419, 420.

Gracian, 1103.

Grainger, *Dr.* James (1721?–1766), 1559, 1991 (1992).

Granom, Mr., 2063.

Gray, Katharine, 2007, 2013.

Great Britain (ship), 1016.

Green, John, 1508.

Green, Jonas, 1202.

Green, Joseph (1701–1765), 2045.

Green, Joseph, author: 144, 279, 280 (1494), 281, 298, 969 (970), 976, 990, 1187 (1188), 1255, 1777, 1921, 1922; mentioned: 20, 975, 997, 1147.

Greenville, *Sir* Richard, 769.

Greenwood, Isaac, 351.

Grew, Theophilus, 1774.

Grierson, Constantia, 95 (97, 1118, 1122, 1128).

'Gripus,' 974.

Grove, *Rev.* Henry, 972.

Growdon, Joseph, 498 (499).

Guido, 1414.

H

'H.,' 733, 1988.

'H.,' Mr., 189 (216).

'H., D.,' 1008.

'H., J.,' 86, 972.

'H., N.,' 1279, 1281.

'H., S.,' 1000.

'H., T.,' 2049.

Subject and Genre Index

Certain categories, like *occasional verse* and *complimentary verse*, which could have been used interminably, have been used only when the poem has not been indexed under at least one other category.

A

acrostic 484, 554, 1243, 1900.
advertisement, poetry quoted in 134, 325, 332, 821, 1287, 1971 (1972), 1973 (1974).
advertisement, rhyming 35, 128, 134, 208, 271, 291, 514, 818, 866, 1097, 1881.
advice 288, 328, 764, 901, 1258, 1916A.
advice to a painter 836, 1304 (1310), 1825.
agriculture 214, 1380, 1526, 1559, 1991.
allegorical 56, 403, 1058, 1180.
almanac verse (see also *Poor Richard* in author index) 332, 386, 390, 580, 671, 848, 861 (867), 869, 870, 871, 967 (1147), 1344, 1402, 1887.
ambition 563.
American nationalism (see also *patriotism, translatio studii*) 164 (cf. nos. 165, 166, 167, 168, 170, 172, 176, 177, 178A), 184 (187, 198, 215, 252A, 253A, 258; cf. nos. 557, 564), 188 (232), 769B, 1062, 1246 (1248), 1732.
anagram 2013.
Anglican ministry 30, 38.
anthem 2008.
art (see also *advice to a painter, ut pictura poesis*) 148, 1381, 1508, 1956.
auction 1580, 1583.

B

ballad 740, 819, 885, 963 (973), 1075, 1413, 1453, 1476, 1604, 1612, 1716, 2035, 2038 (2091), 2074.
batchelor (see also *War of sexes*) 1822 (1990, 2022).
beauty 1524.
Biblical comparisons 1028.
Biblical paraphrase 74, 106, 126, 145, 146 (154), 205, 310, 366, 378, 479, 487, 536, 633, 685, 729, 788, 806, 816, 1089, 1136, 1463, 1465, 1623 (1866A), 2077.
birth-day verse 239.
broadside 517.
burlesque (see also *parody, speech parodied,* and *travesty*) 260, 297.

C

calamity (see also *fire, natural phenomena*) 49.
cantata 1384.
Carpe diem 89, 1168.
carrier's verses (see also *New Year's Verses*) 343, 714, 765A.
catholic 1, 2 (4), 3, 49, 52, 71, 825 (828).
celibacy 336.
character: jealous father, 853; justice of the peace, 42 (874, 877); miser, 196, 873, 1611; minister, 950, 951, 773; officious ladies, 851, 862; old husband and young wife, 307.
charity 1096 (1108).
choice genre (see also *contentment; marriage*) 1090 (1095), 1114, 1119, 1624, 1724, 1951, 1953, 1983, 2005, 2076.

chorus (see *Tune*).

Christmas 33, 34, 385, 668, 1109, 1400, 1794, 1843, 2009.

classical authors: Anacreon 466; Claudian 110, 326; Homer 1012; Horace 61, 430, 432, 438, 469, 476, 488, 702, 734B, 780, 786A (789), 827 (830), 914, 1135, 1137, 1179, 1203 (1204), 1533, 1573, 1602, 1767, 1858, 1892, 1931, 1963; Lucian 375; Martial 985; Menander 1399; Ovid 622, 811; Persius 703; Petronius 107; Phaedrus 820, 1220; Politian 811; Statius 90; Theocritus 108; Xenophon 1056.

colleges (see also *Exercise and commencement verse*): Harvard 60 (65), 66; Philadelphia, Academy of 1160, 1190 (1192), 1205 (1206, 1207, 1212), 1222 (1227, 1229), 1223 (1228, 1230); Princeton 1630, 1821, 1824, 1826, 1859A (1864); Yale 981.

comet 489, 721 (725, 728), 1579 (1589, 1591, 1595, 1600).

commendatory (not personal; see also *complimentary verse*) 122, 169.

commerce 269.

complimentary verse (personal) (see also *encommium*) 60, 64, 89, 93, 434 (436), 1477, 1506, 1769.

conscience 473.

consolation 720.

contentment (see also *choice, happiness*, and *retirement*) 890 (913), 1143, 1156, 1158, 1725.

cosmological poetry 1199.

courtly verse (see also *war of sexes*) 311, 322.

courtship (see also *war of sexes*) 456.

criticism (cf. *literary quarrels*) 25, 38, 48, 51, 153, 183, 192, 217, 298, 1103, 1468.

currency (i.e., paper money) 648, 958, 959 (962), 961 (966), 1921.

D

Death (see also *elegy*) 409, 623, 974, 1126.

Deism 542, 854, 978.

dialect (see also *mock-illiterate*) 349, 850.

dialogue 195, 413, 469, 794, 815, 905, 958, 1863.

Dreams 58, 908 (915, 925).

drink (see also *Temperance*) 101, 295, 472, 524, 1959.

E

Earthquake (see under *natural phenomena*) 1317, 1318, 1382, 1942 (1943, 1944, 1945).

Easter poetry 1253.

Eclipse (see under *natural phenomena*) 31, 1407.

eclogue 265.

education (see also *colleges*, and *Exercise and Commencement Verse*) 24, 28, 35, 134, 726, 965, 1091 (1092, 1111), 1774.

elegy (see also *Braddock* in name index, *Graveyard school, pastoral elegy*, and *Wolfe* in name index) 1, 2 (4), 3, 37, 39a, 40, 57, 75 (77, 78, 80), 79, 81 (82), 99, 127, 141, 143, 152, 163, 189 (216), 236, 263, 294, 335, 396, 404, 419, 420, 448, 454, 455, 484, 494, 495 (497), 498 (499), 528, 529, 530, 534, 535, 544, 558, 630, 636, 716, 717, 727 (734A), 739 (745), 779, 804, 841, 857, 858, 860, 880, 887, 894, 934, 938, 971, 1026, 1031, 1036, 1043, 1057, 1059, 1081 (1093), 1091 (1092, 1111), 1098, 1127, 1133, 1160, 1167, 1205 (1206, 1207, 1212), 1209 (1218), 1232, 1244, 1295, 1326, 1327, 1328, 1345, 1346, 1411, 1424, 1458, 1478, 1484 (1517, 1565, 1570), 1495 (1499), 1496, 1497, 1510, 1521, 1616, 1637 (1656), 1668, 1721, 1775, 1780, 1785, 1791, 1800, 1815, 1818, 1838, 1888, 1889, 1903, 1904 (1911, 1919), 1910, 1933, 1940, 1941 (1966), 1947, 1968, 1970, 1975, 2019 (2020), 2026, 2043 (2046, 2047, 2051), 2050.

encomium (see also *complimentary verse, eulogy*) 386, 401, 756, 770, 1606, 1739.

enigma (and solutions) (see also *paradox, riddle*) 715, 832, 903, 923, 1000, 1396 (cf. 1416, 1437), 1607, 1737.

epigram 393, 394, 395, 405, 465, 583, 609, 624, 879, 889, 950, 951, 1011, 1062 (1065), 1063 (1066), 1064 (1067), 1281, 1437, 1533, 1652, 1674, 1675, 1676, 1762, 2013.

epilogue (see also *prologue* and *Theater*) 356, 408, 693, 1185 (1200, 1543 [revised], 1848 [revised]), 1193, 1223 (1228, 1230, 1240), 1349 (1350, 1358, 1359, 1369), 1733, 1760.

epistolary poem 565, 601, 649, 657, 752, 833, 876, 2025.

epitaph (see also *mock-epitaph*) 138, 264 (268), 334, 387, 459, 525, 576, 701, 837, 859, 941, 949, 981, 1049, 1051, 1052, 1078, 1084, 1232, 1432, 1484, 1678, 1810, 1866, 1946, 2078A.

epithalamium 191, 313, 478, 596, 751, 764, 881, 952, 953, 956, 993, 1069, 1386, 1768, 1965A.

Escatological poetry 64, 67, 112, 1264, 1833.

essay, poetical 810.

essay series (see also under *Franklin* in name index) 107, 110, 428, 490, 1324, 1367.

eulogy (see also *encomium*) 1152.

exercise and commencement verse (see also *colleges* and *education*) 66, 1630, 1681, 1682, 1688 (1926), 1824, 1826, 1859A, 1926 (1929A), 2039 (2040, 2052, 2053).

F

fable (see also *parable*) 139 (151, 223, 906), 161, 185 (303), 338, 516, 642, 848 (cf. 1546), 895, 904, 906, 909 (932), 912, 931, 988 (1117), 1003, 1024, 1068 (1070, 1071), 1076, 1129, 1220 (1231), 1247, 1431, 1672, 1693, 1819, 1827, 1871.

fame 1044.

fancy 776.

fate (see also *Fortune*) 421, 1718.

feminism 425.

fire (see also *calamity, eschatological poetry*) 1, 94, 112, 1967.

flirtation (see also *war of sexes*) 136, 206–7, 240A, 311, 322, 369, 443–4, 561, 820A, 978, 1024, 1025, 1027, 1539, 1915, 1932, 1961, 1963, 1964, 2027.

food 1046, 1048.

fortitude 817.

Fortune (luck) (see also *Fate*) 964.

free verse (see *speech parodied*)

freedom 812.

French and Indian Wars (1689–1763) see *Jenkins' Ear, War of* (1738–42); *French and Indian War* (1755–63); *King George's War* (1744–48).

French and Indian War (1755–63). (See also *Viscount Howe* in name index) 800, 802 (808), 810, 878, 983, 984, 1209 (1218), 1211 (1251), 1220 (1231), 1233 (1234, 1236, 1242), 1235, 1252, 1255, 1259, 1260 (1261, 1265), 1266, 1268 (1270), 1274 (1277), 1278, 1279, 1283 (1285, 1286), 1288 (1289, 1290, 1292), 1291, 1293, 1294, 1299, 1306, 1311, 1314 (1315), 1320 (1323), 1324, 1335 (1336, 1339, 1342), 1336, 1353 (1362, 1365, 1372), 1354 (1355, 1401, 1406), 1364, 1374, 1383, 1390, 1420, 1423, 1425, 1427, 1433, 1434, 1439 (1449), 1443, 1445, 1446, 1458, 1459, 1472, 1473, 1475, 1481, 1482, 1487, 1500 (1503), 1528 (1530, 1538, 1551, 1554), 1529 (1536, 1537, 1540, 1552), 1531, 1541, 1546, 1555, 1557, 1558, 1560, 1569, 1574, 1593, 1617, 1627, 1666, 1667 (1750, 1770), 1685, 1695, 1745, 1750, 1756, 1775, 1776, 1786, 1788, 1791, 1862, 1863, 1864, 1875, 1891 (1901), 1893 (1897), 1894, 1895, 1898, 1929.

French poetry 405, 418, 419, 602, 603, 1698, 1699, 1700, 1701, 1702, 1703, 1704.

friendship 476, 1474, 1783, 1906.

G

gambling 772.
Graveyard school (see also *elegy, melancholy, moon*) 884, 1508, 1548, 1820, 1823, 1912.
Great Chain of Being 1142 (1159).

H

happiness (see also *contentment, retirement*), 317, 918, 920, 1387, 1471, 1689, 1771.
Health 1141.
hymn (see also *chorus, song, tune*) 281, 385, 658, 681, 709, 736, 824, 897, 1037, 1140A,
    1221, 1269, 1448, 1467, 1469, 1531, 1613, 1738, 1787 (1789), 1842, 1869, 1960,
    1995.
hypocrisy 507.

I

imagination (see *fancy*).
imitation (see also *Homer, Horace, paraphrase, translation*) 90, 108 (113), 384, 561, 910,
    981, 985, 1081 (1093), 1091 (1092, 1111), 1100 (1106), 1101 (1107), 1220 (1231),
    1509, 1687, 1736, 1830B, 1841, 1880A, 1880B, 1952, 1964, 2000, 2083; Addison's
    Cato imitated: 431, 693, 872, 1009, 1060, 2089; see also 1172, 1297, 1697 (1705,
    1735); Shakespeare's *Hamlet* imitated: 733, 1126, 1174, 1456, 1553, 1599, 1869A,
    1876.
inbreeding 960.
Indians (see also *French and Indian Wars*) 820B, 1295, 1649, 1670, 1775, 1959, 2083.
industry (see *ship-building*)
Inter-colonial disputes (i.e., between colonies) 330, 1669A.
Irish 320, 349, 610, 669, 927.

J

Jacobite 152, 819, 829.
Jenkins' Ear, War of (1738–1742) 549, 560, 577 (578, 579, 594; cf. 614), 586, 592, 593,
    608, 613, 618, 620, 643, 644, 663 (665), 666, 674, 724.
Journey poem (see *Topographical poetry*).
Judgement Day (see *Escatological poetry*).

K

King George's War (1744–48) 696 (699, 700), 780A (781, 783, 786), 780B (782, **784**,
    785), 786A (789), 789A (790), 792, 795 (796, 799), 805, 815A, 820B, 936.

L

lamentation 318, 933.
Latin poetry 1, 36, 37, 39a, 49, 79, 134, 153, 260, 375, 449, 455, 525, 569, 589, **635**,
    638, 653, 654, 655, 676, 680, 701, 774, 835, 838, 893, 936, 1033, 1189, 1208 (1214,
    cf. 1213), 1210, 1226, 1257, 1266, 1272, 1273, 1275, 1280, 1283, 1373, 1375, 1394,
    1436, 1450, 1488, 1489, 1490, 1493, 1505, 1506, 1577, 1587, 1681, 1776, 1812,
    1821, 1861, 1866A, 1936, 1955, 1958, 1988, 1996, 1997, 2037.
lawyers (see also *social satire*) 185 (303).
lecturers, itinerant 351, 831, 1296 (1301), 1297 (1302, 1319), 1298 (1305, 1321).
Liberty 1532, 1535, 1930.
life 446, 1619, 1680, 1950.

literary quarrels (see also *criticism*) 5, 6, 7, 19 (cf. 21), 25 (cf. 26, 38, 39), 41, 43, 45
(46, 47, 48), 59, 62, 144, 239A, 279, 280, 295 (cf. 297), 296 (cf. 298), 299 (301),
355, 440 (cf. 442, 447, 451), 502 (cf. 508, 513, 518, 601, 604, 650, 651, 656), 602
(cf. 603), 736A (cf. 736B), 739A, 833 (cf. 834, 835, 838), 847, 954, 975 (cf. 976),
979, 980, 1008, 1015, 1018, 1061, 1072 (cf. 1077, 1079, 1080, 1085), 1103, 1143
(cf. 1156, 1158), 1154 (cf. 1155), 1193 (cf. 1201), 1266 (cf. 1267, 1272, 1273, 1275,
1279, 1280, 1281), 1580 (cf. 1583), 1626 (cf. 1631, 1633, 1641), 1669A, 1686,
1711, 1712 (cf. 1727), 1717, 1764, 1795 (cf. 1840, 1850, 1854), 1812, 1873A, 1883
(cf. 1885, 1886), 1908 (cf. 1916), 1956 (cf. 1957), 1967 (cf. 1969), 1976 (cf. 1977,
1978, 1979, 1985, 1994).
literature (see also *criticism*) 398, 1870, 2073.
London—Description 1157.
Lottery 1040, 1859 (1860).
love poetry (see also *war of sexes*) 20, 197A, 296, 333, 424, 441, 469, 496, 645, 855,
883, 891, 902, 1177, 1725A, 1830A, 1880A, 1880B, 1880C, 1881A, 1886A, 1886B.
luxury 864, 917, 967 (1147).

M

madness 509.
manners 662, 1030, 1166.
marriage (see also *mock-proposal, war of sexes*) 16, 178 (186), 482, 483, 863, 930, 1395,
1456, 1491, 1516, 1556, 1563, 1982.
    choice of a husband: 921 (926), 1009, 1245.
    choice of a wife: 868, 1010.
Maryland, description (see also *topographical poetry*) 257, 259.
masonry 491, 500 (cf. 501), 990, 997, 1022, 1041, 1712, 1829 (1830).
mathematics 113A.
medicine (see also *smallpox*) 348, 710, 1045, 1262, 1263, 1457.
melancholy (cf. *Graveyard school*) 50, 382, 1388, 1960.
mock-advertisement 1641.
mock-elegy 374 (377), 1085, 2018.
mock-epitaph 109, 1868.
mock-illiterate (see also *dialect*) 218.
mock-proposal (of marriage) 202 (212, 220, 231, 235).
mock-receipt 317, 719B, 890 (913).
mock-speech (i.e., imaginary speech; see also *speech parodied*) 349, 878.
mock-translation 825 (828).
mock-will 199 (203, 204, 219, 225, 226), 345, 458, 472, 1706.
moon (see also *Graveyard school*) 1677.
morality 286, 305, 315, 421, 441, 468, 473, 543, 864, 905, 991 (998, 999, 1004), 1002,
1153, 1169.
music (see also James Lyon in name index, *tune*) 102, 283, 441, 460 (477), 735, 1385,
1890, 1962, 2012, 2073.

N

natural phenomena (see *earthquake, eclipse*).
nature poetry (see also *pastoral, seasons, weather*) 36, 38a, 184 (187, 198, 215, 252a,
253a, 258), 188 (232), 244 (321), 316, 319, 323, 557, 719, 1187, 1356, 1454, 1759,
1914, 1984.
negro (see also *slavery*) 35, 209 (cf. 211), 360, 361, 730, 1725A, 2062.
New Light (see also *religious, Whitefield* in name index) 598, 619, 661, 667, 753, 821,
1217.

New Year's Verses (see also *Carrier's verses*) 171, 342, 800, 989, 1032, 1110, 1402, 1422, 1799, 1802, 1803, 1845, 1846, 1848A, 1948, 2010.

O

occasional verse (see also *natural phenomena, weather*) official (e.g., a governor entering or leaving a colony): 45 (45A), 69, 83, 72, 83, 91, 92, 93, 156, 157, 158, 159, 233, 234, 245 (256, 261, 300), 255, 257, 259, 266, 308, 313, 329, 339, 381, 422, 474, 948, 968, 1148 (1150, 1176), 1225, 1237 (1238, 1250), 1282, 1329, 1331, 1828, 1831, 1832, 1851, 1878; non-official: 118, 123, 255, 341, 344 (346), 350, 351, 427, 522, 523, 876, 1062, 1202, 1462, 1753, 1823, 1912.

Ode (see also *Sapphic Ode*) 214, 397 (400), 423, 509, 623, 682, 735, 747, 802, 817, 886, 896, 921 (926), 927, 1022, 1069, 1110, 1183, 1232, 1249, 1254, 1335 (1336, 1339, 1342), 1385, 1386, 1400, 1410, 1419, 1420, 1421, 1474, 1483, 1493, 1524, 1627, 1650, 1673, 1712, 1726, 1739, 1749, 1775, 1783, 1788, 1811, 1828, 1846, 1848A, 1852, 1857, 1859A, 1918, 1922A, 1929, 1934.

old age 140.

Opera 63.

P

painting (see *art*).

pair of poems 58, 360 & 361, 482 & 483, 706 & 707, 1100 & 1101 (1106 & 1107), 1317 & 1318, 1387 & 1388.

paper-mill (see also *printing*) 271, 746.

panegyric (see *encomium*).

parable (see also *fable*) 52.

paradox 849, 852.

paraphrase (see also *imitation*) 914, 922, 1056, 1587.

parody (see also *burlesque, speech parodied, travesty*) 562, 1297.

pastoral (see also *pastoral elegy*) 160, 248, 531, 1441, 1442, 1453, 1604, 1625.

pastoral elegy (see also *elegy*, and *pastoral*) 53, 512, 823, 1047, 1094.

patriotism (see also *American nationalism*) 103.

peace 826, 1824, 1926 (1928), 1938.

Pennsylvania, description 103, 182.

pets 280 (1494), 374 (377), 399 (470), 766 (including various examples of the genre), 775, 1868, 1913 (1917), 2028, 2031.

philosophical (see also *cosmological*) 559, 892, 1021.

political (see also *Jacobite*) 18, 19, 27, 29, 42, 87, 103, 164 (cf. 165, 166, 167, 168, 170, 172, 177, and 178A), 272, 274, 282, 284, 287, 302, 341 (347), 344 (346), 350, 358, 376, 410, 411, 462, 480, 577, 648, 820, 882, 1060, 1808, 1884, 1922, 1923, 1924, 2030 (2034), 2035, 2036.

poverty 634.

prayer 922, 1628, 1650.

preaching 704.

press, liberty of 29, 1865A.

pride (see *vanity*).

primitivism, chronological 814 (cf. 1514), 1830B, 2064A.

printing (see also *paper-mill*) 95 (97, 1118, 1122, 1128), 96, 194 (237, 241, 246), 201 (228; cf. 229, 230), 318 (327), 746, 978, 1426, 1999.

prison 121, 1023.

prologue (see also *epilogue* and *Theater*) 352, 354, 407, 734, 843, 1087, 1184 (1199, 1542[revised], 1847[revised]), 1190 (1192), 1222 (1227, 1229, 1239), 1297 (1302, 1319), 1347 (1348, 1357, 1363, 1368), 1686, 1697 (1705, 1735), 1732, 1990A.

prophecy 769A.

Q

Quakers 435, 865, 875.

R

rebus 1271, 1397, 1781, 2002 (cf. 2003), 2033.
receipt (see *mock-receipt*) 317, 1046.
religious (see also *Biblical imitation, Catholic, Eschatological poetry,* and *Whitefield* in
    name index) 30, 35, 73, 114, 115, 125, 221, 262, 402, 429, 565, 590, 625, 670 (675),
    687, 744, 854, 897, 1006, 1019, 1042, 1073, 1139, 1140, 1312, 1313, 1379, 1485,
    1513, 1578, 2016.
retirement theme (see also *contentment*) 265 (285), 649, 702, 919, 996 (1017), 1005,
    1054, 1852, 1905.
rhapsody 244 (321), 433, 928 (942, 943, 945, 946).
riddle (see also *enigma*) 201 (228; cf. 229, 230), 461, 552 (cf. 555), 591 (cf. 611), 601
    (cf. 604), 632, 683, 697 (cf. 705), 719A, 916, 940, 944, 1131 (cf. nos. 1132, 1134).

S

Sapphic Ode 919.
satire 5, 12, 25, 27, 38, 44, 45a, 46, 47, 48, 54, 86, 100, 197, 217, 279, 280, 358, 465,
    519, 568, 574, 580, 610, 643, 661, 666, 667, 736A, 739A, 757, 813, 846, 875, 882,
    910, 958, 959, 960, 979, 980, 1061, 1072A, 1217, 1220, 1262, 1263, 1545, 1572,
    1669A, 1717, 1744, 1795, 1808, 1827A, 1839A, 1870, 1873A, 1908, 1916, 1922,
    1959, 1976, 1981, 2030, 2035, 2036, 2042, 2060 (2061, 2061A, 2064), 2064A,
    2065 (2065A, 2067), 2078 (2087).
Scatological (see also *scurrilous*) 640.
science (see also under *natural phenomena*) 242, 351, 831, 1296 (1301), 1297 (1302,
    1319), 1298 (1305, 1321).
scurrilous (see also *scatological*) 22, 695, 882, 1883, 1916.
Sea voyage 732.
seasons (see also *weather*) 316, 388, 809, 896, 900, 1034, 1072, 1088, 1130, 1547, 1765,
    1844, 1869, 1907, 1909.
sensibility 306.
sentimental verse 76 (84), 243, 1023 (1124).
sermon 309.
ship-building 129 (130).
sickness 262, 760.
sincerity 1925.
slavery (see also *negro*) 116, 291, 1518, 1725A.
Sleep 445.
smallpox (see also *medicine*) 7, 1007, 1719, 1744, 1747, 1761, 2025.
social satire (see also *characters, lawyers,* and *satire*) 468, 856, 1757.
societies 137, 208, 253, 290, 846, 862, 927, 995, 1806.
soliloquy 812, 1009, 1171, 1172, 1382.
song (see also *anthem, hymn, tune*) 399, 440, 442, 500, 503, 504, 593, 689, 738, 750, 791,
    1055, 1123, 1163, 1181, 1262, 1428, 1515, 1625, 1663, 1670, 1720, 1740, 1806,
    1830A, 1865B, 1896, 1930, 2055 (2056, 2057), 2068, 2082, 2090.
sonnet 418, 419.

U

union of colonies 1233.
ut pictura poesis 131 (133), 148, 635, 1125, 1146, 1224, 1276, 1414, 1486.

V

Vanity 517.
vers de société 32, 100, 102, 208, 253, 279, 280, 281, 1436, 1507, 1561.
Virtue 543, 1947A.
Vision 100, 917.

W

War (see *French and Indian Wars* [1689–1763]).
War of sexes (see also *batchelors, courtly verse, courtship, flirtation, love poetry, marriage,* and *women*) 9, 10, 11, 13, 14, 39, 173, 629, 851, 901, 2080.
weather (i.e., storms, hurricanes; see also *seasons*) 73, 238, 243, 462, 939, 1016, 1035, 1050, 1099, 1102 (1104, 1112, 1115, and 1121), 1287, 1379, 1418, 1455.
Welsh 290.
wine 602, 975, 1483, 1795, 1853.
wisdom 276, 1726.
wish genre 464, 762.
wit 683.
women (see also *feminism, war of sexes*) 305, 328, 367, 947, 987, 1142 (1159), 1149, 1175.

PERIODICALS INDEX

For poems reprinted from issues of newspapers which are not extant, see *see also* at the end of listings for the *Boston Gazette, Boston Post Boy, Maryland Gazette, New York Weekly Journal,* and *Virginia Gazette.*

A

American Magazine and Historical Chronicle (Boston, 1743–46) 697–99, 701–05, 708–11, 713, 717–19, 725–27, 729, 734–36, 745–46, 751–52, 755, 759, 764–66, 771, 773–76, 785–88, 794, 799, 809, 817, 824.

American Magazine or Monthly Chronicle (Philadelphia, 1757–58) 1384–89, 1395–1400, 1408–10, 1414–20, 1425–26, 1434–37, 1441, 1450–51, 1462–68, 1472–74, 1483–88, 1505–09.

American Weekly Mercury (Philadelphia, 1719–49) 35, 53, 57, 58, 59, 62, 77, 84, 97, 98, 108, 111, 114, 115, 116, 117, 118, 120, 122, 123, 130, 133, 142, 148, 150, 151, 154, 173, 183, 185, 203, 223, 233, 236, 240, 243, 266, 274, 282, 285, 287, 288, 290, 299, 303, 340, 342, 343, 346, 347, 357, 360, 361, 363, 369, 376, 377, 381, 391, 392, 401, 402, 404, 405, 419, 420, 424, 435, 465, 475, 480, 487, 498, 505, 507, 523, 528, 529, 540, 542, 544, 547, 554, 557, 566, 573, 574, 579, 580, 582, 583, 607, 608, 618, 626, 643, 652, 662, 664, 695, 756, 768, 789, 790.

Annual Register (London, 1758–65) 1690, 1691, 1692, 1892, 1949, 2091.

B

Bee (London) 254.

Boston Evening Post (1735–65) 390, 517, 524, 577, 646, 660, 665, 667, 669, 671, 672, 673, 674, 691, 721, 753, 777, 783, 784, 796, 821, 840, 869, 870, 871, 874, 915, 924, 959, 969, 986, 990, 1016, 1043, 1046, 1086, 1088, 1187, 1217, 1255, 1374, 1402, 1449, 1461, 1471, 1479, 1499, 1536, 1635, 1643, 1696, 1710, 1812, 1816, 1823, 1830, 1840, 1850, 1854, 1859, 1866, 1885, 1903, 1906, 1907, 1910, 1922, 1944, 1965, 1976, 1988, 2005, 2018, 2025, 2026, 2035, 2036, 2041, 2043, 2059, 2065, 2088.

Boston Gazette (1719–65) 12, 76, 80, 82, 85, 89, 94, 102, 131, 136, 138, 144, 172, 175, 180, 186, 190, 197, 214, 255, 264, 298, 316, 322, 323, 331, 370, 429, 443, 444, 459, 478, 488, 490, 495, 499, 504, 510, 520, 585, 806, 808, 811, 816, 826, 946, 948, 956, 967, 976, 1010, 1017, 1033, 1037, 1083, 1124, 1149, 1150, 1166, 1167, 1168, 1242, 1253, 1258, 1260, 1266, 1267, 1272, 1273, 1275, 1276, 1278, 1279, 1280, 1281, 1286, 1304, 1313, 1319, 1321, 1372, 1373, 1403, 1406, 1459, 1480, 1537, 1545, 1568, 1577, 1580, 1583, 1634, 1642, 1664, 1666, 1706, 1707, 1711, 1730, 1763, 1780, 1800, 1877, 1882, 1886, 1897, 1898, 1908, 1916, 1970, 1981, 2021, 2037, 2061, 2069, 2070, 2078, 2084, 2089;
see also: : 148, 351, 360, 361, 1822.

Boston News Letter (1704–65) 1, 2, 3, 4, 36, 37, 38A, 39A, 40, 45, 49, 63, 79, 91, 494, 609, 616, 648, 680, 696, 795, 933, 957, 958, 964, 982, 985, 997, 1041, 1052, 1057, 1114, 1147, 1189, 1208, 1210, 1213, 1214, 1215, 1216, 1226, 1248, 1259, 1277, 1324, 1498, 1501, 1528, 1557, 1573, 1574, 1591, 1638, 1639, 1698, 1699, 1700, 1701, 1702, 1703, 1704, 1709, 1721, 1795, 1796, 1797, 1798, 1875, 1878, 1893, 1900, 1904, 1933, 1936, 1937, 1940, 1950, 1955, 1967, 1969, 1975, 1977, 1978, 1979, 1982, 1996, 2019, 2045, 2046, 2068.

Boston Post Boy (1734–65) 374, 397, 550, 551, 572, 575, 576, 586, 642, 661, 781, 782, 792, 961, 975, 1034, 1071, 1099, 1100, 1101, 1112, 1128, 1195, 1569, 1610, 1636, 1644, 1669, 1680, 1697, 1708, 1720, 1788, 1801, 1806, 1827, 1839, 1861, 1865, 1938, 1945, 1951, 1958, 1997, 2006, 2027, 2030, 2044, 2050, 2071, 2072; *see also:* 620, 630.
Boston Weekly Advertiser (1757–58) 1407, 1500, 1516.
Boston Weekly Magazine (1743) 677, 678, 679, 681, 682, 683.

C

Connecticut Courant (Hartford, 1764–65) 2011, 2032, 2033, 2048.
Connecticut Gazette (New Haven, 1755–65) 1261, 1285, 1292, 1306, 1311, 1312, 1316, 1320, 1338, 1339, 1364, 1546, 1619, 1678, 1743, 1769, 1787, 1810, 1815, 1818, 1822, 1888, 1895, 1917, 2051, 2055, 2058, 2060.

G

General Magazine (Philadelphia, 1741) 589, 590, 591, 592, 593, 594, 595, 596, 597, 598, 599, 600, 611, 612, 613, 614, 619, 620, 621, 622, 623, 624, 625, 628, 629, 630, 631, 632, 633, 635, 636, 637, 638, 639, 640, 641
Gentleman's Magazine (London, 1731–65) 189, 215, 225, 231, 250, 251, 256, 257, 259, 273, 321, 329, 349, 364, 382, 393, 394, 395, 408, 481, 486, 492, 526, 527, 688, 724, 733, 810, 823, 859, 911, 942, 963, 977, 1007, 1081, 1135, 1136, 1137, 1144, 1151, 1164, 1178, 1179, 1183, 1199, 1200, 1204, 1221, 1239, 1240, 1257, 1269, 1270, 1284, 1355, 1356, 1368, 1369, 1370, 1371, 1510, 1559, 1594, 1595, 1603, 1622, 1752, 1786, 1836, 1855, 1862, 1867, 1872, 1873, 1920, 1929, 1935, 1968, 1991, 2090.

H

Halifax Gazette (Nova Scotia, Halifax, file at Mass. Hist. Soc.) 1089, 1108, 1111, 1119, 1121, 1126, 1174, 1175, 1176, 1177, 1225, 1243, 1244, 2063, 2066, 2073, 2075, 2076, 2077, 2079, 2080, 2081, 2082, 2086.

I

Imperial Magazine (London, 1761–63) 1830A, 1830B, 1834, 1839A, 1839B, 1873A, 1873B, 1873C, 1873D, 1873E, 1880A, 1880B, 1880C, 1881A, 1881B, 1886A, 1886B, 1886C, 1886D.
Independent Advertiser (Boston, 1748–49) 888, 889, 890, 891, 892, 894, 899, 900, 901, 902, 905, 934, 935, 936, 937, 939.
The Instructor (New York, 1755) 1249, 1254.

L

London Magazine (1732–65) 226, 235, 237, 258, 265, 279, 280, 281, 359, 383, 396, 407, 436, 457, 474, 506, 627, 644, 689, 716, 723, 730, 731, 732, 737, 738, 740, 741, 742, 743, 747, 748, 749, 750, 754, 758, 831, 949, 950, 951, 971, 984, 1059, 1145, 1165, 1173, 1219, 1220, 1238, 1300, 1314, 1375, 1560, 1604, 1612, 1725, 1736, 1737, 1738, 1753, 1767, 1781, 1841, 1868, 1939, 1952, 1953, 1954, 1960, 1961, 1962, 1966, 1998, 1999, 2000, 2001, 2012, 2038, 2052, 2062.

1522, 1538, 1544, 1570, 1578, 1593, 1629, 1637, 1647, 1648, 1670, 1679, 1685, 1716, 1717, 1723, 1745, 1746, 1748, 1750, 1751, 1758, 1759, 1765, 1776, 1777, 1784, 1791, 1794, 1813, 1820, 1821, 1825, 1842, 1844, 1845, 1846, 1871, 1879, 1914, 1983, 1984, 1989, 2042, 2074.

New York Mercury (1725–65) 1096, 1098, 1102, 1103, 1130, 1138, 1139, 1141, 1142, 1143, 1152, 1153, 1156, 1158, 1162, 1171, 1196, 1206, 1245, 1247, 1274, 1283, 1289, 1299, 1301, 1310, 1317, 1318, 1323, 1331, 1332, 1357, 1358, 1377, 1404, 1432, 1438, 1529, 1542, 1543, 1558, 1579, 1581, 1630, 1646, 1772, 1807, 1847, 1848, 1880, 1899, 2002, 2003, 2023, 2057, 2085.

New York Weekly Journal (1733–51) 74, 276, 301, 308, 317, 328, 341, 344, 350, 367, 384, 399, 421, 441, 452, 458, 470, 471, 502, 508, 511, 512, 513, 518, 521, 531, 536, 546, 549, 552, 555, 558, 559, 561, 562, 563, 564, 569, 581, 588, 601, 602, 603, 604, 634, 645, 649, 650, 651, 656, 657, 658, 659, 666, 670, 684, 862, 877, 910, 940, 960, 962, 966, 968, 970, 972, 974, 978, 979, 980, 982, 1000;
see also: 538.

P

Pennsylvania Gazette (Philadelphia, 1728–65) 101, 103, 105, 109, 121, 124, 129, 134, 143, 157, 161, 162, 166, 167, 169, 174, 178, 181, 182, 184, 194, 195, 196, 204, 212, 222, 228, 229, 230, 232, 234, 238, 242, 252, 260, 268, 270, 272, 275, 277, 278, 286, 289, 295, 297, 300, 304, 324, 326, 327, 334, 335, 337, 338, 345, 351, 355, 362, 365, 375, 385, 386, 387, 389, 398, 414, 415, 416, 417, 418, 427, 430, 449, 479, 485, 497, 509, 530, 538, 578, 584, 587, 606, 610, 653, 654, 655, 676, 685, 686, 694, 722, 739, 805, 812, 818, 830, 854, 861, 865, 866, 867, 886, 917, 918, 919, 920, 921, 922, 943, 998, 1062, 1063, 1064, 1068, 1072, 1073, 1082, 1093, 1140, 1146, 1160, 1184, 1185, 1186, 1190, 1193, 1201, 1205, 1218, 1222, 1223, 1232, 1264, 1265, 1297, 1325, 1326, 1327, 1336, 1347, 1350, 1351, 1352, 1393, 1645, 1665, 1734, 1774, 1799, 1809, 1852, 1857, 1863, 1869, 1870, 1881, 1889, 1890, 1894, 1918, 1926, 1941, 1942, 1947, 1971, 1973, 2015, 2040, 2049.

Pennsylvania Journal (Philadelphia, 1742–65) 668, 675, 687, 700, 714, 720, 728, 760, 761, 762, 763, 769, 797, 800, 893, 896, 908, 938, 941, 999, 1005, 1006, 1038, 1039, 1054, 1074, 1092, 1104, 1105, 1116, 1148, 1191, 1234, 1235, 1236, 1256, 1296, 1298, 1328, 1335, 1348, 1349, 1366, 1394, 1555, 1660, 1681, 1682, 1891, 1972, 1974, 1993, 2039.

Portsmouth Mercury (New Hampshire, 1765) 2064A.

Providence Gazette (1762–65) 1896, 1909, 1921, 1923, 1924, 1925, 1927, 1931, 1943, 1948, 2009, 2010, 2014, 2016, 2017.

S

South Carolina Gazette (1732–65) 200, 201, 205, 206, 207, 208, 209, 210, 211, 213, 218, 219, 220, 221, 224, 227, 245, 246, 247, 248, 249, 253, 262, 291, 292, 305, 306, 307, 309, 311, 312, 314, 315, 320, 330, 339, 352, 353, 354, 356, 368, 373, 378, 379, 380, 406, 411, 412, 413, 438, 439, 462, 467, 473, 482, 483, 503, 514, 515, 565, 567, 568, 570, 571, 663, 690, 692, 693, 706, 707, 712, 715, 757, 767, 770, 779, 791, 801, 813, 814, 829, 836, 837, 841, 845, 846, 847, 853, 857, 858, 860, 868, 880, 887, 927, 928, 955, 1009, 1019, 1021, 1026, 1027, 1028, 1029, 1045, 1047, 1049, 1050, 1097, 1115, 1131, 1132, 1134, 1154, 1155, 1163, 1168, 1170, 1180, 1181, 1209, 1224, 1250, 1262, 1263, 1287, 1303, 1322, 1333, 1334, 1346, 1353, 1380, 1478, 1526, 1626, 1631, 1632, 1633, 1641, 1663, 1667, 1668, 1719, 1729, 1744, 1747, 1749, 1756, 1761, 1762, 1766, 1770, 1771, 1775, 1783, 1793, 1802, 1803, 1811, 1856, 2004, 2031.

Scots Magazine (Edinburgh, 1739–65) 780, 987, 1194, 1198, 1203, 1231, 1237, 1251, 1252, 1268, 1288, 1295, 1315, 1354, 1383, 1456, 1497, 1600, 1655, 1656, 1657, 1658, 1659, 1713, 1714, 1754, 1790, 1874, 1930, 1934, 1992, 2053.

U

Universal Magazine (London, 1747–65) 885, 988, 1053, 1271, 1561, 1609, 1693, 1835, 1849, 1963, 1964, 2054.

V

Virginia Gazette (Williamsburg, 1736–65) 422, 423, 425, 426, 428, 431, 432, 433, 434, 440, 442, 447, 450, 451, 454, 455, 456, 460, 461, 463, 464, 466, 469, 472, 476, 477, 484, 489, 493, 496, 516, 525, 533, 534, 535, 543, 545, 548, 553, 819, 820, 1001, 1002, 1011, 1012, 1013, 1014, 1015, 1018, 1022, 1023, 1025, 1030, 1032, 1035, 1042, 1055, 1056, 1058, 1077, 1078, 1079, 1080, 1085, 1087, 1090, 1106, 1107, 1110, 1293, 1671, 1853, 2049A;
see also: 596, 599, 628, 635, 640, 945.

W

Weyman's New York Gazette (1759–65) 1572, 1618, 1731, 1764, 1773, 1808, 1819, 1911, 1928, 1959, 2022, 2087.
Weekly Rehearsal (Boston, 1731–35) 199, 202, 216, 252A, 271, 318, 325, 332, 348.